NEVER MARRI

Never Married

Singlewomen in Early Modern England

AMY M. FROIDE

OXFORD
UNIVERSITY PRESS

Great Clarendon Street, Oxford OX2 6DP

Oxford University Press is a department of the University of Oxford.
It furthers the University's objective of excellence in research, scholarship,
and education by publishing worldwide in

Oxford New York

Auckland Cape Town Dar es Salaam Hong Kong Karachi Kuala Lumpur
Madrid Melbourne Mexico City Nairobi New Delhi Shanghai Taipei Toronto

With offices in

Argentina Austria Brazil Chile Czech Republic France Greece
Guatemala Hungary Italy Japan South Korea Poland Portugal
Singapore Switzerland Thailand Turkey Ukraine Vietnam

Oxford is a registered trade mark of Oxford University Press
in the UK and in certain other countries

Published in the United States
by Oxford University Press Inc. New York

© Amy M. Froide 2005

British Library Cataloguing in Publication Data
Data available

Library of Congress Cataloging in Publication Data
Data available

Typeset by SPI Publisher Services, Pondicherry, India
Printed in Great Britain
on acid-free paper by
Biddles Ltd.
King's Lynn, Norfolk

ISBN 978–0–19–927060–6 (Hbk.)   978–0–19–923762–3 (Pbk.)

1 3 5 7 9 10 8 6 4 2

To Diana, Terry, and Sophie

Acknowledgements

The best part about finishing this book is reflecting back on the people and institutions that have supported this project. Scholarship is truly a collaborative endeavour, and this book is a prime example of scholarly community. The institutions where I have taught the last eight years—Miami University of Ohio, the University of Tennessee at Chattanooga, and Clark University—have all supported my research, and the opportunity to teach their students has made this a better book. In particular, the students in my seminars on Women and Work and on European Women's History have convinced me that marital status really did matter for women in the past. I would also like to thank the staff of the various archives and libraries where I conducted the research for this book. I would especially like to single out the assistance I received at the Southampton Record Office, the Hampshire Record Office, the Folger Shakespeare Library, the Newberry Library, the York City Archives, and the Borthwick Institute of Historical Research.

I have been incredibly lucky in receiving a generous amount of financial support for this project. Short-term fellowships at the Folger Shakespeare Library in 1998 and the Lewis Walpole Library at Yale University in 2001 allowed me to collect material from diaries, letters, and prints. A Rockefeller Foundation Fellowship at the Newberry Library in 1999 provided a full year to transform the dissertation into a book. Summer fellowships from the UC Foundation at the University of Tennessee—Chattanooga in 2000 and the Higgins School for the Humanities at Clark University in 2002 allowed me to visit archives in Britain to collect data on singlewomen's wills. And a senior fellowship at the Rutgers Center for Historical Analysis in 2003–4 enabled me to finish the book.

Words cannot repay the support and guidance I have received from my dissertation advisors, Cynthia B. Herrup and Judith M. Bennett. The hours, countless letters of recommendation, editorial comments, and helpful advice they have given me have ensured that this book came to fruition. They can take credit for all of the good parts of this project.

Numerous colleagues have provided me with helpful criticism and advice at various stages. I would like to thank the Newberry Library fellows of 1998–9 and 1999–2000, in particular Fran Dolan, Margot Finn, Elliott Gorn, Robin Gray, Jim Grossman, Janine Lanza, Ann Little, Diana Robin, Sean Shesgreen, and Lisa Vollendorf. I am also grateful to the following colleagues who have commented on conference papers, articles, and chapters, and have otherwise supported my work at various stages: Cordelia Beattie, Lynn Botelho, Anna Clark, Margot Finn, Charlotte Goldy, Nigel Goose, Barbara J. Harris, Margaret Hunt, Suzanne Kaufman, Maryanne Kowaleski, Susan Lanser, Beverley Lemire, Amy Masciola, Dana Rabin, Colleen Seguin, Pamela Sharpe, Pat Thane, Bob Tittler, Barbara Todd, Deborah Valenze, Ginger Vaughan, Merry Wiesner, Ronald Witt, and Judith Zinsser. I would like to thank my colleagues in the various History departments at the University of Tennessee—Chattanooga, Clark University, and the University of Maryland–Baltimore County who attended numerous presentations of my work. In particular, I would like to single out Aaron Althouse and Amy Richter for their collegial support.

I would like to thank Oxford University Press for their continued interest in this project over the years. In particular I am grateful to Thomas Lebien for his initial interest, to Susan Ferber for consultation and advice, and to my editor Ruth Parr. Ruth's enthusiastic support for my book and her ability to get it produced in a timely fashion have amazed me. I would also like to thank Anne Gelling and Louisa Lapworth for their assistance. And I owe a debt of gratitude to the anonymous readers for Oxford, who gave me such judicious advice for revising.

Last, but really first, I want to thank my husband Terry Bouton. An excellent historian in his own right, he has delayed his own book so that I could complete this one. He has continually championed my work, always been supportive, and improved this project immeasurably with his editorial and analytical skills. Whether helping me transcribe singlewomen's wills in York, enduring my stony looks while he thanklessly edited my prose, or trying to salvage downloaded documents from the C-Pen, he has been there every step of the way. And at the same time he has helped me produce a book about singlewomen he has also helped me reproduce a new single-woman, little Sophie.

Chapter 2 appeared in an earlier version in Judith M. Bennett and Amy M. Froide (eds.), *Singlewomen in the European Past, 1250–1800*, copyright @ 1999 University of Pennsylvania Press. It is reprinted by permission of the University of Pennsylvania Press.

Contents

List of Tables

1
Introduction

Envision a city street in early modern England, then let your attention settle on the adult women who go about their business that day. You might imagine differences between the women: some are young, some are elderly, a number are prosperously attired, while others appear in more humble dress. In a port town like Southampton or in London you might even glimpse a different race or ethnicity in the face of an African woman or a Jewess. All of these categories might be relevant, but there is another difference between these women, a distinction perhaps subtler than age, class, or ethnicity, but no less significant in early modern England. Married women wear bands of gold on the fourth fingers of their left hands, while never-married women do not. In towns like Chester married women wear white caps covered by broad black hats, while singlewomen simply wear white head coverings.[1] And if we follow these women into their parish churches on a Sunday morning, we find that married and widowed women sit together in the matron's pews, while singlewomen are seated separately. What we see when we look at rings, head coverings, and church seating is marital status, one of the most important distinctions between women in the early modern era, and one that would have been obvious to any contemporary.

In our modern age, when marriage is normative but not expected to be universal, and when married women retain the same legal rights as unmarried ones, it is easy to forget the significance a woman's marital state once held over every aspect of her life. Our present-day preoccupation with class, race, and sexuality has obscured the fact that marital status shaped in profound ways the life experiences of early modern women. This book reintroduces us to marital status as a category of difference, and looks at the women about whom we know the least—single, or never-married, women.[2]

Why should we study singlewomen in the past? Most of our scholarship has assumed that all laywomen married and became wives and mothers in

---

[1] Rupert H. Morris, *Chester in the Plantagenet and Tudor Reigns* (Chester: n.p., 1894), 375.

[2] Marital status was also important to early modern men. Marriage was closely associated with adulthood and full entry into the economic and civic spheres, and a patriarch was, after all, the married head of a family and a household. While I have chosen to focus on singlewomen, more work is needed on the role of single men in the patriarchal societies of the past.

pre-modern Europe. Of course, the religious and social ideal in post-
Reformation England was that all women would marry and have children,
but this ideal diverged notably from the reality.[3] Demographic historians
have shown that significant numbers of single people lived in north-western
European countries such as England, where people married late and a good
number never married at all. For instance, between 1600 and 1750 the
average Englishwoman did not marry until age 26, and men waited even
longer to marry, or until age 28.[4] Since England's population was quite
youthful in this period this means that a large proportion of its people were
single. Moreover, it has been suggested that anywhere from 13 to 27 per
cent of persons born between the years 1575 and 1700 remained single, not
just for a period of their adult life-cycle, but for their entire lives. While
these figures may be a bit high, demographers do agree that at least up to 20
per cent of adults never married.[5] At least one-fifth of men and women in
early modern England did not marry, and yet we know virtually nothing
about this group.

And while these figures are impressive, they might actually be too
conservative. Instead of estimating how many people might have died
never married, we could ask how many women were single at any given
point in time. Thanks to census-like sources such as the Marriage Duty tax
of the 1690s, it is possible to calculate (rather than just estimate) the
numbers of adult single people in early modern England. For instance,
I have found that in 1696, in the port town of Southampton, 34.2 per cent
of adult women were single, while 18.5 per cent were widowed and 47.3 per
cent were married.[6] Amazingly, while most of women's history has
focused on married women, in the late seventeenth century wives actually

[3] In Protestant England some women continued to devote themselves to a single, religious life
even if it meant having to join or establish convents abroad. Nevertheless, these women did not
number more than a thousand or so in the seventeenth century, and so were much less numerically
significant than lay singlewomen. For more on early modern Englishwomen who became nuns, see
Claire Walker, *Gender and Politics in Early Modern Europe: English Convents in France and the Low
Countries* (New York: Palgrave, 2003).
[4] J. Hajnal, 'European Marriage Patterns in Perspective', in *Population in History: Essays in
Historical Demography*, ed. D. V. Glass and D. E. C. Eversley (Chicago: Aldine, 1965), 101–43;
E. A. Wrigley and Roger Schofield, *The Population History of England, 1541–1871: A Reconstruction*
(Cambridge, Mass.: Harvard University Press, 1981), 255.
[5] Clandestine marriages may have artificially inflated this number to some extent. Unfortunately
Wrigley and Schofield did not break down their percentages of single people by sex, so their models
did not predict if women and men were equally likely to remain single. Wrigley and Schofield,
Population History, 255–65. David R. Weir, 'Rather Never Than Late: Celibacy and Age at Marriage
in English Cohort Fertility', *Journal of Family History*, 9: 4 (1984), 340–54, esp. 346.
[6] Southampton Record Office (hereafter SRO), SC 14/2/66a–68b, 70a–74c. These figures are
derived from the Marriage Duty Tax of 1696, the closest source to a census available to early modern
historians. For a full discussion of Southampton's Marriage Duty Tax listings and my methodology
in using them, see Amy M. Froide, 'Hidden Women: Rediscovering the Singlewomen of Early
Modern England', *Local Population Studies*, 68 (Spring 2002), 26–41.

comprised a minority of adult women in this town. And singlewomen, about whom we know so little (far less than about widows), made up one-third of the townswomen. Moreover, this demographic reality was not just limited to Southampton. In a sample of 100 urban and rural communities throughout England in the period from 1574 to 1821, singlewomen comprised on average 30.2 per cent of the adult female population.[7] In urban localities the percentage of never-married women was often even higher than in rural areas. For instance, in the late seventeenth century over half (54.5 per cent) of the women in London were single.[8] We can say with some confidence, then, that at least one-third of urban women were single in the early modern era.

By decentring marriage as the norm in social, economic, and cultural terms, this book critically refines our current understanding of people's lives in the past. The quantitative evidence forces us to question what has hitherto been almost a sole focus on married adults. Until recently married adults have been the primary subjects of historical inquiry. Studies of youth and adolescence, widowhood, and old age are now emerging, but this research has not significantly challenged our assumption that the normative people (or put another way, the people who mattered) in early modern England were husbands and wives. This is surprising, given that we know that early modern women married relatively late and that they lived longer than their spouses, so that they were almost as likely to end their adult lives as they had begun them—without a spouse. A 60-year-old woman might well have spent only twenty years of her life as a wife.[9] If a woman was likely to be unmarried for two-thirds of her lifespan, then why do those of us who work on the early modern period continue to view marriage as the normative state? We have too readily assumed that a woman's life was of little importance until she married. This examination of never-married women will help scholars envision what life was like outside of marriage. Since all women began their adult lives as singlewomen, the lives of never-married women illuminate not only the experiences of lifelong singlewomen, but of all women in the past. By recognizing that the married state was not always the norm—not even necessarily the most important or longest portion of people's lives—this study of never-married

[7] Peter Laslett, 'Mean Household Size in England Since the Sixteenth Century', in Peter Laslett and Richard Wall (eds.), *Household and Family in Past Time* (Cambridge: Cambridge University Press, 1972), 145. Calculations are my own, since Laslett's figures did not distinguish the number of single female children from single female adults.
[8] D. V. Glass, 'Notes on the Demography of London at the End of the Seventeenth Century', *Daedalus*, 97: 2 (1968), 583–4, 586. Such a high number of never-married women was due to the uniquely large number of servants and apprentices in the metropolis.
[9] Most people in this era died in their fifties and sixties. Mary Abbott, *Life Cyles in England 1560–1720* (New York: Routledge, 1996), 135.

women will allow us to view both singleness and marriage from a fuller perspective.

While modern historians of Britain and the United States have been interested in the lives of single men and women, this research has seldom probed earlier than the late eighteenth century.[10] These scholars have construed singleness as a modern phenomenon and have not been as interested in historicizing the subject. In contrast to scholars of the modern era, historians of the pre-modern period had rarely made never-married women their category of analysis until quite recently. Rather, information on singlewomen emerged as a by-product of research on other topics. For instance, propelled by an argument that fertility drove the demographic system of early modern England, and that the timing and incidence of marriage affected this fertility, demographers eagerly tracked female ages at first marriage and the proportions of women who never married.[11] In other words, demographers have shown that when women marry later in life or never marry at all, they produce fewer children, creating a lower overall birth rate. But few demographers have moved beyond calculating sheer numbers of singlewomen, to look at the women themselves.[12]

Historians of women's work have provided the most information on never-married women. This is no surprise, since most never-married women in early modern England would have worked for a period of time before they married, and thus they made up a large proportion of the female labour force. Research on apprenticeship, service, and youth has illustrated the working lives of young, labouring singlewomen in particular, but we still know relatively little about how middling-status and older single-women maintained themselves.[13] Scholars interested in criminal and

---

[10] See e.g. the special issue on spinsters in the *Journal of Family History*, 9: 4 (1984); Lee Chambers-Schiller, *Liberty: A Better Husband* (New Haven: Yale University Press, 1984); Howard Chudacoff, *The Age of the Bachelor: Creating an American Subculture* (Princeton, NJ: Princeton University Press, 1999); Ruth Alexander, *The Girl Problem: Female Sexual Delinquency in New York* (Ithaca, NY: Cornell University Press, 1998).

[11] See Weir, 'Rather Never Than Late'; Roger Schofield, 'English Marriage Patterns Revisited', *Journal of Family History*, 10: 1 (1985), 2–20; and Katherine A. Lynch, 'The European Marriage Pattern in the Cities: Variations on a Theme by Hajnal', *Journal of Family History*, 16: 1 (1991), 79–96.

[12] Exceptions to this include Richard Wall's 'Woman Alone in English Society', *Annales de Démographie Historique*, 17 (1981), 303–17—an examination of the residential patterns of unmarried women in early modern England—and Maryanne Kowaleski's wide-ranging survey of the demographic history of singlewomen in pre-modern Europe found in *Singlewomen in the European Past*, ed. Judith M. Bennett and Amy M. Froide (Philadelphia: University of Pennsylvania Press, 1999).

[13] On female servants, see: Ann Kussmaul, *Servants in Husbandry in Early Modern England* (New York: Cambridge University Press, 1981); Marjorie K. McIntosh, 'Servants and the Household Unit in an Elizabethan English Community', *Journal of Family History*, 9: 1 (1984), 3–23; D. A. Kent, 'Ubiquitous But Invisible: Female Domestic Servants in Mid-Eighteenth Century London', *History Workshop Journal*, 28 (1989), 111–28; and Bridget Hill, *Servants: English Domestics in the Eighteenth Century* (Oxford: Clarendon Press, 1996). On female apprentices, see: K. D. M. Snell, *Annals of the*

immoral behaviours such as prostitution, vagrancy, bastardy, and infanticide have also had something to say about never-married women.[14] Such work, while obviously important, has associated singlewomen with largely negative behaviours, and has perhaps coloured our opinions about never-married women too much.

Recent work in women's history has begun to distinguish among women by marital status and has started to reveal some of the differences between single, widowed, and married women.[15] The latest textbooks devote some space to never-married women. For instance, Sara Mendelson and Patricia Crawford's *Women in Early Modern England* includes ten pages on adult singlewomen, and does not assume that such women were single merely before marriage.[16] And Olwen Hufton's survey text on women in early modern Europe devotes half of a chapter to lifelong singlewomen, as well as incorporating more material on these women into chapters on prostitutes, witches, religious women, and female writers.[17]

Nevertheless, the first book devoted entirely to the subject of singlewomen in pre-modern Europe appeared less than five years ago.[18] With this edited collection, Judith M. Bennett and myself aimed to provide an

Labouring Poor: Social Change and Agrarian England, 1660–1900 (New York: Cambridge University Press, 1985), ch. 6; Ilana Krausman Ben-Amos, 'Women Apprentices in the Trades and Crafts of Early Modern Bristol', *Continuity and Change*, 6: 2 (1991), 227–52; and id., *Adolescence and Youth in Early Modern England* (New Haven, Conn.: Yale University Press, 1994). On single working women, see: Pamela Sharpe, 'Literally Spinsters: A New Interpretation of Local Economy and Demography in Colyton in the Seventeenth and Eighteenth Centuries', *Economic History Review*, 44: 1 (1991), 46–65; and Bridget Hill, *Women, Work, and Sexual Politics in Eighteenth-Century England* (New York: Basil Blackwell, 1989). On women as property-holders and creditors, see: Robert Tittler, 'Money-Lending in the West Midlands: The Activities of Joyce Jeffries, 1638–49', *Historical Research*, 67: 164 (1994), 249–63; Christine Peters, 'Singlewomen in Early Modern England: Attitudes and Expectations', *Continuity and Change*, 12: 3 (1997), 325–45; Pamela Sharpe, 'Dealing With Love: The Ambiguous Independence of the Singlewoman in Early Modern England', *Gender & History*, 11: 2 (July 1999), 202–32.

[14] G. R. Quaife, *Wanton Wenches and Wayward Wives* (New Brunswick, NJ: Rutgers University Press, 1979); Peter Laslett et al., *Bastardy and Its Comparative History* (Cambridge, Mass.: Harvard University Press, 1980); Ruth Karras, *Common Women: Prostitution and Sexuality in Medieval England* (New York: Oxford University Press, 1996); Paul Griffiths, *Youth and Authority: Formative Experiences in England 1560–1640* (Oxford: Clarendon Press, 1996); Rosalind Mitchison, *Girls in Trouble: Sexuality and Social Control in Rural Scotland, 1660–1780* (Edinburgh: Scottish Cultural Press, 1998).

[15] Examples include Sharpe, 'Literally Spinsters', and id., 'Dealing With Love'; Hill, *Women, Work, and Sexual Politics*; Amy Louise Erickson, *Women and Property in Early Modern England* (New York: Routledge, 1993); Judith M. Bennett, *Ale, Beer and Brewsters in England: Women's Work in a Changing World 1300–1600* (New York: Oxford University Press, 1996); and Barbara J. Harris, *English Aristocratic Women 1450–1550: Marriage and Family, Property and Careers,* (New York: Oxford University Press, 2002).

[16] Sara Mendelson and Patricia Crawford, *Women in Early Modern England, 1550–1720* (New York: Oxford University Press, 1998), 165–74.

[17] Olwen Hufton, *The Prospect Before Her: A History of Women in Western Europe*. Vol. I: *1500–1800* (London: HarperCollins, 1995), chs. 7–11.

[18] Bennett and Froide, *Singlewomen in the European Past.*

introductory and comparative look at never-married women in pre-modern Europe in order to spur more research on the subject. Since this time some excellent work on singlewomen in England has begun to appear, much of it focused on the medieval period. Judith Bennett has examined what we can learn about the interests of young singlewomen, as well as concerns about them, through the voices of maidens in late medieval songs. Cordelia Beattie has looked at the residential and economic options for women without husbands. And two recent books have illuminated ideas about and the experiences of young singlewomen. Kim Phillips's theory that maidenhood was represented as the perfect age for women in medieval England illustrates why it is important to think about women outside the framework of marriage.[19] Although this work on singlewomen in medieval England is provocative and breaking new ground, it has not entirely moved away from our conventional notions of marital status in the past. It either focuses on young, life-cycle singlewomen rather than lifelong ones, or, in Beattie's case, still groups singlewomen and widows together into the category of unmarried.

Research on never-married women in the early modern period is more scarce. Pamela Sharpe has contributed important studies of how working singlewomen maintained themselves, and Christine Peters has found that, despite the Reformation's promotion of marriage and de-emphasis of celibacy, wills and inheritance strategies reveal that a single life was a common and perhaps growing possibility for rural Englishwomen at this time. The late Bridget Hill also recently produced *Women Alone: Spinsters in England, 1660–1850*.[20] This is an excellent survey of much of the secondary literature on poor and working women, many of whom were single. Hill also covers many of the literary depictions of singlewomen for the period after 1700. Nevertheless, her primary focus is not on the early modern period, nor is the book based on original, archival research.

The study of never-married women is enjoying a promising beginning, but we are still sorely in need of original studies and research based in the

---

[19] Judith M. Bennett, 'Ventriloquisms: When Maidens Speak in English Songs, c. 1300–1550', in Anne L. Klinck and Ann Marie Rasmussen (eds.), *Medieval Women's Song: Cross-Cultural Approaches* (Philadelphia: University of Pennsylvania, 2002), 187–204; Cordelia Beattie, 'A Room of One's Own? The Legal Evidence for the Residential Arrangements of Women Without Husbands in Late Fourteenth-and Early Fifteenth-Century York', in Noel James Menuge (ed.), *Medieval Women and the Law* (Woodbridge: Boydell Press, 2000), 41–56, and id., 'The Problem of Women's Work Identities in Post Black Death England', in James Bothwell et al. (eds.), *The Problem of Labour in Fourteenth-Century England* (York: York Medieval Press, 2000), 1–19; Katherine J. Lewis, Noel James Menuge, and Kim M. Phillips (eds.), *Young Medieval Women* (New York: St Martin's Press, 1999); Kim M. Phillips, *Medieval Maidens: Young Women and Gender in England 1270–1540* (New York: Palgrave/Manchester University Press, 2003).

[20] Sharpe, 'Literally Spinsters' and id., 'Dealing With Love'; Peters, 'Single Women in Early Modern England'; and Bridget Hill, *Women Alone: Spinsters in England, 1660–1850* (New Haven, Conn.: Yale University Press, 2001).

archives. We also need more studies of never-married women in the early modern era, a period that this book argues was one of change for lifelong singlewomen in particular. And we still know relatively little about never-married women in urban settings, despite our knowledge that they often migrated to towns to support themselves.

This book seeks to provide some of that original research into the lives of urban singlewomen in the early modern period; but perhaps more importantly, it shows how such women can serve as a new interpretative category that also changes how we think about many of the larger issues germane to English society in the early modern period. For instance, singlewomen force us to examine patriarchy in a new light. Focusing on women who never married calls into question how we have studied women almost solely in relationship to the nuclear family. This book reframes the history of women in the early modern period by uncovering a significant proportion of women who did not perform the roles of wives and mothers. This means that by definition singlewomen have to be studied both as individuals as well as in relationship to the family. While the ideal in a patriarchal society such as early modern England may have been for women to dedicate themselves to conjugal and maternal roles, in reality not all women could or chose to do so. These women were legal adults, free from the control of a male relative, but at the same time they did not enjoy the privileges English society afforded wives, mothers, and widows. This book will argue that while gender is an integral category to understanding patriarchy, marital status was just as crucial in the early modern era.

Focusing on singlewomen also changes the way in which we view the nuclear family and kinship in early modern England. Family historians who have focused on the significance of the nuclear family and household in early modern England have perhaps unintentionally dismissed the importance of kinship ties in the period. Singlewomen reveal the importance of a wider definition of family and of the ties of kinship in early modern England. People who did not live in a nuclear household—singlewomen and men, orphans, widows and widowers, and abandoned or separated spouses—by necessity relied upon the material and emotional support of siblings, aunts and uncles, cousins, nephews, and nieces. Once we cease to view married adults as the norm and realize that a great proportion of people in early modern England were unmarried we find that spouses and children did not always form the most important connections in people's lives. Kinship also appears more significant when we attend to life-cycle. When a woman was single or widowed she might well have activated ties of kinship, friendship, or neighbourhood that she did not need to rely on during her married years. Thus, kinship was significant both to women who never married as well as to women who spent portions of their lives unmarried.

The study of singlewomen also has much to tell us about the history of urban economies and societies. Despite the large numbers of never-married women who migrated to towns, urban historians have largely neglected the positive and useful roles performed by such women in England's towns. Rather, urban historians have generally focused on male merchants and guildsmen, who comprised a minority (albeit a powerful one) of urban inhabitants. While social historians have examined the disorder attributed to young women who never married, we still have little sense of the economic, social, and civic contributions singlewomen also made to urban areas. While some of the best research in women's history has focused on the work performed by women in the past, we have much left to learn about how women contributed to the economy by other means, such as property holding, moneylending, and philanthropy. We also understand little about how women may or may not have been included within the definition of the urban citizenry. In other words, urban history is incomplete without taking into account the role of the numerically significant singlewomen in early modern towns.

An examination of never-married women also sheds light on the historical construction of a marginalized group. Modern historians have had a tendency to write as if 'spinsters' were a new 'problem' in the nineteenth century. Contrary to such assumptions, these women emerged into the popular consciousness as early as the second half of the seventeenth century. Of course, before this contemporaries had recognized that some women in their society were not marrying, but once the numbers of singlewomen began to increase in the seventeenth century these women became recognized as a societal group for the first time. Negative depictions soon followed this public recognition, with singlewomen being labeled and scorned as 'spinsters' and 'old maids'. Although these stereotypes were pejorative, recognition did result in contemporaries acknowledging and discussing the social and economic position of never-married women in England for the first time. This resulted in a paradoxical position for singlewomen by the eighteenth century: they were recognized, but not entirely accepted. How did never-married women respond to the stereotypes about them, and were the representations of their lives accurate? We have paid very little attention to the words of singlewomen themselves. The experiences and struggles of never-married women in the past have much to tell us about the emergence of minority groups in society.

Before we turn to these issues, a discussion of terms, sources, and methodology is necessary. For the purposes of this study I define a singlewoman as an adult woman who has never been married (although she might later marry). This is the definition and compound spelling that was used in early modern England. Contemporaries referred to such women interchangeably as 'singlewomen' or 'spinsters', and less frequently as 'maids', 'virgins', and 'never-married' women. I prefer the term 'singlewoman' to that of 'spinster', since the latter has pejorative connotations that originated in the later seventeenth century and are still with us today. Even more confusingly, present-day demographic historians only use the term 'spinster' to refer to women above the age of 45 who have never married.[21] But in the early modern period people did not reserve the term 'spinster' for just older women who had remained single. Rather, in the seventeenth century once a female was in her mid-teens she would stop being referred to as a girl or child and start being called a 'spinster'.[22] People in the early modern era also referred to women as 'singlewomen' or 'spinsters' even though they might later marry. To avoid the confusion over differing early modern and modern meanings of the word 'spinster', I have chosen the term 'singlewoman'. At times when it is necessary to differentiate between women who have not yet married and women who never marry, I use the term *life-cycle* singlewoman for the former and *lifelong* singlewoman for the latter. I also use 'never-married women' as a synonym for 'singlewomen'. And I only use the term 'unmarried' to refer to singlewomen along with other groups of women without husbands, such as widows and abandoned wives. This book does not focus on widows in early modern England—save for comparative purposes—because as Chapter 2 will demonstrate, the experiences of never-married and widowed women differed dramatically at this time.[23]

[21] Most demographers prefer to use the age of 45 or 50 to define a woman as a spinster, since they argue that few women marry or produce children after this age. Susan Cott Watkins, 'Spinsters', *Journal of Family History*, 9: 4 (1984), 310.

[22] There were many competing definitions of maturity in the early modern period—legal, religious, and social. A woman was able to marry at 12 but was not of legal age until 21. But when she reached her mid-teens contemporaries expected a labouring singlewoman to economically maintain herself and she was able to participate fully in religious life. Ben-Amos says that entry into service occurred in the mid-teens and that young adults began to earn an adult wage between the ages of 15 to 18. Ben-Amos, *Adolescence and Youth*, 39, 74. Wright found that 16 was the mean age at which children became religious communicants and tithe-payers. See S. J. Wright, 'Easter Books and Parish Rate Books: A New Source for the Urban Historian', *Urban History Yearbook* (1985), 38. In Southampton this also seems to have been the age at which young adults became godparents. The seventeenth-century Revd William Gouge believed that childhood ended at the age of 14, at which time an individual entered the stage of 'youth', when he or she commonly left home to enter into service or apprenticeship. William Gouge, *Of Domesticall Duties*, 2nd edn. (London, 1626), 296.

[23] There is also a much more abundant literature on English widows than on singlewomen. It includes Charles Carlton, 'The Widow's Tale: Male Myths and Female Reality in Sixteenth and Seventeenth Century England', *Albion*, 10: 2 (1978), 118–29; Barbara J. Todd, 'Widowhood in a Market Town: Abingdon, 1540–1720', D.Phil. thesis, University of Oxford (1983), and her 'Demographic Determinism and Female Agency: The Remarrying Widow Reconsidered...Again', *Continuity and Change*, 9: 3 (1994), 421; Jeremy Boulton, 'London Widowhood Revisited: The Decline of Female Remarriage in the Seventeenth and Early Eighteenth Centuries', *Continuity and Change*, 5: 3 (1990), 323–56; Caroline Barron and Anne Sutton (eds.), *Medieval London Widows, 1300–1500* (New York: Hambledon Press, 1994); and Sandra Cavallo and Lyndan Warner, *Widowhood in Medieval and Early Modern Europe* (New York: Longman, 1999).

The never-married women in these pages range from poor servants and labourers to wealthy rentiers and gentlewomen. My primary focus is on urban singlewomen who came from the families of craftsmen, tradesmen, urban professionals, and gentry. I supplement this with information on urban labouring women. This means that rural singlewomen and servants, about whom we already know more, are not at the centre of this book. Hill, Peters, and others have already started to look at rural singlewomen, and their findings provide some instructive comparisons to my own throughout this book.[24]

When researching a neglected topic such as women who never married, I chose to leave no stone unturned, and this has led me to use a wide range of sources. While Bridget Hill has stated that there is little evidence on spinsters, this book attests that this is simply not the case.[25] Rather, I have sometimes had to be choosey about what examples and stories I had room to include. The following chapters make use of administrative and financial records kept by urban authorities, tax records, probate records, ecclesiastical court depositions, and proceedings from secular courts such as the courts of quarter sessions, the courts leet, and borough courts. Other chapters that rely on family papers, diaries, memoirs, and personal writings are by necessity skewed toward the more prosperous and educated singlewomen who were able to write and leave glimpses of their lives behind on paper.

This book is primarily urban in focus; because never-married women frequently migrated to towns, they are easier to find in urban sources. I have chosen not to make London an integral part of this story, because the capital was so exceptional. Rather, to provide a more representative picture of the experiences of singlewomen, I have focused my research on the provincial towns of early modern England. My evidence comes from many towns, but primarily from Southampton, Bristol, Oxford, and York. These four towns were all quite different in economic function, size, and prosperity, so they provide a range of contexts for studying never-married women. For example, Southampton was a port town that suffered an economic downturn during the early modern period. Its population fell to 3,000 persons in the late seventeenth century. The town fathers did not permit singlewomen to live alone or work independently at the beginning of the period.[26] But in

[24] B. Hill, *Women Alone*; Peters, 'Single Women in Early Modern England'; and Judith Spicksley, 'The Early Modern Demographic Dynamic: Celibates and Celibacy in Seventeenth-Century England, D.Phil. thesis, University of Hull (2001).
[25] B. Hill, *Women Alone*, 14.
[26] See Amy M. Froide, 'Marital Status as a Category of Difference: Singlewomen and Widows in Early Modern England', in Bennett and Froide (eds.), *Singlewomen in the European Past*, and id., 'Singlewomen, Work and Community in Southampton, 1550–1750', Ph.D. dissertation, Duke University (1996), 242–302.

the eighteenth century, as the town transformed into a genteel resort, a small number of single tradeswomen began to spring up on the High Street. In contrast, the larger port town of Bristol saw its fortunes rise as it became the gateway for the Atlantic trade in the mid-seventeenth century. The town's population grew too, from 12,000 inhabitants in 1600 to 20,000 in 1670. Nevertheless, Bristol's wealth was concentrated in the hands of male merchants and mariners, and opportunities for singlewomen to apprentice themselves into a range of trades diminished in the 1600s.[27] Oxford enjoyed modest prosperity in the early modern era, despite the ravages of the Civil Wars and a decline in university admissions. In the mid-seventeenth century the town's citizens numbered above 8,000. Oxford's economy revolved around the provision of goods and services to the university community. While service trades were usually conducive to female employment, Oxford did not allow singlewomen the freedom to trade independently or to join the guilds. Many instead maintained themselves by investing in college properties or lending money.[28] York was the provincial centre of the North, and as such boasted a large population of about 11,000 inhabitants in the early seventeenth century. Although York's role as an ecclesiastical and political centre had diminished due to the Reformation, the city continued to serve as a social centre for the northern gentry. Opportunities in service and trade may have been more open to women here than in other towns, but only in a relative sense.[29]

This book covers the period from roughly 1550 to 1750; a span of time during which England became Britain and individual females who were single became known as 'spinsters' or 'old maids'. Nevertheless, most of the evidence dates from 1600 onward, and an attentive reader will find a few examples that post-date 1750. By examining the entire early modern era, I am able to show that this was an important period of transformation for never-married women in terms of economic and civic opportunities as well as in cultural depictions.

Just as my source base has been necessarily eclectic, so has my methodology, for the two influence one another. A historian of women must be conversant with many fields: legal, economic, family, demographic, cultural, and intellectual history. The various chapters of this book are informed by the different theories, debates, and methodologies of these fields. With my emphasis on archival sources, scholars will recognize the

---

[27] David H. Sacks, *The Widening Gate: Bristol and the Atlantic Economy, 1450–1700* (Berkeley: University of California Press, 1991); and Ilana Krausman Ben-Amos, 'Women Apprentices in the Trades and Crafts of Early Modern Bristol', *Continuity and Change*, 6: 2 (1991), 227–52.

[28] Alan Crossley (ed.), *The Victoria County History: A History of the County of Oxford*, vol. IV: *The City of Oxford* (Oxford, 1979).

[29] Diane Willen, 'Guildswomen in the City of York, 1560–1700', *The Historian*, 46 (1984), 204–18.

influence of social history in these pages. In addition, many of the ideas in this book are indebted to feminist theory and theories of difference. Most influential to me have been Judith Bennett's theories of continuity and change in women's history, Joan Scott's theorization of gender as a category of analysis, and Elsa Barkley Brown and Adrienne Rich's ideas on difference.[30] Several of the following chapters also benefit from the tools of literary theory—in particular, an awareness of all sources as constructed texts and how individuals, in this case singlewomen, represented themselves through the act of writing.

The reader will find the chapters of this book to be more thematic than chronological. Chapter 2, 'Marital Status As a Category of Difference: Singlewomen and Widows', establishes the importance of marital status as a differentiating factor between women in early modern England; a category of difference as significant as class or gender for women at this time. This chapter sharpens our definition of singlewomen by revealing the critical differences that separated the experiences of *never-married* women and what I call *ever-married* women (wives and widows). It illustrates how singlewomen and widows cannot be lumped together into one group, because their residential, economic, and poor-relief options differed markedly. In particular, I show how widows enjoyed more employment and welfare options due to their accepted roles as householders and deputy husbands, while singlewomen did not earn such privileges.

Chapter 3, 'Single But Not Alone: The Family History of Never-Married Women', looks at family history from the perspective not of the marital couple, but of the singlewoman. This chapter examines the social relationships of women who did not have husbands or children, and thus did not fulfill the roles of wife and mother that were assigned to women in this patriarchal society. It illustrates the significance of kinship ties to single people, and in particular the importance of female kin, such as sisters and nieces, to singlewomen, who were largely woman-identified in their relationships. I also explore the important roles that never-married women played in their natal families and the inheritance strategies of women without spouses and children. Ultimately this chapter shows that, contrary to our cultural assumptions, singlewomen were by no means isolated individuals, bereft of social relationships or marginal to their families.

---

[30] Judith M. Bennett, 'Medieval Women, Modern Women: Across the Great Divide', in David Aers (ed.), *Culture and History 1350–1600: Essays on English Communities, Identities, and Writing* (Brighton: Harvester Wheatsheaf, 1992), 147–75; Joan Scott, 'Gender: A Useful Category of Historical Analysis', in *Gender and the Politics of History* (New York: Columbia University Press, 1988); Elsa Barkley-Brown, 'Polyrhythms and Improvisations: Lessons for Women's History', *Signs*, 15: 2 (1990); Adrienne Rich, 'Compulsory Heterosexuality and the Lesbian Continuum', in *Blood, Bread, and Poetry: Selected Prose, 1979–1985* (New York: Norton, 1986), 23–75, and 'Compulsory Heterosexuality and Lesbian Existence', *Signs*, 5 (1980), 631–60.

Chapters 4 and 5 examine the economic and civic lives of singlewomen and the contribution these women made to the urban milieu. Chapter 4, 'A Maid Is Not Always a Servant: Singlewomen in the Urban Economy', explores how early modern officials attempted to prescribe the economic lives of never-married women, excluding them from independent trades and demanding that they labour as dependent, residential servants. This chapter shows how many singlewomen challenged these limited roles by attempting to establish themselves as independent tradeswomen. I conclude by arguing that economic options for singlewomen opened up in the eighteenth century. My findings challenge the historiographical notion that all middle-class women withdrew from work in this period. Attention to marital status reveals that while married women may have moved away from work outside the home, the same was not true for singlewomen. Chapter 5, 'Women of Independent Means: The Civic Significance of Never-Married Women', examines the importance of middling-status singlewomen as property holders, rentiers, and moneylenders. I also examine how singlewomen took upon themselves the duties and privileges of urban citizens, even to the point of claiming the franchise in some towns and demanding inclusion among political oath-takers in others.

The last two chapters look at the cultural history of singlewomen, including how never-married women were depicted in the popular imagination and how such women in turn represented themselves. Chapter 6, 'Spinsters, Superannuated Virgins, and Old Maids: Representations of Singlewomen', illustrates how ideas about never-married women changed over the early modern era, and in particular historicizes the emergence of the 'spinster' stereotype. Lifelong singlewomen were largely effaced in the sixteenth century, but by the mid-seventeenth century they became recognized as a social group referred to as 'spinsters'. By the latter part of that century negative stereotypes about never-married women emerged, such as the derided and scorned 'old maid'. I look at why these stereotypes emerged when they did, and why they were particular to England. Chapter 7, 'The Question of Choice: How Never-Married Women Represented Singleness', utilizes diaries, letters, memoirs, and autobiographical poems to explore, first, why some women remained single for life, and second, how such women represented themselves and their singleness. I examine how never-married women viewed their own singleness, and how these women negotiated society's perceptions about them. This finding is indicative of the overall experience of singlewomen in the early modern era. Women who never married at best faced a lack of conceptual space for women of their marital status, and at worst confronted harassment and downright antipathy. Nevertheless, many singlewomen strove, at times with admirable success, to create a place for themselves in a patriarchal world that paradoxically made use of their time, talents, and money, but then insisted there was no space or need for women who never married.

The Epilogue, ruminates on these themes for never-married women in the early modern period. Contrary to Bridget Hill, who has argued that the position of spinsters changed little over this period, one of the findings of this book is that there were significant transformations in how singlewomen were viewed and in the roles available to them.[31] And yet there were also some nagging continuities in the marginal status of never-married women, continuities so strong that they last until today.

[31] B. Hill, *Women Alone*, 11.

2
Marital Status as a Category of Difference: Singlewomen and Widows

When Fanny Burney's novel *Camilla* appeared it featured a singlewoman, Mrs Mittin, who provided a telling comment on the importance of marital status to women in her time. She confided to a close friend: 'Do you know, for all I call myself Mrs., I'm single ... The reason I'm called Mrs. is ... because I'd a mind to be taken for a young widow, on account everybody likes a young widow; and if one is called Miss, people being so soon to think one an old maid, that it's quite disagreeable.'[1] Mrs Mittin knew what present-day historians of women have often ignored—although a singlewoman and a widow were both unmarried women, people in early modern England did not at all think of these two groups of women in the same ways. This crucial distinction is one that most historians of women have overlooked in our preoccupation with comparing married to unmarried women. We have privileged the distinction between married and unmarried women for primarily two reasons. First, widows and singlewomen both lived without husbands, as opposed to (most) married women. And second, all unmarried women, or *femes soles*, enjoyed an independent legal status that wives, or *femes coverts*, surrendered upon marriage.[2] Merging singlewomen and widows into one category, and taking the experiences of widows as representative of both groups of women, we have too often left the unique experiences of never-married women unexamined.[3]

---

[1] Fanny Burney, *Camilla* (London, 1796, reprint, Oxford: Oxford University Press, 1999) Book VI Ch. X, 469.

[2] In other words, both adult singlewomen and widows shared the ability—lost to wives under the legal doctrine of coverture—to make contracts, to own and dispose of property, and to sue or be sued in a court of law. Some English towns did extend the status of *feme sole* to married women engaged in trade. And some courts did treat married women as *femes soles* if they wanted to hold such women liable for their criminal behaviour (for as *femes coverts* wives were not legal adults and thus were not legally culpable for their actions). But these were exceptions to the general rule. See Amy Louise Erickson, *Women and Property in Early Modern England* (New York: Routledge, 1993), 24, 30, 100, 146; Carole Z. Wiener, 'Is a Spinster an Unmarried Woman?', *American Journal of Legal History*, 20 (1976), 27–31.

[3] The French historian Olwen Hufton's path-breaking piece, 'Women Without Men: Widows and Spinsters in Britain and France in the Eighteenth Century', *Journal of Family History*, 9: 4 (1985), 355–76, is indicative of how scholars have grouped singlewomen with, and subsumed them

Our tendency to see widows as representative of all unmarried women is especially problematic since, at any given time in early modern England, never-married women outnumbered widows in the population. Peter Laslett's sample of 100 rural and urban communities throughout early modern England reveals that while widows made up 14.9 per cent of the adult female population, singlewomen were twice as numerous, comprising 30.2 per cent of adult women. And as mentioned in chapter 1, I have found that in Southampton widows made up 18.5 per cent of adult females while never-married women comprised 34.2 per cent.[4] Since singlewomen formed a larger proportion of the female population than did widows, we have been generalizing from the experiences of a smaller group to the experiences of a larger one. Moreover, in so doing we misrepresent how contemporaries in early modern England viewed women of different marital states. Today we differentiate women with men (usually wives) from women without men (widows and singlewomen); but in the early modern period people distinguished between women who were, or had been, wives and mothers of legitimate children, and women who were, and had been, neither. Marital status was an important differentiating factor between women, but the significant difference in the past was not between married and unmarried women; rather, it was between what Judith Bennett and I have called *ever-married* (women who had been married at some point in their lifetimes, and thus, both wives and widows) and *never-married* women.[5] This distinction was a result of the very disparate roles of widows and wives on the one hand, and singlewomen on the other, in a society where the conjugal household was the basis of social, economic, and political thought and structure.

The differing experiences of ever-married and never-married women make sense in light of the prominence of the conjugal household and family

under, widows. Even Amy Erickson, whose attention to marital status led her to divide her book on women and property in early modern England into separate sections on maids, wives, and widows, sometimes muddled these groups. Two of her chapters in the section on widows, 'How Lone Women Lived' and 'Lone Women's Wills', merge together the experiences of both widows and singlewomen: Erickson, *Women and Property*. For a recent defence of studying singlewomen and widows as one group, based on medieval English sources at least, see Cordelia Beattie, 'A Room of One's Own? The Legal Evidence for the Residential Arrangements of Women Without Husbands in Late Fourteenth- and Early Fifteenth-Century York', in Noel James Menuge (ed.), *Medieval Women and the Law* (Woodbridge: Boydell Press, 2000), 41–56.

[4] Peter Laslett, 'Mean Household Size in England Since the Sixteenth Century', in Peter Laslett and Richard Wall (eds.), *Household and Family in Past Time* (Cambridge: Cambridge University Press, 1972), 145. Calculations are my own. Southampton Record Office (hereafter SRO), SC 14/2/66a–68b, 70a–74c. For more on singlewomen in Southampton's 1696 Marriage Duty Tax assessments, see Amy Froide, 'Hidden Women: Rediscovering Singlewomen in Early Modern England', *Local Population Studies*, 68 (Spring 2002), 26–41.

[5] See introduction to Judith M. Bennett and Amy M. Froide (eds.), *Singlewomen in the European Past, 1250–1800*, (Philadelphia: University of Pennsylvania, 1999).

in early modern English society. Early modern England was a patriarchal society in which contemporaries thought of women in terms of their familial roles: as daughter, wife, mother, and widow. The position of women who had married was clear: wives assisted their husbands in the running of households, and widows, by virtue of being the deputies of their deceased husbands, headed households. But contemporaries did not conceive of singlewomen as heading or even assisting in running households of their own. Rather, women who had never married were expected to remain in a dependent position, in which they lived as daughters or, if their parents were deceased, as sisters, kin, or servants in another male's household. The only acceptable role for the never-married woman was as a household dependant, not as an independent female head of household, outside the control of a father or master. This was a serious problem for the many singlewomen who could not or did not live as dependants. Widows had a public and independent place within the patriarchal society; never-married women did not.

Marginalized singlewomen faced more scrutiny and operated under more disadvantages than did widows, who at least enjoyed a sanctioned social role.[6] This chapter illuminates the differing experiences of singlewomen and widows throughout various communities in early modern England by focusing on three areas—residential options, employment, and poor relief—which best illustrate the differences between ever-married and never-married women. We will find that while singlewomen and widows may have shared a theoretical legal status, never-married women laboured under practical disadvantages that meant that they seldom enjoyed the residential, employment, and welfare opportunities of ever-married women. While such distinctions between ever-married and never-married women were the rule, we will also see how age and social status allowed a small number of singlewomen to achieve a 'widow-like' status, so that they experienced contingently the opportunities reserved customarily for matrons who had married.

Residence

Singlewomen and widows had very different residential options available to them. For one thing, widows had more alternatives from which to choose. The dominance of the nuclear family and household in early modern England meant that once a husband died, his widow did not return to

---

[6] Widows also encountered difficulties in a patriarchal society such as early modern England; however, both the positive and negative experiences of widows have been studied much more. For the literature on early modern widowhood see Chapter 1.

her natal family or go to live with her husband's family. Instead, she became the head of her deceased husband's household.[7] In assuming the role of head of household a widow gained authority over the house, the family, the servants and apprentices, and the family business. She had earned this role by marrying and helping to create a household, which it was her responsibility to continue after her husband was gone. This pattern of nuclear households is evidenced by the 70 per cent of households in early modern England that were headed by married couples, as well as the 12.9 per cent (the next most common arrangement) headed by widows.[8] Of the residential options a widow entertained upon her spouse's death, heading her own household was the most popular. For example, between 72 and 79 per cent of widows headed their own households in eighteenth-century Lichfield, Stoke-on-Trent, and Corfe Castle.[9] In the port town of Southampton it was customary for a widow whose husband left her with property to take over his lease and remain in the family home. This was the case in 1705 when the widow Elizabeth Rowte took out a new lease on a tenement in French Street (that her husband John Rowte had originally leased in 1679), and continued to head a household made up of herself and several adult children.[10] Of course, poverty prevented some widows from establishing their own households, but even poor widows had options. They might move in with kin (such as adult children, siblings, or even parents if they were young), with friends, or board in another family's home. By opening their homes to lodgers or boarders, some poor widows retained their headship of households. And some widows co-headed households with other women who lived without husbands. For example, in 1696 widow Flood and widow Weeks lived together with Weeks's two children in St Lawrence's parish, Southampton. These two widows shared household expenses and housework, and perhaps provided emotional as well as material support to one another.[11] Even if they could not always exercise it, widows enjoyed the privilege of living on their own, or at least heading a household with another woman, and the majority chose to do so. Widows made use of the independence their marital status gave them. If poor, they still had the option to retain their household and bring in lodgers, or to lodge them-

    [7] E.g. Barbara Todd found that while only 4% of married male testators left their dwelling houses to their children, fully three-quarters of these testators expected their wives to become the head of household. Barbara J. Todd, 'Widowhood in a Market Town: Abingdon, 1540–1720', D.Phil. thesis, University of Oxford (1983), 8, 256; Laslett, 'Mean Household Size', 125–6.

    [8] Laslett, 'Mean Household Size', 147.

    [9] Richard Wall, 'Woman Alone in English Society', *Annales de Demographie Historique*, 17 (1981), 313. Wall examines the living arrangements of widowed and never-married women using population listings from the Staffordshire towns of Lichfield (1695) and Stoke-on-Trent (1701), as well as the rural community of Corfe Castle, Dorset (1790). Calculations are my own.

    [10] SRO, SC 4/3/359.

    [11] SRO, SC 14/2/66a, b.

selves with other women—for widows, no matter what their social status, had earned to right to live outside a male-controlled household. And if more prosperous, widows could opt to establish their own households, where they could gather around them whichever children, servants, relatives, and friends they could accommodate.

The residential situation of a never-married woman was quite different from and far more limited than that of a widow. Because a lifelong singlewoman did not engage in a wedding ceremony there was never a definitive public moment when she became a householder in her own right. And precisely because she had not married, a singlewoman had not earned the privilege of setting up her own household.[12] While widows were in charge of 12.9 per cent of households in early modern England, never-married women headed only 1.1 per cent.[13] There were twice as many singlewomen than widows in England, but they headed only a tiny fraction of households. It was rare for a never-married woman, especially a younger or poorer one, to be in charge of her own household. Richard Wall has found that a singlewoman under the age of 45 typically lived as a dependent daughter in her parents' household until they died; then she went to live as a servant, lodger, or relative in someone else's home. Only between 4.5 and 5.9 per cent of singlewomen below age 45 headed their own households.[14]

While the focus here is on the residential options of urban singlewomen, housing difficulties for never-married women did not end at the town walls. Bridget Hill has detailed the equally difficult circumstances faced by rural singlewomen. She argues that the enclosure movement disproportionately affected lone women who lived on small plots of land, where they erected illegal cottages and subsisted by grazing animals on common land and gleaning.[15]

Contemporaries expected never-married women to live as dependants in the households of their fathers, male relatives, or masters, and those who did not do so caused local authorities a good deal of worry. One reason for this expectation was the assumption that a singlewoman was a young woman, and contemporaries believed that young people were in need of

[12] It is difficult to judge when the adulthood of never-married women began. For more on this issue see Amy Froide, 'Old Maids: The Lifecycle of Singlewomen in Early Modern England', in L. A. Botelho and Pat Thane (eds.), *Women and Ageing in British Society Since 1500* (New York: Longman, 2001).

[13] Laslett, 'Mean Household Size', 147.

[14] Wall found that between 43.9 and 53.8% of never-married women below the age of 45 lived with at least one parent, while between 30.2 and 39.4% lived as a servant, between 5.4 and 11% lived as a lodger, and between 3 and 7.6% lived with some other relative. Wall, 'Woman Alone', 311.

[15] Bridget Hill, *Women Alone: Spinsters in England, 1660–1850* (New Haven, Conn.: Yale University Press, 2001), 18.

discipline and authoritarian control.[16] From at least the fifteenth century, and continuing well into the seventeenth century, municipal authorities throughout England issued edicts against never-married women who lived independently of fathers or masters, or in other words, outside a family or male-headed household.[17] In 1492 the civic officers of Coventry ordered that 'no singlewoman . . . take or keep from henceforth houses or rooms to themselves, nor that they take any room with any other person, but that they go into service'.[18] A century later, in 1582, the officers of South-ampton's court leet defined the single female objects of their concern as charmaids, or 'maid servants that take chambers and so live by themselves masterless and are called by the name of charwomen which we think not meet or sufferable . . . '[19] In other sixteenth- and seventeenth-century towns, such as Norwich, the town fathers issued orders against young people living 'at their own hand'. Almost all of those prosecuted under such orders were younger singlewomen from the labouring classes and female servants, who lived either on their own or in female-headed households.[20]

Town fathers worried about independent singlewomen for various reasons. Diane Willen believes the authorities in York were concerned about never-married women living on their own because they thought such women 'represented a threat to the patriarchal social order', by living outside the authority of the household and a male master.[21] Some local officers raised suspicions about the morality of singlewomen who lived alone, and accused them of serving as a bad example. In 1584 Manchester's court leet railed against 'women being unmarried [who] be at their own hands . . . also abusing themselves with young men and others having not any man to control them to the great dishonour of God and evil example of others'.[22] Urban authorities, such as those in Manchester, assumed that sexual immorality would be the by-product of any never-married woman

---

[16] Griffiths says that 'the household and service were the most widely discussed forms of disciplining youth' in early modern England. Paul Griffiths, *Youth and Authority: Formative Experiences in England 1560–1640* (Oxford: Clarendon Press, 1996), 13. These institutions served the same purpose for singlewomen, whether young or old.

[17] Concern over independent singlewomen was by no means limited to England. See Bronislaw Geremek, *The Margins of Society in Late Medieval Paris* (New York: Cambridge University Press, 1987), 221; and Merry E. Wiesner, 'Having Her Own Smoke: Employment and Independence For Singlewomen in Germany, 1400–1750', in Bennett and Froide (eds.), *Singlewomen in the European Past*.

[18] Cited in P. J. P. Goldberg (ed.), *Women in England c. 1275–1525* (New York: Manchester University Press, 1995), 212.

[19] F. J. C. and D. M. Hearnshaw (eds.), *Southampton Court Leet Records A.D. 1578–1602*, Southampton Record Society, 2 (Southampton, 1905–6), 236.

[20] Griffiths, *Youth and Authority*, 358, 381–2.

[21] Diane Willen, 'Women in the Public Sphere in Early Modern England: The Case of the Urban Working Poor', *Sixteenth Century Journal*, 19: 4 (1988), 561.

[22] J. P. Earwaker (ed.), The *Court Leet Records of the Manor of Manchester*, Vol. 1: *1552–1686* (Manchester, 1884), 241; Griffiths, *Youth and Authority*, 380.

living on her own. Officials elided singlewomen who lived in their own lodgings with prostitutes who rented lodgings from which they plied their trade. The line between a singlewoman who worked and lived on her own and a prostitute became a thin one.[23] This seems to have been purposeful, since it allowed urban authorities to control any independent woman under the guise of moral policing. These urban ordinances caused the morality of all never-married women to be called into question and created a precedent for legislating and controlling singlewomen's sexuality. Such sexual control is something we will also see in the bastardy laws discussed below.

Town officials addressed in the strictest terms the supposed social and moral threat posed by never-married women living on their own. When Southampton's officials failed to compel independent singlewomen back into household dependency, they forced the women to leave the town. In 1609, for example, they told the charmaid Elizabeth Green to put herself into service within two weeks or to depart from Southampton. In this manner, Southampton's assembly prosecuted fourteen charmaids between 1607 and 1608, ten between 1609 and 1610, and nine more between 1615 and 1616.[24] While enforced departure was a common threat in Southampton, singlewomen in Norwich who took chambers or otherwise lived out of service were more commonly incarcerated in the local Bridewell, or house of correction, where they would be whipped and set to work.[25]

Persecution of singlewomen whose only 'crime' was to live and work on their own was no accident. Scholars have noted the intense fear of disorder expressed by Tudor and early Stuart contemporaries. The targets of this fear were often poor, female, and young: those people who seemed to threaten a social order run by adult, married males of middling and elite

[23] See Ruth Karras, 'Sex and the Singlewoman', and Sharon Farmer, '"It Is Not Good That [Wo]man Should Be Alone": Elite Responses to Singlewomen in High Medieval Paris', both in Bennett and Froide (eds.), *Singlewomen in the European Past*, for how singlewomen and prostitutes were conflated in the Middle Ages. Goldberg believes that Coventry's ordinance forbidding single-women to live on their own was aimed at prostitutes: P. J. P. Goldberg, *Women, Work, and Life Cycle in a Medieval Economy: Women in York and Yorkshire c.1300–1520* (Oxford: Clarendon Press, 1992), 155–6.

[24] J. W. Horrocks (ed.), *Assembly Books of Southampton 1609–10*, Southampton Record Society, 21 (Southampton, 1920), 59; id. (ed.), *Assembly Books of Southampton 1602–8, 1609–10, 1611–14, 1615–16*, Southampton Records Series, 19, 21, 24, 25 (Southampton, 1917, 1920, 1924, 1925); W. J. Connor (ed.), *The Southampton Mayor's Book of 1606–1608*, Southampton Records Series, 21 (Southampton, 1978).

[25] These punishments may have differed because the Norwich singlewomen who were accused of being 'out of service' were commonly residents of the town, while the residential status of South-ampton's charmaids is not always possible to discern. Those who can be identified as residents were less likely to be told to depart. Griffiths, *Youth and Authority*, 380; Amy Froide, 'Single Women, Work, and Community in Southampton, 1550–1750', Ph.D. dissertation, Duke University (1996), 269–70. Bridewells were used to incarcerate petty offenders, including those who were 'idle' or anyone who had run away from service or refused to serve. Joanna Innes, 'Prisons For the Poor: English Bridewells, 1555–1800', in Francis Snyder and Douglas Hay (eds.), *Labour, Law, and Crime: An Historical Perspective* (New York: Tavistock Publications, 1987), 70, 74, 85.

status.[26] The never-married women who found themselves the subject of much local legislation were not only from the lower classes, but also young, female, and of an anomalous marital status in a society that privileged the marital state. Singlewomen might well have been the early modern patriarch's worst nightmare—encompassing multiple characteristics of disorder all at once. Nevertheless, views of never-married women do seem to have modified over the early modern era. By the 1640s urban authorities became less overtly concerned about independent singlewomen, and punishments of such women waned, although they did not disappear completely. Intriguingly, although the antipathy toward them was lessening, there was no consequent increase in the numbers of never-married women living on their own. Even at the end of the seventeenth century only 8 per cent of singlewomen (twenty-two out of a total of 292 possible singlewomen) headed their own households in Southampton. If we consider another twenty-one possible singlewomen living with unrelated persons as 'co-household heads', then 15 per cent of singlewomen headed their own households. But this small percentage does not even compare to the 86 per cent of widows who headed or co-headed their own households in the port town.[27]

As the above figures indicate, a minority of singlewomen did manage to form their own households. These women shared three characteristics: advanced age, the absence of any living parent, and elevated social status. When urban authorities legislated against singlewomen living on their own, they were assuming that all women married and that any woman who was single was also young. But not all women did marry in early modern England, and for older singlewomen living with a parent was not always an option (since they might very well be deceased), nor were positions in service always available or consonant with a woman's social status. These lifelong singlewomen were the ones most likely to establish their own households.

Two events enabled a never-married woman to establish her own household. The first was passing the age of menopause, which would have signified the end of any assumption that a singlewoman would inevitably marry, produce a family, and assist in running her husband's household. Menopause and older age may have also signalled a rise in autonomy for the

[26] The period from *c*.1560 to 1640 is now recognized as one of socio-economic upheaval in England (characterized by high population growth, inflation, unemployment, increasing poverty, and vagrancy), which resulted in much contemporary worry about disorderly elements in society. On a crisis in gender relations, see: Susan D. Amussen, *An Ordered Society: Gender and Class in Early Modern England* (New York: Oxford University Press, 1988); Michael Roberts, 'Women and Work in Sixteenth-Century Towns', in P. J. Corfield and D. Keene (eds.), *Work in Towns 850–1850* (New York: Leicester University Press, 1990), 86–102; David Underdown, 'The Taming of the Scold: The Enforcement of Patriarchal Authority in Early Modern England', in Anthony Fletcher and John Stevenson (eds.), *Order and Disorder in Early Modern England*, (New York: Cambridge University Press, 1985). On youth and disorder, see: Griffiths, *Youth and Authority*, 6–7, 13, and ch. 7.
[27] SRO, SC 14/2/66a–68b, 70a–74c.

singlewoman, thus allowing her to live more independently.[28] For instance, in a sample of three eighteenth-century communities in Staffordshire and Dorset, only between 4.5 and 5.9 per cent of singlewomen under 45 years of age headed their own households, but between 36.4 and 40 per cent of singlewomen aged 45 and over headed their own households. Age, in other words, resulted in an eight- or ninefold increase in the number of single female householders.[29] Forty-five is the age demographers have chosen to differentiate between life-cycle and lifelong singlewomen, but it does seem close to the age at which contemporaries decided a never-married woman might acceptably live on her own. For instance, in Coventry officials were explicit that 'no singlewoman... under the age of fifty years, [should] take or keep from henceforth houses or rooms to themselves'.[30]

The second event that allowed a never-married woman to set up her own household was the death of a surviving parent. This circumstance heralded the end of a singlewoman's tenure as daughter, as well as the loss of a parental household in which to reside. The small but significant number of single female householders in seventeenth-century Southampton all shared the circumstance of their surviving parent's recent death. Barbara Richards was 38 years old when she leased her own town house in 1705. Her mother had died in 1698, and the messuage that Richards leased had been her mother's before she died. A few years after their widowed mother died, Elizabeth and Joanna Shergold, who were 47 and 39 years old respectively, leased a large house together in 1721.[31] And in 1733 a 49-year-old Ann Goodridge was living in her own house one year after she had served as her father's executrix.[32] An older singlewoman, who had neither a parent's nor a husband's household to live in, may have now resembled a widow, and like a widow now had the privilege of living on her own.[33] Nevertheless, there was no distinct age at which a singlewoman might strike out on her own. Instead, it seems she had to judge what her own family and community

[28] Contemporary literature placed menopause between the ages of 40 and 50. Patricia Crawford, 'Menstruation in Seventeenth-Century England', *Past & Present* (1981), 65–79. Keith Thomas has theorized that advancing age may have resulted in rising female authority. Keith Thomas, 'Age and Authority in Early Modern England', *Proceedings of the British Academy*, 62 (1976), 205–48.
[29] Wall, 'Woman Alone', 311.
[30] Earwaker, *Court Leet Records of Manchester*, 241. For more on singlewomen and the significance of middle age, see Amy Froide, 'Old Maids', in Botelho and Thane (eds.), *Women and Ageing in British Society.*
[31] SRO, transcript of the parish registers of Holy Rood (29 July 1667, 1 Aug. 1674, 3 Apr. 1682).
[32] SRO, D/ABC 1/1, fos. 56v, 59.
[33] Much more rarely, age could also affect the householder status of widows. For example, in 1613 Margaret Griffin was widowed and living in her brother's house in Southampton. Griffin was young and had no children, so Southampton's authorities treated her more like a singlewoman than a widow. They did not allow Griffin the option of living wherever she chose, but instead told her brother that she must either leave Southampton or put herself into service by Michaelmas. *Assembly Books of Southampton 1611–14*, 66.

would condone. This may have left many never-married women in their thirties and forties unsure of their options, and at a loss if they had no family or master with which to reside.

While advanced age and parental demise were sufficient reasons for a singlewoman to become a householder, middling-to-elite social status was a necessary factor. It is telling that all of the never-married women who headed their own households in seventeenth-century Southampton were not only mature in years, but also of independent and ample means. For example, Barbara Richards was the daughter of a Southampton gentleman, who supported herself by lending money when she began to lease a house of her own.[34] Elizabeth and Joanna Shergold, also the daughters of a South-ampton gentleman, employed themselves in trade and kept a boarding house for young ladies. The latter occupation required them to have their own residence, so together they rented one of the largest buildings in Southampton.[35] Singlewomen like Richards and the Shergold sisters had the means to support themselves, a matter of considerable importance to civic officers. Early modern towns did not want to play host to singlewomen who might become economic charges as they aged and who had no family on which to rely for assistance. Through various measures town fathers discouraged any but the prosperous from establishing households in their towns.[36]

Nevertheless, not all of the singlewomen who had the economic means to set up their own households chose to do so. Sometimes they opted to live in the households of relatives or friends. For example, the Southampton singlewoman Jane Bracebridge lived in the household of her kinsman Robert Richbell, despite the fact that she was mature, well-off, and enjoyed the partial ownership of two houses in which she could have lived on her own.[37] Why did Bracebridge choose to live as a dependant? Perhaps she had heard too many stories about the harassment of independent singlewomen, or she too felt the concern contemporaries voiced over the virtue of never-married women living on their own. Or, as we shall see in the next chapter, she may have enjoyed the companionship. Whatever the reason, a widow could legitimately maintain her own household and her neighbours would not give it a second thought, but a never-married woman only did so contingent on her age, financial means, and reputation.[38] And even then

---

[34] SRO, SC 7/1/21 (1703); SC 4/3/360a & b, 453.

[35] SRO, D/MC 10/11, 8a & b.

[36] The 1662 Settlement Act stipulated that if newcomers to a town were questioned within 40 days of their arrival they could only remain if they had rented property worth at least £10 a year. Paul Slack, *The English Poor Law 1531–1782* (Basingstoke: Macmillan, 1990), 36.

[37] Hampshire Record Office (hereafter HRO), 1697 B6; SRO, SC 14/2/37a.

[38] Charles Carlton, 'The Widow's Tale: Male Myths and Female Reality in Sixteenth and Seventeenth Century England' *Albion*, 10: 2, (1978), 126.

her kin and community might not approve of such an arrangement. Younger and poorer singlewomen were in an even more constrained situation; they seem to have never enjoyed the full freedom or choice to live on their own.

Employment

If the residential options available to singlewomen were more limited than those enjoyed by widows, never-married women fared even worse in employment opportunities. Widows enjoyed the most extensive economic rights and privileges of any working women in the early modern period. Most women living in English towns had a difficult time breaking into formal trades, which were often organized into male-run gilds and companies in this period. In Southampton, for example, women were denied regular apprenticeship and entry into the freedom (a status which conveyed the right to trade in the town). Other towns were slightly more open to female apprentices and mistresses, but women never operated on equal terms with men. Nevertheless, wives often worked as partners in their husbands' businesses, and both gild and civic officials permitted widows to continue the trades of their deceased husbands. By virtue of their status as 'deputy husbands', widows in towns like York and Southampton formed the majority of women independently engaged in formal trades.[39] The widow Judith Delamotte, for example, carried on her husband's cloth trade and even expanded the family business, becoming one of seventeenth-century Southampton's most successful businesswomen.[40] Not only did widows inherit their husbands' trades, but urban authorities also on occasion allowed widows to succeed to their husbands' public offices, which provided them with a source of both income and prestige. In 1586 Southampton's assembly allowed widow Alice Harvey to assume the office of a porter for her lifetime.[41] Widow Harvey had to hire a male labourer to do the actual carrying, but she did appropriate a portion of the fees collected for the service, and thus was able to maintain herself.

The widows of wealthy craftsmen, merchants, and officials benefited from economic privileges, but less wealthy widows and wives found employment in informal and casual work. Ever-married women engaged in

---

[39] Diane Willen, 'York Guildswomen, 1560–1700', *The Historian*, 46 (Feb. 1984), 204–18, esp. 209.

[40] *Assembly Books of Southampton 1615–16*, 1–2.

[41] Porters carried goods from ships anchored in the harbour to storehouses and cellars in Southampton. A. L. Merson (ed.), *Third Book of Remembrance of Southampton 1514–1602*, Southampton Records Series, 8 (Southampton, 1965), 41.

various stages of textile production; they worked as petty retailers of food, alcohol, and other small goods; they ran lodging houses and alehouses; and they assisted the sick and the poor. Urban authorities often regulated the widows and wives who worked in these informal employments, but by doing so they also condoned their work. For instance, in 1650 Southampton's assembly questioned the widow Anne Janverine about her huckstering, and decided to allow her to retail 'fish, salt, candles, butter and other victuals provided that she [did] not sell any other thing and [did] not forestall, regrate or do any other thing contrary to the law or order of the town'.[42] Sometimes town fathers not only allowed but actively recruited working widows and wives. In York and Southampton civic officers regularly paid widows and wives for distributing relief to the poor, instructing poor children and 'idle' singlewomen in a trade, assisting in the births of illegitimate and poor children, nursing the sick, and laying out and burying the dead.[43] In London and Salisbury widows and wives comprised the majority of women who let out lodgings, retailed food, brewed and sold beer, and managed alehouses.[44] Officials in Southampton, Salisbury, and many other communities regularly granted licenses to work as victuallers, tipplers (sellers of ale), and alehouse-keepers to poor widows in particular. The predominance of widows among such licensees can be explained by the fact that local officials used such casual work as a form of poor relief for needy widows.[45] Urban officials could give licenses to anyone they wished, but they singled out widows; and in so doing they deemed widowed female householders especially worthy of economic assistance.

Town officials not only allowed widows to engage in both formal and informal trades, they also doled out more active assistance to these women. When widows did not possess the money or goods necessary to continue the family business, they were sometimes able to borrow money from local authorities in order to establish a livelihood. Testators in provincial towns

[42] SRO, SC 2/1/8, fo. 69v. To forestall was to buy up goods before they reached the market in order to sell them again for profit, and to regrate was to buy up goods to sell them again at a higher price. Local authorities frowned on both practices because they supposedly increased the cost of food and goods.

[43] SRO, PR 9/15/5; Willen, 'Women in the Public Sphere'.

[44] Widows and wives comprised virtually all of the female hawkers, caterers, and victuallers in early modern London. Peter Earle, 'The Female Labour Market in London in the Late Seventeenth and Early Eighteenth Centuries', *Economic History Review*, 2nd ser., 42: 3 (1989), 339. Wright found that petty retailing was particularly suited to poor wives and widows, and that widows frequently engaged in victualling. Sue Wright, ' "Churmaids, Huswyfes and Hucksters": The Employment of Women in Tudor and Stuart Salisbury', in Lindsay Charles and Lorna Duffin (eds.) *Women and Work in Pre-industrial England*, (London: Croom Helm, 1985), 108, 110.

[45] Paul Slack, 'Poverty and Politics in Salisbury 1597–1666', in Peter Clark and Paul Slack (eds.), *Crisis and Order in English Towns 1500–1700: Essays in Urban History*, (London: Routledge & Kegan Paul, 1972), 182, 190; Judith Bennett, *Ale, Beer, and Brewsters in England: Women's Work in a Changing World, 1300–1600* (New York: Oxford University Press, 1996), 56 and n. 75; Willen, 'Women in the Public Sphere', 560, 564–5.

often endowed loans or grants of money to individuals (usually young men) starting up in a business or trade. In 1670 Southampton's assembly reiterated that only those persons holding the freedom to trade in the town (that is, men) were to receive such assistance, but in practice widows also received loans. Between 1641 and 1721, 560 people received money from Mr Lynch's endowment, twenty-two of whom were women—all widows. The widows obtained loans of £10 a piece, the same amount that men received.[46] While widows made up only 4 per cent of those persons receiving money from Mr Lynch's gift, they did relatively well, since they comprised at most 14 per cent of the adult population in Southampton. Widows were the only women acknowledged as legitimate recipients of business loans in Southampton.

This is not to say that widows always found themselves welcome in the urban economy. A widow who remarried and attempted to continue in her prior husband's occupation could encounter opposition. In 1674 Southampton's assembly, after hearing various complaints from the hatters against Mrs Lyne, told her that she had to forebear from selling any hats within the town because she had 'no right to the trade'; she had forfeited it by remarrying. Nor could a widow practise a trade different from that of her deceased husband. Protests against such women even came from fellow widows, as was the case in 1718, when Southampton's assembly ordered widow Fry not to sell any more grocery or other wares upon the complaint of widow Dummer and other grocers' widows.[47] These examples show that Southampton's authorities did not hesitate to restrict the trading activities of widows on occasion. But local authorities dealt with widowed women on an individual basis. This was very different from how local officials treated working singlewomen, whom they declined to help, and in fact punished as a group.

Working women who never married faced many disadvantages, for they enjoyed neither the economic toleration nor the economic assistance extended to working widows. Singlewomen obviously could not inherit a trade or office from a husband, and it was not customary for fathers to leave their businesses to their daughters. Some never-married women did learn skills and work in their parents' shops, while a few others even apprenticed themselves into a formal trade. But most of these women did not enjoy the possibility of independently exercising these trades. This was because in early modern England to be a master or mistress in a trade also meant being a householder. Just as local authorities believed that a singlewoman should reside as a dependant in someone else's household and not be an

---

[46] SRO, SC 2/1/8, fo. 261v; SRO, D/MC 7/1, 6/1, 8/1; SRO, D/MC/7/1.
[47] SRO, SC 2/1/8, fo. 307 and SC 2/1/9, fo. 521.

independent householder, so they also believed that the only appropriate economic role for a never-married woman was a subordinate one. A never-married woman was encouraged, even expected, to work for her family, other relatives, or as a servant in a master's household, but she was not supposed to establish a business of her own or work independently as widows did. Even when a singlewoman worked with her siblings, if they were male or widowed, urban authorities viewed her as a dependent worker. For example, in 1697 the singlewoman Ann Faulkner and her widowed sister Mary Stotes jointly inherited their mother's trade. The following year 'widow Stotes and her sister' paid a Stall and Art fee (an annual licensing fee that allowed those without the freedom to trade in the town). But the tax assessors in Holy Rood parish didn't even bother to mention Faulkner when they assessed the widow 'Mrs. Stotes' stock in trade' at a value of £12. 10s.[48] In the eyes of Southampton's officials, widow Stotes was an independent tradeswoman, but the singlewoman Ann Faulkner was a dependent worker, sometimes noted as Stotes's sister, and sometimes not mentioned at all.

As the sisters Mary Stotes and Ann Faulkner illustrate, even though singlewomen shared the legal status of *feme sole* with widows, and thus had the legal ability to trade, in practice urban authorities allowed widows to engage in formal trades but not never-married women.[49] When singlewomen tried to exercise their *feme sole* status they met with opposition. In other towns besides Southampton legal theory and local economic practice also diverged sharply.[50] For instance, Mary Prior has found that while Oxford's officials tolerated the business activities of both married women and widows, 'the independent singlewoman had no place in the Oxford commercial community'.[51] As we will see in Chapter 4, while widows formed a consistent minority of those individuals who paid the Stall and Art fees to trade in Southampton each year, only one singlewoman did so before the 1680s. And even Mary Sherwood, who inherited her widowed mother's shop and trade in 1639, enjoyed a very brief stint as the only officially acknowledged single tradeswoman in Southampton, since she died the following year.[52]

[48] HRO, 1697 A48; SRO, SC 6/1/73, SC 14/2/97. See Ch. 4 for more on Stall and Art fees.

[49] Katherine Kittredge also notes that it was beneficial for a singlewoman in early modern England to 'remain attached to a widow, since in this way she could share in economic opportunities unavailable to her as a single woman'. Katharine Ottaway Kittredge, '"Tabby Cats Lead Apes in Hell": Spinsters in Eighteenth Century Life and Fiction', Ph.D. dissertation, SUNY, Binghamton (1991), 71.

[50] In her study of working women in Oxford, Mary Prior noted that 'whilst common law might not hinder singlewomen and widows from trading, borough custom might do so'. Mary Prior, 'Women and the Urban Economy', in her *Women in English Society: 1500–1800* (New York: Routledge, 1994), 103.

[51] Ibid. 110–12.

[52] SRO, SC 6/1/50; HRO, 1641 A100/1.

If Sherwood had lived she would have most likely shared the treatment that Mary Shrimpton Jr. received from Southampton's assembly. In 1649 the Justices of the Peace examined the widow Shrimpton and her daughter Mary Jr. about the theft of two cheeses from a shop. They decided that Mary Jr. 'appeared to be an idle and suspicious housewife and therefore sent [her] to the workhouse'.[53] Eight years later Mary Jr. again aroused the disapproval of the town officials, but this time for very different behaviour. The assembly gave her 'one month's space to put off and dispose of her sackcloth and whalebone which she has now in her house and custody and from that time forward to forbear to use the trade of bodice making unless she be employed by the freemen of the town'.[54] While Shrimpton had at first appeared too idle to Southampton's authorities, now she seemed too industrious and independent, and the officers punished her for both behaviours. Mary Shrimpton Jr. illustrates the difficult position in which singlewomen found themselves—they were punished for not supporting themselves, but they were also penalized for working independently in formal trades.

One option for a never-married woman like Shrimpton was to find work in the informal and casual trades such as victualling and huckstering that employed so many wives and widows. But even in these occupations never-married women were treated differently from their ever-married sisters. Widows made up the majority of women working as tipplers and alehouse-keepers, but singlewomen were less active in these trades. In early modern London, out of a sample of fifty-three women engaged in catering or victualing, thirty-two were wives, eighteen were widows, and only three were never married.[55] In Southampton it was not until 1739 that Mary Smith became the first singlewoman to keep a licensed alehouse in the early modern era.[56] Ever-married women could gain licenses to victual, but never-married women usually could not. If it was the case that urban officials reserved licenses for alehouse-keeping and tippling for those persons they deemed worthy of help, it is not surprising to find so few singlewomen in these occupations. As we shall see, contemporaries did not usually number never-married women among the 'worthy' poor.

Singlewomen found a few more employment opportunities in huckstering, or selling small goods and victuals, than they did in tippling or alehouse-keeping; but the handful of never-married women who made a

---

[53] SRO, SC 9/3/12, fo. 25. 'Housewife' was an occupational term as well as an indicator of marital status, which explains why town officials used it to describe a singlewoman.
[54] SRO, SC 2/1/8, fo. 132.
[55] Earle, 'The Female Labour Market', 339, Table 10.
[56] SRO, SC 6/1/98.

living by petty retailing in towns like London and Southampton never
compared to the consistent number of ever-married women who did so.[57]
Perhaps the clearest example of the relative economic privilege of widows is
apparent in the starkly different manner in which Southampton's officials
treated petitions to trade made by widows and singlewomen. In 1607 Mrs
Ecton and her stepdaughter appeared before Southampton's assembly,
where Mrs Ecton asked if 'her daughter [might] be admitted to open a
shop above the Bar and sell small wares by retail'. The assembly's response
was an unequivocal no—they were unwilling to permit the singlewoman to
establish herself independently in trade.[58] Things were very different when,
in the summer of 1629, widow Tirrell came before the same assembly
asking if she might be allowed to sell goods in the town. The local
authorities had a different response for Tirrell, whom they allowed to
'have free liberty, license, and toleration from henceforth to retail all sorts
of saltfish and herring within this town'.[59] Even though Ecton's daughter
and widow Tirrell were both *femes soles*, and despite the fact that Ecton's
daughter had family backing for her venture (which made her a good
economic risk), Southampton's officials favoured the widow and frowned
on the singlewoman.

    If a never-married woman found herself unwelcome in formally organ-
ized and more casual trades, and did not have a family member for whom
she could work, then her most likely option was to enter into service. This
was exactly the type of subordinate economic position for singlewomen that
contemporaries encouraged, for it placed them under the roof and control
of a master or mistress.[60] Unfortunately for never-married women, good
service positions were not always to be found. For instance, a rising
population, unemployment, poverty, and a youthful age-structure made it
difficult to find a position in service at the turn of the seventeenth century.
And even if one had a position in service, it was precarious—servants were
often dismissed, and sickness or pregnancy could lead to the loss of one's
position.[61] In addition, lifelong singlewomen might not want, or be able, to
remain in service for their entire working lives. Never-married women
who would not or could not maintain themselves through service struck
out into various types of day labour or other independent occupations,

---

[57] Earle, 'The Female Labour Market', 339, Table 10.

[58] *The Southampton Mayor's Book of 1606–1608*, 102.

[59] SRO, SC 2/1/6, fo. 237.

[60] According to the Statute of Artificers (1563), people without independent trades could be
compelled into service. But the majority of those punished for being out of service were young
women. For instance, 80% of such cases in Norwich dealt with women. Griffiths, *Youth and
Authority*. 358.

[61] Ibid., 360; Bridget Hill, *Servants: English Domestics in the Eighteenth Century* (Oxford:
Clarendon Press, 1996), 95–9.

and in doing so ran afoul of local authorities. In Southampton such women were called 'charmaids', and in Norwich they were referred to as 'out of service', or in other communities as 'out of place'.[62] The assumption was that singlewomen should be employed as the servants of adult males, which was their proper 'place' in both the economic and social meanings of the word.

Just as early modern towns punished never-married women for attempting to set up their own households, town fathers also prosecuted singlewomen for working independently or in occupations other than service. The opposition that these day labourers, or charmaids, faced offers some of the clearest evidence of the official antipathy toward independent, working singlewomen. Never-married women in Norwich who were found 'out of service' were given the option of incarceration in the local Bridewell or finding a position in service within a set period of time.[63] In the late sixteenth and early seventeenth centuries Southampton's officials issued repeated proclamations against charmaids who kept 'themselves out of service and [worked] for themselves in diverse men's houses'.[64] Southampton's authorities did not stop at general pronouncements against independent working women, for they also singled out and punished individual singlewomen for working outside of service. These women would 'disappear' from their employers' homes after a reprimand or punishment, but then inevitably re-entered casual employment until the next time they came to the attention of the authorities. For instance, between 1608 and 1616 Southampton's beadles arrested Elizabeth Quinten for working as a charmaid at four separate times. In 1609 Quinten briefly responded to town pressure by getting a job as a servant; in 1615 she was thrown in the cage (a prison for petty criminals); and by 1627 she was resorting to petty thievery to sustain herself.[65] Like many other working singlewomen, Elizabeth Quinten lived a precarious life on the economic margins—moving from job to job, eking out a living, and trying to avoid the notice of the authorities.

Economic legislation was specifically crafted with social considerations in mind so that singlewomen would not compete with householders, and so

---

[62] Griffiths, *Youth and Authority*, 71, 353. A charwoman was someone who did 'char' work such as cleaning, laundering, or other household chores for a daily wage. However, in Southampton at least, town officials seemed to have used the word 'charmaid' to refer to women who performed any kind of day labour. They targeted singlewomen (char*maids* more specifically than char*women*) who neither lived with a master nor worked for that master for a contractual period of time.

[63] Griffiths, *Youth and Authority*, 354.

[64] *Southampton Court Leet Records A.D. 1578–1602*, 186.

[65] *Assembly Books of Southampton 1602–8*, 98; *1609–10*, 3; *1615–16*, 11; and R. C. Anderson (ed.), *Books of Examinations and Depositions 1622–44*, Southampton Record Society, 31 (Southampton, 1931), 15. For similar examples of repeat offenders in Norwich see Griffiths, *Youth and Authority*, ch. 7, esp. p. 351.

that never-married women would have no option but to work for someone else (and preferably in that person's household). For instance, Manchester's court leet railed at the 'inconvenience' caused by 'singlewomen... at their own hands [who] do bake and brew and use other trades to the great hurt of the poor inhabitants having wife and children'.[66] Never-married women, in other words, were discouraged from trading independently because they might compete with married male householders, who plied their trades to support their families. By living and working on their own, singlewomen were assuming the privileges of householders, which their communities did not think they deserved. Since contemporaries believed that never-married women were not proper householders and had no children to support, they were seen as unnecessary competition and so were not allowed to trade. This situation is similar to what Merry Wiesner has noted for Germany, where spinner's wages were purposely kept low so that singlewomen could not support themselves on their own, and thus would have to move into the household of some male master or artisan and work for him.[67] The work of never-married women was never restricted for purely economic reasons; such restrictions had as much to do with social expectations about who was a legitimate, independent worker, and in early modern Europe single-women were not viewed as such.

Despite the considerable opposition they faced from local officials, a few intrepid singlewomen did manage to work independently in early modern towns. As we will see in Chapter 4, this was not common until the late seventeenth century. And just as age and social status were mitigating factors that allowed a few singlewomen to set up their own households, these same characteristics enabled some never-married women to work independently. For instance, almost all of the single tradeswomen in Southampton were middle-aged as well as being householders and property holders in their own right. In other towns it was also singlewomen of at least middling social status who established themselves as independent traders. In Oxford it was the daughters of former mayors who broke into the male-dominated millinery trade.[68] In London and Edinburgh it was never-married women from middling families—the daughters of merchants, ministers, and significant tradesmen—who independently plied the trades of milliner, mantua-maker, and shopkeeper.[69]

---

[66] *Court Leet Records of Manchester*, 241. This 1584 ordinance was reissued in 1589 and once more. Griffiths, *Youth and Authority*, 357.

[67] Merry E. Wiesner, *Women and Gender in Early Modern Europe* (New York: Cambridge University Press, 1993), 99.

[68] Prior, 'Women and the Urban Economy', 112.

[69] Margaret R. Hunt, *The Middling Sort: Commerce, Gender, and the Family in England, 1680–1780* (Berkeley: University of California Press, 1996), ch. 5; Elizabeth C. Sanderson, *Women and Work in Eighteenth-Century Edinburgh* (New York: St Martin's Press, 1996), ch. 3.

Moreover, the few singlewomen who established their own businesses also did so without any public or charitable assistance. When widows established their own businesses they had somewhere to turn for business assistance. As noted above, between 1641 and 1721 twenty-two widows in Southampton received loans from Mr Lynch's charity. Eleven more widows also received economic aid from the charity endowed by John Steptoe in 1675. While this may seem a small figure it is still significant, because not one singlewoman received a business loan during the same period. Moreover, never-married women often had to pay exceptionally high fees to trade. In Southampton most male and widowed female traders paid 2*d.* each year for the privilege to trade in the town. But Jane Zains, one of the first singlewomen to pay Stall and Art so that she could trade as a linen-draper, paid a fee of 2*s.* 6*d.* This sum was fifteen times more than what most men and widows paid.[70] In other words, those singlewomen who managed to ply an independent trade never did so on equal terms with widows. If a never-married woman was old enough to resemble a widow, if she had her own household, and if she was wealthy enough to establish her own business and pay the discouragingly high trading fees, then urban officials might turn a blind eye to her trading. Nevertheless, civic officers were not going to assist or encourage a singlewoman in taking on the role of a householder and an independent tradesperson. As was the case with residential options, a few never-married women managed to carve out an independent space for themselves, but they only did so contingently, and not because they were viewed as legitimate tradespeople, worthy of the same privileges as others.

When urban authorities allowed widows to continue in their husbands' trades, licensed widows and wives to engage in casual employment, and assisted widows in establishing their own businesses, they acted not out of any conviction that ever-married women had the right to engage in trade, but because they believed in supporting the household and the family economy. If a wife worked in a by-employment or assisted her husband, then authorities viewed her as helping to maintain her household, rather than functioning as an individual worker. A widow was the deputy of her deceased husband, and if she could support herself and her children through her trade, then her family and her household would not become an economic burden on the town. By tolerating and even assisting the business activities of ever-married women town fathers aided in the maintenance of a family and a household.[71] These same officials regularly chose

---

[70] Froide, 'Single Women, Work, and Community', 282; SRO, SC 6/1/70–73.

[71] Roberts also believes that 'widows' rights to engage in trade and production seem . . . to have rested on the assumed priority of family survival'. Roberts, 'Women and Work', 91.

not to assist, and even to oppose outright, never-married women who worked for themselves. If they allowed singlewomen to trade, the town fathers believed that they would be supporting never-married women in independent and aberrant roles, since they expected these women to confine themselves to subordinate residential and economic positions within a household. Put simply, early modern people did not think of singlewomen as heads of household, even if in reality some were, and thus they saw no reason to support such women as independent workers.

Poor Relief

Widows not only had more economic opportunities open to them than did singlewomen, but if they were unemployed, widows also had an easier time than never-married women in securing poor relief. As with employment assistance, parochial officials dispensed poor relief in accordance with paternalistic beliefs about who was or was not a worthy recipient of aid. Widows typically found themselves included among the 'deserving poor', along with orphans, the aged, sick, or lame, as well as householders over-burdened with children. Because widows were usually either elderly, or young and 'overburdened' with children for whom they were the sole support, widowed women were some of the most common recipients of poor relief from the local parish. For instance, in the villages and towns of early modern Norfolk widows comprised an average of 50 per cent of those receiving poor relief.[72] Likewise, in the town of Abingdon (Oxon) widows were the largest group of poor relief recipients.[73] And in Southampton widows comprised two-thirds of the persons receiving money from the poor rates at the end of the sixteenth century.[74]

Widows also figured among the most common beneficiaries of assistance from private charities and almshouses. Each year seven poor people in Southampton received new clothing from the endowment of John Cornishe. In the years between 1617 and 1636 ever-married women described as widows and goodwives received at least three to four of these gowns (the remainder went to aged men), and sometimes, as in 1625, all of the gowns went to ever-married women. The women who lived in Southampton's numerous almshouses were also usually widows. For example, in 1675 the widow Mary Jenkins was living in the lower almshouse in St Mary's parish

[72] Tim Wales, 'Poverty, Poor Relief and the Life-Cycle: Some Evidence from Seventeenth-century Norfolk', in Richard M. Smith (ed.), *Land, Kinship and Life-Cycle* (New York: Cambridge University Press, 1984), 361, 377.
[73] Todd, 'Widowhood in a Market Town', 5.
[74] SRO, SC 10/1/5, 10.

when she petitioned Southampton's justices for some assistance because she was suffering from 'the [skin] disease called the King's Evil'.[75] Widows also made up a considerable proportion of the inhabitants of almshouses in York and Aldenham (Herts.). Outside of England, institutions for poor women also seem to have catered largely to widows rather than to never-married women.[76]

While needy widows were thus able to obtain various types of assistance, local officials expected singlewomen to shift for themselves. In an age that did not comprehend systemic unemployment, young and single individuals found themselves characterized as the 'able-bodied' or 'undeserving' poor. Paradoxically, civic officials required singlewomen to work and support themselves, but at the same time they limited these women's employment options and channeled them into less remunerative and less autonomous occupations, thus giving never-married women little control over their work or the length of their employment. Employment conditions such as these meant that singlewomen sometimes found themselves in need of relief, but they did not often get it.

Only a small number of never-married women figured in various lists of poor relief recipients compiled by urban authorities. For example, in 1552 the officers of St Michael's and St John's parish in Southampton provided assistance to four widows, seven men, four wives, sixteen children, but not to any known singlewomen.[77] Similarly, the census of the poor conducted by Norwich in 1570 identified forty never-married women as paupers, but only six of the forty obtained relief. By comparison, out of the 177 poor widows living in Norwich in the same year, sixty-four received financial assistance.[78] The likelihood of widows obtaining more relief than never-married women was even more striking in the seventeenth-century community of Aldenham. Here widows formed 48 per cent of those receiving assistance, but singlewomen averaged an incredibly small 4.5 per cent of the poor relief recipients.[79]

---

[75] SRO, SC 2/1/6; D/MC 1, 2; SC 9/1/19.

[76] Willen, 'Women in the Public Sphere', 563; W. Newman Brown, 'The Receipt of Poor Relief and Family Situation: Aldenham, Hertfordshire 1630–90', in Richard M. Smith (ed.), *Land, Kinship and Life-Cycle* (ed.), (New York: Cambridge University Press, 1984), 414. Hans Christian Johansen, 'Never-married Women in Town and Country in Eighteenth-Century Denmark', in John Henderson and Richard Wall (eds.), *Poor Women and Children in the European Past* (New York: Routledge, 1994), 202.

[77] SRO, SC 10/1/1. Three women whose marital status cannot be identified also received relief, some of whom may have been singlewomen.

[78] J. F. Pound (ed.), *The Norwich Census of the Poor*, Norfolk Record Society, 40 (Norwich, 1971). Calculations are my own. The census also includes 43 daughters over the age of 14. Nineteen of these single daughters lived in households that received relief payments, but such relief was assisting the household and not these singlewomen in particular. Out of an additional 63 women in the census whose marital status cannot be identified, 30 obtained economic assistance.

[79] Brown, 'The Receipt of Poor Relief', 412.

Historians of early modern England have largely characterized the 'deserving' poor as women, but the above examples caution against such a generalization. Ever-married women, and especially widows, made up the majority of women counted as the 'deserving' poor, but never-married women most definitely did not.[80] In terms of early modern poor relief, marital status mattered as much as gender. And the focus on marital status seems to have continued into the modern era. In 1835 the First Report of the [New] Poor Law Commissioners stated that singlewomen were not to be considered 'as members of families maintained by allowances, nor entitled to relief as distinct claimants'.[81]

While parish officials assisted poor parents and their young children, they did not extend that assistance to teenagers and young adults who were still living at home and not yet married. The contemporary correlation between singleness and 'undeserving' poverty is illustrated by the predicament of the Veere family of Southampton. In 1697 the parish officers of St Mary's gave widow Veere 2s. 6d. because she was otherwise unable to support herself and her young children. But the officers granted this money to widow Veere on the condition that she would make her eldest son and daughter 'go abroad into service'.[82] The churchwardens of St Mary's felt it was necessary to provide for poor widows and their young children, but not for their equally poor, but able-bodied, daughters and sons, whom the officers believed were capable of supporting themselves. In Norwich, children deemed old enough to be in service (14-year-old boys and 15-year-old girls) were ordered out of their mothers' households.[83] Likewise, in Aldenham and Terling (Essex) the parish officers refused to aid young people who could go into service, dispensing relatively little to individuals between the ages of 15 and 30, those who were old enough to leave home but not yet married.[84] Moreover, for women who never married—and so could not hope to earn the economic assistance officials extended to the heads of households—the years they spent without relief extended far beyond the age of 30.

The Norwich census of the poor provides a telling illustration of how urban officials singled out never-married women for punishment rather

---

[80] A. L. Beier, 'Vagrants and the Social Order in Elizabethan England', *Past & Present*, 64 (1974), 6–9; Slack, 'Poverty and Politics in Salisbury', 166; Wales, 'Poverty, Poor Relief and the Life-cycle', 361. For instance, Wales argues that women comprised an average of 63 % of all poor-relief recipients in his sample of Norfolk villages and towns. Nevertheless, 50 % were widows, while only the remaining 13 % was made up of wives and singlewomen. Calculations are my own.

[81] Cited in B. Hill, *Women Alone*, 97.

[82] SRO, PR 9/15/2.

[83] Griffiths, *Youth and Authority*, 381, 383.

[84] Brown, 'The Receipt of Poor Relief', 418–19; Pamela Sharpe, *Adapting to Capitalism: Working Women in the English Economy, 1700–1850* (Basingstoke: Macmillan, 1996), 109.

than for assistance. The census listed all paupers in the town, whether they received relief or not. It also included some singlewomen whom officials did not characterize as paupers, but whom they nevertheless chose to 'note' in the census. These included ten never-married women identified as harlots, three maids living with unrelated individuals whom officers either noted or ordered to depart, and four 'grass maids', a term for singlewomen who had given birth to bastards or who lived in common law unions. Three other 'grass women' did make it into the category of pauper. While officials found they could not fit these singlewomen into conventional categories for never-married females, such as servant or daughter, they also did not view most of these women as potential recipients of poor relief. Just as we saw with the ordinances against singlewomen living on their own, the sexual behaviour of never-married women was of particular interest to urban authorities.

As part of the 'undeserving' or 'able-bodied' poor, singlewomen were not ignored, but in contrast to the economic assistance obtained by widows, never-married women received more punitive attention.[85] Urban governors preferred to force poor singlewomen into compulsory labour, rather than giving them monetary aid. Communities throughout England enrolled young girls and singlewomen in pauper apprenticeships where they learned skills such as sewing, spinning, and housewifery.[86] After the passage of the Poor Law Act of 1598 (re-enacted in 1601) unemployed singlewomen in towns like Norwich were set to work on stocks of raw materials such as flax, hemp, and wool.[87] Towns such as Salisbury and Southampton set up workhouses for the poor in the early seventeenth century. In 1632 Southampton's Corporation established a workhouse wherein twenty resident children and up to forty other compulsory day workers (including adult singlewomen) would be forced to make bonelace, or to knit, card, and spin.[88]

Most historians agree, however, that schemes to set able-bodied paupers to work never successfully employed many people, singlewomen included. Instead, local authorities did a much better job incarcerating and punishing those who did not find employment. Alongside workhouses (and often in

[85] Historians of vagrancy have most often characterized the able-bodied poor as young, single males and have not paid much attention to singlewomen. Paul Slack found that out of a sample of 3,000 vagrants in the seventeenth century one-fourth were singlewomen, but he did not discuss female vagrants to any degree. Paul Slack, *Poverty and Policy in Tudor and Stuart England* (London: Longman, 1988), 98. A. L. Beier noted that in his sample of vagrant arrests just over half were of single males, but does not discuss the arrests of women. Beier, 'Vagrants and the Social Order', 6–9. The title of Beier's synthetic work on vagrancy in early modern England—*Masterless Men* (London: Methuen, 1985)—indicates his focus on male vagrants.

[86] A. J. Willis (comp.), and A. L. Merson (ed.), *A Calendar of Southampton Apprenticeship Registers 1609–1740*, Southampton Records Series, 12 (Southampton, 1968); Pamela Sharpe, 'Poor Children as Apprentices in Colyton, 1598–1830', *Continuity and Change*, 6: 2 (1991), 253–70.

[87] *The Norwich Census of the Poor*, 19.

[88] Slack, *Poverty and Policy*, 180–1; SRO, SC 2/1/6, fo. 254ᵛ.

the same building) towns established houses of correction for those persons deemed particularly idle, unwilling to work, or more generally 'lewd'. Southampton's officers installed a house of correction, or Bridewell, in their workhouse. Here the governor and his officers incarcerated and 'corrected' (or punished, usually by whipping) idle, vagrant, and incorrigible persons. Then they set these 'idle' paupers to work.[89] Women consistently made up a majority of the prisoners in Hampshire's house of correction (situated in the county town of Winchester) between 1680 and 1750. Indeed, women vastly outnumbered men in most of the urban Bridewells of seventeenth- and eighteenth-century England. Robert Shoemaker estimates that 69.3 per cent of the inhabitants in the houses of correction near the capital were female, and most of those unmarried.[90] These houses of correction were designed for exactly the sorts of petty crimes associated with singlewomen: prostitution, living out of service, petty larceny, idle or disorderly behaviour, and bastard bearing. For example, in the summer of 1706 Joanne Fisher was residing in Hampshire's house of correction 'for living an idle and disorderly life and [for being] out of service'.[91] Although Fisher may not have been able to find work due to the limited employment options of never-married women like herself, the authorities only recognized her idleness and disorderliness, and not her possible poverty. They punished this singlewoman instead of offering her any assistance.

This is not to say that the poverty of never-married women always went ignored and unassisted. Certain characteristics guaranteed particular singlewomen a place among the 'deserving' poor. Sickness, infirmity, old age, or motherhood enabled a poor singlewoman to appear worthy of at least temporary aid. For instance, in 1696 widow Beele and her never-married daughter Alice received assistance from the churchwardens of St Mary's parish, Southampton, who judged both women to be 'very poor and sickly and not able to earn their maintenance'. Significantly, just a year earlier the parish officers had been willing to support widow Beele but not her daughter. What had elevated Alice Beele to the status of 'deserving' poor was her illness, not simply her poverty. The churchwardens granted Alice half of the 4*s.* that they provided to her mother each month. Following the same logic, the parish officers extended relief to the singlewoman Ann Call in her mid-teens because she was 'unable to get her livelihood' due to a

---

[89] Slack, *Poverty and Policy,* 180–1; Wales, 'Poverty, Poor Relief and the Life-cycle', 379, 386; SRO, SC 2/1/6, fo. 254v.

[90] Innes, 'Prisons For the Poor', 100; Robert Shoemaker, *Prosecution, Punishment, Petty Crime and the Law in London and Rural Middlesex, c. 1660–1725* (Cambridge: Cambridge University Press, 1991), 185.

[91] HRO, Q 9/1/1–256.

crippled left leg. But in 1725 the parish officers apprenticed the 19-year-old Call against her will to a silk thrower, who twice absconded and left her without provision.[92] In this case, Call's infirmity had been worthy of temporary assistance, but the parochial officers eventually decided Call's singleness overshadowed her disability, and so they forced her to work instead of providing her with regular relief over her lifetime.

While sickness or disability might merit a never-married woman some aid, old age was the characteristic that entitled these women to the most relief. For example, Elizabeth Downer of Southampton received a significant amount of assistance in the form of money, food, and lodging throughout the 1730s, when she was in her seventies and eighties. All six of the pauper singlewomen who received relief according to Norwich's census were over 40 years of age, and half of them were also sick or 'lame'.[93] Advanced age allowed some singlewomen to establish their own households and businesses just as widows did. Similarly, old age allowed never-married women to resemble ever-married women by entitling them to the same poor relief that widows enjoyed. This does not mean that the majority of elderly singlewomen in need received assistance, however. It is significant that, even though never-married women outnumbered widows in the population, the number of widows who obtained poor relief was always much higher than the number of never-married women.

In addition to sickness and old age, certain life events allowed singlewomen to earn temporary economic assistance. Local governors rewarded never-married women who opted to enter into one of the dependent or traditional roles contemporaries urged on all women. In other words, singlewomen on the verge of becoming servants, wives, and even mothers were sometimes able to obtain a measure of parochial relief. In Southampton parish officers paid 15s. for a pair of stays for Robert Butcher's daughter when she went into service. Likewise, the community of Aldenham offered monetary help to children who left home to become servants.[94] Southampton's churchwardens were also willing to disburse large sums of money when poor singlewomen decided to alter their marital status and become wives. For example, Holy Rood parish paid £3.5s. 6d. for the marriage of one Wellow's daughter, and Mary Chandler received £3.1s. to clothe herself on her marriage day.[95] Chandler was the illegitimate daughter of singlewoman Elizabeth Chandler—a continual thorn in the side of Southamp-

[92] SRO, PR 9/15/2; SC/AG 6/1, #238.
[93] SRO, SC/AG 8/6/1; *Norwich Census of the Poor*. For more examples, see B. Hill, *Women Alone*, 99.
[94] SRO, SC/AG 8/6/1; Brown, 'The Receipt of Poor Relief', 418. For more examples, see B. Hill, *Women Alone*, 101.
[95] SRO, SC/AG 8/6/1.

ton's governors. It seems that Southampton's churchwardens were willing to pay dearly to encourage the second generation not to repeat the mistakes of the first.

Intriguingly, one of the most common times for never-married women to receive relief from the parish (at least by the eighteenth century) was when they were pregnant or the mothers of young children.[96] Parochial and town officers paid out large amounts of money to assist single mothers in giving birth, in finding clothes for new babies, and in nourishing mother and child, at least through the first few months. For example, the officers in Holy Rood parish, Southampton, paid £2.15s. 2d. for Mary Andrew's lying in and for clothing her child. This amount was comparable to the amount (£2.8s.) a widow like Eleanor Metcalf received in parish relief for the entire year. Although singlewomen did not regularly reside in Southampton's almshouses, never-married women with children found lodging in houses for the poor. In 1746 Mary Benson, alias Edminston, and her illegitimate daughter were staying in a house in St Mary's that was 'made use of for lodging poor persons of the said parish'.[97] Likewise, single mothers in eighteenth-century London found that parish assistance and institutions such as hospitals and workhouses, which were normally intended for the more 'deserving' and moral poor, provided them with a temporary 'safety-net' in their time of need. These examples back up John Gillis's finding that, by the eighteenth century, 'a pregnancy, previously something to be kept quiet, now became an instrument for securing either marriage or parish maintenance'.[98]

On the surface it seems odd that singlewomen would receive aid after giving birth to illegitimate children. It was, after all, by this act that these women accomplished what authorities most feared and tried to avoid—the creation of disorder. The single mother had taken it upon herself to create a family outside of the bonds of marriage and the male-controlled household, thereby disrupting the social order. She had also disrupted the economic order by producing a child, and thus a family, who might very well become an economic burden on the community. Much like today, people in early modern England saw single mothers as undeserving and immoral, and as such they were punished, usually by banishment or a yearlong stint in the

[96] Long ago Ivy Pinchbeck also noted this conundrum. She said that single motherhood was 'the only means of escape from the inadequate allowances supplied by the parish'. *Women Workers and the Industrial Revolution, 1750–1850* (London: Virago Press, 1981), 81, cited in B. Hill, *Women Alone*, 103.

[97] SRO, SC/AG 8/6/1; SRO, SC 9/4/347.

[98] Tim Hitchcock, '"Unlawfully begotten on her body": Illegitimacy and the Parish Poor in St Luke's Chelsea', in Tim Hitchcock, Peter King, and Pamela Sharpe (eds.), *Chronicling Poverty: The Voices and Strategies of the English Poor, 1640–1840* (New York: St Martin's Press, 1997), 70–86; John Gillis, *For Better, For Worse: British Marriages, 1600 to the Present* (New York: Oxford University Press, 1985), 115.

house of correction.[99] But at the same time paternalistic town fathers could not desert a child in need, even if that child was illegitimate. Bastards and single mothers benefited from this contradiction. Such a paradox is understandable, especially if we see it as yet another example of how the family and household were favoured over the individual in early modern England. While single mothers were not wives, they could, by giving birth, become mothers; if so, they then resembled widows with children to support. With the birth of a child a single mother became the de facto head of a family and household, and as such she was entitled to more assistance than a singlewoman on her own. While local officials were willing to ignore a solitary woman, they were less likely to neglect a child who, while illegitimate, was still one of the deserving poor. Single mothers throughout England benefited from their association with deserving children, although for how long is unclear.[100] For example, in 1743 Southampton's All Saints parish was offering relief to Argentine Long's 2-year-old bastard, but not to the singlewoman herself (who bore two further illegitimate children in 1748 and 1751).[101] In the same way that never-married women managed to establish their own households and work independently, such women earned economic assistance contingently, and not legitimately. A singlewoman might receive assistance while pregnant and nursing, but this was because poor mothers were legitimate recipients of poor relief, not because singlewomen were. When a never-married woman became a mother she exposed one of the loopholes in the early modern poor-relief system, a loophole that was the very concern of local authorities.

Only one sort of benefactor looked especially benevolently on poor singlewomen no matter what their age and condition. Never-married women did not have to be sick, disabled, or old, nor did they have to seek service, marriage, or motherhood to obtain relief from other singlewomen; they merely had to be single. In 1741 singlewoman Susanna Shreckenfox bequeathed £20 to the 'poor widows, maids, and decayed housekeepers' of Holy Rood parish, Southampton. Shreckenfox distinctly mentioned the three marital states of women, noting that widows, singlewomen, and wives might all be in need. In her 1697 will Jane Bracebridge focused purely on women of her marital status, stipulating that four to six servant maids from Southampton should carry her 'corpse to the grave and that they each [should] have a hood and gloves and 2s. 6d. in

[99] Mark Jackson, *New-Born Child Murder: Women, Illegitimacy and the Courts in Eighteenth-Century England* (New York: Manchester University Press, 1996), 31.

[100] On the (sometimes generous) support given to single mothers, see Hitchcock, '"Unlawfully begotten"', 73–5; and Pamela Sharpe, '"The bowels of compation": A Labouring Family and the Law, *c*.1790–1834', both in *Chronicling Poverty*, 92–3, and n. 27.

[101] SRO, SC/AG 8/3/1; transcript of the All Saints parish registers (16 Aug. 1741, Nov./Dec. 1748, 7 July 1751).

money'.[102] Shreckenfox and Bracebridge were both relatively wealthy singlewomen, suggesting that never-married women of all classes may have been particularly aware of how difficult it was for a singlewoman to maintain herself. Only other never-married women recognized that singleness could be enough of a detriment in itself to merit economic assistance.

As this examination of residence, employment, and poor relief has shown, a woman's marital status was a key determinant of how she would live her life. When a woman married she lost legal, economic, and social independence, but she also gained protection and earned certain privileges from both her family and the local community. By virtue of being a wife, a mother, and her husband's deputy, a widow earned the right to head a household. An ever-married woman could live where she wished, support herself through various trades, or receive financial assistance if she could not. But never-married women merited no such assistance or privileges. Town governors limited where singlewomen could live, in what trades they could work, and the circumstances under which they might claim poor relief. These constraints meant that never-married women were much more socially and economically vulnerable than ever-married women. By fulfilling neither the role of wife nor mother, a singlewoman earned neglect or even outright repression in early modern England. This serves as a caution against romanticizing the supposed independence of all singlewomen in the past.

This chapter has shown how the experiences of women in early modern England suggest that there is another category of difference to attend to in our examinations of women in pre-modern Europe. Women's historians have long acknowledged the differences of gender, have become comfortable examining the differences of class, and more recently have become attuned to differences in race and sexuality, but we have not fully explored one of the critical differences between women—that of marital status. While most of us have acknowledged that married women's lives were unlike those of unmarried women in many ways, such a binary distinction is incomplete. Not only did married women differ from unmarried women, but the lives of ever-married women also contrasted with those of never-married women. Widows, wives, and singlewomen all experienced life differently in early modern England, but it was perhaps the singlewoman's experiences that were the most distinct from those of other women. Certainly we do not want to confine our understanding of women in early modern England (or any other region or time, for that matter) to the experiences of only those women who conformed closely to the roles sanctioned by their patriarchal societies. We must, therefore, pay clearer

---

[102] HRO, 1741 A119; 1697 B6.

attention to how marital status differentiated the experiences of women in the past, and how women who never conformed to the roles of wife and mother lived and sometimes even thrived. The following chapters will elucidate the lives of such women.

3
Single But Not Alone: The Family History of Never-Married Women

How different does the history of the family in early modern England look when we place the single person at its centre rather than the marital couple? This is a question that we have only just begun to contemplate. After years of emphasizing the nuclear family, historians are beginning to entertain new ideas about family and kinship in the early modern era. Naomi Tadmor has recently questioned what the term 'family' even meant in eighteenth-century parlance. Her work suggests that the concept of the nuclear family is more familiar to modern historians than it would have been to people in the past. This chapter adds to this reassessment of family history by exploring the concept of the 'singlewoman's family'.[1] When we look at family through the prism of singleness, the nuclear family lessens in importance. Focusing on women who did not have husbands or children allows us to turn away from the reified concept of the nuclear family, with the conjugal couple at its core, and instead investigate a range of other important relationships. First, a focus on singlewomen allows us to rediscover the significance of sibling relationships in the past. Second, it reveals the importance of female kin to other women. For never-married women in particular, the most important bonds were the ones they forged with their mothers, sisters, and nieces, and to a lesser extent more distant female kin. Third, singlewomen were not strangers to the nuclear family and household. This chapter argues that, without the labour and financial support of never-married women, which has gone largely unacknowledged and thus has been forgotten over time, many so-called 'nuclear families' would not have survived or thrived in the past. The assistance of singlewomen did not end with their deaths, either. The last section of this chapter examines how inheritance looks different through the prism of singleness. In the absence of biological children, the question of the single person's heir was fraught with both conflict and complexity in early modern England.

One of the more common assumptions about never-married women in the past is that these women led empty lives because they did not marry and

---

[1] Naomi Tadmor, *Family and Friends in Eighteenth-Century England: Household, Kinship, and Patronage* (Cambridge: Cambridge University Press, 2001), 22, 23, 33, 37, and *passim*.

produce families of their own. Singlewomen have been imagined as isolated and lonely individuals, bereft of what we assume to be an individual's primary relationships: those with spouses and children. But in a society where widowhood was common, child mortality high, and single-sex socializing the norm, we may have overestimated the relative significance of spouses and children in early modern England. When we look at the evidence about singlewomen in the past we find them embedded in various social relationships. The wills made by singlewomen illustrate this particularly well. Much of this chapter is based on five samples of singlewomen's probated wills for the period 1550 to 1750. Four of the samples are from the provincial towns of Bristol, Oxford, York, and Southampton, and for comparative purposes another sample covers both urban and rural parishes in the county of Hampshire.[2] While probate evidence can be biased toward the wealthy, the wills sampled here represent never-married women from across the social spectrum, with a particular emphasis on women whose families engaged in a craft or trade.[3] The purpose of making a will was to ensure the certain distribution of a testator's estate. This means that singlewomen of all socio-economic backgrounds, and not just the wealthy, may have been more inclined to make a will since they had no clear heir. In addition to wills, this chapter relies on family papers, letters, diaries, and memoirs. These sources are necessarily biased toward literate and elite

[2] The sample of singlewomen's wills from Bristol was taken from a set of indexes for the years 1610–1760 and an unpublished transcript of wills proven between 1749 and 1751 held in the Bristol Record Office. I chose 40 of the most complete wills out of the approximately 50 or so extant and consulted them on microfilm. I chose a sample of 40 Oxford singlewomen's wills out of the approximately 92 extant wills proved in the Oxford diocese between the years 1550 and 1775. I consulted only those wills that were copied into register books and thus available on microfilm at the Centre for Oxfordshire Studies. These wills were found in the *Probate Records of the Courts of the Bishop and Archdeacon of Oxford, 1516–1732*, 2 vols., and the *Probate Records of the Courts of the Bishop and Archdeacon of Oxford 1733–1857*, 2 vols. (1997). The sample of singlewomen's wills from York is derived from those proved in the Prerogative and Exchequer courts of the Archbishop of York, as well as the courts of the Dean and Chapter of York. A sample of 50 wills proven between 1620 and 1750 was chosen from the indices of the Yorkshire Archaeological Society Record Series and the manuscript indices held in the Borthwick Institute of Historical Research, where the microfilmed wills were also consulted. The Southampton will sample consists of all the extant wills made by singlewomen between 1550 and 1752 and proved in the Winchester diocese and archdeaconry courts. There are 35 extant wills, 27 of which were made by self-declared singlewomen or spinsters, while an additional eight were servants and/or shared the surname of their siblings. The Hampshire sample of wills is derived from the approximately 825 singlewomen's wills proven in the Winchester diocesan courts between 1570 and 1750. From these I chose a random sample of 45 wills. Both the Southampton and Hampshire will sets were consulted on microfilm held in the Hampshire Record Office.

[3] Amy Erickson also has found that singlewomen with modest and even 'tiny' estates still made wills. Amy Louise Erickson, *Women and Property in Early Modern England* (New York: Routledge, 1993), 209. For example, the estates of single female testators from Southampton ranged from £2 to £274 in value (excluding one woman's estate that was worth over £3,000). This compares to the estates of single female testators in Hampshire, 42 of which ranged from £4 to £190 in value, plus another three that were worth between £314 and £536.

women and their families, but I have used them in tandem with court depositions from the Consistory (or Bishop's) court of Winchester diocese and from Southampton's Sessions court, in order to illustrate the social relationships of singlewomen from various socio-economic backgrounds.

One of the first myths about never-married women that can be put to rest by consulting their wills is the assumption that they lacked a full network of social relationships. Table 3.1 illustrates the wide range of people who received legacies from or served as executors and trustees for single female testators. Singlewomen mentioned twenty-five different types of social relationships in their wills, ranging from parents and siblings to more distant kin such as nieces, nephews, aunts, uncles, in-laws, and cousins. They also included friends, godchildren, pastors, employers, land-ladies, and servants. Singlewomen's wills stand in stark contrast to those made by married men. Married men focused primarily on providing for their nuclear families in their wills, but when we do not assume that married men were the norm, probate evidence reveals the common signifi-cance of kinship in early modern England. For instance, singlewomen were not the only testators likely to leave legacies to a wide range of family and friends. Cicely Howell found that those individuals who had fulfilled their familial obligations, such as grandparents, widows, and widowers, as well as those who had no such obligations, such as bachelors and never-married women, left legacies to a wider 'kin-circle'. And Barbara Harris has shown that extended kin were common in the wills of childless wives from the aristocracy.[4] Unmarried and childless persons, singlewomen among them, were able to commemorate their kinship ties at death; it was married men who were actually the most distinct from everyone else.

A degree of caution is needed when looking at singlewomen's wills for evidence about social relationships. While it is tempting to assume that wills provide a list of all the primary relationships in an individual's life, this is not necessarily the case. Those persons who had already obtained or did not receive legacies from the testator were likely to be absent, as well as those who had died before the individual made her will. This is the reason why so few parents are mentioned in these probate samples, even though a single-woman's parents may have been some of the most important people in her life. Even younger relatives can be missed. For example, the Southampton

---

[4] Cicely Howell, 'Peasant Inheritance Customs in the Midlands, 1280–1700', in Jack Goody, Joan Thirsk, and E. P. Thompson (eds.). *Family and Inheritance: Rural Society in Western Europe, 1200–1800* (New York: Cambridge University Press, 1976), 141; Barbara J. Harris, *English Aristocratic Women 1450–1550: Marriage and Family, Property and Careers* (New York: Oxford University Press, 2002), 190–1, 201–3. Extended family and friends also 'figured prominently' in the lives of medieval priests, who were of course single men. Jacqueline Murray, 'Kinship and Friendship: The Perception of Family by Clergy and Laity in Late Medieval London', *Albion*, 20: 3 (1988), 376.

Table 3.1. Social relationships mentioned in five samples of singlewomen's wills

Social relationship	Bristol N = 40	Oxford N = 40	Southampton N = 35	York N = 50	Hampshire N = 45
Mother	1	4	3	7[b]	5
Father	1	1	2	0	3
Sister	18	17	23	23	29
Brother	14	11	14	17	17
Niece	12	12	18	19	18
Nephew	16	12	15	13	17
Sibling's child (sex unknown)	6	6	8	6	7
Aunt	1	2	0	7	5
Uncle	2	2	0	4	6
Kinswoman or female cousin	18	12	10	19[c]	14
Kinsman or male cousin	14	9	7	17	12
Kin (sex unknown)	0	5	1	2	5
Sister-in-law	6	8	6	5	3
Brother-in-law	5	2	8	6	12
Female (relationship unknown)	15	10	19	22	16
Male (relationship unknown)	15	8	17	19	15
Female friend	8	4	5	3	5
Male friend	11	5	12	8	4
Landlady	1	0	1	0	0
Goddaughter	1	1	1	2	4
Godson	1	2	1	1	4
Master	1	1	4	0	0
Mistress	1	1	0	1	1
Female servant or nurse	6	4	6	10	10
Male servant	0	3	1	0	0
Fellow servant	0	1	0	1	0
Betrothed	0	0	0	0	2
Child[a]	1 (male)	0	1 (female)	0	1 (female)

[a] Foster son of Bristol singlewoman, bastard child of Southampton singlewoman, and future stepchild of Hampshire singlewoman; [b] includes one stepmother; [c] includes one grandmother. When it was possible to establish the more precise relationship of an individual, I assigned that person to their respective category (e.g. nephew, aunt) rather than to the kinswoman/man category.

Source: Sample of singlewomen's wills from Bristol, Oxford, Southampton, York, and Hampshire. See n. 2.

singlewoman Alice Zains died in 1701, bequeathing her sizeable estate of about £240 to various nieces and nephews, a brother-in-law, a widowed sister, and a brother.[5] From her will it appears that Zains had two sisters and one brother, but other records reveal that she had also had a never-married sister named Jane. These two sisters had lived together, jointly run a linen-drapery business, and held property together. Nevertheless, Jane Zains had died two or three years prior to her younger sister Alice, and so Alice Zains's will is silent on perhaps the most primary relationship in her life. Keeping in mind such limitations, wills still provide the best picture of the spectrum of never-married women's social relations.

Singlewomen's social relationships were also significantly female-centred, according to their wills. The majority of legacies bequeathed by never-married women in all five probate samples went to other women. Moreover, greater than half of the single female testators from Southampton and Hampshire remembered more women than men in their wills, while 60 per cent of singlewomen from Bristol and York and as many as 70 per cent from Oxford did so. Overall, single female testators were the most women-identified testators in the early modern era, more so than even widows or single men.[6] This female-centred perspective is not just limited to probate evidence but also appears elsewhere. For instance, although historians and biographers associate her with her father, the canon of Lichfield, Anna Seward's own feelings about kin differed. The lifelong singlewoman and poet mentioned only women when she reflected back on the most important relationships in her life. The female kin who had sustained her and whom she had lost by the age of 45 included: 'my sister, crushed in the blossom of our youth, by the pale hand of death . . . my mother, in all the energies of her high and generous spirit; [and] my beauteous Honora [Seward's foster sister], as in the golden days of her prime, when her affections were warm, and artless as her

---

[5] Hampshire Record Office (hereafter HRO), 1701 A107.

[6] This is based on a random sample of 45 wills derived from the 273 extant wills made by Southampton widows between 1570 and 1750 and proven in the Winchester diocesan courts. Adequate information for this analysis was only available in 30 of the wills, so not all 45 were used. The 30 wills reveal that widows privileged female legatees only slightly more than male ones. Twelve left more legacies to women than men, 11 left an equal number of bequests to each sex, and seven named more male legatees than female ones. A probate sample of 28 Southampton bachelors from the early modern period reveals that they left more legacies to men than to women. Only 12 of 28 single men gave legacies to more women than men, while eight gave bequests to an equal number of men and women, and another eight gave more legacies to men. Nevertheless, single men did remember sisters more than brothers, nieces more than nephews, and fellow female servants more than male ones. The latter may have been girlfriends. For example, Richard Smith left a bequest of £15 to Eleanor Hayler, the servant of Sir Thomas Bishop, because 'he said she was his betrothed wife and intended to marry her if he lived'. HRO, 1614 B69/1-3.

bloom.'[7] The significance of parents and siblings to singlewomen like Seward is the focus of the next section.

Natal Families

Natal families were where singlewomen began and frequently remained for a good portion, if not all, of their lives. It is not surprising, then, that the relationships never-married women had with their parents and siblings were among their most significant. Wills can be useful in revealing these bonds, but the age at which a singlewoman made her will determined whether she would mention her parents or not. As Table 3.1 illustrates, relatives of an older generation appeared less frequently in singlewomen's wills than did lateral kin or those of a younger generation, because female testators were on average middle-aged or elderly and their older kin had predeceased them. Interestingly, however, wills show us that the parental bond did not end with death. Never-married women frequently mentioned that they wished to be interred near or with their fathers or mothers. Many singlewomen were like Isabel Harrison of York, who asked to be buried 'as near the place where my father and mother were buried as . . . conveniently may be'.[8]

The bonds between mothers and their never-married daughters were particularly strong. Adult singlewomen often remained at home with a parent, who was more commonly a widowed mother than father. For example, the Southampton widow Elizabeth Manfield, who died in 1632, left all of her belongings to her daughter Elizabeth Jr., 'in recompense of the pains she [has] taken about me'.[9] If a singlewoman predeceased her mother, she frequently relied on her maternal parent to execute her will and named her as a primary heir. When Elizabeth Whislad of Southampton died, she bequeathed a house to her widowed mother Eleanor as well as making her the executrix and residuary legatee of her will.[10] It was more likely for a mother to die before her single daughter, however, and such deaths could leave singlewomen bereft. Ann Hanson was so upset when her mother died that she followed her to the grave, just three months afterwards, 'being heart broke, as she declared, with trouble at the death of her mother . . .' She

[7] A. Constable (ed.), *Letters of Anna Seward: Written between the Years 1784 and 1807*, 6 vols. (Edinburgh, 1811), i. 258.
[8] Borthwick Institute of Historical Research (hereafter BIHR), Probate Register vol. 36, fo. 298, Isabell Harryson, (29 Jan. 1620).
[9] HRO, 1632 B31/1.
[10] HRO, 1723 A119. (Whislad's will is misnumbered; she died in 1732.)

asked to be buried near her mother in the choir of Silkstone church in Yorkshire.[11]

Because mothers and single daughters often spent so much of their lives together, mothers commonly appointed these daughters as their executors and made them their primary heirs. For example, when the widow Anne Ockleford of Southampton died she left furniture to her son and a single daughter who lived at a distance from her, and left only a token bequest to her married daughter. Ockleford then left the residue of her goods, chattels, personal estate, and lands, as well as the executorship of her will to her never-married daughter Martha, who resided with her.[12] While some widows may have made their resident daughters their executors for convenience's sake, others showed a real preference. In 1708 Elizabeth Rowte of Southampton died and in her will appointed her daughter Mary as her executrix. This was despite the fact that Rowte had another never-married daughter and a son living with her, as well as married sons in Southampton.[13] And as we will see in Chapter 4, mothers and adult single daughters not only resided together, they also were often business partners.

The time they spent together, the work they did together, and the trust that developed between mothers and single daughters meant that they were frequently implicated in criminal activities together.[14] In 1725 the Southampton clothworker, Philip Guillum, complained that his stepdaughter Mary Jackston had beaten him and 'broken his head in several places' without any provocation. It turned out that Guillum had 'barbarously beaten' his wife, and Jackston protested that she lashed out only to protect her mother.[15] In 1630 one mother-and-daughter team, Jane De La Haye and her never-married daughter Margaret, faced indictments together for an assault and battery upon a married woman in Southampton.[16] In 1683 the same town authorities implicated Eleanor Speed and her daughter Elizabeth in a theft of linen from His Majesty's storehouse, and they bound over both mother and daughter to give evidence against Alice Tyler for the same crime. Ten years later Alice Tyler was accused of stealing goods again, this time with her never-married daughter Jane.[17] Mothers and daughters who committed property crimes together were in some sense simply illegal versions of mother–daughter business partnerships.

[11] 'The Journal of Mr. John Hobson', in *Yorkshire Diaries and Autobiographies*, Surtees Society, 65 (1877), 321.

[12] HRO, 1729 B39.

[13] HRO, 1708 A108.

[14] R. C. Anderson (ed.), *The Books of Examinations and Depositions 1622–27*, Southampton Record Society, 29 (Southampton, 1929), 65, 68.

[15] Southampton Record Office (hereafter SRO), SC 9/4/113.

[16] R. C. Anderson (ed.), *The Books of Examinations and Depositions 1627–34*, Southampton Record Society, 31 (Southampton, 1931), 71.

[17] SRO, SC 9/3/14, fos. 48ᵛ, 105ᵛ.

Of course, we should not romanticize all relationships between mothers and daughters. In 1741 Mary Jeffreys complained to the Southampton JPs that her mother Jane Jeffreys had beaten her several times and threatened to kill her, and 'in particular... that she would cut [her] flesh from her bones'.[18] While most of the evidence concerning mother–daughter relationships reveals both close and positive ties, the Jeffreys women show that there were some exceptions to this rule.

Evidence of relations between fathers and single daughters can be more difficult to find, but the information that comes from court depositions suggests more of a power struggle than was common in mother–daughter relationships. For instance, fathers of younger singlewomen often appeared in disputes surrounding matrimony, either angry at daughters choosing inappropriate partners or exasperated at daughters who would not marry according to their wishes. Of course, mothers may have also quarrelled with their daughters over marital plans, but if the father was still alive he was more likely than the mother to appear in a court case concerning the matter. For example, in 1582 John Legatt came to Sydmonton, (Hants.), where his daughter Edith was residing, and tried to betroth her to one of her suitors, but she wept and asked for more time to think about it. Her father feared Edith had 'been turned by some lewd folk [in that household] there, she being but a girl', and he said 'if she would not be betrothed to Anthony that she would not have any part of his goods'. According to Legatt, his daughter later contracted herself to Anthony Dalby without any compulsion from him, although he admitted that at the time 'she went aside and wept a little'.[19] In 1577 Edmund Haylles of Somerset sent his daughter Anne all the way to Southampton, instructing her to stay there as long as it 'pleased' him. Anne Haylles explained to the Southampton JPs that her father expected her 'to learn to exercise her needle and to pay for her meat and drink...' She added that her father had sent her from home because she had many suitors and he did not like any of them.[20]

While life-cycle singlewomen struggled with fathers over courtship, lifelong singlewomen struggled with their fathers over issues of dependence. It was not uncommon for women who never married to efface their identities and talents by dedicating their lives to their fathers. For example, Anna Seward spent the first fifty years of her life living with and keeping house for her father Canon Seward of Lichfield. She also nursed him through years of ill health. Although she did not seem to question her

---

[18] SRO, SC 9/4/238.
[19] HRO, 21M65 C3/8, 425–6.
[20] G. H. Hamilton and E. R. Aubrey (eds.), *Books of Examinations and Depositions 1570–1594*, Southampton Record Society, 16 (Southampton, 1914), 33.

duty, she did acknowledge the tension she felt between pursuing her literary talents and caring for her father's person and household.[21]

It is perhaps not surprising that parents were significant in the lives of singlewomen, but siblings were equally, if not more, important. While death tended to absent parents from the latter years of a never-married woman's life, her siblings (and, to a lesser extent, cousins) were likely to share her entire lifespan. Family historians have not focused enough on sibling relationships, although a recent collection by several historians of modern Britain has provided a fresh impetus in this direction.[22] The lack of historiography is unfortunate, since ties between siblings were some of the most long-lasting and deep relationships that early modern people enjoyed. This was especially true for never-married women. For these women, the primacy of sibling relationships was never challenged or supplanted by husbands or children. While we might assume that an individual's siblings were significant during their early years, probate evidence reveals that sisters and brothers continued to hold an important place in the lives of older singlewomen as well. In fact, siblings were the most prominent relatives in all five samples of never-married women's wills.[23] Siblings did not appear equally in these wills, however, for the number of sisters was substantially more than the number of brothers (see Table 3.1). As many as two-thirds of the single female testators from Southampton and Hampshire remembered their sisters in their wills, and about 45 per cent of those from Oxford, Bristol, and York did so. Brothers surfaced rather less—in as few as 27.5 per cent of Oxford singlewomen's wills and as many as 40 per cent of Southampton singlewomen's wills—while appearing on average in 35 per cent of the wills made by never-married women from Bristol, York, and Hampshire.

Adult singlewomen were able to maintain close ties to their siblings throughout their lifespans. Some did so by residing with their siblings for long periods of their adult lives. Elizabeth Carter, although better known as one of the learned women later referred to as Bluestockings, spent a good part of her correspondence in the 1740s reporting on domestic life with her

---

[21] Margaret Ashmun (ed.), *The Singing Swan: An Account of Anna Seward and Her Acquaintance with Dr. Johnson, Boswell & Others of Their Time* (New Haven, Conn.: Yale University Press, 1931), 173–4.

[22] Leonore Davidoff et al., *The Family Story: Blood, Contract and Intimacy, 1830–1960* (Harlow, Essex: Longman, 1999).

[23] Keith Wrightson also found that testators who had no children of their own were more likely to leave bequests to their siblings. Keith Wrightson, 'Kinship in an English Village: Terling, Essex, 1550–1700', in Richard M. Smith (ed.), *Land, Kinship, and Life-Cycle* (New York: Cambridge University Press, 1985), 313–32. Grassby found the same in his study of bachelor business-men. Richard Grassby, *Kinship and Capitalism: Marriage, Family and Business in the English-Speaking World, 1580–1740* (New York: Cambridge University Press, 2001), 219, 238, and Table 6.3.

siblings. Carter, the daughter of a clergyman, grew up in Deal. Her mother died when she was only 10 years old, and she quickly became a surrogate mother to her younger siblings. Her letters mention walks with her youngest sister, 'working my eyes out in making shirts for my brother', her sister Peggy's marital plans, and minding a younger stepbrother and stepsister while her stepmother was away. In a 1746 letter to her friend Catherine Talbot, Carter revealed the type of feelings a singlewoman might harbour for her siblings: 'My sister's illness did indeed affect me beyond any thing I ever met with in my whole life, not merely from the thoughts of losing her, though a most melancholy loss it would have been, but from the apprehension of her suffering such excessive pain.'[24]

Other singlewomen were able to remain close to their sisters and brothers despite living far apart. From her early twenties Nancy Woodforde no longer resided near her siblings, but still maintained intimate ties with them through correspondence and regular visits. Her uncle, the Revd James Woodforde, recorded in his diary the frequent letters that passed between Nancy and her two brothers, the brothers' regular visits to see their sister, and what a pleasure it was to see Nancy and her brothers appear so happy 'in each other'. In 1786 uncle and niece spent three months in Somerset visiting their kin. While there Nancy spent time with her sister Juliana, but over time Juliana 'talked so much about Nancy having to leave' that it made the latter 'exceedingly low'.[25] Two years later Juliana came down with the measles, and Nancy was very worried about her sister. Family in Somerset sent a series of letters, each more urgent than the one before, urging Nancy and her uncle to come visit so that Juliana could see her sister. Nancy cried all night and Woodforde wrote that 'no two sisters could love one another more', but Nancy was suffering from a leg injury and could not travel. Juliana sent a poignant gift of a red morocco purse filled with a silver locket and some coins. The gift's resemblance to a last bequest made Nancy even more uneasy. When her brother William sent a note berating her for not visiting Juliana's deathbed, Nancy was so upset she 'vomited a great deal'. Two months after Juliana Woodforde's initial illness, the much-feared news of her death arrived. Nancy sought some solace in buying mourning clothes and in the company of female friends, but the loss of her sister was significant.[26]

[24] Revd Montagu Pennington, *A Series of Letters Between Mrs. Elizabeth Carter and Mrs. Catherine Talbot from the year 1741 to 1770*, 3rd edn. (London, 1819), 49, 129, 157, 255, 124; Sylvia Myers, *The Bluestocking Circle: Women, Friendship, and the Life of the Mind in Eighteenth-Century England* (Oxford: Clarendon Press, 1990), 45.
[25] John Beresford (ed)., *The Diary of a Country Parson: The Rev. James Woodeforde 1758–1781* (Oxford: Oxford University Press, 1926), ii. 215, 271.
[26] Ibid. iii. 9, 11, 13, 19–23.

A lack of personal writings by most singlewomen makes it difficult to assess emotional intimacy in the past. Nevertheless, there is an abundance of circumstantial evidence that shows how never-married women cared for their sisters. In her will Frances Parkinson of Southampton left her also single sisters, Anne and Margery, £30 each and provided annuities of £2–£4 for her three married sisters.[27] When Phoebe Gander of Southampton died in 1742 she bequeathed all but £37 out of £220 to her two married sisters and their children, and made one of those sisters her sole executrix.[28] Grace Hildyard of York left £100 to her single sister Dorothy Hildyard, and the same amount to her ever-married sister Sarah Scott, while she left the smaller sum of £30 to her ever-married sister Elizabeth Ellis and an annuity of £4. 10s. to another single sister, Ann Hildyard.[29] These examples illustrate how singlewomen bequeathed larger legacies to single and widowed sisters, who probably had more financial need than married ones.

While never-married women had close relationships with sisters no matter what their marital status, the most meaningful ties were with their also single sisters. Never-married women ran in families, and single sisters often came in pairs or multiples.[30] A look at the families of London writers and printers reveals this. For example, the novelist Henry Fielding had four sisters who never married. In the late 1740s Ursula, Catharine, Sarah, and Beatrice Fielding were middle-aged sisters sharing a residence in Westminster. A letter written by Ursula reveals a cheerful existence: 'Kitty is at work, Sally is puzzling about it and about it. Bea is playing on her fiddle, and Patty scribbling.' Between 1750 and 1751 three of the sisters died, having never married. This led Sarah Fielding, who was an author like her brother, to move in with an unrelated singlewoman, the writer Jane Collier. The Fielding women were not uncommon; William Hogarth had two never-married sisters, and Fanny Burney's two aunts, Ann and Rebecca, were lifelong singlewomen. Two of Daniel Defoe's daughters, Hannah and Henrietta, also never married.[31]

Never-married sisters also populated the provinces. It is possible to identify at least fifty pairs of single sisters (who were in their thirties or

---

[27] HRO, 1615 B37.

[28] HRO, 1742 A65.

[29] BIHR, Dean and Chapter Wills, reel 1252, Grace Hildyard (Aug. 1741).

[30] Lee Chambers-Schiller also found that pairs of single sisters were common in the nineteenth-century USA, and she attributed this to 'changes in the middle-class family and to the transformation of American society'. But my evidence shows that this phenomenon was not particularly American or modern. Lee Chambers-Schiller, *Liberty, A Better Husband: Singlewomen in America: The Generations of 1780–1840* (New Haven, Conn.: Yale University Press, 1984), 128.

[31] Linda Bree, *Sarah Fielding* (New York: Twayne Publishers, 1996), xii, 12; Claire Harman, *Fanny Burney: A Biography* (New York: Knopf, 2001); Paula Backscheider, *Daniel Defoe: His Life* (Baltimore, Md.: Johns Hopkins Press, 1989), 527.

older) in early modern Southampton alone. Most commonly there were two single sisters in a family, but Mr Kemp, the keeper of nearby Carisbrooke Castle, had six single daughters. There was Ann, aged 31; Dorothy, aged 28; Mary, aged 26; Joanne, aged 24; Dowsabell, aged 22; and Elizabeth, aged about 16.[32] While the Kemp sisters were all still of marriageable age, other families included several lifelong singlewomen. In 1597 Captain James Parkinson died in Southampton, leaving behind a widow, two sons, a married daughter, and eight unmarried daughters—Bridget, Alice, Elizabeth, Frances, Anne, Margery, Jane, and Barbara.[33] Four years later Elizabeth Parkinson, who was probably in her twenties, died, having never married. From Elizabeth's probate documents it is apparent that her younger sister Jane had died a singlewoman sometime before her.[34] Fourteen years after Elizabeth's decease, her sister Frances also died without ever having married.[35] Frances was probably in her late thirties or early forties at this time. Since their father's death eighteen years before, only two Parkinson daughters (Alice and Bridget) had married. But another four had died never married, and another two yet living had remained single. Of these two, Anne was 34 and Margery 33 years old. Whether the various Parkinson sisters remained single due to the example of their elder sisters or by circumstance is unclear. But what is apparent is that these never-married sisters provided material support to one another through their various bequests and, one would surmise, emotional support as well.

Many single sisters effectively created an alternative conjugal couple, by residing, working, and worshipping with each other rather than with husbands. William Blundell explicitly acknowledged the alternative conjugality of his single sisters, Winifred and Frances. When Frances Blundell went to visit his mother-in-law, William wrote begging for her return, saying, 'You have taken from my sister Winifred a husband...'[36] The Blundell sisters resided together for three decades of their adult lives, beginning in the 1640s. This was quite common in the early modern era. For example, in 1692 Louise Bretin made both her sisters, Jane and Perrette Bretin, who were 'now dwelling with her', her heirs and joint executrices.[37] In Southampton never-married sisters like the Bretins almost always lived together. Jane and Anne Barrow set up house in Holy Rood parish in 1692

---

[32] HRO, 21M65 C3/11, 448.
[33] A. L. Merson (ed.), *The Third Book of Remembrance of Southampton 1514–1602*. 3 vols. Southampton Records Series, 8 (Southampton, 1965), 115.
[34] HRO, 1601 AD29/1–2. Elizabeth Parkinson's administration provides the names and ages of her sisters.
[35] HRO, 1615 B37.
[36] Margaret Blundell (ed.), *Cavalier: Letters of William Blundell To His Friends, 1620–98* (London: Longmans, Green and Co., 1933), 55.
[37] HRO, 1692 A11.

and moved together to All Saints Infra by 1695. This was the same parish where Elizabeth and Ann Waller held property together in the 1720s.[38] Never-married sisters not only provided companionship for one another, but as we will see in Chapter 4 they were often business partners as well. Other never-married sisters, like Susan and Mary Fleetwood, attended Nonconformist churches together. And when the Fleetwood sisters moved from Southampton to Winchester, they migrated together.[39] Elizabeth Goodridge of Southampton made her sister Ann Goodridge her primary heir and executrix.[40] These examples illustrate the various ways in which single sisters relied on each other, both in a material sense and for companionship.

While evidence of the practical bonds between never-married sisters is more forthcoming, we can read them alongside sources produced by literate and elite women that are more explicit about the emotional bonds between single sisters. Writing to her niece about the death of her sister Cassandra, Jane Austen said: 'I have lost a treasure, such a sister, such a friend as never can have been surpassed. She was the sun of my life, the gilder of every pleasure, the soother of every sorrow, I had not a thought concealed from her, and it is as if I had lost a part of myself'.[41] Although Austen lived in Southampton fifty years after the never-married women referred to above, it is not a great leap to think that the women who came before her felt the same way about their sisters. Austen's words are also strikingly similar to those of Anna Seward. Writing to her friend Mrs Cotton to condole about the loss of another female friend, Seward said she understood her loss for this day was 17th March, 'the birth-day of my lovely long-deceased sister, who died in her 19th year—"a fair flower soon cut down on our fields..."—yet does not my heart forget this day, which gave to life an amiable creature, who shed the light of joy over many of my youthful years... Time balms sorrow...'[42] Seward wrote these words a quarter of a century after her sister Sarah's decease; despite her aphorism, time evidently had not eased her sorrow.

The bonds that never-married women forged with their sisters did not end when and if their sisters married. Anna Seward wrote that her friend

[38] SRO, SC 14/2/49, 71 and SC 14/2/326.

[39] SRO, transcript of the Above Bar Independent Chapel registers (6 Mar. 1736).

[40] HRO, 1715 A42.

[41] Deirdre Le Faye (ed.), *Jane Austen's Letters* (New York: Oxford University Press, 1995), quoted in Terry Castle, 'Sister-Sister', *London Review of Books*, 17: 5 (3 Aug. 1995), 3–6. In her review, Castle suggested that the relationship the Austen sisters enjoyed could be seen as a 'romantic female friendship'. And she proposed that bonds between female siblings could have been among the more passionate and intimate in a woman's life. Although Castle did not make any overt assertions about Austen's sexuality, the *London Review of Books* advertised her review with the words: 'Terry Castle: Was Jane Austen Gay?'

[42] Constable, *Letters of Seward*. ii. 59.

Miss Hinckley had recently died, because 'the excessive affection she had always felt for her sister, married some three years since', caused her to throw all her energies into nursing her sick sibling. While Miss Hinckley's sister recovered, she herself passed away at the age of 38. Seward exclaimed: 'Alas! What a violent wrench from meridian life, the pleasures of health, and the indulgent kindness of a generous brother and numerous friends! Since her sister's marriage, she used to be often with me. Her society was pleasant, and I shall long regret her loss.'[43] Just as Miss Hinckley's devotion to her sister did not end upon her sister's marriage, the same was true for how married women felt about their single sisters. For example, Anne Donnellan, a singlewoman who resided with her mother and stepfather in eighteenth-century London, was able to gain financial independence thanks to her generous married sister. When her sister's husband received a substantial inheritance the couple decided to turn her dowry over to Donnellan, so that she could support herself outside of marriage.[44]

The continued importance of married sisters to singlewomen meant that they often forged important ties with their sisters' spouses. This helps explain the presence of brothers-in-law in some singlewomen's wills—23 per cent of single female testators from Southampton mentioned them, as did 27 per cent of those from Hampshire. Since wives could not own property or make contracts, never-married women who wanted to bequeath property to their married sisters sometimes chose to appoint their brothers-in-law as legatees or executors.[45] For example, Sarah Page of Southampton left most of her estate to her married sister Anne Arrowsmith, and made her 'loving brother-in-law' Charles Arrowsmith her executor.[46] Brothers-in-law also provided much of the same assistance to singlewomen that fathers or brothers might do. For example, in 1592 Christian Colson was arguing with Alice Oate in the street of Bursledon (Hants.). When Oate began to beat her, Colson's brother-in-law William Arnold came to her defence.[47] Similarly, when Henry Newcombe's sister-in-law Anne Mainwaring found herself in financial difficulties, she asked him to lend her £5 'to save her cow that is just taken from her'. Although he did not have the money and would have to borrow it, he conceded 'we are of kin and so I have some tie to help her'. Newcombe provided his sister-in-law with £2

---

[43] Ibid. iii. 114.
[44] Myers, *Bluestocking Circle*, 38.
[45] The fact that never-married women could leave property directly to their brothers perhaps explains why never-married women remembered their sisters-in-law in their wills to a lesser extent. They often provided such women with only a token gift, such as the 1s. Mary Rowte left to her brother's widow Delariviere Rowte. HRO, 1745 A101.
[46] HRO, 1706 A79.
[47] HRO, 21M65 C3/10, 207.

of the £5 she needed, and although he did not expect it, she paid him back three years later.[48]

Married sisters and their husbands also commonly provided short- and long-term residences for adult singlewomen. For instance, Averine Ham lived with her brother-in-law, William Lile, as his servant in Southampton.[49] On a higher social scale, brothers-in-law also housed singlewomen but did not expect domestic service in return. Walter Claverley recorded the frequent visits made by his sisters-in-law in the first years after he married Julia, the daughter of Sir William Blackett. In 1707 his wife's sisters Elizabeth and Frances came for a visit and also left their sister Isabella to stay for three months. Next came sister Arabella for a three-month stay. A few years later the two eldest sisters, Betty and Frances, visited for two weeks. While they were with Claverley, their three younger sisters, Arabella, Dina, and Nancy, also came to stay. The next year Betty and Frances were again visiting for three months, and this time Claverley made a point of recording that his sisters-in-law had enjoyed 'their board here free'. It seems that the bonds between Julia Claverley and her six single sisters had a material cost for this brother-in-law.[50]

Close proximity between never-married women and their brothers-in-law could also cause more than financial annoyance. For example, several neighbours in Upton Grey deposed that Thomas Lipscomb had 'lived incestuously' with Margery Lee, his wife's sister, when Margery had resided with the couple.[51] Lipscomb was not the only example of a man attracted to his wife's single sister. This could make life difficult for a singlewoman who chose to reside with, or had no other place to live than with, a married sister.

The complicated relationships never-married women sometimes had with their brothers-in-law provide some context for why these female testators might try to circumvent the coverture of their married sisters. Although married women could not own property according to Common Law, many never-married women stipulated that legacies bequeathed to their married sisters should go directly to them, and not to their sisters' husbands. This led to several strategies on the part of single female testators. In Oxford singlewomen chose not to name their brothers-in-law as executors or residuary legatees. In Southampton never-married women's wills specified that they wanted their legacies paid directly to their *feme coverte* sisters. For example, when Mildred Arnold, a successful Southampton

[48] Thomas Heywood (ed.), *The Diary of the Rev. Henry Newcombe*, Chetham Society, 18 (1847), 31–2.
[49] HRO, 21M65 C3/11, 414.
[50] 'Memorandum Book of Sir Walter Claverley, Esq.', in *Yorkshire Diaries and Autobiographies*, Surtees Society, 77 (1886), 114–33.
[51] HRO, 21M65 C3/10, 89.

apothecary, made her will in 1667, she left £5 to her sister Joanne 'for her own use'. She added that Joanne's husband should have 'no power over it'. In 1752 Elizabeth Compton also tried to protect her sister's inheritance. First, Compton left most of her estate to two male trustees and instructed them to sell her lands and pay the profits to her sister Mrs Catherine Jones for life. Second, she stated that her married sister's 'receipt for the same notwithstanding her coverture shall be a good and sufficient discharge to my said trustees'.[52] In other words, Compton said her sister's signature for the legacy was binding, although legally *femes covertes* could not sign contracts.

While Compton was the only single female testator in Southampton to set up a trust for the benefit of married female kin, a significant number of singlewomen in Bristol did so. For example, Ann Martin died in 1751 holding at least three houses in the port town. She appointed three men, one distiller and two merchants, to hold her property in trust and to periodically pay the rents and profits from her properties to her two sisters and a nephew. She ordered the trustees to pay the proceeds into her married sister Elizabeth Edwards's 'own and proper Hands, for her own separate and distinct use, so as her said Husband shall not have anything at all to do therewith or intermeddle thereabouts, and the Receipt alone of my Sister Elizabeth notwithstanding her said Coverture shall be Good and Effectual Discharge to my said Trustees'. She also ordered that, upon her sister's death, the proceeds should go to her own 'nearest relations', thereby ensuring her sister's husband would not inherit Martin family property.[53]

It is not clear how we should interpret Ann Martin's actions. The brother-in-law that Martin did not want 'intermeddling' with her estate already occupied one of her Bristol houses, and his son was one of Martin's three heirs. Did Ann Martin dislike men? Was she against non-relatives inheriting her property? Or was she merely in a spat with her brother-in-law? While we will never know for sure, it is worth noting that Martin was not unique in trying to leave bequests directly to a married female relative. A few widowed female testators in Southampton also attempted to leave bequests directly to married women. Amy Erickson has also found examples of female (both single and widowed) testators who used various legal devices to ensure that bequests would remain in the hands of women. And even some early modern businessmen left money to married female relatives for their own separate use.[54]

---

[52] HRO, 1667 B1; 1752 A20.

[53] Bristol Record Office (hereafter BRO), unpublished transcript of will, Ann Martin, (10 July 1751).

[54] Erickson, *Women and Property*, 214; Grassby, *Kinship and Capitalism*. 87, 348.

When a singlewoman's sister became widowed the two sometimes became even closer. Never-married women lived and conducted business with widowed sisters, albeit to a lesser extent than with single sisters. Susannah Shreckenfox of Southampton and her widowed sister Elizabeth Plant inherited property together from their widowed mother, and jointly purchased more land.[55] This land became a sore point, for in her will Shreckenfox made the point that 'her sister [had] had no right to dispose [in her will] of the said estate since it was purchased with their joint moneys'. Despite her irritation, Shreckenfox's ties to her widowed sister won out in the end. She did not alter her sister's bequest, and she asked to be buried in the St John's burial place, 'as near to her widowed sister Elizabeth Plant as possible'.[56]

While never-married women were particularly close to their sisters, abundant evidence exists of the close relationships many enjoyed with their brothers. Nevertheless, these sibling ties differed, because while singlewomen and their sisters were on a level playing-field in terms of gender, in the case of their brothers they were not. This may account for why singlewomen's relationships with their brothers seem to be characterized more by material assistance, while ties with sisters were characterized as much by companionship and emotional support. And as is often the case, differences of opinion over material matters also led to tensions between brothers and their single sisters.

Adult singlewomen most often received assistance from their brothers in the form of a home. When Cassandra Willoughby's eldest brother reached his majority he took her away from their stepfather's household to keep house for him. At the young age of 17 Willoughby found herself the mistress of Wollaton Hall in Nottinghamshire. Although her brother died a year later, she stayed on to keep house for her younger brother, Thomas, until he married. Cassandra Willoughby continued to assist her married brother and his family until her early forties.[57] As this example illustrates, the single sister–brother relationship was characterized by mutual assistance. Although contemporaries may have emphasized the brother's role in providing a home for a single sister, we can note that she was providing her brother free housekeeping as well.

In addition to a home, brothers also provided financial assistance to their single sisters. Lucy Porter, a lifelong singlewoman from Lichfield and the stepdaughter of Samuel Johnson, finally achieved residential and financial independence in mid-life when her brother left her a fortune

[55] HRO, 1693 A103; SRO, SC 14/2/256.
[56] HRO, 1741 A119.
[57] A. C. Wood (ed.), *The Continuation of the History of the Willoughby Family*, by Cassandra, Duchess of Chandos, vol. 2 (Eton, Windsor: Shakespeare Head Press, 1958), pp. xiii, 125–41.

of nearly £10,000. Porter, who had resided and run a bookshop with Dr Johnson's mother, used her inheritance to build herself a home.[58] Another helpful brother was Adam Eyre, whose financial difficulties after the Civil Wars did not stop him from fulfilling his duty to his single sister. The government owed him £688 that he never received, and he was forced to borrow to get by. And yet in 1646 he reported paying £180, or the residue of his sister's portion, to his new brother-in-law James Wostenholme. A month later he cast up his accounts and recorded annual expenses of £100 but an income of only £30 per annum. Eyre had dutifully paid the portion due his sister, even though it was six times his annual income.[59]

Filial assistance was just as important lower down the social scale. For instance, in 1624 Elizabeth Warton, a servant in the Southampton suburb of St Denys, found that some of her master's silver spoons had gone missing. Her brother James spotted the spoons at a local inn and alerted his sister, so that she was able to recover the goods.[60] When Amis Fox left the house of John Wade (her lover and probable master) she found refuge in the Southampton home of her brother Simon, where she gave birth to her illegitimate child.[61] Helen Hawksworth of Hinton Ampner (Hants.) had her marriage negotiated by her brother William, despite the fact that her father was still alive. Helen's suitor lived in another parish, and William rode to see him, something her father may not have been able to do himself.[62] Because lifelong singlewomen were likely to outlive their fathers, this meant that their brothers had even more of a likelihood to serve *in loco parentis*.

As family patriarch, a singlewoman's brother could be protective but also authoritarian. This resulted in relations between brothers and sisters that were not always so rosy, and there is plenty of evidence of tensions between eldest brothers and their never-married sisters in particular. For example, the relationship between Ann Pitt and her brother William (the future Lord of the Privy Seal) reveals how sibling conflicts could evolve over the life-cycle. Out of a family of seven children, Ann and William were each other's special favourites. During the early 1730s William wrote letters to 'his dear little jug', telling her 'every man may have girls worthy his attention, but few, sisters so conversible as my dear

---

[58] Ashmun, *Singing Swan*, 21; Constable, *Letters of Seward*, i. 116–17.
[59] Adam Eyre, 'A Diurnal', in *Yorkshire Diaries and Autobiographies in the Seventeenth and Eighteenth Centuries*, Surtees Society, 65 (1877), 72, 81, 352–3.
[60] Anderson, *Books of Examinations and Depositions 1622–27*, 41.
[61] F. J. C. and D. M. Hearnshaw, (eds.), *Southampton Court Leet Records A.D. 1603–1624*. Southampton Record Society, 4 (Southampton, 1906–7), 512.
[62] HRO, 21M65 C3/8, 306.

Nanny'.[63] In 1737, when Queen Caroline died and Ann lost her place as maid of honour at court she and her brother set up house together in Pall Mall. Four years later Ann went to France for a long visit with friends. William condoned such visits if they were for her health, but was not as sanguine about their duration. In 1742 he moved to more modest bachelor quarters, because he was unable to keep up his household without his sister's assistance. When Ann returned to England in 1744 it is significant that she chose to stay with friends rather than live with her brother once again. Although William 'made a gallant effort at reconciliation', Ann complained that he had tried to control her movements and had unnecessarily let it be known in public that he 'allowed' her an annuity of £200. Here we see the unenviable position of a singlewoman. Financial and residential dependence on a brother, even a generous one such as William Pitt, translated into a loss of autonomy for the sister. In 1751 William wrote to Ann claiming that he 'never expected absolute deference or blind submission, only a degree of deference' on her part. William contradicted Ann's perception that 'to satisfy me you must live with me as my slave', and said he had merely asked her 'to shape her life in some degree to his'.[64] Brother and sister did not view her situation in the same light.

Fortunately for Ann Pitt, she was able to maintain her independence by obtaining another position at court, this time as Keeper of the Privy Purse to her royal highness as well as governess to young Princess Augusta. Back in France in the 1750s, Ann and William were once again writing affectionate letters to one another, and in 1754 William was able to report to Ann that Hester Granville had consented to make him a husband and 'gives you a sister'. Ann returned to England in 1757 with the assistance of her 'kind brother', and she was very conscious of how 'very disagreeable and embarrassing it must be to him to have me in France'. (Britain was at war with France and William Pitt was head of the British government). Ann even stayed with her brother and new sister-in-law for some months afterward, but relations began to decline again in 1759. Ill and wishing to be with family, Ann journeyed from Bath to London, where her brother refused to see or lodge her due to his workload. Ann wrote before she left, 'I will not dissemble that I am very much disappointed and mortified in not having seen you', but she accepted his excuse.[65]

Now that William Pitt was married, with a family of his own and an important career, he did not seem to have time for his sister as he once did when he wanted her to keep house for him. Not only did William fail to see

[63] Sir Tresham Lever (ed.), *The House of Pitt: A Family Chronicle* (London: Wyman & Sons, 1947), 68.

[64] Ibid. 91–2.

[65] Ibid. 127, 130.

his sister's continuing need for familial intimacy, he also was less than sympathetic to her financial worries. In 1760 Ann was delighted to obtain a government pension for her service to the royal family. William refused to empathize with his never-married sister's financial predicament, and could only voice his shame at seeing his surname placed on the pensions list. Ironically, a year later William accepted a pension and a new peerage. Ann wanted to send her brother a copy of his previous letters to her on the subject of pensions, but her friends restrained her from doing so. Ann and William Pitt both seem to have been stubborn, controlling, strong-willed people, and it is perhaps no surprise that they clashed. Nevertheless, although they may have had similar characters, they were not equals. The two illustrate how gender, social status, and marital status combined so that this male peer and his commoner sister occupied very different social positions vis-à-vis one another.

William Pitt was not the worst brother in his family by far. His elder sibling, Thomas, enjoyed that honour. When Thomas got into money trouble in 1754 his single sisters, Elizabeth and Mary, were affected more than he was. He wrote to his brother William: 'My sisters will be separated when I go into Cornwall [the location of the family estate] . . . I wish to God some way may be thought of to provide for them, for I must repeat it, either of them living with me is extremely disagreeable, and having so many uneasinesses in the world it is too much to have my home, my retirement made uneasy to me'.[66] In addition to refusing to house his sisters, Thomas never paid his sister Mary her portion. When her nephew Thomas Jr. attained his majority he found himself in 'acrimonious discussions' with his aunt Mary, who 'demanded money which she maintained was owed her by her recalcitrant brother'. It appears that Mary's 'demand' was a fair one, for her nephew settled with her in 1759. At this point Mary was about 34, well past the normal age of marriage for the gentry, but still capable of bearing children and marrying. Mary Pitt, however, never married; the delay in receiving her portion may well have led to her lifelong singleness.

Mary's sister Betty was treated even more harshly by their brother Thomas. The 'fair Betty Pitt' (as contemporaries termed her) had a series of non-marital relationships in the 1750s. Commenting on them, Horace Walpole wrote that 'her very first slip was with her eldest brother'. If it is true that Thomas Pitt sexually abused his younger sister, then his refusal to let her reside with him and to maintain her was doubly cruel. Betty's brother William did provide her with a house and a generous annuity after Thomas dropped her, but she was angry at William for reducing her allowance when he found out about her sexual affairs. In her mid-to-late forties Betty

---

[66] Ibid. 87.

married John Hannam, who was both younger and richer than herself. Poignantly highlighting her lack of money, and perhaps her age, Betty wrote to her brother William: 'And as he can have no possible inducement in my situation to ask my hand but the most disinterested affection, I have reason to flatter myself with the hopes of a great share of felicity, under the protection of a man of his superior understanding and merit'.[67] When siblings were unavailable, either literally or emotionally, singlewomen like Betty Pitt might marry, but others looked to relatives or extended kin.

Kinship

Relationships with their family of origin were some of the most primary to singlewomen, but bonds of kinship were not limited to immediate family members. Extended kin also played active roles in the lives of never-married women. The experiences of singlewomen contradict a historiography that until recently held that kinship ties in early modern England were generally 'loose, narrow, and shallow', and thus relatively unimportant compared to the bonds of nuclear family and of neighbourhood. Scholars based this theory primarily on quantitative research that used parish registers and population listings to reconstitute families.[68] Recent scholarship has questioned static demographic studies that have reified the nuclear family and have conflated family and household in the English past. And research is showing that household composition continually changed over time (with supposedly nuclear families full of extended and step-kin), and that co-residence was not required for meaningful ties to exist between kin.[69]

Some historians have examined kinship through other types of sources, such as probate evidence. But because they have looked primarily at the wills of married men, theories about early modern kinship have been almost exclusively male-focused.[70] The few historians who have utilized women's wills have found that women's bequest strategies were quite different from

---

[67] Ibid. 98.

[68] Howell, 'Peasant Inheritance Customs', 141; Wrightson, 'Kinship in an English Village', 321, 324; David Cressy, 'Kinship and Kin Interaction in Early Modern England', *Past & Present*, 113 (Nov. 1986), 38–69; Peter Laslett, *The World We Have Lost: England Before the Industrial Age*, 2nd edn. (New York: Scribner, 1971); Peter Laslett and Richard Wall, *Household and Family in Past Time* (Cambridge: Cambridge University Press, 1974).

[69] Examples include Miranda Chaytor, 'Household and Kinship: Ryton in the late 16th and early 17th centuries', *History Workshop Journal*, 10 (1979), 25–60; Davidoff et al., *The Family Story*; and Tadmor, *Family and Friends*.

[70] David Cressy's 'Kinship and Kin Interaction' examined the wills of yeomen, tradesmen, and male clothiers; Howell's 'Peasant Inheritance Customs' used a sample of 207 wills, 193 of which were made by married men; Wrightson's 'Kinship in an English Village' used 192 wills, 140 of which mentioned children and 116 a female spouse.

men's, particularly because they remembered a much wider range of kin. For example, Richard Vann's examination of female testators in the town of Banbury (Oxon) revealed that after 1650 women began to take on the role of 'kinship expert'. Although never-married women and widows always left more legacies to kin, friends, and servants than did men, over the eighteenth century women began to leave two to three times more bequests to these individuals than did men.[71] This suggests that a wider range of sources, more qualitative methods, and attention to difference (especially in terms of gender and marital status) will reveal that kinship ties in early modern England were much more significant than we once thought.

Indeed, because singlewomen did not marry and form nuclear families, their wills are exceptionally good sources for revealing the prominence of early modern kinship. Table 3.1 reveals the range of extended kin who figured prominently in these women's wills. Single female testators from Hampshire and the towns of Bristol, Oxford, and York actually mentioned aunts and uncles a little more than parents, especially fathers. Aunts and uncles often appeared because of the fostering or quasi-parental role they performed for singlewomen. A number of never-married women lived some portion of their lives in the households of their parents's siblings. For example, Margaret Jenkins alias Jenkinson, whose parents lived in London, was 'educated, trained, and brought up' from the age of 2 until she was 20 by her aunt and uncle in Southampton.[72] Aunts and uncles also helped their nieces by providing them with portions or property. The Southampton baker George Downs left property to a never-married niece and a nephew, as well as monetary legacies to six other single nieces and six single nephews.[73] The Southampton widow Mary Carteret bequeathed two houses and the George Inn to her five nieces. Such property helped maintain at least one lifelong singlewoman, for Carteret's niece Frances Gollop was still single twenty-eight years after she had received her inheritance.[74]

A marital case from Winchester's consistory court reveals the parental power that singlewomen's uncles could wield. In 1567 William Coles brought a case against William Hodges, the father of his betrothed, Christian Hodges. It seems that Hodges did not want his 14-year-old daughter to marry Coles and so hid her away to prevent it. While William

---

[71] Richard Vann, 'Wills and the Family in an English Town: Banbury 1550–1800', *Journal of Family History*, 4: 4 (1979), 366–7. Vann's findings contradict Wrightson's assertion that 'women did not vary from men on the grounds of sex alone in their recognition of kin'. Wrightson, 'Kinship in an English Village', 325. Amy Erickson also found that women gave more bequests to extended kin than did men. Erickson, *Women and Property*, 211.

[72] *Books of Examinations and Depositions 1570–1594*, 55.

[73] SRO, SC 4/4/536/1.

[74] SRO, SC 4/4/491/1–2.

Hodges had never condoned the relationship between Coles and his daughter, his brother John had furthered the affair and allowed Coles and his niece to contract themselves in his home. John Hodges admitted that he had asked his brother if he would agree to the contract, but when William said his daughter was 'too young', John had decided to hide the betrothal from him. Christian Hodges claimed the betrothal was against her wishes and that she had only gone through with it after her uncle called her 'horse shit and baggage and harlotry' and threw his dagger in fury. William Hodges believed that his brother had usurped his parental role. He told his daughter that her uncle 'will make thee say that the crow is white, but if I have thee once away, I will make thee say as it please me'.[75]

Never-married women not only enjoyed close ties with their aunts and uncles, but they also played a significant role as aunts themselves. It is clear that the role of the 'maiden aunt', so common in modern Anglo-American society, was actually of early modern (if not earlier) origin. Singlewomen were encouraged to help other children and families if they did not have ones of their own. Aunts who fostered their nieces and nephews or bequeathed property to them fulfilled a maternal role, one of the most defining and encouraged roles for the early modern woman. Through their assistance to their siblings' children, never-married women discovered one of the most appreciated and condoned positions available to them, that of the surrogate mother.

The extended kin who figured the most prominently in the lives of singlewomen were the children of their siblings. Nieces and nephews were the relatives most frequently mentioned by single female testators from Bristol, Oxford, and Southampton. And they came second to siblings as the kin who appeared most often in York and Hampshire singlewomen's wills. As with the case of siblings, however, kinship was gendered. In Southampton, York, and Hampshire never-married women mentioned nieces in their wills more than nephews. In Oxford the gender balance was equal, and only in Bristol did singlewomen remember nephews more than nieces.[76]

While some singlewomen had close relationships with their nephews, the bonds between maiden aunts and their nieces were amongst some of the strongest in their lives, second only to singlewomen's ties to their sisters. Relationships between never-married aunts and their nieces were a common feature of eighteenth-century English literature, such as in Bernard Mandeville's prose dialogues *The Virgin Unmask'd: or, Female Dialogues*

---

[75] HRO, 21M65 C3/4, 75, 84–90, 106, 124–5, 222.
[76] This gender difference may not be definitive, however, because singlewomen also mentioned children of siblings with no reference to their gender.

Betwixt an Elderly Maiden Lady, and her Niece (1709).[77] These ties also appear in the wills of never-married women, who as a group mentioned and made more bequests to nieces than to nephews. As Table 3.1 reveals, singlewomen in Southampton, York, and Hampshire remembered nieces more frequently; in Oxford they remembered nieces and nephews equally; and only in Bristol did they name nephews more than nieces. Nieces also appeared more than nephews within individual singlewomen's wills. For instance, of the twenty-one single female testators in Southampton who remembered their siblings' children, ten named more nieces than nephews, six referred to an equal number, and only five mentioned more nephews than nieces. Similarly, in the Hampshire probate sample, thirteen single-women named more nieces than nephews, another four remembered an equal number, and eight named more nephews than nieces. In addition to remembering nieces more, never-married women frequently made some of their largest bequests to them. For example, when Mildred Arnold died in 1667 she left legacies to thirty-one family members and friends, but her largest bequest was to Mary Arnold, the daughter of her brother William.[78]

It was also common for a never-married woman to make her niece her primary beneficiary (see Table 3.2). When Mary Smith of Southampton died in 1705 she left 'all her goods, chattels, and effects' to her niece Elizabeth Smith. Smith also stipulated that if her niece came 'to any poverty before she [arrived] at age 16 or the day of marriage', her executrix was to assist her.[79] As we will see in Chapter 4, some never-married aunts practised trades or kept shops of their own that they passed on to their nieces. For instance, when Elizabeth Aldridge of Fareham died in 1725 she bequeathed her dwelling house and millinery shop to her niece Ann Leach and made her sole executrix.[80] Singlewomen also frequently made some of their more personal bequests to their nieces. For example, Elizabeth Whislad of South-ampton left only two pieces of personal jewellery in her will—a gold chain to her mother and a diamond ring to her never-married niece Mary Rowcliffe.[81] In 1741 Grace Hildyard of York left money to her mother and siblings. But she bequeathed more personal gifts, such as 'one scepter broad of gold which was given me many years ago by my late dear father to keep in his memory', to her niece Elizabeth Ellis, and 'a gold ring which has a locket with my late dear father's hair in it' to her niece Sarah Scott.[82]

---

[77] Amy Erickson also found that 'nieces were a particular favourite' of single female testators. Erickson, *Women and Property*, 217. For examples in literature, see Katherine Ottaway Kittredge, '"Tabby Cats Lead Apes in Hell": Never-married Women in Eighteenth-Century Life and Fiction', Ph.D. dissertation, SUNY, Binghamton (1991), 273–4, 337–47.

[78] HRO, 1667 B1.

[79] HRO, 1705 P105.

[80] HRO, 1725 P2/1–2.

[81] HRO, 1723 A119.

[82] BIHR, Dean and Chapter Wills, reel 1252, Grace Hildyard (Aug. 1741).

Table 3.2. Primary beneficiaries of single female testators

Bristol N = 40	Oxford N = 40	Southampton N = 35	York N = 50	Hampshire N = 45
Sister [7]	Sister [12]	Sister [11]	Sister [8]	Sister [14]
Nephew [7]	Niece [7]	Niece [6]	Brother [6]	Niece [9]
Brother [6]	Mother [4]	Brother [3]	Niece [6]	Nephew [8]
Niece [4]	Kinswoman [4]	Nephew [3]	Kinswoman [5]	Brother [6]
Man [3]	Brother [3]	Brother-in-law [2]	Kinsman [5]	Male friend [6]
Kinswoman [3]	Kinsman [3]	Master [2]		
Sister's children [3]	Female Friend [3]	Male friend [2]		

Source: See Table 3.1.

Another reason why singlewomen chose to provide for their nieces and nephews was that they were frequently their godchildren as well. The role of a godparent was to step in and help raise the godchild if he or she was orphaned or in need, and single female testators seem to have taken this responsibility to heart. Never-married women most often served as godparents to the children of their siblings. Frances Parkinson of Southampton left her goddaughter Frances £4 and her godson Augustine £2, amounts that were in the middle range of the sums that Parkinson bequeathed to her nieces. Ellen Seager of Fordingbridge (Hants.), left £5, two ewes, two lambs, and four yards of woollen cloth to her godchild Ellen Plomley, who also was her niece.[83] The largest bequests in Seager's will went to her niece and nephew, who were also her godchildren. Although the two were both biological and spiritual kin to Seager, her will illustrates that godchildren may be invisible in some singlewomen's wills if a woman emphasized biological over spiritual kinship. This, and the fact that godparenting declined after the Reformation, perhaps explains why godchildren appeared in only 8 per cent of singlewomen's wills from Hampshire, and in only 2 per cent of the wills from Southampton and not at all in the wills from Bristol, Oxford, and York.[84]

The range of extended kin with which singlewomen enjoyed close ties did not stop at the siblings of their parents or the children of their siblings. Cousins were the third most common legatees of single female testators from Southampton and Hampshire. And in York they were the fourth most common. In Oxford single female testators mentioned cousins more than friends or in-laws. And in Bristol kinswomen equalled sisters as the most common legatees in singlewomen's wills. One of the reasons why cousins were so plentiful in the wills of never-married women is that contemporaries used the term to refer to any relative other than a parent, sibling, spouse, or child. For example, the diarist Ralph Josselin used the term 'cousin' to refer to his sister's son, the children of aunts and uncles, and a cousin's spouse.[85] Singlewomen's wills also reveal that they employed the terms 'kins(wo)man' and 'cousin' synonymously, in addition to using the terms to describe a wide range of kin. The casual and vague nomenclature used to refer to relatives once led some historians to argue that kin ties were relatively loose and insignificant in early modern England, but Naomi Tadmor has recently presented a different perspective. She sees the wide use of the term 'cousin' as proof of the inclusive and flexible nature of

---

[83] HRO, 1615 B37 and 1621 A59.

[84] In the village of Terling (Essex), testators mentioning godchildren decreased over the sixteenth century, and almost disappeared in the following century. Wrightson, 'Kinship in an English Village', 324.

[85] Cited in Tadmor, *Family and Friends*, 150–2.

kinship. Kin ties were not insignificant; rather, they were more widespread and more adaptable than modern-day concepts of kinship, which have become more defined and restrictive.[86]

Singlewomen often were quite close to what we might term 'distant' kin; that is, relatives other than parents, siblings, and siblings' children. For example, Jane Maidman of Portsmouth left the residue of her real and personal estate to her executrices Sarah and Mary Maidman, who were the single daughter and widow of her father's nephew.[87] Cicily Hodgson of York bequeathed all her goods to her 'cousin Isabel Hodgson in regard her hath look to and kept me in my sickness when none else of my friends would help me'.[88] Elizabeth Ireland of Bristol made a number of bequests to her two female cousins, Joanna and Mary Gough. The codicil to her will read: 'as for my particular Friends Joanna and Mary Gough who have so agreeably co-habitated with me so many years, I desire may be given to them [various household goods and that] they may have the sole possession and free use of my dwelling house one whole year after the day of my decease'.[89] Gracill Roberts asked to be buried with her cousin Katherine Palmer in Jesus chapel, just outside Southampton.[90] Such a request shows unusual closeness between kinswomen, since most singlewomen asked to be buried near their parents, and to a lesser extent, their sisters.

Some context for why extended kin received bequests from single female relatives is provided through examining how contemporaries described the duties of kinship. For example, Matilda Hopkins was abetted in a love affair by her kinswoman Alice Goddyn, who approved of the match and let the couple meet at her home. Although Hopkins's father disapproved of her lover, her relative Thomas Thorpe of Winchester believed it was right for Matilda and Edmund Bedham to marry if they had contracted themselves to each other. He told the couple that, 'for my wife's sake because she is somewhat of kindred unto [Matilda] I will bestow somewhat of household stuff on you', and that he would try to persuade Matilda's father and brother to her side.[91] Kin could also assist singlewomen in other ways. Rose Michenar lived as a servant with her aunt for a few years until they argued over her wages. Michenar left and went to the house of John Garye of Boyatt, who was 'somewhat of kindred' to her. Garye allowed Michenar to

[86] Cressy, 'Kinship and Kin Interaction', 66; Tadmor, *Family and Friends*, ch. 4, esp. 117–21.
[87] HRO, 1740 A110.
[88] BIHR, Probate Register 46, fo. 112, Cicilly Hodgson, (21 May 1644).
[89] BRO, unpublished transcript of wills, Elizabeth Ireland, (9 Feb. 1749/50).
[90] HRO, 1643 AD43.
[91] HRO, 21M65 C3/7, 47, 51, 53–5. For the important role that kin played in negotiating the marriages of their relatives, see Diana O'Hara, *Courtship and Constraint: Rethinking the Making of Marriage in Tudor England* (Manchester: Manchester University Press, 2000), esp. chs. 1 and 3.

stay with him for a few months, 'for kindred's sake', until she found another position in service.[92] Rose Michenar's story illustrates how singlewomen felt they could rely upon the help of certain individuals by claiming ties of kinship, even if both parties only knew that they were 'somewhat' related. These examples show how extended kin were more active in never-married women' lives than we might have guessed, providing emotional, practical, and material assistance.

Singlewomen's wills also indicate that geographical distance did not necessarily diminish the importance of kinship. David Cressy has posited that kinship was a relationship that could lie dormant and then could be activated by a relative at any time; for never-married women this was definitely the case.[93] Singlewomen were more prone to 'activate' distant ties of kinship (whether that distance was spatial or familial), since they did not have closer kin such as husbands and children. Whether this activation was due to opportunity or necessity varied by individual, but distant kin appear in many of the wills made by singlewomen. For example, Elizabeth Compton of Southampton left half of her estate to her married sister and her sister's family in the parish of Freemantle.[94] While Compton was a wealthy woman who obviously had contacts beyond Southampton, never-married women of more modest means also remembered long-distance relatives. Mary Yeomance of Southampton, who died with an estate worth £24, left three of her five legacies to her nieces Susannah and Joy Yeomance in the Sussex town of Chichester, and one to another niece, Jane Yeomance, who lived in Portsmouth.[95]

Surrogate Kinship

As we have seen, singlewomen were particularly woman-identified in their relationships, with sisters and nieces holding the most primary place in their lives. Never-married women were also woman-identified in their relationships with non-kin. If a singlewoman did not have a mother, sister, niece, or female cousin in her life, she would opt to live and sometimes work with an unrelated woman. This woman was usually also single, or, to a lesser extent, widowed. Although these women were not blood relations, they became, in effect, the 'surrogate kin' of singlewomen. Never-married

[92] HRO, 21M65 C3/8, 198–9.
[93] Cressy, 'Kinship and Kin Interaction', 47.
[94] HRO, 1752 A20.
[95] HRO, 1693 A133. Wrightson also found that the kin mentioned by testators in Terling did not always live in the same village; e.g. 24% of kin living outside Terling resided over 15 miles away. Wrightson, 'Kinship in an English Village', 326.

women created households and mutually supportive relationships with other unmarried women during their lifetimes, and upon their deaths frequently made these women their heirs. For instance, when Sarah Piesley of Oxford made her will she bequeathed to 'Deborah Marcham, Oxford spinster, and now living with me all my household goods, stuff and implements, together with all my plate, rings, jewels, wearing apparel, as also my ready money, bills, bonds, notes of hand, wood, coal, and all my effects whatsoever'.[96] Not only did Piesley live with Marcham and designate her as her heir, she also made Marcham the executrix of her will. When Joane Northell, a Bristol bone-lacemaker, died in 1672 she left both money and property to various nieces and other female relatives. But she also bequeathed one-third of her entire estate, as well as all her household goods, to Joane Rowlings, a fellow bone-lacemaker. Northell was particularly interested in Rowlings's well-being, specifying that she could sell or pawn any of the goods bequeathed to her if she was in need. Jane Green, also of Bristol, made bequests to five people in her will. Four of them were female friends, three of whom were married or widowed. But it was her 'loving friend Elizabeth Hopkins, Bristol, singlewoman' whom she made her residuary legatee and sole executrix.[97] As mentioned above, when Sarah Fielding's three sisters died she went to live, not with her famous brothers, but with Jane Collier, a fellow single female author. The governess Agnes Porter lived her last years as a temporary lodger with various kin and friends, including Mrs and Miss Lucy Lloyd. She found her final resting place in the Lloyd family burial plot. In death, the never-married Agnes Porter was literally adopted by this other family of unmarried women and laid to rest with them.[98] Such evidence indicates how material assistance and companionship were common practice between unrelated single-women.

The question of how to interpret such female–female relationships has generated much debate. On the one hand these could have been friendships, and on the other they could have been what we would today define as lesbian relationships. The historiography of lesbianism in early modern England is rapidly expanding.[99] Scholars have cautioned against anachron-

---

[96] Centre for Oxfordshire Studies (hereafter COS), Will 100.59 Sarah Piesley, (16 Jan. 1785).

[97] BRO, W 1672/41 Joane Northell (1672) and W 1665/18 Jane Green (27 January 1665).

[98] Jeanna Martin (ed.), *A Governess in the Age of Jane Austen* (London: Hambledon Press, 1998).

[99] Emma Donoghue, *Passions Between Women: British Lesbian Culture, 1668–1801* (New York: HarperCollins, 1993); Patricia Crawford and Sara Mendelson, 'Sexual Identities in Early Modern England: The Marriage of Two Women in 1680', *Gender & History*, 7 (1995), 362–78; Margaret R. Hunt, 'The Sapphic Strain: English Lesbians in the Long Eighteenth Century', in Judith M. Bennett and Amy M. Froide (eds.), *Singlewomen in the European Past, 1250–1800* (Philadelphia: University of Pennsylvania Press, 1999), 270–96; Elizabeth Wahl, *Invisible Relations: Representations*

istically applying the modern category of 'lesbian' to the past, and have concluded that there probably was no lesbian self-identity in the early modern period. Rather, what has become the focus are the sorts of behaviour that might indicate a 'lesbian-like' relationship. This is a term Judith Bennett has coined to describe women who 'lived in circumstances that allowed them to nurture and support other women', and who resisted heterosexual marriage, but who may not have necessarily 'engaged in certifiable same-sex genital contact'.[100] Scholars differ on whether such behaviour must be sexual or erotic, or whether emotional intensity can be regarded as having the same importance as physical intimacy. Historians have endeavoured to find examples of female–female relationships in the past, assuming, like scholars of race and gender, that historical bias has prevented us from detecting such minority subjects. For the early modern period a number of cases of 'female husbands' have been identified: women like Anne Poulter, who, under the name and guise of 'James Howard', married Arabella Hunt and lived with her for a short while before her sex became known.[101] But the number of identified couples remains small. We need to more fully pursue female relationships in sources such as letters and wills in order to write a true social history of lesbianism in the period.

More evidence has been forthcoming from literary critics, who have focused on the discourses and representations of female–female desire in the sixteenth through eighteenth centuries. Scholars such as Harriette Andreadis and Valerie Traub have persuasively shown that early modern people recognized that desire could exist between women. The lesbian was invisible, not so much because female–female desire was unacknowledged, but because such desire was not threatening to a phallocentric model of sexual intercourse. Nevertheless, female–female desire was not generally condoned, even if it was acknowledged. This means that early modern discourses about such desire were often coded or subtle, leaving them open to multiple interpretations and debate.

If one believes that female–female desire existed in the past, then two singlewomen who resided together and bequeathed their property to each other look like a lesbian couple; but if one is not inclined to believe this, then such women look like friends. For my purposes, however, this debate is moot. What is most important is that some never-married women

---

of Female Intimacy in the Age of Enlightenment (Stanford, Cal.: Stanford University Press, 1999); Judith M. Bennett, '"Lesbian-Like" and the Social History of Lesbianisms', *Journal of the History of Sexuality*, 9: 1–2 (2000), 1–24; Harriette Andreadis, *Sappho in Early Modern England: Female Same-Sex Literary Erotics, 1550–1714* (Chicago: University of Chicago Press, 2001); Valerie Traub, *The Renaissance of Lesbianism in Early Modern England* (Cambridge: Cambridge University Press, 2002).

[100] Bennett, '"Lesbian-Like"', esp. 9–10, 14.
[101] Crawford and Mendelson, 'Sexual Identities in Early Modern England'.

identified their ties to unrelated women as the primary relationships in their life. In terms of social relationships, such singlewomen could take the social place of a husband for one another; whether they also took the sexual place would merely provide further evidence of the primacy of their relationship.

The Significance of Singlewomen To Their Families

So far we have been examining the individuals who were significant in the lives of early modern singlewomen, but we also need to recognize how important never-married women were to others, in particular their kin. Singlewomen were not marginal to their families, as a nuclear-family centred approach has implied. Rather, never-married women were frequently at the very centre of what we have perhaps mistakenly thought of as the nuclear household. Historians of north-western Europe have posited that new households were created when a couple got married. But household formation was not just dependent on marriage. If it was, how should we account for the significant number of men who set up households before they married, or for those who did so and never married? If we look more closely, we will notice the crucial role played by never-married sisters. The sister–brother couple may have been a close second to spouses in respect to households headed by a male and female.

The analogy between a household led by a brother and sister and one led by a marital couple was an obvious one to early modern people. On 11 May 1726 James Fretwell noted in his diary that he had brought his sister with him to Norton, to begin housekeeping in a house that his father had purchased from a kinsman. James was 26 years old and Mary was 21. He concluded this notation with: 'I observe it was the same day on which my father was married.' It is telling that Fretwell associated the start of his father's marriage with the beginning of his own co-residence with his sister. In May 1733 Fretwell's sister Mary married Thomas Routh. Routh was a Pontefract grocer who had courted her years earlier, but due to parental disapproval the match had been delayed. Two years after his sister's marriage Fretwell sold his house at Norton, 'designing to leave that place, being weary of living with servants only, since my sister had left me'. Fretwell went on to share his home with a cousin, Elizabeth Atkinson, whom he described as 'an old maid', and in 1759 he took in his difficult niece Mary Woodhouse as a housekeeper.[102] James Fretwell never did marry, but spent his entire life heading a household with the help of various single female kin. Similarly,

---

[102] 'A Family History begun by James Fretwell', in *Yorkshire Diaries and Autobiographies*, Surtees Society, 65 (1877), 182, 204, 212–13, 225, 242–3.

the painter Sir Joshua Reynolds lived with his sister Frances for twenty-four years, 'until she was supplanted by her [two] nieces', one of whom stayed with him until his death. On one occasion he wrote to his friend Bennett Langton that his sister was at his house in Richmond and his niece was visiting family in Devonshire, 'so that I am quite a batchelor'. While we might think of the never-married Reynolds as a perpetual bachelor, he only described himself as one when his female relatives were not his home companions.[103] Other historians have also noted that men of the middling sort benefited from the housekeeping skills, monetary loans, and companionship of their single sisters, but we have not recognized just how common and necessary this phenomenon was in the early modern period.[104]

While singlewomen enabled bachelor brothers to establish households, others helped so-called 'nuclear' family households to be successful. Scholars have begun to question the self-contained nature of the nuclear family implied by sources like population listings. When we look at other sources, such as family papers and correspondence, we find that the nuclear family was not so distinct from the larger kin group. If anything, the household formed a semi-permeable barrier that allowed kin to freely move in and out. Marital couples with children commonly benefited from the material, emotional, and financial assistance of a never-married sister. A perusal of diaries, letters, and memoirs illustrates the significant role played by singlewomen in their families. For example, Hester Mulso's mother died when she was in her early twenties, which led to her taking over as mistress of her father's household. Then, when her clergyman brother married, Mulso went to live in his household to assist his wife and help with their children. It was not until her early thirties that Hester Mulso created her own nuclear family and household by marrying John Chapone. But Chapone died a year later, and Hester moved back to her brother John's house. She spent only one year of her life as a wife and mistress of her own household; the rest she devoted to her father's and her brother's families.[105]

William Blundell was explicit about the important role played by his never-married sisters in sustaining his family. The Blundells were Catholic, which meant that when William inherited the family estate in 1638, two-thirds of it was forfeit to the crown. But William's monetary problems were assuaged when his never-married sister Emelia, who lived with him and his wife at Crosby Hall (Lancs.), died in 1640. Emelia made her brother the

---

[103] John Ingamells and John Edgecumbe (eds.), *The Letters of Sir Joshua Reynolds* (New Haven, Conn.: Yale University Press, 2000), 111, 264.

[104] See Grassby, *Kinship and Capitalism*, 80–1, and Margaret R. Hunt, *The Middling Sort: Commerce, Gender and the Family in England, 1680–1780* (Berkeley: University of California Press, 1996), esp. ch. 3, 'Middling Daughters and the Family Economy'.

[105] Myers, *Bluestocking Circle*, 77–8, 117–19, 143–4.

executor of her will and left him 'all her monies, bonds, and other worldly goods'.[106] William had two other single sisters, Winifred and Frances, who continued to reside in his household. The 1640s proved to be a rough decade for the family. William fought for Charles I in the Civil Wars, and as a result the Blundell estate was sequestered and William had to flee to Wales. Despite the interruptions, William and his wife Anne had produced a large household of seven children by 1649. They eventually had a total of fourteen children, ten of whom survived infancy. The household and the children benefited from the inclusion of William's two sisters. When Blundell purchased his estate back in 1653, he had to spend £1,109, nearly half (£520) of which his sisters Winifred and Frances supplied. In later years Winifred and Frances never asked their brother to pay their portions, instead each received a modest £25 a year from him.

The significance of Winifred and Frances to the Blundell household was more than merely financial. In 1654 Frances went to visit her sister-in-law's family, who wanted to keep her with them. William hastily wrote to his mother-in-law to fend off this disaster: 'But give me leave to lament humbly the damage you have done to my Family. You have taken from my sister Winifrid a husband, from [my daughter] Milly a Tutoress, a companion from my wife, and from myself a most excellent player of shuttlecock'.[107] Blundell's words reveal the multiple positions that a singlewoman could hold within a family. Rather than being 'superfluous' or a 'burden', Frances (or Franke, as her brother called her) Blundell was a treasured companion to her also single sister, to her brother, to her sister-in-law, and to her nieces and nephews.

Winifred and Frances Blundell also illustrate the types of surrogate mothering performed by never-married women for their extended families. The Blundell sisters helped their sister-in-law maintain the large household and estate at Crosby. Frances tutored all of her nieces in reading, writing, and housewifery, and perhaps in the Catholic religion, since seven of the nine girls became nuns. The example of Winifred and Frances Blundell undoubtedly influenced their nieces' views on Catholic singlehood and the decision to eschew marriage, although the nieces pursued their piety within the cloister rather than as laywomen in the home. The Blundell aunts also assisted their secular nieces and nephews in setting themselves up in life. In 1667 Frances travelled with her married niece, Emelia Butler, and her husband when they went to Ireland to claim their inheritance. Six years later William called on his sister, that 'ancient maid in Ireland', to take another of his daughters to the continent to be professed as a nun. By this time Frances was also caring for the next generation in the family, in

---

[106] Blundell, *Cavalier: Letters*, 1–292, 8.   [107] Ibid. 55.

particular, her great-nephew Edmund Butler. William noted, 'my sister Frances hath made herself his nurse, his Servant, his mistress, his mother indeed. Her money and pains and patience have been freely extended to him and on his behalf'.[108]

Frances Blundell was not only a surrogate mother, she also became a proxy wife for her brother late in life. By the late 1670s Frances's sister Winifred Blundell was deceased. Her brother William's wife Anne also died in 1685. Having lost their respective 'spouses', William and Frances lived out their days in a brother–sister household. William wistfully described their life to his daughter Bridget, saying that, when in a good humour, 'the venerable Mistress Frances, Regent', would give him advice, tell him his faults, and perhaps mend his clothes, but would not give him coffee or be gay and pleasant as Bridget had once been.[109] A 67-year-old Frances was with William when he died in 1698. She had spent her entire life residing with and heading households with her siblings, rather than with a husband.

While Frances Blundell was an exceptional helpmeet to her kin, she was not unique among never-married women. The Byrum family, who lived in Manchester a century later, provides another example of the significant roles played by singlewomen in their families. The physician and scholar John Byrum had five sisters who never married: Anne, Dorothy, Elizabeth, Ellen, and the youngest, Phebe, to whom he was closest. Sarah Brearcliffe was the only one of John's sisters who married, but she gave birth to four lifelong singlewomen. John's wife (and cousin) Elizabeth Byrum also had a never-married sister, named Ann. Her other sister, Mary, married and produced three single daughters. And John and Elizabeth themselves had two daughters who never married, named Elizabeth and Dorothy (known to the family as Beppy and Dolly). In just two generations the Byrum family produced fifteen women who never married.

The Byrum singlewomen were an integral part of the extended family. In the 1720s John Byrum was away at Cambridge and in London, leaving his wife with four children under the age of 10. He may have felt he could do so because into the breach stepped his never-married sisters. Phebe, in particular, lived with his wife and assisted her. She served as nurse and companion to her brother's family and took part in her nephew's education. When his daughter Nelly died while he was away, John received the news, not from his wife, but from his sister Phebe and sister-in-law Ann. He wrote to his wife hoping she would be comforted by the 'friends around her'.

Phebe Byrum was as close to her bother as she was to his family. John sometimes referred to his sister Phebe as 'my wife', and in a joint letter to his wife and Phebe he complained of being absent from his 'dear wives'. John

---

[108] Ibid. 126, 141, 152.   [109] Ibid. 284.

x78   *Single But Not Alone*

and Phebe were also business partners in the instruction of shorthand. As
early as 1723 Phebe sent her brother missives written in shorthand and
requested steel pens from London. In 1733 she was in Bath when the
younger daughter of a JP and a gentleman expressed an interest in learning
shorthand from her. She wrote to John to ask if she should teach them. In
1742 John wrote to Phebe, his 'dearly beloved sister' and the 'Grand
Mistress' of the art of shorthand. It seems that John had gone to London
to get a patent on the shorthand system he and his sister had created. He
reported that their 'shorthand Bill' had passed in the Commons without
opposition. John sent his sister a copy of 'An act [of Parliament] for securing
John Byrum, Master of Arts [and fellow of the Royal Society], the sole right
of publishing, for a certain term of years [twenty-one], the Art and Method
of Short-hand, invented by him'. While John told Phebe the bill was 'hers',
'just as I would call everything that I can call my own yours', one wonders
what Phebe Byrum thought of having her name excluded from the patent.

　　How do we reconcile the assumption that never-married women in the
past were a blight or burden on their closest kin with the presence of lifelong
singlewomen in so many families? Would not the Blundells and Byrums
have tried to marry off their single female kin if their marital status was a
negative circumstance for the family? The Verney family, members of the
gentry in the seventeenth century, shed some light on this question. Ralph
Verney never tried very hard to find suitable partners for his sisters, because
their portions cost him money. When his sister Penelope (or 'Pen') found a
very suitable marriage partner in George Thorne, Ralph said he was unable
to pay her dowry and refused to put up security for the future payment of
her £1,000 portion. He merely offered £60 a year until he could pay the
larger sum, and when the Thorne family asked for the more reasonable rate
of 8 per-cent interest, or £80 a year, he again baulked. Ralph told his wife
that he thought Pen could not get her portion 'out of my estate . . . for I am
well assured neither law nor equity will give it her'.[110] Not only do his
words hardly reflect any sense of fraternal duty or kindness, they also reveal
no concern about having a lifelong singlewoman in the family. Thanks to
her brother, Pen lost her suitor. She did eventually marry a cousin, but Pen's
lack of a portion was to lead to difficulties in her marriage and trouble with
her in-laws. Her sister Susan Verney's marital negotiations were strikingly
similar. Ralph managed to decrease his share of her £1,000 portion to £400
in cash. He refused to sell off any of his property to pay Susan's inheritance,
and the 'money' he did offer her was in the form of a 'desperate' debt owed
to him by a political enemy. Ralph Verney illustrates how brothers in the

[110] Miriam Slater, *Family Life in the Seventeenth Century: The Verneys of Claydon House* (New York: Routledge, 1984), 92–7, 102–3.

early modern era viewed the marriage of their single sisters as a trade-off. On the one hand they would no longer be responsible for a dependent sister, but on the other they had to part with money, in the form of their sister's portion, in order to get them married.

While popular stereotypes implied that a spinster or 'old maid' was an embarrassment to her family as well as a burden on it, most kin seem to have realized that a single female relative was in reality a significant asset. Never-married women were the housekeepers, child-minders, nurses, teachers, business assistants, and moneylenders for their families. Perhaps the question we should really be asking is why any family in the period would have let all its female members marry. Of course, being useful and being acknowledged as useful are two different things. In her study of the Verney family Miriam Slater suggested that a singlewoman was in the position of 'a perennial supplicant who had little possibility of returning favors; this placed her in an untenable position in a society which placed high priority on reciprocation'.[111] But this statement misses all of the ways in which singlewomen performed the reciprocal duties of kinship. When never-married women such as Frances Blundell and Phebe Byrum nursed, cleaned, cooked, raised, taught, and funded their siblings' families, they participated in the familial web of reciprocity.

Inheritance

Moreover, the support and assistance a singlewoman provided to her family even continued after her death. Through their inheritance strategies, never-married women continued to support their relatives long after their demise. Janet Finch and Jennifer Mason have posited that 'bequeathing property allows people to define their kin network and confirm who counts and how much'.[112] Singlewomen in early modern England most definitely used their wills as a means to define their social relationships and their place in the extended kin group. A never-married woman's last will and testament can be read as an autobiographical text that explains how she wanted to present her life (at the moment of her death), how she hoped to display her relationships, and how she wished to perpetuate her memory. A legacy from a never-married woman was significant not only in material but also in emotional terms. Bequests not only allowed a singlewoman to assist those important to her, they also let her symbolically realize the bond she had

---

[111] Slater, *Family Life*, 85,

[112] For a summary of the anthropological explanation of the symbolic nature of inheritance, see Janet Tinch and Jennifer Mason, *Passing On: Kinship and Inheritance in England* (New York: Routledge, 2000), 1–3, 11, 14–15.

with a particular relative or friend. Every time an individual looked at something bequeathed to them or benefited from property that they had inherited, they would hopefully remember the never-married woman who had made it all possible. For singlewomen, who did not have children to perpetuate their memory, the bequeathing of goods may have been that much more significant. It was a way for childless individuals to ensure that they lived on in the recollections of their extended families.

While most never-married women were more than happy to use bequests as a means to assist their kin, some families were more grasping than grateful when it came to the assets of their single female relatives. For instance, when the Revd James Woodeforde's father died he left everything to his two sons and to his unmarried sister Jane. Nine years later Woodforde noted that his 'aunt Jane of Bath' had died and bequeathed all of her estate to her maid Betty, which was 'a great disappointment to my uncle Tom and family'. In this case the loss of a never-married aunt was not the cause of their sorrow; rather, it was the loss of her inheritance. This vignette sums up the situation in which singlewomen found themselves on their deathbeds. Without biological children of their own, they were expected to assist their natal families rather than exercising some autonomy over how they bequeathed their estates. Woodeforde's aunt Jane chose to make another singlewoman her heir, but her extended family expected her to leave everything to her brother Tom and his family.[113] What we need to ask is why aunt Jane's brother and his family assumed her estate would go to them.

This brings up the question of exactly who was a singlewoman's heir. Naming an heir was a more complicated prospect for a single person than for a married person with children, because it was unclear who was the heir of a person with no spouse and no direct descendents. Custom dictated that the heir was the nearest of kin, but it was not always evident who this was for a single person; and whether a never-married woman chose to follow this custom was another story altogether. If a singlewoman died while still a minor, her share of the parental assets was redistributed among her remaining siblings. Wills reveal that this was also commonly the case when an adult singlewoman died rather young. For example, when Elizabeth Parkinson died in 1601 her inventory included money due her 'by reason of the death of Jane her sister for her parte according to the will of their father which was everie sister survyvinge the other and not married or of the age of 21 yeres at the tyme of her deathe to be distributed amongest them equallie, which to the said Elizabeth parte of 200li comes to 25li 10s'.[114]

[113] Beresford, *Diary of a Country Parson*, i. 107–9, 282.
[114] HRO, 1601 AD 29/1.

When never-married women in Hampshire died intestate, or without naming an executor in their will, court officers named brothers, and to a lesser extent mothers, as administrators of these women's estates. By doing so the ecclesiastical courts were naming a singlewoman's parents and siblings as her next of kin. For example, in 1584 Agnes Godwin died in the house of her master in the Southampton suburb of St Mary's. While Godwin's master compiled the inventory of her goods, court officers granted the administration of those goods to her brother Richard, even though he lived some distance away in the town of Bishop's Waltham.[115]

When singlewomen reached a more advanced age they favoured a wider range of people as their primary heirs. This was sometimes out of necessity, if their siblings had died before them, but for other never-married women it was a choice. When a singlewoman had a large estate, the issue of inheritance was especially contentious. The case of Mary Wandesford, a member of the Yorkshire gentry, sheds some light on this situation. Wandesford died in 1726, leaving a sizeable estate (consisting of various properties as well as over £1,200 in South Sea stock and annuities) to endow an institution for Anglican singlewomen in York. She chose to make a statement with her money: she wanted it to benefit women who shared her marital status. Wandesford's family was not so happy with her philanthropic bent, however. Her nephews contested her will, claiming that, as the nearest of kin, they stood to inherit their kinswoman's estate, her testamentary wishes to the contrary. In 1737, more than a decade after her death, the Court of Chancery finally upheld Mary Wandesford's will. In the final event, the Court found in her favour because English law allowed a testator to dispose of her estate to whomever she wished. It was custom, and not law, that dictated that a singlewoman's heir was her sibling or her sibling's children.

Although some singlewomen were like Wandesforde and chose not to leave their estates to their kin, most single female testators favoured their siblings. Table 3.2 illustrates the most common heirs of never-married women. Between 79 and 86 per cent of single female testators in Bristol, Southampton, and Hampshire recognized a sibling or a sibling's child to be their primary heir. In York and Oxford the proportions were slightly lower, but were still a significant 50 and 61 per cent respectively. Table 3.2 also shows that never-married women especially favoured their female kin. Sisters were overwhelmingly the primary beneficiaries of single female testators in all five samples. The second most common heir was also a woman, in this case the daughter of a sibling. Nieces were the second most common heirs in singlewomen's wills from Oxford, Southampton and

---

[115] HRO, 1584 AD23.

Hampshire, the third most common in York, and the fourth most common in Bristol.

Some never-married women informally adopted their nieces and made them their heirs. For example, in 1714 Jane Tilliard of Oxford left her copyhold lands to her niece Catherine. Tilliard also set up a trust for her niece, and required her executor to provide her with 'good and sufficient meat, drink, washing and lodging during and until such time as her trustees' should begin paying the rents to her use. Tilliard's last request was for her executor and trustees to be 'careful in her [niece's] education'.[116]

In general, single female testators left their larger bequests to women, and the majority designated females as their primary heirs.[117] For instance, 68.6 per cent of single female testators from Southampton left their largest legacies to women, as did 60 per cent from Hampshire; and in York it was 54.3 per cent. But the most female-identified testators were in Oxford, where 72.7 per cent named women as their primary beneficiaries. The least female-identified singlewomen were from Bristol, where 48.8 per cent left their largest bequests to women, and even here the numbers were close to equal.

Why did singlewomen favour women in their wills? Some may have bequeathed more to women because these were the most important people in their lives. For women who did not have husbands or sons there were no relationships to mitigate the largely homosocial world of early modern England. A singlewoman's life could be almost entirely spent in female company and devoted to female relationships, and the wills of never-married women reveal this. Other singlewomen seem to have favoured women in their wills as a way of compensating for how inheritance customs benefited men, especially eldest sons.[118] A particularly clear example of this is provided by the noncupative will of the Hampshire singlewoman Joan Moodye. Moodye left her lease of freehold land and her largest bequest to her sister. But when the men helping Moodye make her will asked how much she would give her brother, she said 'nothing since he would have enough if he lived to it [from his father]'. Moodye also left twenty sheep to her sister's daughter, Joan Bellchamber, and another eight sheep to her sister's son, Nicholas Bellchamber. When the men asked if Nicholas should get twenty sheep like his sister, Moodye said no. When one of the men complained, and

---

[116] COS, W 208.126, Jane Tilliard, (28 Jan. 1716).

[117] The monetary worth of bequests has to be estimated because the value of real estate, household, and personal goods is usually unclear in wills and because inventories, which provide valuations, do not survive as often as wills from the early modern era. The lack of an inventory makes it especially difficult to assess the value of what a residuary legatee received.

[118] Amy Erickson found that both widows and never-married women gave larger bequests to women than to men, but that singlewomen favoured female legatees even more than did widows. Erickson, *Women and Property*, 215–17.

said 'nay Joan give him 20', she firmly refused again.[119] Joan Moodye used her will as an opportunity to compensate her sister and niece for the lesser inheritances women commonly received in comparison to their brothers.

The one clear exception to the female-focus of singlewomen's wills was their choice of executor. While a majority of never-married women's legatees were female, their executors were more likely to be male. As Table 3.3 shows, even though sisters were the most common executors in all of the probate samples except for Bristol, the remaining executors were overwhelmingly male. Brothers were the second most likely executors appointed by never-married women, followed by male friends, kinsmen, brothers-in-law, and nephews. And while relatives outnumbered non-kin among singlewomen's legatees, executors were less likely to be related to a single female testator. In four out of five of the probate samples male friends were the first, second, or third most likely executor appointed by never-married women. This meant that singlewomen differed from widows in their choice of executor. Widows in Southampton and in Abingdon, for example, were most likely to choose kin to handle their estates—either an unmarried daughter or a married daughter and son-in-law.[120] Widows could entrust their estates to their children, but never-married women did not have this option.

How should we account for singlewomen's preference for male executors in the midst of largely female-focused wills? Never-married women were not unique in this regard: bachelors and widows also were likely to appoint male executors. It seems that contemporaries felt that men had more legal knowledge, resources, and contacts to ensure that they could successfully carry out their duties as executors. This would explain why the overseers and trustees appointed by singlewomen were also primarily male. Perhaps, then, what is surprising is not the number of men that served as the executors of never-married women, but the large minority of women that did so. It is also not clear why singlewomen chose non-kin as executors.[121] It may well indicate that never-married women recognized that their estates were more difficult to execute because they had no clear heir, and that they did not want to privilege any one relative over another. When it came to the question of where to bestow their inheritance, singlewomen had much more freedom of choice than testators with responsibilities for spouses

---

[119] HRO, 21M65 C3/10, 132–5, 138.

[120] Daughters and sons-in-law were the executors for about half of the widowed testators in Abingdon. Barbara J. Todd, 'Widowhood in a Market Town, Abingdon 1540–1720', D.Phil. thesis, University of Oxford (1983), 305.

[121] Of course, some of these men could have been relatives who did not share a surname with the deceased and who were not identified as kin in the probate document. Nevertheless, since single female testators usually recognized their kin this is unlikely to have been true in most cases.

Table 3.3. Most common executors named by single female testators

Bristol N = 40	Oxford N = 40	Southampton N = 35	York N = 50	Hampshire N = 45
Male Friend [7]	Sister [12]	Sister [9]	Sister [7]	Sister [11]
Man [6]	Niece [4]	Brother [6]	Brother [6]	Brother [8]
Niece [4]	Woman [4]	Male friend [4]	Male friend [5]	Male friend [8]
Sister [3]	Brother [3]	Master [3]	Kinsman [4]	Brother-in-law [5]
Brother [3]	Nephew [3]	Brother-in-law [2]	Kinswoman [4]	Niece [3]
Nephew [3]	Male friend [3]			
Master [3]	Kinswoman [3]			
Female friend [3]				
Kinsman [3]				

Notes: 'Kinsman' and 'Cousin' are treated as synonyms.

Source: See Table 3.1.

and children. Nevertheless, such testamentary freedom led to legal complexities and competition among prospective heirs.

When we view the history of the family through the prism of singleness it requires us to rethink the notion of family and kinship for all of early modern English society. Historians have noted that young people often 'activated' ties of kinship when they migrated and searched out jobs as servants and apprentices. Nevertheless, tapping the networks and resources of kinship was not simply a product of the life-cycle. This was something that lifelong singlewomen and men, widows and widowers, orphans, abandoned spouses, and married people without children also frequently did. Ties of kinship would have been significant to most people, at some point in the life-cycle, in early modern England.

When we stop looking only for the nuclear family and instead open our view to the extended family, we find that singlewomen were firmly entrenched in familial networks. Never-married women may have not created new families, but they sustained existing ones. In fact, we have largely missed or neglected the significant role of never-married women in helping to sustain nuclear families. Singlewomen were integral to the financial, material, and emotional success of their parents, siblings, nieces, nephews, and other kin. And in return, never-married women could claim assistance. The realization that singlewomen were embedded in their extended families allows us to dismiss the stereotype of the isolated, lonely spinster; rather, many never-married women may even have welcomed a rest from the duties of kinship. Early modern singlewomen did not live in the age of the individual. Many may not have even thought of themselves as single or solitary women, but rather as part of their collective families.

This chapter has also revealed the female-centred nature of never-married women's lives. Singleness seems to have run in families, for where there was one never-married woman there were often two or more single sisters. The relationships that were commonly the most significant to never-married women were those with their mothers, sisters, and nieces. It was these women who received the largest bequests in never-married women's wills, and who were likely to be a singlewoman's primary heir. Female friends could be as important as female kin to other never-married women. Friends and non-kin, such as landladies and servants, could become 'surrogate kin' to singlewomen without family members. Rather than never-married women lacking significant and intimate relationships because they did not have husbands and children, they created and nurtured important and close relationships with other women, both kin and non-kin. While never-married women were by necessity the most female-focused in their relationships, married women and widows may have been so to a lesser degree. Further research on all women's social relationships in the homo-social society of early modern England is needed.

In this chapter we have examined the singlewoman's family; in the next we will look at the singlewoman's economy. We turn from the social experiences of women who were not part of a marital couple to the economic experiences of women who were not part of the household economy in the traditional sense. Just as never-married women forged alternative social relationships, they also had to insinuate themselves into new employment sectors and economic opportunities. It is this economic history of urban singlewomen in particular that we will now examine.

4

A Maid Is Not Always a Servant: Singlewomen in the Urban Economy

If you visited a linendraper on Southampton's High Street in the 1690s you might go to the shop run by Jane and Alice Zains, a pair of never-married sisters. The sisters had been born into a family of haberdashers and hatters, which meant that they were familiar with the making and sale of clothing and accessories, but they chose to strike out into a new facet of the clothing trade when they set up as linendrapers. Unlike a haberdasher, a linendraper was a more specialized shopkeeper, selling linen and ladies clothes made up from linen such as kerchiefs and smocks, and unlike a hatter, the linendraper sold instead of made goods. After Jane died some time around 1698 her sister Alice continued to run their shop, and seems to have done so quite successfully. In her 1701 will Alice bequeathed £240 in cash, as well as apparell, jewellery, household and shop goods, and £12 in store debts due to her. One of the major beneficiaries of Alice Zains's will was her never-married niece Elizabeth Wheeler. Wheeler inherited all of her aunt's household goods, and more significantly £50 worth of shop goods. This inheritance enabled Elizabeth Wheeler to take over her aunts' business and ensured that the linendrapery shop continued to be run by a singlewoman in the family. Despite her aunts' assistance, Wheeler encountered obstacles to her trade, in the form of Southampton's authorities. In 1702 the town's court of quarter sessions presented her for working as a linendraper without having served a formal apprenticeship in the craft. Wheeler, the daughter of a cutler, had not chosen to follow her father's craft. She had found work as a servant early in life, but by her forties was plying the linendrapery trade she had learned informally from her aunts. Wheeler persevered in her occupation, agreeing to pay a particularly high entry fine that allowed her to trade in the port town.[1] The authorities, evidently assuaged by Wheeler's not insubstantial finances and her membership in a prosperous local family, allowed her to trade unmolested from then on. Unknowingly, Wheeler was a milestone; she was the last singlewoman in early modern Southampton to encounter official harassment for attempting to work independently. With

---

[1] Hampshire Record Office (hereafter HRO), 1701 A107.

the advent of the eighteenth century, economic opportunities were improving for the urban singlewoman.

The experiences of the Zains sisters and their niece Elizabeth Wheeler underline many of the factors that influenced the work of never-married women in the towns of early modern England. They show how singlewomen worked outside of the family economy, and what work meant to women who did not have husbands to support them and the identity of motherhood to fill their time. They illustrate which trades were open to never-married women and what cultural, legal, and practical obstacles constrained singlewomen's occupational choices. They show how women who never married acquired the skills and capital to trade, as well as how opportunities for work changed over a never-married woman's life-cycle. And they illustrate how economic options for singlewomen altered over the early modern period.

This chapter explores issues like these by examining the work of never-married women in several provincial towns, with a special focus on the port town of Southampton. First I look at domestic service, and then move on to the occupations open to lifelong and middling-status singlewomen. Then I analyse the factors that allowed some women to function as independent tradeswomen, in particular, social status, age, the assistance of female kin, and the local economy. Lastly, I argue that economic opportunities for singlewomen opened up at the end of the seventeenth century, rather than decreasing, as they seem to have done for married women of the middling sort. Attention to marital status reveals that a history of women's work based only on married women is not applicable to all women in the past.

Service is the occupation most often associated with singlewomen, by both historians today and contemporaries in the early modern era. There has been a good amount of historical research done on domestic service, and in fact these studies have provided much of the information we have about young singlewomen in particular. Because of this extensive scholarship, the following section only briefly discusses the occupation of domestic service before moving on to the other economic options open to never-married women.[2]

---

[2] This discussion is based on the following literature: Ann Kussmaul, *Servants in Husbandry in Early Modern England* (New York: Cambridge University Press, 1981); Marjorie K. McIntosh, 'Servants and the Household Unit in an Elizabethan English Community', *Journal of Family History*, 9: 1 (1984), 3–23; D. A. Kent, 'Ubiquitous But Invisible: Female Domestic Servants in Mid-Eighteenth Century London', *History Workshop Journal*, 28 (1989), 111–28; Graham Mayhew, 'Life Cycle Service and the Family Unit in Early Modern Rye', *Continuity and Change*, 6: 2 (1991), 201–25; Bridget Hill, *Servants: English Domestics in the Eighteenth Century* (Oxford: Clarendon Press, 1996); and Tim Meldrum, *Domestic Service and Gender 1660–1750: Life and Work in the London Household* (New York: Longman, 2000). Two studies of youth that by necessity also examine servants are: Ilana Krausman Ben-Amos, *Adolescence and Youth in Early Modern England* (New

It could be argued that service was not so much a particular job description as a stage of life in early modern England. In England, as opposed to southern European countries such as Italy, domestic service was seen as an occupation for young people in their teens and twenties. It was something one did before marrying and establishing a household and (ideally) becoming one's own master (or in the case of a woman, the master's wife). Service was not only structured by age, it was also gendered. While it was a common occupation for both sexes, in towns it became increasingly a feminized one. For example, 55 per cent of servants in late seventeenth-century Southampton were female, as were an astonishing 81 per cent of servants in London. Not only were most servants female, a good proportion of adult singlewomen were servants. For instance, 27 per cent of single females (both minors and adults) living in Southampton were servants, while 40 per cent of never-married women in London were in service.[3] Not all servants found work in urban environments, however. In the early modern period England was still largely rural, and many singlewomen found work as servants in husbandry. Such work might include dairying as well as harvesting, haymaking, and gleaning.

Much of the scholarship on domestic service has focused on the positive and negative conditions of such employment. In many respects singlewomen benefited from their time in service. For example, service provided women with multiple skills. Servants were not yet confined to domestic tasks in the early modern era, which meant that an urban maidservant would, in addition to jobs such as cleaning, sewing, and cooking, assist in child-rearing and in the family craft, or in running the family shop or tavern. A female servant's wages were never high (and were always less than those of a male servant), but the occupation could be worthwhile not for the salary but for the room, board, and clothes that servants received in kind. Because a maidservant did not have day-to-day expenses she was often able to save up her wages for a dowry or, if she never married, for her future maintenance. This meant that servants often served as modest moneylenders. The time outside her natal home also allowed a female servant to make social contacts with masters, mistresses, and fellow servants, and enabled her to mature and learn to live apart from her family.

Historians of a feminist bent in particular have emphasized the negative aspects of service. Despite all the functional and useful attributes of this

Haven, Conn: Yale University Press, 1994), and Paul Griffiths, *Youth and Authority: Formative Experiences in England 1560–1640* (Oxford: Clarendon Press, 1996).

[3] Southampton Record Office (hereafter SRO), SC 14/2/66a–68b, 70a–74c; Peter Earle, *The Making of the English Middle Class* (Berkeley: University of California Press, 1989), 219, Table 8.4, and id., 'The Female Labour Market in London in the Late Seventeenth and Early Eighteenth Centuries', *Economic History Review*, 2nd ser., 42: 3 (1989), 339.

occupation, there were also many disadvantages. Female servants in urban locales, as well as most in rural areas, lived and worked in the household of their master or mistress. The master or mistress functioned *in loco parentis*, and as such he or she disciplined the servants as well as caring for them and training them. Female servants often disliked the control their masters had over them, and what they perceived as unreasonable treatment and requests. This resulted in a very high turnover rate, with servants rarely working for an employer for more than a year, and some working for just a few months in one household before they moved on. Servants were household dependants in a subordinate position, and they seldom had any influence over their working hours, conditions, or tasks. For some domestics these circumstances chafed, but for female servants the working environment could be much worse. Maidservants also had to face the possibility of sexual harassment and abuse. Sleeping in the same house, if not the same room, with an unrelated man meant that a master, his son, a male servant, apprentice, or boarder had ample opportunity to court, if not seduce or rape, a maidservant. Those female servants who found themselves pregnant were often put out of service, whether they desired to leave the occupation or not. A pregnant maidservant was a public sign that a master could not keep his household in order, or that he was the cause of such disorder, and as such she was not welcome. Single mothers, even after they delivered, also found it difficult to work as a servant and head a family. In England servants were expected to be single and to live in the master's household—provision was not made for spouses or children.

While it is true that many never-married women were servants at one time or another, not all women chose to remain in an employment that emphasized their dependence and subordinate status. Moreover, for lifelong singlewomen service was not always a possibility in later life. Older women who never married found that, with age, they could not perform all the menial duties that families expected of their (usually young and able-bodied) female servants. Women who never married exposed the inherent contradiction of domestic service in England: it was the preferred employment for all singlewomen, but it was only a life-cycle occupation. Service was also not an option for singlewomen of middling status, who found their finances unequal to supporting them if they had no husband or family, but who believed such a job was beneath them. Rather than domestic service, then, this chapter will focus on the economic alternatives for lifelong and middling-status singlewomen who needed to make a living.

Never-married women whose fathers were craftsmen, tradesmen, or professionals often found they needed to support themselves. Some of these women had parents who provided them with an education or training to ensure that they would be able to maintain themselves if need be. Other women pursued training or skills on their own or later in life. Women of the middling sort who attempted to move into formal, skilled parts of the economy found themselves confronting the rules and regulations of companies or gilds well into the eighteenth century. To enter a craft a singlewoman had to serve an apprenticeship; nonetheless, young women never served formal apprenticeships in anywhere near equal numbers to young men. For example, females comprised only 3 per cent of formal apprentices in sixteenth-century Bristol and early seventeenth-century Salisbury, and between 3 and 7 per cent of formal apprentices in England in the early eighteenth century (this is in contrast to the high number of females who served pauper apprenticeships, that did not necessarily teach a trade but instead were a form of service).[4] While their numbers were not high, a minority of females did manage to indenture themselves into a wide variety of trades, such as goldsmithing, watchmaking, printing, pewtering, ironmongering, and blacksmithing.

While all kinds of crafts accepted at least a few single female apprentices, the majority of never-married women who wished to serve apprenticeships found it easiest to do so in trades that contemporaries considered appropriately feminine. For instance, in the first half of the eighteenth century female apprentices in the counties of Surrey, Bedfordshire, Warwickshire, and Wiltshire congregated in trades such as mantua making, tailoring, millinery, weaving, sempstry, gloving, coat-making, stay-making, shoemaking, lace-making, housewifery, and shopkeeping. Similarly, the singlewomen who apprenticed themselves in the Sussex towns of Chichester and Lewes, as well as in Greater London, did so in the mantua making, millinery, gloving, tailoring, and sempstry trades.[5] In Edinburgh most girls took apprenticeships to learn skills such as lace-making, embroidery, button-making, and mantua making. By the eighteenth century the most common apprenticeship for women in the town became shopkeeping, which included the making as well as the selling of clothing. Gender was not the only issue faced by would-be female apprentices, for social status was of equal weight for daughters of the middling sort up. In London these women entered into what contemporaries deemed 'genteel' trades such as millinery, mantua making, and shopkeeping. For some singlewomen these

[4] Ilana Krausman Ben-Amos, 'Women Apprentices in the Trades and Crafts of Early Modern Bristol', *Continuity and Change*, 6: 2 (1991), 229, 246; Sue Wright, ' "Churmaids, Huswyfes and Hucksters": The Employment of Women in Tudor and Stuart Salisbury', in Lindsey Charles and Lorna Duffin (eds.), *Women and Work in Pre-industrial England* (London: Croom Helm, 1985), 103. For overviews of female apprenticeship in the early modern era see Ben-Amos, *Adolescence and Youth in Early Modern England* and K. D. M. Snell, *Annals of the Labouring Poor* (Cambridge: Cambridge University Press, 1985), 270–319.
[5] R. Garraway Rice, *Sussex Apprentices and Masters 1710 to 1752*, Sussex Record Society, 28 (London: Mitchell, Hughes & Clarke, 1924).

trades provided a modicum of independence and a way to maintain themselves, but for never-married women of genteel status such occupations may well have represented downward mobility.[6]

While singlewomen were allowed to learn a craft through apprenticeship, the expectation was that after their training they would use their skills to work for a master craftsman or with a husband. Many 'servants' were actually singlewomen who were skilled in a craft and working for a master, and many husbands sought out a wife who had skills to assist them in their trade. But for women who never married it was unclear if they could practise their craft independently. For much of the early modern era it was difficult (but not impossible) for urban singlewomen to establish themselves as mistresses or independent tradeswomen.

One of the obstacles was that all women—single ones included—rarely enjoyed membership in the 'freedom', which conferred the right to trade in most provincial towns. For example, between roughly 1550 and 1750 not one woman obtained the freedom in Southampton, as well as in Exeter, Newcastle upon Tyne, and Norwich. The latter town explicitly ruled out the participation of single tradeswomen. Here, 'no singlewoman could set up any shop within the city without the sanction of the authorities and unless she were freeborn [daughter to a freeman of the town]'.[7] In York never-married women also faced barriers to trading. While some widows were members of the baker's gild, young singlewomen were not able to enter the trade.[8] In the market town of Abingdon (Oxon) only one never-married freewoman appeared in the town records before the mid-eighteenth century. The exception to the rule was a 28-year-old singlewoman named Elizabeth Muns, who in 1644 paid a fine of 4s. (higher than the normal 2s. 6d. fee) to become a 'freewoman'. She based her claim upon her apprenticeship to her glover father.[9] It is unclear why Muns was such a rarity; was it tenacity on her part, or good connections?

[6] Elizabeth C. Sanderson, *Women and Work in Eighteenth-Century Edinburgh* (New York: St Martin's Press, 1996), 83, 87–94; Margaret Hunt, *The Middling Sort* (Berkeley: University of California Press, 1996), 83, 90–1.

[7] Madeleine Hope Dodds (ed.), *The Register of Freemen of Newcastle Upon Tyne*, Publications of the Newcastle Upon Tyne Records Commission. 3 (Newcastle: Northumberland Press, 1923); Margery M. Rowe and Andrew M. Jackson (eds.), 'Exeter Freemen 1266–1967', *Devon and Cornwall Record Society*, extra series 1 (Exeter, 1973); SRO, SC 3/1/1–2; SC 3/5/1; Percy Milligan, 'The Freemen of Norwich 1714–1752', *Norfolk Record Society*, 23 (Norwich, 1952); id., *The Register of the Freemen of Norwich 1548–1713* (Norwich, 1934), esp. p. xv. Women also did not enjoy the freedom in sixteenth-century Wells. Dorothy Shilton and Richard Holworthy, 'Wells City Charters', *Somerset Record Society*, 46 (London, 1932).

[8] Diane Willen, 'York Guildswomen in the City of York, 1560–1700', *The Historian*, 46: 2 (1984), 208–9.

[9] Barbara J. Todd, 'Widowhood in a Market Town: Abingdon 1540–1720', D.Phil. thesis, University of Oxford (1983), 181.

Despite significant obstacles, a few never-married women like Elizabeth Muns did attempt to trade on their own, but lack of access to apprenticeships and to the freedom meant that most singlewomen could not hope to be their own mistresses. Throughout the seventeenth and early eighteenth centuries it was common for singlewomen in various towns to be prevented from trading independently. For example, in 1649 Southampton's assembly warned Barbara Midwinter alias Winter, 'a bonelacemaker being a single-woman and a stranger', to depart the town within a fortnight. Although Midwinter had a trade to sustain herself, she was not welcome to practise it or to remain in the town. As we saw in Chapter 2, in 1657 the same assembly ordered that Mary Shrimpton be allowed 'one month's space to put off and dispose of her sackcloth and whalebone, which she has now in her house and custody, and from that time forward to forbear to use the trade of bodicemaking, unless she be employed by the freemen of the town'.[10] Shrimpton was welcome to work, but she could not hold the freedom in Southampton, which meant that she had to work for a freeman and not as her own mistress.[11]

Southampton was not alone in its harassment of single tradeswomen in the seventeenth and early eighteenth centuries. In Portsmouth never-married women numbered among those punished for trading without having served apprenticeships from the 1660s through the 1720s. Similarly, in 1624 the singlewoman Elizabeth Winstanley was presented in the town of Liverpool for 'using the faculty of a free woman, not being free'. Never-married women trying to break into the shopkeeping trade also found it rough going in the town of Nottingham. Mary Kitchen, Ann James, and Mary Keeling were presented in the 1680s for trading as grocers without having served seven-year apprenticeships, while Mary Hart was presented for trading as a linendraper.[12]

Singlewomen were not the only persons to face a penalty for trading without apprenticeship or the freedom, but they were the only individuals who had little or no access to formal trade. All men could obtain the freedom if they had the ability to pay for the privilege, and wives and widows were allowed to trade with or in place of their husbands. Because singlewomen did not have these privileges, some had to resort to bribery. For example, in 1701 Katherine Eglisfield presented a plate to the fraternity

[10] SRO, SC 2/1/8, fo. 132.
[11] SRO, SC 9/3/12, fo. 25.
[12] Adrienne B. Rosen, 'Economic and Social Aspects of the History of Winchester 1520–1670,' D.Phil. thesis, University of Oxford (1975), 312. Robert East (ed.), *Extracts from Records in the Possession of the Municipal Corporation of the Borough of Portsmouth* (Portsmouth, 1891), 62, 68, 102; James A. Picton, *City of Liverpool: Selections from the Municipal Archives and Records* (Liverpool, 1830), 186; *Records of the Borough of Nottingham*, 4 (London, 1889), 327, 329, 331.

of merchant tailors in Carlisle. The plate was engraved with the words: 'in gratitude to ye fraternity of merchant taylors in Carlisle by Mrs. Katherine Eglisfield 4 July 1701.' Local legend stated that Eglisfield was a stay-maker with whom the gild had chosen not to interfere, and she seems to have recompensed them for their silence. Nevertheless, not all singlewomen had the wealth or clout to bribe their way into trading independently. Forty years later, in the same town of Carlisle, Martha, the daughter of Joseph Robinson, was accused by the glover's gild of having undertaken 'to cut and sew and follow our trade having no right or privilege to do the same to the great damage of this occupation'. Although living in the same location, Robinson was not as lucky as Eglisfield, for she was told to cease trading.[13]

While single tradeswomen faced a hostile economic climate for much of the early modern period, circumstances began to change in the eighteenth century. In Southampton, for example, the ban on singlewomen trading independently ended at the turn of that century. As mentioned above, in 1702 Elizabeth Wheeler was the last recorded singlewoman that the town prosecuted for trading without serving an apprenticeship. Wheeler differed from most of the single tradeswomen who had been cited before her; even after appearing in court she continued to trade. She did have to pay a £2 penalty for trading illegally, and an even heftier fee of £5, yet there was an important distinction between the first and second sums: the £5 fee was not a punishment for illegal activity, but rather a 'Stall and Art' fee that allowed her to ply her trade for a year. Even though Wheeler was not the very first singlewoman to trade independently in Southampton, a clear change had occurred; after her indictment in 1702 no other singlewoman paid a penalty for trading in Southampton. Thus, Elizabeth Wheeler was something of an innovator, a leading example of a new phenomenon in late seventeenth-and early eighteenth-century Southampton—the independent and prosperous single tradeswoman.

It is possible to track changes in the numbers of single tradeswomen over time by searching through the lists of unfree traders that many towns in early modern England compiled. The custom of licensing people who did not enjoy the freedom to trade was common in towns such as Liverpool and Nottingham. In Canterbury such traders were known as 'intrantes', in Shrewsbury they were called 'tensors', and in Winchester non-free traders paid 'artificer's money'.[14] In Southampton non-free traders paid a 'Stall and

---

[13] R. S. Ferguson and W. Nanson, *Some Municipal Records of the City of Carlisle*, Cumberland and Westmoreland Antiquarian and Archaeological Society, extra series, 4 (Carlisle, 1887), 144, 212.

[14] *City of Liverpool*, 174; *Records of the Borough of Nottingham*, 158; Kay E. Lacey, 'Women and Work in Fourteenth and Fifteenth Century London', and Diane Hutton, 'Women in Fourteenth Century Shrewsbury', in *Women and Work in Pre-industrial England*, 44, n. 130, 86; Rosen, 'History of Winchester', 105, 109, 175–6.

Art' fee for the privilege of setting up their stall or shop and practising their art or trade.

As we saw in Chapter 2, Southampton established barriers to single-women working on their own in the sixteenth and seventeenth centuries. Not surprisingly then, few never-married women figured in the Stall and Art lists in these centuries. Wives figured in the Stall and Art lists hardly at all, although it is possible that some of the men who paid the fee were paying for their wives (in this instance coverture would have effectively erased married women from the official record). The handful of women who paid the trading fee in this period were almost all widows. Even though widowed women comprised the smallest proportion of the adult female population, their independent economic activity dwarfed that of wives and singlewomen. In 1730, out of 339 people paying Stall and Art, thirty-six were women, all but four of whom were widows. Twenty years later 352 people were paying to trade. While the number of non-free traders in Southampton had remained stable, the total who were female had almost doubled, to sixty-five. And among the women widows still predominated, comprising at least fifty-one of the females who paid Stall and Art.[15]

Before the 1680s only three singlewomen paid Stall and Art to trade in early modern Southampton. The first was Eleanor Beeston, who in 1611 paid 6*d.* to trade as a huckster. From other sources it is apparent that Beeston was a singlewoman and that she made her living as a charmaid, working in a variety of casual occupations including selling both herbs and sex. The next singlewoman to appear in Southampton's Stall and Art rolls was Elizabeth Wheat in 1620. She was followed twenty years later by Mary Sherwood, a daughter who inherited her mother's shop in Holy Rood parish. As we saw in Chapter 2, however, Sherwood only lived another year to trade on her own, so she did not alter the absence of single trades-women to any large degree.

Changes began at the end of the seventeenth century for never-married women who wanted to trade in Southampton. Rose Penford, whom poll tax records show was the single daughter of John Penford, paid 2*d.* in Stall and Art in 1682. Then in 1694 the first woman identified as a 'spinster' appeared in the lists. This was Jane Zains, who paid 2*s.* 6*d.* to ply the linendrapery business mentioned at the outset of this chapter.[16] From this point on singlewomen began to trickle into the lists, with perhaps one or two appearing each year until the 1730s, when somewhere between four to

---

[15] SRO, SC 6/1/91, 108. In 1730 339 people paid Stall and Art in Southampton, of whom 36 were women—32 widows, 3 singlewomen, and 1 woman of unknown marital status. In 1750 352 individuals paid to trade, and of these 65 were women—51 widows, 10 singlewomen, and 4 women of unknown marital status.

[16] SRO, SC 6/1/70.

fourteen never-married women were paying Stall and Art to trade in Southampton each year. The total number of singlewomen was always small, but their ranks grew over time. Of the thirty-two never-married women I have identified in the Stall and Art rolls in the period 1550 to 1750, fully thirty of them appeared after 1680. We need to be cautious about focusing on one or two successful businesswomen and generalizing about their representativeness. Nevertheless, there were virtually no single businesswomen in Southampton before 1690, and there were at least ten to twenty in each decade afterwards. Change, while slow, was clearly occurring.

While Southampton's officials finally allowed singlewomen to participate as traders by the end of the seventeenth century, they still penalized this group of women. Single tradeswomen differed from other non-free traders in that they incurred an extra cost that most others avoided; they had to pay exceptionally large Stall and Art fees. In the sixteenth century officials charged most female traders at the rate of either 4*d*. or 6*d*. a year, while 12*d*. was the average assessment for a tippler, even into the mid-seventeenth century. By the late seventeenth and into the eighteenth century, the customary Stall and Art payment actually fell to 2*d*. Nevertheless, single-women often had to pay more, sometimes much more. In 1694 South-ampton's court leet charged Jane Zains 2*s*. 6*d*. to trade as a linendraper, and in the next two years she paid the even higher rate of 5*s*. Her fee was fifteen to thirty times larger than that paid by the men and widows who appeared in the Stall and Art lists. The court leet officers sometimes assessed men and widows at comparably high amounts, but these men and women were wealthy exceptions, whereas all singlewomen, no matter what their status, were charged the higher Stall and Art fees.[17] Never-married women also differed from others who paid Stall and Art because they frequently had to pay a large entry fine the first year they traded, which then fell to a smaller, customary sum in subsequent years. For instance, in 1739 court officers assessed the singlewoman Mary Smith 1*s*. 2*d*., although by the next year Smith paid the more common 2*d*. fee. When Elizabeth Wheeler took over her aunts' trade she paid £5, the largest sum ever assessed a singlewoman who traded annually in Southampton. But by the following year officials charged her at the usual rate of 2*d*.[18] Large entry fines and higher than average annual assessments served to discourage, but not totally bar, single-women who attempted to enter into business in Southampton after 1690.

---

[17] The men who paid large Stall and Art fees in the early seventeenth century numbered among the wealthiest inhabitants in the town. I would like to thank Mark Newmark for this information.
[18] SRO, SC 6/1/98, 70–4.

What kind of trades did these never-married women practise? Many of the singlewomen who set up businesses in eighteenth-century Southampton entered into shopkeeping. Some, like the Zains sisters, were linendrapers; others, like Elizabeth Smart, were grocers.[19] Jane Martin became one of Southampton's more prominent shopkeepers in the 1740s. The town officials described her as making a living as a seller of and dealer in linen and millinery wares (such as ribbons, laces, gloves, and caps). Between 1729 and 1741 Martin continually appeared as a plaintiff in the town's civil court, suing for money owed her by customers. In 1741 Martin prosecuted Elizabeth White for obtaining goods at her shop by fraud. The list of goods stolen by White indicate what kind of wares that Jane Martin sold: yards of coloured linen, a yard of cambric, a silk handkerchief, several yards of ribbon, including some expensive silver ribbon, and a pair of cotton gloves. Jane Martin was quite successful in her business. She owned property in two of Southampton's parishes for at least twenty years, paid a fine for transporting her wares by iron-bound carts (something only the large-scale traders did), and was numbered among a select group of householders who contributed to the repair of St Michaels Church in the 1740s.[20] Milliners were considered among the luxury traders of their time, so it is not surprising that a successful milliner would have had such an income. What is surprising is that Jane Martin was a singlewoman.

Jane Martin was by no means rare as a never-married woman in the clothing trade, but selling clothes generated more wealth than did making them, and most singlewomen did the latter. In London close to half (44 per cent) of the never-married women who maintained themselves by means other than service did so by making or mending clothes. Some seamstresses worked independently. For instance, in Portsmouth one of the few single tradeswomen in the town was allowed to open a seamstress's shop in 1690. While women of all classes found work making clothes, the millinery, sempstry, and mantua making trades were the jobs deemed acceptable for the 'daughters of respectable people'.[21] In Oxford never-married women were prominent among mantua makers; those who sewed the newly fashionable mantuas or loose gowns without stays. Bespoke clothes were a male preserve regulated by the gild system, but singlewomen were able to insinuate themselves into the market for ready-made fashions in the late seventeenth century because it was too new to be controlled by the gilds. In

[19] SRO, SC 2/1/9, 521.
[20] SRO, SC 9/1/124; SC 7/1/22–3; SC 6/1/101–8; SC 9/4/261–261a; SC/AG 8/6/1.
[21] Earle, 'The Female Labour Market', 339, 344; *Records from... Borough of Portsmouth*, 196; Earle, *Making of the English Middle Class*, 159–60, 217; Bridget Hill, *Women, Work and Sexual Politics in Eighteenth Century England* (Oxford and New York: Basil Blackwell, 1989), 95.

Leeds a Miss Darnton had a millinery shop, and Elizabeth Parker worked in the trade of mantua making. In Colchester the Misses Reeve and Wood ran a millinery business on the town's High Street for two decades. Single-women in this town made and sold women's clothes, while men's clothes remained a male preserve.[22] This was not necessarily the case in Southampton, however. Elizabeth Bracebridge was a member of a prominent cloth-trading family in the town. In 1707 she was living in lodgings when she reported that a large amount of goods had been stolen from her. They included 'five or six yards of black drugget [a wool blend], a piece of broadcloth made into a petticoat...about 12 yards of fine black cloth made into a parsons gown...about three yards of gray broadcloth made into a man's coat', and several other items of apparel.[23] It seems that Elizabeth Bracebridge earned a living not only by making petticoats for women, but also by making gowns and coats for men.

Gloving was another trade in which singlewomen commonly found employment. In Southampton Anne Goodridge began to trade as a glover when her father died in 1732. She was a 48-year-old singlewoman at the time.[24] In the market town of Abingdon the only woman to gain the freedom before the mid-eighteenth century was the glover Elizabeth Muns. In Woodstock, the Oxfordshire town nearest the estate of Blenheim Palace, Elizabeth Heath inherited her family's gloving trade.[25] Many never-married women in Ludlow engaged in gloving; a number of the single-women who were able to maintain their own households there were gloveresses, and a majority of never-married women who resided with their parents or in lodgings also worked in the glove trade. Singlewomen such as Mary Southern and Margaret Stanway even lodged kinsmen who engaged in glove production.[26] Usually never-married women worked for male masters, but in Ludlow the case was reversed among single female glovers.

While the sempstry, millinery, and gloving trades were important occupations for urban singlewomen, they were not the only ones available. In the eighteenth century never-married women looking for a business that would provide them with independence and would not require much of a capital outlay could turn to the new and expanding field of female

[22] Mary Prior, 'Women and the Urban Economy: Oxford 1500–1800', in her *Women in English Society 1500–1800* (London: Methuen, 1984), 110–14; *Extracts from the Leeds Intelligencer*, Thoresby Society, 33 (Leeds, 1935), 176, 219; Shani D'Cruze, "To acquaint the Ladies": Women Traders in Colchester c.1750– c.1800', *The Local Historian*, 17: 3 (1986), 158–61.

[23] SRO, SC 6/1/98–9, 106, 108; SC 9/1/101.

[24] SRO, SC4/4/479/1.

[25] Centre for Oxfordshire Studies (hereafter COS), W.216.254 Elizabeth Heath (1777).

[26] Todd, 'Widowhood', 45; Susan Wright, ' "Holding Up Half the Sky": Women and Their Occupations in Eighteenth-Century Ludlow', *Midland History*, 14 (1989), 56, 58, 65.

education. Singlewomen just starting out as teachers often ran their schools out of their lodgings. For example, in 1744 a singlewoman styling herself 'Madesmoiselle Roland' moved from London to Bath, where she took up lodgings with a Mrs Lewis. Once ensconced, she advertised in the *Bath Journal* her intent to instruct young ladies in dancing and speaking French, at either her lodgings or in their own homes. Roland was part of the movement of girl's schools out of London and into the provinces. In 1764 Leeds boasted a boarding school run by a Miss Robinson and a Miss Steel.[27] Boarding schools like this one required more money and space, compared to teaching a few day students out of lodgings. Schools for the daughters of the middling classes quickly sprang up in resort and county towns where the gentry spent the season. Many of these schools were established and managed by never-married sisters, like the popular boarding school run by the Misses Sophia, Harriet, and Ann Lee in eighteenth-century Bath.[28] Mary More and her younger sisters (including the future author Hannah More) established one such school in Bristol in 1757. They were so successful that after five years they built themselves larger premises.[29] The Shergold sisters of Southampton shared a similar success. In the early eighteenth century Elizabeth and Joanna Shergold leased one of the largest buildings in the port town for their boarding school for young ladies.[30]

Another early modern teaching opportunity that was available to never-married women in particular was the position of governess. In her recent book on singlewomen Bridget Hill noted that teachers, governesses, and companions were all occupations that were suitable for genteel women with insufficient finances to avoid employment. A lifelong singlewoman might work in all three occupations over her lifespan. As Hill showed, although the pathetic figure of the governess was a common focus of nineteenth-century literature, this occupation was not new in the modern era.[31] Opportunities for these positions increased in the late eighteenth century, as families below the elite also began to employ women to educate and care for their children. Scholars have emphasized the social marginality of the companion and the governess, who, while educated and genteel, were also servants, but we have missed how the marital status of these women

[27] *The Bath Journal*, 1: 23 (30 July 1744); *Leeds Intelligencer*, 164.
[28] Susan Skedd, 'Women Teachers and the Expansion of Girls' Schooling in England, c.1760–1820', in Hannah Barker and Elaine Chalus (eds.), *Gender in Eighteenth-Century England: Roles, Representations and Responsibilities* (New York: Longman, 1997).
[29] Janet Todd (ed.), *A Dictionary of British and American Women Writers 1660–1800* (Totowa, NJ: Rowman & Allanheld, 1985), 224.
[30] SRO, D/MC 10/8a & b.
[31] Bridget Hill, *Women Alone: Spinsters in England 1660–1850* (New Haven Conn.: Yale University Press, 2001), 54–66.

exacerbated their marginal position. The irony was that lifelong single-women without husbands and children performed the roles of surrogate spouse and mother in return for a wage.

By the early eighteenth century educated and middling-class single-women who earned money by teaching, such as Lee and Hannah More, also began to see writing as an employment option. While there were no female writers of note in Southampton until Jane Austen lived there at the turn of the nineteenth century, other provincial towns were home to never-married women who made a living in this way.[32] As Cheryl Turner has pointed out, writers were free from apprenticeships, initial capital outlays, and entry frees, which may have made this a desirable occupation for singlewomen, despite the high failure rate.[33] Never-married women were prominent amongst the earliest professional writers, most likely because writing required time and space to oneself, something a wife or widow with children and a household had in short supply. Writing was also a vocation often pursued in tandem with other trades. For instance, in the 1740s Mary Latter lived in Reading, where she and her widowed mother ran a linen-drapery and millinery business in Butcher Row. After her mother's death Latter also took in boarders. It was only when her business faltered that Latter gathered together the literary fruits of her youth and, with the help of local patrons and subscribers, published *The Miscellaneous Works, in Prose and Verse, of Mrs. Mary Latter* (1759).[34] Similarly, Mary Chandler com-bined shopkeeping and writing in eighteenth-century Bath. In 1734 she published *The Description of Bath. A Poem*, a collection of poems she had been writing since she was a young woman. Chandler was more secure about her business than about her literary abilities. In her dedication she claimed: 'I would rather choose to be taken notice of as one that deals honestly in trade, and behaves decently in the relations of life, than as a writer. Since I am conscious I have a better right to the first, than the last character'.[35] Despite her misgivings, Chandler's volume went through six editions by 1744, and while Chandler's shop no longer stands in Bath's Abbey yard, her poetry is still known to us. Like Latter and Chandler, Jane Barker published a collection of verse written in her youth, and she went on to become one of the first English novelists, penning such works as *Love Intrigues* (1713) and *A Patch-Work Screen for the Ladies* (1723). Barker combined writing with other occupations. Early in life she had supported

[32] Elizabeth Child, '"To Sing the Town": Women, Place, and Print Culture in Eighteenth-Century Bath' *Society for Eighteenth Century Studies*, 28 (1999).

[33] Cheryl Turner, *Living by the Pen: Women Writers in the Eighteenth Century* (London and New York: Routledge, 1992), ch. 4, esp. 79.

[34] J. Todd, *A Dictionary of Women Writers*, 190–1.

[35] Ibid. 80–1; Mrs Mary Chandler, *The Description of Bath. A Poem*, 3rd edn. (London, 1736).

herself by managing estates in Lincolnshire and by inventing a treatment for the gout that she sold out of apothecary shops in London.[36]

A smaller number of singlewomen managed to insinuate themselves into non-feminized trades. For instance, while Jane Barker sold receipts to apothecaries, Mildred Arnold of Southampton was an apothecary herself. Sarah Martin was a gingerbread-maker who travelled regionally to fairs like that held in Southampton to sell her wares. The bookselling trade included a good number of widows of booksellers, but few singlewomen, who had to enter the trade on their own instead of inheriting the businesses of their spouses. Nevertheless, one singlewoman in Ipswich printed and sold books for nearly half a century, between 1728 and 1776.[37] Some singlewomen printed engravings rather than texts. While Anne Hogarth started out in the drapery trade with her sister Mary, she eventually became the agent for her brother, the engraver William Hogarth. After her brother's death Anne inherited the copper plates for his famous engravings and helped his widow sell his prints.[38] Another woman who practised what might seem an unlikely trade for a singlewoman was Mary Rowte, who was an iron-monger. Rowte came from a family of ironmongers—her father John, youngest brother Thomas, and widowed mother Elizabeth had all worked in the craft. When her mother died in 1708 Mary Rowte was 35 years old. She began to pay Stall and Art to trade in Southampton as an ironmonger in her own right, something she did into the 1740s. Actually ironmongery was not a difficult trade for a singlewoman like Mary Rowte, since ironmongers sold (rather than made) iron tools, most of which were household utensils such as tongs, cooking pots, and nails. These were goods with which women would have been familiar and which they would have been able to lift and move. Mary Rowte was able to become prosperous in the ironmongery trade. She died in 1745 at the age of 72, leaving an estate worth over £100, an amount that places her among the provincial middle class.[39]

How should we explain the success of the never-married women so far discussed? Why were some singlewomen able to enter into new and non-feminized trades? The experiences of Southampton's single tradeswomen

[36] Carol Shiner Wilson (ed.), *The Galesia Trilogy and Selected Manuscript Poems of Jane Barker* (New York: Oxford University Press, 1997), pp. xxi, xxiv, 116–18.

[37] H. R. Plomer et al., *A Dictionary of Printers and Booksellers 1726–1775*, (Oxford: Oxford University Press, 1932).

[38] Jenny Uglow, *Hogarth* (New York, 1997), 23, 152–3, 239, 695, 700.

[39] SRO, SC 4/4/479/2–5 and SC 9/4/321; HRO, 1708 A108 and 1745 A101. My assessment of Rowte's wealth is based on the wealth categories that Craig Muldrew derived from data on seventeenth-century King's Lynn. According to this scale Mary Rowte was a member of the provincial middling class, due to her ownership of property and her estate valued at more than £100. Craig Muldrew, *The Economy of Obligation* (New York: MacMillan, 1998), 70–3, Table 3.2.

provide some answers. These women shared several characteristics, including wealth or high social status, advanced age, and assistance from other women, all set against the background of a changing urban economy at the end of the seventeenth century. I will look at each of these factors in turn and at how they improved the chances of singlewomen working for themselves.

A distinguishing characteristic of the never-married women who paid Stall and Art to trade in Southampton was that they tended to be of high social status. Prohibitively high entry fines and annual Stall and Art fees precluded any but prosperous singlewomen from independently trading there. Because they did not have to pay high entry fines and annual fees, there was a wider socio-economic range among the male and widowed female traders. There was another reason why most single tradeswomen were relatively prosperous; it was expensive to start up in business or trade. It took a minimum of £100–£200 to set up a shop in this period. These steep costs precluded all but the daughters of master craftsmen, shop-keepers, merchants, and professionals from establishing themselves in business.[40] Daughters of clergymen and of the landed gentry might also go into trade, but many of these singlewomen did not wish to work with their hands, because they feared this would lessen their gentility. In Southampton the never-married women who paid Stall and Art were from some of the town's more prominent mercantile and professional families. Elizabeth and Joanna Shergold were the daughters of a merchant and the sisters of a self-styled gentleman. They paid Stall and Art yearly from 1718 to 1744 for being tradeswomen and keepers of a boarding school for young ladies. Ann Goodridge surfaced in the Stall and Art lists in the mid-eighteenth century and traded as a glover. She owned a house large enough for the Congregational church to rent for special occasions, and in 1747 she executed the will of her brother Moses, who had achieved the title of gentleman. Ann Fleming began to pay Stall and Art annually in the 1730s. At this time she was one of a select group of Southampton inhabitants who kept a coach house, and she held property assessed annually at the substantial level of £8.[41] It seems that if a singlewoman enjoyed some material resources local officers did not perceive her independence as such an economic or social threat, and saw that it was to their benefit that she work and support herself; otherwise they might end up supporting her. To this end Southampton's officials ceased harassing such prosperous tradeswomen by the turn of the eighteenth century.

[40] Hunt, *Middling Sort*, ch. 5, esp. 90–1; Ian Mitchell, 'The Development of Urban Retailing 1700–1815,' in Peter Clark (ed.), *The Transformation of English Provincial Towns 1600–1800* (London: Hutchinson, 1984), 270–7; Earle, *Making of the Middle Class*, 166–75, and 'Female Labour Market,' 344; Sanderson, *Women and Work*, 96–100.

[41] SRO, D/MC/10/11; D/ABC 1/1 and D/Z 459/4; PR 7/5/1 and SC 14/2/337.

The second factor that aided a singlewoman in establishing a business was advanced age. It is possible to identify the ages of twenty of the thirty singlewomen who set themselves up as independent tradeswomen in Southampton between 1680 and 1750. When they began trading, four of these singlewomen were at least in their twenties; two were at least in their thirties; nine were at least in their forties; four were at least in their fifties; and one was in her sixties.[42] This means that 80 per cent of these single tradeswomen began their careers in middle or old age. This was partly due to practical considerations. One of the reasons singlewomen began to work independently when they were older is that their parents had died by this time and they no longer had someone else to support them or for whom they could work. Many single daughters also were freed from caring for an aged and dying parent by the time they reached middle age. As we saw in the last chapter, singlewomen also commonly inherited money or a trade upon the death of parents or other kin, such as aunts. This means that it was common for a single businesswoman to have advanced into her third or fourth decade before she could begin trading in her own name. For example, Elizabeth Shergold was 40 years old and her sister Joanna 32 when their mother died and left her estate and business interests to her single daughters. Four years later the sisters were paying Stall and Art to trade in their own name. Similarly, Ann Goodridge did not begin trading independently as a glover until both her parents were deceased, at which time she was 48 years old.

These single tradeswomen challenge the characterization of old age as a time of retirement from the world, and from economic activity in particular.[43] Scholars of aging note that people in the past retired because their declining physical and mental capacities left them less able to participate in various activities, and because contemporaries believed that elderly people deserved some rest after an active life. Singlewomen, however, may have experienced something akin to retirement in their early years as household dependants, and so they preferred to become more, instead of less, involved in their communities as they aged. Indeed, many never-married women initially entered the economic sphere at an age when we might think of people retiring today. For example, in 1742 Catherine Woods began trading in Southampton at the age of 52; she died only three or four years later. Mary Sibron did not begin working independently until she was well past modern retirement age; she began paying Stall and Art when she was 68 years old.[44] There was no mandatory or common age of retirement in the

---

[42] SRO, SC 6/1/68–108.

[43] For more on this topic, see my essay 'Old Maids: The Lifecycle of Singlewomen in Early Modern England', in L. A. Botelho and Pat Thane (eds.), *Women and Ageing in British Society Since 1500* (New York: Longman, 2001).

[44] SRO, SC 6/1/101, 106; transcript of St Michael's Parish Register (1690, 1745).

early modern era (and the poor were probably never able to retire), so the singlewomen who worked in their later years were not anomalies for doing so. Rather, it was these women's late entry into trade that was distinctive. It was also common for singlewomen to work up until their deaths. Jane and Alice Zains continued to work in their linendrapery business until they died in 1698 and 1701, respectively.[45] Although prosperous, these two women never retired. The psychological benefit of work may explain why wealthy singlewomen began to ply a trade in their later years and continued to work until their deaths, even though there was no financial need to do so. Ann Goodridge began working on her own when she was nearly 50, despite her recent inheritance of a considerable estate from her father, that included a house and a large sum of money. Women such as Goodridge suggest that financial need was only one of the important benefits that work provided to older singlewomen.

The advanced age of Southampton's single tradeswomen may also account for the town's acceptance of them. As discussed in Chapter 2, the barriers to never-married women living and working on their own lessened as these women reached 40 or 50 years of age, and were thus beyond marriageable age and no longer had parents to care for them. Age also imbued all early modern people, never-married women included, with respectability and authority. Town officers may have believed that an older singlewoman, like all aged persons, enjoyed the benefit of wisdom that came with advancing years. In official eyes such wisdom rendered an aged singlewoman capable of establishing her own household and, as a householder, running her own business. In effect, older singlewomen began to look a lot like older widows, who had always been allowed to head their own households and work for themselves.

While elevated social status and advanced age were necessary factors for a singlewoman to engage in trade, they were not sufficient. A never-married woman interested in trade also needed skills, capital, and goods to establish herself in business. Shopkeepers needed to be able to read, write, do accounts, and have a working knowledge of their goods and their market, while dressmakers and seamstresses had to be able to sew skillfully. Women who set themselves up in a shop had to find a likely space, fit it out with furniture, drawers, and measures, establish an accounting system, and purchase a stock of merchandise.[46] Where would a woman learn to do such things?

We know that some singlewomen learned a trade from their fathers, albeit informally, and then assisted in the family craft or shop. And it seems

[45] SRO, SC 6/1/73, 74; SC 14/2/68b, 72; HRO, 1742 B73.
[46] For a more detailed description of setting up in trade, see Sanderson, *Women and Work*, 74–107.

that some never-married women who took advantage of the changing economy did so with the blessing and help of their fathers. One of the Southampton fathers who seemed to recognize his daughter's abilities in trade was Richard Cornelius. In 1667 he left his paper mill to his daughter Dumer, and 'in lieu thereof' a cash settlement to his son.[47] While it is not clear if Cornelius intended his daughter to run the business, there are other more explicit examples of daughters who worked in their own enterprises with the aid of their fathers. In 1746 the town granted Ann Grove a new lease of Godshouse Tower, which had been held by her father before her. Grove planned to use the tower as a hospital or lodging house for wounded and sick French prisoners who were quartered in Southampton at the time. Other women in the town were running lodging houses for prisoners, and Ann Grove saw an opportunity and wanted to benefit economically from it.[48] Anne Martin was another Southampton entrepreneur whose successes were tied to her father. Just four years after Frederick, Prince of Wales, came to bathe in the sea at Southampton, Martin invested in the town's growing reputation as a spa, and in 1754 became the owner of a bathhouse in St Michael's parish.[49] Anne Martin's bathhouse was on the west shore of the town, coincidentally near to where her father John Martin opened the largest bathing establishment in Southampton as well as a space for promenading and socializing called the Long Room in 1761. The venture was a family one, and was handed down from father to daughter. By 1771 a visitor to Southampton cited Anne Martin as both the proprietor of several baths and the Long Room.[50]

Singlewomen who did not receive assistance from their fathers in setting up a trade or training in a craft could opt for a formal apprenticeship. In the latter case they often received mentoring from other never-married women. Singlewomen in Sussex learned the trade of mantua making from mistresses who were also often unmarried (single or widowed). For example, Elizabeth Gravet and Mary Puxty worked together as mantua makers in the town of Lewes, and between 1711 and 1716 trained three never-married women in their trade. In the town of Chichester the webs of female mentorship extended even further. Here there were four mantua makers and one seamstress who apprenticed anywhere from one to six singlewomen at a time. The case of Frances Heberden and Mary Bettesworth, both singlewomen from Chichester, provides the best example of how never-married

[47] SRO, SC 9/3/13 fo. 31ᵛ.
[48] SRO, SC 2/1/10, fos. 146, 171; *Calendar of State Papers Domestic, 1702–03*, 530.
[49] Alison Wells, 'Southampton in the Spa Period', BA thesis, University of Southampton (1980), 6; SRO, SC 9/2/4.
[50] Adrian Rance, *Southampton: An Illustrated History* (Portsmouth: Milestone Publications, 1986), 78–9.

women formally passed on skills to one another. Heberden, a mantua maker and milliner, took on a female apprentice nearly every year between 1705 and 1711. The fourth woman Heberden trained was Mary Bettesworth, who in 1709 paid the large sum of £20 to apprentice herself with Heberden. It seems likely that both Bettesworth, who paid £20, and Ann Willis, who paid £30, received some kind of advanced training in comparison to female apprentices who paid substantially less. In any case, Bettesworth went on to become a mistress herself. Ten years after her apprenticeship Mary Bettesworth had established her own mantua making establishment in Chichester and was herself training young women in the profession. Between 1719 and 1727 Bettesworth took on a new apprentice every four years, training only one protégé at a time, and receiving substantial premiums that rose from £19 to £26 over the 1720s. Between the never-married mistresses Heberden and Bettesworth, ten singlewomen became skilled in the trade of mantua making in Chichester in the first quarter of the eighteenth century.[51] This is a substantial number of singlewomen in one trade for a town of 4,000 people, and even more significantly, these women all had ties to one another since they came out of two workshops. Heberden's mantua making workshop would have stood out in Chichester as a large household and business comprised of singlewomen.[52]

While the mantua makers of Chichester learned their trades through apprenticeship, most never-married women did not train formally in a craft. But there was an informal method by which singlewomen could acquire a trade, that is, through the education and assistance that female family members provided to younger women. In Southampton some of the town's most successful singlewomen received the instruction and aid that allowed them to establish themselves in trade from their mothers, aunts, and sisters. And, most interestingly, female relatives fully intended that these never-married women should run their own businesses, rather than work for a father, brother, or husband.

Widowed mothers performed an especially critical role for singlewomen who wanted to work in a craft or run a shop. Mothers could provide the training and instruction needed by a daughter attempting to establish herself in trade. In the town of Ludlow young women generally learned their trades from their mothers.[53] The same was often true in Southampton. For example, Mary Rowte's father was an ironmonger, but he died relatively young and his wife Elizabeth took over the family trade. While

---

[51] *Sussex Apprentices and Masters*, 2, 4, 19, 30, 38, 47, 54, 75, 78, 87, 99, 103, 112, 113, 117, 146, 158, 192, 195, 209.

[52] Chichester's population was 4,030 in 1739. Alexander Hay, *The History of Chichester* (London: Longman, 1804), 573.

[53] Wright, ' "Holding Up Half the Sky," ' 58,

Mary's widowed mother formalized the instruction of her son Thomas through a public apprenticeship, she evidently did not limit her tutelage just to him. When widow Rowte died in 1708 she left her son Thomas some of her shop goods, but to her daughter Mary she bequeathed all 'the goods, chattels, wares, and merchandises that are in my shop and warehouse, also in the little shop and in the press in the fore gallery, and all my millstones . . . out of which I desire her to pay my debts and the remainder to take for herself'.[54] Mary Rowte's receipt of more ironmongery equipment and goods than her brother illustrates how, even though Thomas had been formally apprenticed in the trade, Mary must have 'informally' learned the same skills from their mother. Mary Rowte, as stated above, began to trade on her own as an ironmonger when her mother died in 1708, and she continued to work into the 1740s.

Mothers not only provided training in a craft, they also often bequeathed the equipment, goods, or cash necessary for their never-married daughters to establish themselves in business. When Mary Arnold died in 1650 she left property and various household goods to her sons and daughters. Only to her never-married daughter Mildred did she offer any trade goods; that is, any goods Mildred could 'make appear she [had] any interest or right unto by laying out her money toward the paying for it'. While widow Arnold's husband had been a tanner, she seems to have practised a different trade, one that she passed on to her daughter. When Mildred died seventeen years later she had numerous glass bottles, cupboards for these bottles, flagons, earthenware, and gallipots (earthenware pots) in her inventory— the type of equipment used by an apothecary.[55] These goods may well have been the ones she had received from her mother two decades earlier to assist her in that trade.

Some mothers specifically indicated their desire for their daughters to follow them into trade. When Mary Page died in 1702 she left the residue of her estate to her three younger children, Mary, Josiah, and Elizabeth. But she stipulated that 'if my daughter Mary be willing to keep on the employment I now use' and 'breed up my other two children . . . she shall have the use and benefit of all my goods until the time' the other children are grown.[56] Widow Page was most likely involved in some facet of the cloth-working trade, as were most of the Pages in Southampton. She may have been uncertain of her daughter's willingness to continue in the trade, but she did not question her ability or skill to pursue this craft, nor the appropriateness of a singlewoman working independently to support her siblings.

---

[54] HRO, 1708 A108.   [55] HRO, 1650 A2; 1667 B1.   [56] HRO, 1702 A58.

In towns all over England trades and businesses passed not just from father to son but also from widowed mother to never-married daughter. Many daughters worked with their widowed mothers and then took over the trade in their own name upon the death of their parent. In the market town of Abingdon (Oxon) widows frequently passed on their trades to their single daughters. The widowed milliner Elizabeth Lydford chose to hand over her shop to her daughter Susanna Williams instead of to her son Richard, also a milliner. Williams plied her mother's trade for another ten years until she was murdered in the shop, sadly strangled by the very laces she independently sold.[57] Similarly, Mary Latter and her mother ran a linendrapery business together in Reading in the 1740s. By 1748 Latter was sole proprietor of the Butcher Row business, since her mother had died sometime earlier.[58] In Southampton the widow Ann Faulkner established herself in trade after receiving a £10 loan from a local charity in 1695. Both of widow Faulkner's daughters, the singlewoman Ann Jr. and the widow Mary Stotes, lived and worked with her. When widow Faulkner died in 1697 her two daughters served as co-executrices of her will and together received the residue of their mother's estate. The following year Ann Faulkner Jr. and Mary Stotes appeared in the Stall and Art lists as partners in trade, having taken over their mother's business. Similarly, Mary Langford died in 1734 and left the residue of her goods to her daughter Betty, whom she made her executrix in preference to her son. Within a couple of years Betty Langford was paying both Stall and Art to trade in Southampton, and tax on the shop that she had inherited from her mother.[59] Girl's schools were also often run by mothers and daughters and gradually passed on to the next generation. In Witney (Oxon) the daughters of Mrs Wells took out a newspaper advertisement announcing: 'The Misses Wells, encouraged by the many assurances of support received since the lamented death of their late Mother, beg to inform their friends they purpose continuing the SEMINARY.'[60]

Mothers were not the only female kin to provide legacies that allowed singlewomen to establish themselves in trade. As we saw in Chapter 3, never-married aunts were likely to grant some of their largest bequests to their single nieces. Such legacies usually took the form of cash or real property, but they could also consist of the capital and goods to set up a business. For instance, when Alice Zains of Southampton died in 1701 she

[57] B. Todd, 'Widowhood', 206.

[58] J. Todd, *Dictionary of Women Writers*, 190–1.

[59] SRO, D/MC 8/1, 16; HRO, 1697 A48; SRO, SC 6/1/73; HRO, 1734 A72; SRO, SC 6/1/96; SC AG 8/6/1.

[60] Skedd, 'Women Teachers', 109, 112–13, and *Jackson's Oxford Journal*, 25 Apr. 1812, quoted in Skedd.

had many siblings, cousins, and other kin, but she bequeathed all her household goods and £50 in shop goods to her never-married niece Elizabeth Wheeler. In the 1701 Stall and Art rolls the clerk, noting that Alice Zains had died, substituted the name of Elizabeth Wheeler for her aunt's.[61] With the stroke of a pen the Zains' linendrapery business had passed down to another single female in the family.

Not only did singlewomen receive the necessary training and assistance to set up a business from female kin, they also formed business partnerships with other women. Never-married women were most likely to engage in trade with another never-married sister. As we saw in the last chapter, singlewomen often had at least one other sister who also remained single. These siblings commonly inherited their parents' properties and businesses together. Indeed, at least half of the single businesswomen in Southampton had a never-married sister who either engaged in trade with them or who independently carried out another occupation. The singlewoman Mary Smith and her sisters appeared as traders in Southampton for the first time upon their mother's death in 1739. The sisters kept an ale or tippling house that boasted a popular billiard table.[62] The majority of partnerships between tradeswomen in eighteenth-century Edinburgh were also made up of sisters or other relatives. For instance, the three Wilson sisters worked as milliners, while Jean Campbell and her sister made lace collars, and Agnes English took her niece Miss Cadell and a friend Miss Brodie into her millinery business.[63] In Oxford, Sarah, Mary, and Elizabeth Bleay did 'all jointly and together carry on the business of innkeeping' in the 1750s.[64] Business partnerships made up of sisters were also very common in London. Hester Pinney sold lace out of the Exchange with her sisters, and William Hogarth's sisters Mary and Anne ran a linendrapery shop for which he engraved an elaborate business card. Fanny Burney had two spinster aunts, Ann and Rebecca Burney, who lived near Covent Garden where they ran Gregg's Coffee House until at least their late fifties.[65] Margaret Hunt suggests that women frequently entered into partnerships because they had insufficient capital to establish a business on their own, and 'perhaps also to safeguard their title in case of marriage'.[66] If the sisters never married, the partnership usually only broke up when one of them died.

[61] HRO, 1701 A107; SRO, SC 6/1/74.
[62] SRO, SC 6/1/98–101. Legal or administrative records normally recorded the name of a widow in preference to a singlewoman, but since Mary Smith's name appeared in the records while her sisters went unnamed it seems they were all single as she was.
[63] Sanderson, *Women and Work*, 85, 99.
[64] COS, W 214.341, Sarah Bleay (8 Oct. 1760).
[65] Pamela Sharpe, 'Dealing With Love: The Ambiguous Independence of the Singlewoman in Early Modern England', *Gender & History*, 11: 2 (July 1999), 202–32; Uglow, *Hogarth*, 23, 152–3, 239, 695, 700; Claire Harman, *Fanny Burney* (New York: Knopf, 2001), 98, 152.
[66] Hunt, *Middling Sort*. 134, 144, n. 48.

This was true in Southampton as well, where Jane and Alice Zains jointly ran a linendrapery shop until Jane's death in 1698, after which Alice ran the business on her own until her own death in 1701. Likewise, Elizabeth and Joanna Shergold ran their enterprises together for almost thirty years. Joanna, who was the younger sister by eight years, died some time between 1746 and 1747, but Elizabeth continued to run their various business interests until her demise in 1756.

If a never-married woman's business partner was not another single sister, a widowed sister was the next most likely person. When Ann Faulkner Jr. and her widowed sister Mary Stotes inherited their widowed mother's business together, for example, it was the widowed sister who received top billing. In 1698 'widow Stotes and her sister' began to pay Stall and Art as partners in trade. In the same year Southampton's tax collectors assessed only Mrs Stotes for the two sisters' £12 10s. worth of stock in trade.[67] This example raises an important and frustrating point. The early modern records probably reveal only a portion of the singlewomen who engaged in trade. Many more never-married women were the silent partners of widowed sisters, brothers, or other kin, and never appeared in the sources. Some singlewomen may have even hidden their gender to escape notice, and thus regulation or repression. For example, Pamela Sharpe has found that Messrs Suter and Sansom, woolcard-makers in late eighteenth-century Colchester, were in reality the married woman Mary Suter and the single-woman Hannah Sansom.[68] For singlewomen trying to break into an economy in which they had never been welcome, a trading partnership, especially one of sisters, presented a united front, and one that perhaps appeared more acceptable to town officials who worried about the social propriety of lone women in the workplace. Such partnerships may have also been psychologically helpful to singlewomen attempting to enter into a traditionally chilly work climate.[69]

Sometimes the custom of female entrepreneurship ran in an extended family, for when several single businesswomen came from the same kin group, it is difficult to put this down to coincidence. For instance, the Southampton milliner Jane Martin, was related to Anne Martin, who owned several bathhouses in the town. The Bracebridge family boasted even more single businesswomen than did the Martins. Jane Bracebridge,

[67] SRO, SC 14/2/97.

[68] Pamela Sharpe, *Adapting to Capitalism: Working Women in the English Economy 1700–1850* (New York: St Martin's Press, 1996), 12.

[69] Lee Chambers-Schiller provides examples of single sisters who worked together in the early nineteenth-century USA, and says that parents believed the company of siblings ensured 'safety, propriety, and companionship' for these women. Lee Chambers-Schiller, *Liberty, A Better Husband: Single Women in America: The Generations of 1780–1840* (New Haven, Coun.: Yale University Press, 1984), 74, 122.

whose father was a woolendraper, loaned money at interest and dabbled in the cloth trade. When she died in 1697 she left a legacy to her never-married cousin Elizabeth Bracebridge. In 1707 the same Elizabeth Bracebridge was living in lodgings and making both men's and women's clothing. Another relative, the widow Helen Bracebridge, also traded in Southampton. In 1748 Helen passed down her business to her 25-year-old daughter Ann, who worked independently at least into the 1750s, when she married. Female assistance, or at least the precedent of other single tradeswomen, was the critical factor in the families who produced a number of female traders.

It is significant that virtually all of the successful single businesswomen in eighteenth-century Southampton received some type of assistance from their female relatives. Women knew first-hand how difficult it could be to trade independently. Because of this knowledge many women made it a priority to assist their female kin, especially those who were single. Widows and singlewomen passed on or shared valuable skills, equipment, and capital with their single female relatives. Widowed mothers and aunts offered the help that fathers usually provided for their sons: setting up the next generation in trade. Although fathers may have helped their daughters, the records only yield a handful of examples of paternal assistance. This is in comparison to the large amount of evidence illustrating the help that female relatives provided to singlewomen. It was difficult and costly for both men and women to set up in trade, but since women did not receive the male support that their brothers enjoyed, female assistance was critical to women's success.

Historians such as P. J. P. Goldberg and Pamela Sharpe have posited that economic independence led some women to choose not to marry.[70] Many of Southampton's successful single tradeswomen never married and may provide some evidence for this hypothesis. A good number of these women were still of marriageable age when they began trading. For example, Ann Faulkner was only in her twenties when her mother died and she and her widowed sister took over their mother's business, but she died without ever marrying. Those singlewomen who began to work independently in their thirties and forties could still have married; they often lived to a ripe old age, and there were instances of women marrying in their sixties and seventies. Mary Rowte began trading as an ironmonger at the age of 35, but she did not die for another thirty-seven years. Elizabeth Shergold worked with her widowed mother until she turned 40, and then spent three decades running

---

[70] P. J. P. Goldberg, *Women, Work, and Life Cycle in a Medieval Economy: Women in York and Yorkshire c.1300–1520* (Oxford: Clarendon Press, 1992); Pamela Sharpe, 'Literally Spinsters: A New Interpretation of Local Economy and Demography in Colyton in the Seventeenth and Eighteenth Centuries,' *Economic History Review*, 44: 1 (1991), 46–65.

various businesses with her sister into her seventies. She lived to be 82 years old. As daughters from wealthy families and successful businesswomen in their own right, Mary Rowte and Elizabeth Shergold must have been desirable marriage partners. If it is possible to say that any woman in the early modern era chose to remain single, the evidence points to women like these two. Mary Rowte and Elizabeth Shergold may have made their own choice to never marry, or they may have been persuaded to do so by their mothers, who passed their trades down to them. Likewise, singlewomen such as Alice Zains and Jane Bracebridge may have convinced their nieces and cousins to remain single by assisting them in setting up a trade. Once provided with a means to maintain themselves, single tradeswomen lost one of their primary incentives for marrying, namely economic security. These women encountered no financial trade-off when they decided to forsake both marriage and a male provider. Indeed, marriage and coverture would have limited their ability to trade. Whatever reasons these women had for remaining single, one thing is clear: they knew that, thanks to their mothers, aunts, and sisters, they had the skills and the means to support themselves.

Whether they chose to forgo marriage or not, the never-married women who entered into trade or business were able to substitute a work identity for that of wife or mother. While it was not unheard of, in the early modern period it was much less common for a woman to be referred to by her occupational status than by her marital status.[71] In Southampton, for example, in rare instances a clerk would note the trade in which a widow engaged, but it was not until the eighteenth century that Southampton's officials endowed a singlewoman with a recorded work identity. In 1733 Anne Goodridge purchased a mortgage of a house in St Lawrence's parish.[72] From other sources it is apparent that Goodridge was a singlewoman, but in this document the clerk did not record her marital status; rather, he referred to her by her occupational status of glover. A few years later Jane Martin brought a criminal suit against Elizabeth White, and in the sessions papers the Southampton JPs referred to Martin interchangeably as both a spinster (her marital status) and a milliner (her occupational status).[73] It seems that, in these particular sources, the occupation of these singlewomen was of as much pertinence as their marital status; although in Goodridge's case it is

---

[71] Cordelia Beattie has usefully pointed out that historical sources were crafted with different intentions, therefore some records are more likely to refer to women by their occupational status while others listed marital status. Her work focuses on medieval records such as the poll taxes, but her point can be applied to the early modern era as well. Cordelia Beattie, 'The Problem of Women's Work Identities in Post Black Death England,' in James Bothwell et al. (eds.), *The Problem of Labour in Fourteenth-Century England* (York: York Medieval Press, 2000), 1–19.

[72] SRO, SC 4/4/479/2.

[73] SRO, SC 9/4/261–261a.

less clear why her investment in a mortgage would lead to her being named as a glover. Elizabeth Sanderson has found that in eighteenth-century Scotland women of all marital states also enjoyed occupational designations, such as shopkeeper, milliner, and merchant.[74] This, of course, does not mean that women only began to possess a work identity when male officials decided they did. But the repercussions of having a recognized public work identity were momentous, especially for a singlewoman, who did not possess the identities of wife or mother and therefore was without a meaningful and useful position in contemporary eyes. A recognized economic role allowed the never-married woman to fill a niche in early modern society. This was a change for singlewomen in the eighteenth century.

The fourth factor that aided the appearance of single tradeswomen in Southampton was the changing economy. Until the late seventeenth century Southampton was economically depressed and offered little employment for singlewomen. Shipbuilding and the transportation and trade of luxury goods never employed many women in the town. Widows and wives were able to find work in the provisioning of the ships and visitors that came into the harbour and market, but as we saw in Chapter 2, singlewomen faced barriers to entering such victualling trades. Southampton's cloth industry had also fallen on hard times by the mid-seventeenth century, meaning that the textile work that had employed many never-married women was no longer an option. But, beginning in the later seventeenth century, Southampton's economic fortunes began to recover as the town became a social centre for the Hampshire gentry. In the eighteenth century Southampton transformed into a fashionable spa and bathing resort, drawing ever more paying visitors, who even included royalty.[75]

At the same time that this economic growth was occurring singlewomen began to gain a foothold in Southampton's formal economy. This was not just a coincidence. While the town's officials in no way encouraged or aided working singlewomen, they did cease their harassment of independent single traders. But why would the local government suddenly permit never-married women to trade independently in Southampton after a century of exclusion and harassment? There are several possibilities. First, Southampton's population had been decreasing over the seventeenth

---

[74] Sanderson, *Women and Work*, 75.
[75] Historians have relatively ignored the early modern period of Southampton's history because the town was not as prosperous or as nationally important as in the medieval and modern eras. The available literature includes: the articles by L. A. Burgess and Elsie Sandell in J. B. Morgan and Philip Peberdy (eds.), *Collected Essays on Southampton* (1961), 66–81; F. J. Monkhouse (ed.), *A Survey of Southampton and its Region* (1964), 218–31; A. Temple Patterson. *A History of Southampton 1700–1914* (Southampton, 1966), 1–101; and Rance. *Southampton: An Illustrated History.* Also see my dissertation: Amy M. Froide, 'Singlewomen, Work, and Community in Southampton, 1550–1750', Ph.D. dissertation, Duke University (1996).

century, and was at a low point by the beginning of the eighteenth. In 1596 the town's inhabitants numbered around 4,200, but one hundred years later this had fallen to around 3,000. The population rose slowly thereafter, reaching only 3,300 by the 1750s.[76] Fewer people meant less economic competition, and actually resulted in a need for workers that seems to have benefited working singlewomen. Secondly, as stated above, Southampton's economy was improving. The lack of people and the increasing number of jobs created a demand for labour, so there was no longer a need to stifle the competition created by singlewomen. And thirdly, as the economic basis of the town transformed from long-distance trade to leisure, new occupations sprang up to cater to visiting gentry and bathers. As discussed above, contemporaries deemed these new trades appropriate for gentlewomen, and many of them depended upon skills that were considered traditionally feminine, such as the millinery, linendrapery, mantua making, and gloving trades. In addition, new economic sectors such as female schooling and bathhouse keeping had yet to be regulated by the civic or gild authorities, and thus women were able to enter into these areas. Single tradeswomen who lived in early eighteenth-century Southampton entered into an environment short on labour and full of new trades that were either appropriate for women or relatively unregulated. All of these factors made for a relatively rosy economic outlook for the wealthy, older singlewoman; but only if she had initiative, for the town did not actively assist her.

The improving economic options for Southampton's working single-women may not have been an isolated occurrence. There is some evidence that this was not just a local change but one that was part of a more general trend throughout England's provincial towns. For instance, Mary Prior has traced a similar opening up of opportunities for never-married women in eighteenth-century Oxford. She found that for much of the early modern era singlewomen in Oxford were not allowed into the Tailors' Company, and thus were barred from the bespoke clothes-making trade. But in the late seventeenth century never-married women took advantage of a change in fashion that popularized more loose-fitting gowns, that were not fitted with stays and thus could be ready-made to fit any figure. Singlewomen began to make these mantuas, creating a space for themselves in Oxford's economy. The Tailors' and Mercers' Companies attempted to suppress the growing numbers of milliners and mantua makers, and prosecuted various single-women in these trades during the early 1700s. Ironically, the Mercer's Company, which had not allowed singlewomen to join its ranks, decided by the mid-eighteenth century that the only way to control mantua makers and milliners was to require them to become members of the gild. But by

---

[76] Rance, *Southampton*, 63; Monkhouse, *Survey of Southampton*, 228.

this time many never-married women refused to join an institution that had once excluded them; they were now prospering without paying the hefty gild dues.[77] Just as in Southampton, singlewomen found a niche for themselves, but they did so without any encouragement or assistance, and only by their own initiative.

The range of jobs open to singlewomen also increased in other towns during the eighteenth century. In the eighteenth century Ludlow served as a provincial social centre and was home to a thriving glove trade, which created jobs for women as shopkeepers, mantua makers, milliners, hatters, and glovers. In reference to Ludlow, Susan Wright has argued that 'by [this] period society obviously tolerated the single woman who lived alone and who wished to pursue a career, provided that she was adequately trained and did not encroach too much in overtly male spheres of work'.[78] Margaret Hunt attributes the rise in economic options for working women throughout London and other towns to the 'consumer revolution' of the eighteenth century—an increase in consumption due largely to the new goods and profits that resulted from Britain's world trade. For example, singlewomen in the capital found jobs selling books and newspapers, retailing imported luxury goods such as chinaware, silks, and tea, and running boarding schools for the daughters of merchants and urban gentry.[79] The single female writers discussed earlier also took advantage of the expanding reading and subscribing public in the eighteenth century. An economic and social revival in England's provincial towns, what historians have termed an 'urban renaissance', and an expanding consumer base provided singlewomen throughout urban England with increased economic options.

If economic opportunities for urban singlewomen were increasing in the late seventeenth century this runs counter to one of the standard hypotheses about Englishwomen's economic history. Almost a century ago Alice Clark posited that direct economic involvement for women of the middling sort began to decline from the seventeenth century onward.[80] While some historians have disagreed with the timing of such a decline more than with the concept of decline per se, and others have shown that we cannot generalize about a decline since occupational alternatives for women varied by region and community, the thesis has yet to fall.[81] This chapter shows

[77] Prior, 'Women and the Urban Economy,' 110–14.

[78] Wright, '"Holding Up Half the Sky"', 56–7.

[79] Hunt, *Middling Sort*, 145.

[80] Alice Clark, *Working Life of Women in the Seventeenth Century*, 3rd edn. (New York, 1992), 11–12, 96.

[81] For work that nuances or challenges Alice Clark's thesis of decline, see Earle, 'The Female Labour Market'; Eric Richards, 'Women in the British Economy Since About 1700: An Interpretation', *History*, 59 (1974), 337–57; Michael Roberts, 'Words They Are Women, Deeds They Are Men', in *Women and Work in Pre-Industrial England*; Sharpe, *Adapting to Capitalism*, 7–8 and epilogue; Wright, '"Holding Up Half the Sky,"' 56–7.

that we also cannot generalize about a decline for all women, but that we must differentiate between the work experiences of never-married and ever-married women. Actually Alice Clark was more attentive to marital status than those of us who have used her work. She was the first to point out that singlewomen's opportunities for economic independence actually improved at the same time that she believed the situation worsened for married women. Clark was primarily interested in the changes in the family economy and in the productive contribution of wives; thus, she emphasized the negative changes she saw in *married* women's lives, which is the part of her theory upon which historians have seized. In this case, the problem is not with Clark but with our reading of her. There is no evidence that singlewomen's economic opportunities declined in the seventeenth century; we have simply assumed it, and our assumptions seem to have been wrong. Whether Clark's hypothesis that married women saw a decline in economic opportunities is upheld or not, singlewomen of the middling sort at least had a different experience. For them, the final years of the seventeenth century and the first half of the eighteenth century were years of increasing opportunity.

Of course, not all singlewomen were able to take advantage of these increasing opportunities. And even those women who were prosperous, mature, and sufficiently well trained were still channelled into particular trades in which men were not interested, either because they were not considered lucrative enough or because they were gendered feminine. The single tradeswomen discussed here were often considerably better off than other never-married women, and frequently numbered among the more prosperous traders in provincial towns. They were a minority, but an important one, whose existence attests to the courage and persistence of singlewomen who refused to limit their economic options to service, and who pushed against the long-standing constraints and prejudices against never-married women working for themselves. These women were willing to work to support themselves; they only asked that they be allowed to control their own labour. These single tradeswomen served as pioneers and examples for other working singlewomen, and stood as proof that never-married women could be useful, productive citizens. The issue of singlewomen's civic significance is the topic of the next chapter.

5

Women of Independent Means: The Civic Significance of Never-Married Women

The singlewomen described in the last chapter contributed to early modern town life through their participation in the urban economy. This was only one of the ways in which never-married women enhanced their urban communities. While town fathers focused on the negative characteristics of poor and humble singlewomen, such as vagrancy, being out of service, and having children out of wedlock, never-married women of the middling sort went unnoticed. These more prosperous women were not the target of public harassment, but at the same time their positive contributions were not acknowledged by the urban authorities. This chapter uncovers the effaced but significant contributions of middling singlewomen to the provincial towns in which they lived. These women played an important role in urban communities as property holders, as private and public creditors, as householders, as tax- and ratepayers, and as philanthropists. At the same time that contemporaries began to portray never-married women from the middling sort as useless and functionless 'old maids', many of these women were performing the roles of upright householders and citizens, and assisting both their neighbours and their urban governments. Largely because contemporaries seldom acknowledged or minimized their roles, the civic significance of never-married women to the urban milieu of the early modern era has been erased. This chapter will show that, rather than being a problem or nuisance, middling singlewomen performed important civic functions and contributed to the success of early modern towns.

The first two sections of this chapter look at how never-married women served an important economic role as property holders and rentiers and as private and public moneylenders. The third and final section examines how singlewomen functioned as urban citizens—paying taxes, extending charity, signing political oaths, and sometimes even voting and holding office. But first we need to look at how never-married women acquired the wealth that allowed them to function as urban citizens.

One of the most significant factors for a woman who never married was that, by definition, she had no husband to maintain her and so she had to support herself. As we have seen, singlewomen often maintained themselves through work, but there were other alternatives. Amy Erickson reminds us that, 'historically, the most important component of wealth was not wages, but inheritance'.[1] Many never-married women, particularly those of middling and elite status, but also women hailing from more modest family backgrounds, inherited something from family, employers, friends, and neighbours. While smaller portions provided the working singlewoman with some added security and perhaps a nest egg for the future, larger legacies supplied never-married women with life incomes, thus making work unnecessary. The latter route was not a passive one, however, because inherited wealth, whether in the form of real estate or money, had to be well managed to see a woman through sixty years or more of singlehood.

Parents were the primary source of inherited wealth for singlewomen. Parents from all socio-economic groups tried to leave something, however small, to help set their children up in life. Some children might acquire a legacy during the lifetime of their parents, but for most it came when a parent died. Parents sometimes stipulated that a daughter should receive her inheritance when she married, but historians have begun to show that many parents recognized that not all daughters would marry, or that they might not marry at a young age. A majority of wills from the early modern period state that a daughter's legacy should be paid at marriage, or a particular age, whichever came first. For example, Christine Peters has found that in the second half of the sixteenth century testators in the archdeaconry of Essex were most likely to leave bequests to their daughters when they reached a particular age rather than at marriage. An almost equal number timed bequests to go to daughters at a certain age or upon marriage, whichever came first. But only 20 per cent of testators tied a daughter's inheritance to her marriage only. Inheritance customs did vary by region. In the diocese of Worcester, Peters discovered that 40 per cent of testators favoured leaving bequests to daughters upon marriage, while a third bequeathed legacies to daughters at a certain age, and the remainder timed legacies for a particular age or upon marriage.[2] While the proportions did vary, the majority of singlewomen inherited at adulthood and not at marriage. For women, the age of inheritance was usually 16, 18, 20, or 21 (for men it was 21, or more commonly their mid-twenties).[3] These findings are significant, because

[1] Amy Louise Erickson, *Women and Property in Early Modern England* (New York: Routledge, 1993), 3.

[2] Christine Peters, 'Single Women in Early Modern England: Attitudes and Expectations', *Continuity and Change*, 12: 3 (1997), 333, Table 1.

[3] Ibid. 334; Richard Vann, 'Wills and the Family in an English Town: Banbury 1550–1800', *Journal of Family History*, 4: 4 (1979), 362; Amy M. Froide, 'Single Women, Work and Community in Southampton, 1550–1750', Ph.D. dissertation, Duke University (1996), 305 and n. 3.

they illustrate that contemporaries did not assume that women would marry. And for women who subsequently never did, a parental legacy was the largest, and perhaps only, endowment that they received for their future security.

Most singlewomen, then, could expect to inherit parental wealth some time in early adulthood. Those who lived in towns might also expect to inherit portions roughly equivalent to those of their brothers. This was because merchants, tradesmen, and urban professionals did not usually practice primogeniture like the landed elite. Instead of giving more to elder sons than to other sons and daughters they engaged in partible inheritance. Burgage (freehold land in urban areas) and leasehold property was usually divided among several children. And even if daughters inherited personal property, such as household goods and money, rather than real property, Amy Erickson has shown that daughters and sons still received portions of equal value. What differed was not the worth of these legacies, but what comprised them.[4]

Moreover, even if a father privileged an eldest son in his will, a widowed mother did not necessarily do so in hers. Many widows chose to use their wills as a means to balance out the inheritances of their children. Overall, widows usually favoured younger children over older ones, and daughters over sons.[5] For example, when the Southampton widow Mary Page died in 1702 she left her son Thomas the token of a silver tankard and divided the residue of her estate among her three younger children, Mary, Josiah, and Elizabeth. Page made her daughter Mary her executrix, in preference to her eldest son, and entrusted the rearing of her two youngest children and the continuance of her trade to Mary. In return for these responsibilities, Mary received the benefit of the entire estate until it was time for Josiah and Elizabeth to be apprenticed.[6] Another widow from the town, Elizabeth Guillum, bequeathed 1s. each to her two married daughters and one son, in token of legacies they had already received, but she left £80 to her daughter Mary, who was still single.[7] These wills show that while a father's primary thoughts may have been to establish his heir in both marriage and an occupation, his actions allowed his widow to look out for younger, female, and single children. In fact, one of the main reasons to make a will at all was to lessen the unequal effects of primogeniture upon the remaining children.[8]

---

[4] Erickson, *Women and Property*, 68–78.
[5] See Froide, 'Single Women, Work, and Community', ch. 7, esp. 310–12 and Table 10.
[6] Hampshire Record Office (hereafter HRO), 1702 A58.
[7] HRO, 1715 A43.
[8] Erickson, *Women and Property*, 78.

There was another means by which legacies could be balanced out between siblings. Fortunately for daughters, especially single ones, parents were not the only people from whom a person inherited wealth. Other kin, in particular grandparents, aunts, uncles, cousins, and siblings, provided never-married women with legacies. For example, in 1559 Nicholas Le Neve left his Southampton blacksmith's shop and all his wares and tools to his eldest son. To his two other sons he provided tokens in recognition of legacies already received. To his only daughter Agnes he left a mere 6s. 8d. If we limit our sights to parental legacies only, it seems that Agnes was severely disadvantaged in comparison to her brothers when it came to the family inheritance. But if we expand our field of vision to include legacies from kin, we find that in the same year that Agnes's father made his will, her maternal grandmother's will noted that Agnes had inherited the deed to a house in Southampton from her grandfather. A similar case was that of the Southampton merchant Thomas Goddard, who left his daughters portions considerably less than those he bequeathed to his sons. But when Goddard's eldest son Henry died just seven years later he left £58 to his sister Joan, as well as £38 to his sibling Alice. Acknowledging the inequitable inheritance strategies of his father, Henry bequeathed only £13 between his two brothers. In this case, a brother rather than a father ensured that Joan and Alice Goddard received an equitable amount of the family estate.[9]

Kin sometimes left bequests to never-married women to allow them to remain single. We have already seen how the Southampton singlewoman Alice Zaines left her linendrapery business and shop goods to her never-married niece Elizabeth Wheeler. Zaines chose her niece to continue the female-run family business, and provided her with a trade that allowed her to maintain herself without a husband. Similarly, Gertrude Savile received a substantial legacy in 1730 from a cousin who had died far off in the service of the East India Company. Savile recorded in her diary that she took 'a little pride and pleasure in his distinction of [her]'. This inheritance had a significant material as well as psychological effect on Savile's life; it allowed her to establish her own household for the first time at the age of 40. With her legacy she rented a house near her brother's family in Yorkshire, and when he died she purchased the leasehold to a London residence on Great Russell Street.[10] The next section looks at such property holding by single-women.

[9] Edward Roberts and Karen Parker (eds.), *Southampton Probate Inventories, 1447–1575*, Southampton Records Series, 34–5 (Southampton, 1992), 154–9, 183–4.

[10] Alan Saville (ed.), *Secret Comment: The Diaries of Gertrude Savile 1721–1757*, Thoroton Society Record Series, 41 (Devon: Kingsbridge History Society, 1997), 19, 219–20, 231; *The Account Books of Gertrude Savile, 1736–58*, Thoroton Society Record Series, 24 (Nottingham: Thoroton Society, 1965), 100–1, 107.

Property Holders and Rentiers

This section examines the inheritance and acquisition of real property by never-married women. In particular, it looks at the property held by single-women in the provincial towns of Southampton, Bristol, Oxford, and York. Because female property holding in early modern towns is largely under-studied, there is little opportunity for comparison, so these findings are more of a beginning on which I hope others will build.

It is striking how common it was for urban singlewomen to hold property. The wills of never-married women who lived in the provincial towns of Southampton, Bristol, Oxford, and York in the early modern period illustrate this. In Southampton, 44.7 per cent (seventeen out of thirty-eight) of single female testators between the years 1550 and 1750 bequeathed real property. This compares to slightly lower proportions of single female property holders in other provincial towns: 30 per cent (twelve out of forty) in Bristol; 32.5 per cent (thirteen out of forty) in Oxford; and 22 per cent (eleven out of fifty) in York.[11] These examples reveal that from just under one-fourth to one-half of urban singlewomen held real estate at the time of their deaths.

The proportion of never-married women holding property in urban communities can be compared to that of women in general. Maxine Berg has found that in eighteenth-century Birmingham and Sheffield 47 per cent of women held real property.[12] Penelope Lane's study of Leicestershire towns reveals that 23.7 per cent of all female testators in Ashby de la Zouch and 38 per cent of those in Hinckley between the years 1750–1835 bequeathed real estate.[13] This means that singlewomen held property in similar proportions to all women. Their *feme sole* status does not seem to have benefited them, but neither does their lack of a husband seem to have hindered them.

A singlewoman who bequeathed real estate when she died had acquired this property in one of two ways during her lifetime: either she had inherited it or she had purchased it through her own means. Never-married women commonly inherited real property. The estates of urban families

---

[11] This discussion of singlewomen's property holding is based on samples of singlewomen's wills from early modern Southampton, Bristol, Oxford, and York. For an explanation of how these samples were created, see Chapter 3, n.2.

[12] Maxine Berg, 'Women's Property and the Industrial Revolution', *Journal of Interdisciplinary History*, 24: 2 (Fall 1993), 241.

[13] Penelope Lane, 'Women, Property and Inheritance: Wealth Creation and Income Generation in Small English Towns, 1750–1835', in Jon Stobart and Alastair Owens (eds.), *Urban Fortunes: Property and Inheritance in the Town 1700–1900* (Burlington, Vt.: Ashgate, 2000), 186 and Table 8.2.

largely consisted of leasehold and burgage property, types of land tenure not burdened by Common law rules of primogeniture.[14] These properties also could be easily divided among several children. For instance, in 1726 Christopher Fleet of Southampton was able to bequeath four houses in Southampton to his five children—a son and four daughters. Christopher Fleet's never-married daughter Anne and his married daughter Jane Rice jointly inherited a messuage with a wash-house, garden, and the use of a pump.[15] Urban singlewomen who primarily inherited leasehold and burgage property seem to have held real estate more than their rural sisters, where land was often held by customary tenure.[16]

The real estate an urban singlewoman was most likely to hold was a house, or in early modern terminology, a messuage or tenement. In Bristol, nine out of twelve singlewomen who bequeathed real estate left houses, as did ten out of thirteen in Oxford and eight out of eleven in York. Houses were useful to singlewomen for two reasons. They served as a home for a never-married woman without family, and they were an easy piece of property to rent out for profit. For example, Anne Wright of York had her own dwelling-house in Micklegate as well as three other houses that she rented out to others to maintain herself.[17]

In addition to houses, urban singlewomen held urban garden plots, suburban lands, and rural farms. Three out of twelve (25 per cent) singlewomen who held property in Bristol, four out of thirteen (31 per cent) in Oxford, and five out of eleven (45 per cent) in York mentioned lands in their wills. For example, in 1682 Jane Bosvile took out a lease on the garden in Oxford's guildhall court, paying 15s. rent per annum. And in 1715 the singlewoman Mary Chillingworth paid 2s. for part of the Jews Mount (the name for Oxford's castle mound), which she leased for much of the eighteenth century.[18] Never-married women also held buildings out of which they worked, such as shops or inns. Martha Hawks was listed as paying rent for the Feathers public house in the 1693 Oxford town rental. Hawks continued to lease this property into the mid-eighteenth century.[19] Women in the resort town of Bath leased shops, cellars, butteries, and stables from the corporation from the late seventeenth century onward. In

---

[14] Erickson, *Women and Property*, 24, 78.

[15] Southampton Record Office (hereafter SRO), D/PM Box 100.

[16] Peters, 'Single Women', 335–7. Judith Spicksley has also found that only 7% and 6% of singlewomen in Cheshire and Lincolnshire respectively held arable or pasture land. Judith Spicksley, 'The Early Modern Demographic Dynamic: Celibates and Celibacy in Seventeenth-Century England', D.Phil. thesis, University of Hull (2001), 230.

[17] Borthwick Institute of Historical Research (hereafter BIHR), Dean and Chapter Wills, reel 1245, Anne Wright (1670).

[18] H. E. Salter (ed.), *Oxford City Properties*, Oxford Historical Society, 83 (Oxford: Clarendon Press, 1926), 151, 29–40, 210–11.

[19] *Oxford City Properties*, 7–29, 142, 233.

1718 Elizabeth Sheyler even leased the building from which she ran Sheyler's Coffee House in Cheap Street.[20]

Not only were never-married women likely to hold certain types of urban property, they were also likely to hold it in certain ways. Single female testators more frequently mentioned leasing property than owning it. Only in Bristol were the proportions equal: three singlewomen who made wills mentioned leasing property and three mentioned owning. This compares to Oxford, where seven single female testators held leases, compared to two who held copyholds and two who held freeholds. In York four never-married women who made wills had leased property while two owned it. And in Southampton three female testators mentioned leases while two mentioned freeholds. Nevertheless, since most urban property was held by leasehold, in this regard singlewomen were no different from the men and widows who also held urban property.

What did distinguish never-married women was that they were frequently co-heiresses, which meant that they often held urban properties as tenants in common. Nearly one-fourth (or twenty-eight out of a sample of 125) of singlewomen who held real estate in early modern Southampton did so with another person, and at least sixteen of these women obtained property jointly through inheritance.[21] In the majority of these cases (eighteen out of twenty-eight) never-married women held property with their siblings, especially other single sisters. For example, in the 1640s and 1650s the never-married sisters Margery and Jane Exton held property together in at least three Southampton parishes.[22] Singlewomen also owned or leased property with brothers, widowed sisters, and married sisters and their husbands. For instance, Ventham Spencer, tailor, left a house in the same town to his single daughter Mary and his son Ventham Jr. as tenants in common.[23] If a singlewoman was not a joint or common tenant with a sibling, she was likely to hold real estate with a widowed mother, father, or another relative. Only two never-married women in

[20] Bath Record Office (Furman's) Repertory of Deeds, etc. (1776).

[21] The sources for the sample of singlewomen who held property in Southampton include: 38 extant wills and inventories made by Southampton singlewomen between 1570 and 1752; J. M. Kaye, 'The Cartulary of God's House Southampton', *Southampton Record Series*, 19–20 (Southampton, 1976); the 1617 survey of town lands and tenements (SC 4/1/2); the 1738–46 corporation rental (SC 4/1/7); the Book of Entry of Leases (SC 4/1/5); an unpublished calendar of corporation leases; an unpublished calendar of various deeds, bonds, and agreements; an unpublished catalogue of deeds to various parishes in Southampton; the unpublished topographical lists to various areas and parishes in Southampton (all unpublished calendars are held in the SRO); Scavage Books (SC 5/17/1–35); Assessment Books (SC 14/2/1–35, 39, 43, 55–61, 83–8, 97); Land Taxes (SC 14/2/118–124a, 126–8, 156, 158–9, 188–91, 193–7, 199–200, 223–30, 232–5, 255–61, 263, 265–70, 298–306, 356–63, 365b–70); and other miscellaneous town records.

[22] SRO, SC 14/2/18, 21, 24, 27–28a (1647–57).

[23] SRO, D/Z 185/1.

Southampton held property with an unrelated man, and none did so with an unrelated woman. Another reason for the custom of joint tenancy was that urban authorities sometimes required a co-signer when a singlewoman acquired property. These women would have been likely to take out leases with another person, especially a male relative. For example, when Penelope Bernard leased Southampton's woolhouse, her father John (a former mayor) held the property along with her.

Although our focus on primogeniture in British history has led us to assume that males inherited real estate over female kin, in provincial towns the opposite was sometimes the case. For example, in 1572/3 one Manchester clothier who had a son chose to bequeath to his daughter Alice 'the house I have lately builded, with the garden thereto belonging, in the Deansgate, to her and her heirs'.[24] Similarly, in 1696 the Southampton clothworker William Wallistone bequeathed £100 and a messuage to his daughter Dorothy, while he left only £20 to his son William.[25] And when Mary Carteret died in 1680 she left a house in Southampton to her niece Mary Fowke, another tenement to her niece Frances Gallop, and the reversion of the George Inn to her niece Katherine Fowke. Carteret's brother was the only male kin to inherit any of her real property, for she favoured her female relatives overall.[26]

The fact that so many single female testators held urban property is all the more surprising given that towns were not necessarily keen to lease property to never-married women. Town rentals, or lists of property leased out by corporations, included very few singlewomen. And those who did succeed in holding town leases were likely to have inherited a lease of the property rather than have taken a lease out on their own. For example, Southampton singlewomen held only 3 per cent (fifteen out of 510) of extant town leases granted between 1550 and 1750, even though these women comprised 14–19 per cent of the town's adult population.[27] And in over a third of these cases (six out of fifteen) the never-married woman had not applied for the lease herself, but had inherited it from her father. It seems that Southampton's corporation was not eager to rent to singlewomen. It could not control whether never-married women inherited town leases from their kin, but it could control how many singlewomen took out leases on their own initiative. The never-married woman who inherited a town lease had to renew it in her own name and pay a fine. For

---

[24] J. P. Earwaker (ed.), *The Court Leet Records of the Manor of Manchester...1552–1686; 1731–1846*, (Manchester, 1884), i. 152, n. 1.

[25] SRO, SC 4/4/430/2.

[26] HRO, 1680 A21/1.

[27] These population figures are based on the 1696 Marriage Duty Tax assessments. SRO, SC 14/2/66a–74c.

example, in 1738/9 Elizabeth Smith paid £15 15s. when she took out a forty-year lease on a messuage and garden in St John's parish, which the town had previously leased to her father, Richard Smith.[28] In Elizabeth Smith's case the corporation lacked control over who held the town lease, but in only nine other instances in the early modern era did Southampton choose to lease town property directly to a never-married woman.

The property holding opportunities for singlewomen in Chester seem to have been equally chilly. In 1639 Elizabeth Walton petitioned the city council for the tenancy of a house held by the city, but almost three years later Walton asked the assembly to accept her surrender of the lease for the tenement and to return the substantial entry fine of £30 that she had paid, since 'she had not yet obtained possession' of the property. Her request was denied due to lack of information. Six months later she had to again petition the council for her entry fine, as well as the £20 rent she had paid for the tenement, because 'so far she had not yet been given possession of it and in the meantime the house had fallen and the land was worn out with tillage and ill husbandry'. By Christmas 1642 the assembly finally agreed to return her entry fine, but without interest. This was three-and-a-half years after Walton's original request to lease the corporation-owned house.[29] While Chester's city council did give Walton a lease, they took her money without helping to put her in possession of the property. Walton's situation is indicative of Maria Cioni's finding, that inheritance of property did not necessarily lead to property holding on the part of women. As she has said, 'it was one thing to be named a beneficiary, and quite another to receive and keep the estate, especially when the heir was a woman'.[30]

In towns where land was held by customary tenure (as opposed to freehold or leasehold tenure), single female property holders seem to have benefited. The sixteenth-century court leet records from Manchester are replete with examples of never-married women inheriting urban property, as well as paying fines and swearing fealty to the lord of the town.[31] For instance, in 1586 Elizabeth Gee, the daughter of a deceased clothier inherited from her father a plot in Mylnegate which was divided into two tenements or dwelling-houses. In court Elizabeth Gee was sworn to the lord of the manor of Manchester, and was admitted a tenant by fealty and payment of 6d. to the steward for a relief.

---

[28] SRO, SC 4/3/493.

[29] Margaret Groombridge (ed.), 'Calendar of Chester City Council Minutes 1603–1642', *Record Society of Lancashire and Cheshire*, 106 (Blackpool: F. Taylor, 1956), 201, 210–11.

[30] Maria Cioni, *Women and Law in Elizabethan England, With Particular Reference to the Court of Chancery* (New York: Garland, 1985), 86.

[31] See examples from 1559, 1561, 1573, 1590 in *Manchester Court Leet Records*, i. 43, 49, 69, 152; ii. 48.

Manchester's authorities did not assist or encourage the economic activity of singlewomen, but they also did not stand in the way if they could find no reasonable objection against women with money. For example, in 1555 the jury presented Elisabeth, daughter of Richard Shalcrosse, as the heir of her grandmother, and as such she was to be given a burgage in Manchester's market-place, 'unless better evidence be brought in to the contrary afore the next court'. Elisabeth's father had lately lived in this property, and perhaps the town preferred his stewardship to his daughter's. But after a year of delay the court declared Elisabeth Shalcrosse of lawful age and lawful heir by right of her mother, and stated that she owed her 'suit of fealty and [was] to pay heriot and relief to the lord according to custom'.[32]

Despite the discouragement or hostility singlewomen faced when trying to hold urban property, their numbers did increase over time. For instance, I have found at least 125 singlewomen who were holders of real property in early modern Southampton.[33] Only two of these never-married women were property holders for the fifty years between 1550 and 1600. The number of singlewomen who held property in Southampton rose throughout the seventeenth century, however, and increased even more rapidly in the early eighteenth century. For instance, between 1650 and 1699 a total of twenty-one singlewomen paid parliamentary assessments on twenty-one buildings, three pieces of land, and seven personal estates (ready money, investments, or goods).[34] Their number doubled in the first half of the eighteenth century, when forty-seven never-married women paid land tax on sixty-one buildings, four pieces of land, and seven personal estates. And these numbers are merely a minimum due to the notoriously high levels of under-assessment in the land tax.[35] The evidence from Southampton corroborates Berg's findings for Birmingham and Sheffield and Lane's for Leicestershire's small towns: singlewomen increased their power over urban real estate throughout the eighteenth century, rather than the opposite, as previous research had suggested.[36]

Although the numbers of never-married women who held property were small, it is significant that they well outnumbered the single tradeswomen in early modern Southampton. For instance, only two women listed as 'spinsters' paid a Stall and Art fine to trade in the town before the 1680s,

[32] Ibid. ii. 3–4; i. 23, 29

[33] This number is a minimum only. A complete examination of the wills made by fathers and widows who bequeathed real property to their daughters in early modern Southampton would doubtless turn up more singlewomen who inherited property.

[34] SRO, SC 14/2/1–35, 39, 43, 55–61, 83–8, 97.

[35] SRO, SC 14/2/118–370, *passim*. On the land tax, see Donald E. Ginter, *A Measure of Wealth: The English Land Tax in Historical Analysis* (Montreal: McGill–Queens University Press, 1992), and Peter Earle, *The Making of the English Middle Class* (Berkeley: University of California Press, 1989), 374 and n. 11.

[36] Lane, 'Women, Property, and Inheritance', esp. 172–5.

compared to twenty-nine never-married women who held property there. And while thirty singlewomen traded independently in the town from the 1680s onward, this was less than a third of the ninety-five never-married women who held real estate. Since three times as many never-married women held property rather than worked independently, this suggests that Southampton's authorities accepted the economic activity of single female property holders and rentiers earlier and more readily than that of single tradeswomen. This could have been because property holders and rentiers were more likely to be of middling status, or from artisanal, trade, and professional backgrounds, as well as from prominent local families; but most single tradeswomen were too. Moreover, not all single female testators who held property were wealthy. For example, Southampton's property holders included women like Eleanor Dickinson, whose inventory revealed that she was worth a mere £13.[37] In fact, only seven out of the seventeen singlewomen who held property in the town had estates worth over £100. The same was true in York, where women of modest means could be property holders, such as Mary Dawson, who held one-third of a lease of a farm, and Margaret Allen, who held a house that she lived in and was able to bequeath.[38]

Another reason why town authorities may have condoned rentiers more than tradeswomen was the assumed passive economic nature of property holding. Theoretically, female property holders only had to venture infrequently into the public sphere to collect rents and sign leases, compared to the more active and public nature of women who worked in the market-place and in the shops along the High Street. Just how passive these single female rentiers really were is up for debate, however. For example, while the sisters Jane and Margery Exton inherited some of their real estate from a brother, they also sought out and purchased other properties in at least three different Southampton parishes. The sisters maintained themselves as rentiers by letting out three of their properties during the 1640s and 1650s.[39] Other singlewomen actively sought out property in which to invest, rather than passively inheriting it. In 1752 Elizabeth Compton already occupied a house in one Southampton parish when she bought a capital (large) messuage in another for £1,400. She died later that same year possessed of an estate worth over £3,200, with real estate comprising nearly half of her substantial wealth.[40] Singlewomen not only purchased or leased property to maintain themselves off of rents, but also ran businesses out of their

[37] HRO, 1646 A19.
[38] BIHR, Dean and Chapter Wills, reel 1250, Mary Dawson (1713) and reel 1251, Margaret Allen (1729).
[39] SRO, SC 14/2/18, 21, 24, 27–28a.
[40] SRO, D/PM Box 100/10; HRO, 1752 A20.

properties. In Southampton Elizabeth Langford leased a shop from which she traded, and the Shergold sisters used their capital messuage in the town's High Street as a boarding school for young ladies.[41] This was true in other towns as well. The sisters Mary, Elizabeth, and Sarah Bleay held various tenements in Oxford and jointly kept the Sun Inn out of one of them.[42] These singlewomen were not passive, retired rentiers.

Other never-married women were downright shrewd in their acquisition of real property. In 1736 Mary Lacy, of Bishops Waltham, came before the Hampshire J Ps and enrolled a deed in her own name and that of her sister Katherine (who was also a singlewoman). In the deed Mary laid claim to Lomer manor and rectory, which Mary Bone, a singlewoman from Corhampton parish, had devised to Lacy's mother and thereafter to William Moore and his heirs. Lacy asserted that her mother was now dead and that William Moore was a papist, and by act of parliament was 'made incapable of having the premises or rents'. So, in accordance with the act, she enrolled her claim to the land she thought rightfully belonged to her and her sister.[43] Mary Lacy provides a good example of how an assertive singlewoman could exploit a legal loophole to acquire property that would not have originally descended to her. Never-married women such as these turn the notion on its head that property holding was always a passive economic activity.

As property holders, never-married women put down roots and became part of their urban communities. They became respectable householders and sometimes rentiers. Middling singlewomen were not urban problems; they were not transients or drains on the poor relief system. Instead, as we will see below, they were the very people whose property was taxed to pay the poor rates and keep up the town infrastructure.

Moneylenders

While never-married women held real property more than we may have assumed, it was even more common for never-married women to control personal property. Such personal estate could include household goods, clothing, jewellery, plate (silver spoons, bowls, plates, and tankards), stock in trade, livestock, and money, whether in the form of credit instruments or cash. Personal property was not necessarily any less important to a never-married woman's livelihood than real estate; in fact, it was often a more flexible and practical inheritance. Household goods and furniture enabled a singlewoman to fit out her lodgings or her own home. Clothes, jewellery,

[41] SRO, SC/AG 8/6/1; D/PM Box 55; D/MC 10/11.
[42] Centre for Oxfordshire Studies (hereafter COS), W 214.341 Sarah Bleay (1759).
[43] HRO, Q 1/12, fos. 143^v–145.

and plate could adorn her person or house, and could just as easily be converted into money.[44] Stock in trade could assist a single tradeswoman. Livestock, such as cows and sheep, could be sold or rented out; the latter being a common practice among servants who inherited animals from kin.[45] And, of course, a monetary legacy enabled a never-married woman to maintain herself, either through its purchasing or its investing power.

Singlewomen frequently turned money into an investment. After apparel and linen, the most common personal property listed in a Southampton singlewoman's will was money, in the form of credit instruments. This money was rarely 'ready' (or on hand), but rather was comprised of money on loan. Banks were not available until the Bank of England was established in the 1690s, and even then only elite or London-based singlewomen invested in the Bank and other public institutions.[46] So early modern singlewomen in provincial towns with money to invest loaned it out locally to both private individuals and town governments.

Historians have been aware of the role of women as local moneylenders for some time. Most of this research has focused on widows as the prominent extenders of local credit.[47] What we know about single female lenders comes from the study of exceptional individuals such as Joyce Jeffries, Elizabeth Parkin, and Hester Pinney.[48] It is still unclear if these wealthy women were representative of singlewomen who loaned money. Elizabeth Parkin, for instance, held a personal fortune of nearly £30,000 due to inheriting her family's substantial ironmongery business around 1740. From then on she actively managed her wealth by investments in loans,

---

[44] Beverly Lemire, *Dress, Culture and Commerce: The English Clothing Trade Before the Factory, 1660–1800* (New York: St Martin's Press, 1997).

[45] Marjorie McIntosh, 'Servants and the Household Unit in Elizabethan England', *Journal of Family History*, 9: 1 (1984), 3–23.

[46] Sir John Clapham, *The Bank of England: A History* (New York: Macmillan, 1945), 275, 281, 288.

[47] Studies of female creditors in England include, B. A. Holderness, 'Credit in English Rural Society Before the Nineteenth Century, With Special Reference to the Period 1650–1720', *Agricultural History Review*, 24: 2 (1976), 97–109, and id., 'Widows in Pre-Industrial Society: An Essay Upon Their Economic Functions', in Richard M. Smith (ed.), *Land, Kinship and Life-Cycle* (New York: Cambridge University Press, 1984), 423–42; Craig Muldrew, 'Credit and the Courts: Debt Litigation in a Seventeenth-Century Urban Community', *Economic History Review*, 46: 1 (1993), 23–38, and id., *The Economy of Obligation* (New York: MacMillan, 1998), ch. 8. Studies of female creditors in Europe include, James B. Collins, 'The Economic Role of Women in Seventeenth-Century France', *French Historical Studies*, 16: 2 (Fall 1989), 437–70; William Jordan, *Women and Credit in Pre-Industrial and Developing Societies* (Philadelphia: University of Pennsylvania Press, 1993).

[48] See Robert Tittler 'Money-lending in the West Midlands: The Activities of Joyce Jeffries, 1638–49', *Historical Research*, 67: 164 (1994), 249–63; B. A. Holderness, 'Elizabeth Parkin and Her Investments, 1733–66: Aspects of the Sheffield Money Market in the Eighteenth Century', *Transactions of the Hunter Archaeological Society*, 10: 2 (1973), 81–7; Pamela Sharpe, 'Dealing With Love: The Ambiguous Independence of the Single Woman in Early Modern England', *Gender & History*, 11: 2 (July 1999), 209–32.

the coal industry, real estate, and public projects such as turnpikes. Her biggest loan amounted to £11,000. This section provides some context for women like Elizabeth Parkin by examining groups of single female creditors rather than isolated individuals. It looks at the role of urban singlewomen as moneylenders in provincial towns such as Southampon, as well as Bristol, Oxford, and York. In these towns it was never-married women and not widows who were the more significant lenders of money.

In Southampton an impressive 45 per cent (or seventeen out of thirty-eight) of single female testators mentioned money they had on loan at the time of their deaths. And this is merely a minimum, since wills did not necessarily record all debts. Inventories did record them, but they survive for only fifteen out of the thirty-eight women. Out of these fifteen inventories, eight include loans or sums owed to the deceased singlewoman. This means that both wills and inventories reveal that the same percentage of Southampton singlewomen (nearly half) had loaned their money out.

Moneylending by never-married women was not a phenomenon unique to Southampton. In Bristol 42 per cent (or twenty-one out of fifty) of single female testators had loaned money. In Oxford a similar 43 per cent (or eighteen out of forty-two) of singlewomen mentioned debts due to them at the time of their deaths. And in York the percentage was slightly higher: 44 per cent (or twenty-two out of fifty-five) of single female testators had loaned money out.[49] In the disparate towns of Southampton, Bristol, Oxford, and York a consistent 42–45 per cent of urban singlewomen engaged in moneylending during the early modern period.

We might expect the single female testators who loaned money to be wealthy; however, these women represented a relatively broad social spectrum. Single female lenders in Southampton left estates ranging from just £2 to over £3,000, and the majority, or twenty-two out of thirty-eight women, were worth £100 or less. Never-married women who loaned money in Bristol held estates worth as little as £3 and as much as £600. In Oxford single female lenders had estates ranging from £8 to over £567, while in York never-married women who loaned money were worth anywhere from £2 to £413.[50] Again, in Southampton about a fourth of the

[49] For Bristol, I chose a sample of 50 wills and inventories made by singlewomen who died between the years 1613 and 1751. For Oxford, I chose a sample of 42 singlewomen's probate documents proved between 1600 and 1786. For York, I chose a sample of 50 wills and inventories made by singlewomen between 1619 and 1750. For more on these samples see Chap. 3, n. 2.

[50] Inventories survive for only 13 of the 38 single female testators in Southampton. For the remaining 25 women I had to estimate their worth based on the bequests they mentioned in their wills. The 21 single female moneylenders from my sample of Bristol wills almost all had extant inventories, so it was relatively simple to learn the value of their estates. Inventories have not survived for the singlewomen from Oxford or York, however, so I have made the best possible estimates of their worth based upon the legacies mentioned in their wills. These estimates are

single female testators were in service. Since some single female lenders left
estates worth less than £10, and given the sizable minority of moneylending
servants, it is obvious that wealth was not a prerequisite for never-married
women to loan money.

The amounts that singlewomen loaned also varied, but could be quite
significant. For example, Southampton had lenders such as the servant
Agnes Godwin, who had 7*s.* due to her, as well as Elizabeth Parkinson,
who advanced the significant amount of £210 to five different debtors.[51]
Until the recent case studies of women like Joyce Jeffries and Hester Pinney,
it was assumed that single female creditors only extended small loans.[52] The
urban singlewomen examined here reveal that Jeffries and Pinney were not
unusual in investing large sums. Over half (seven out of thirteen) of the
never-married women from Southampton who mentioned the value of
their credits had loaned between £50 and £210. This can be compared to
Bristol, where, out of twelve wills that listed amounts due to the testator,
five singlewomen had loaned out £10 or less, four women £40 or less, and
three had extended even larger sums. For instance, Susan Harmer's will
listed two bonds, one for £100 and one for £150, that her nephews owed
her. Unlike Southampton and Bristol, Oxford's single female testators did
not as a rule list the value of the debts owed to them, but the evidence for
York is better. Here singlewomen loaned out relatively more modest sums
than their counterparts in Bristol or Southampton: most (nine out of
sixteen) had £20 or less due to them. Nevertheless, even York boasted single
female lenders like Elizabeth Peacock, who in 1630 had loaned out over
£110.[53] To put the value of these loans in perspective, a female servant in an
early modern town would have earned about £3 a year, as well as room and
board (which would have doubled the value of her salary). This means that
a loan of between £50 and £100 was a significant sum of money for a
singlewoman in a provincial town to hold.

The single female lenders who appeared in Southampton's common
court also had loaned out substantial sums. If their loans were not repaid,
these women had the option to sue their debtors in the town's civil court.[54]

---

minimums; they do not include real estate or goods for which I could not venture a value, which
means that these women could have been worth more. I could determine an approximate value for
the estates of all but two (of the 22) single female testators in York. For Oxford, I could determine
approximate estate values for only half (9 out of 18) of the single female testators.

[51] HRO, 1584 AD 23 and 1601 AD 29/1.

[52] Women have been characterized as providers of small or 'domestic' loans. Erickson, *Women
and Property*, 81; Jordan, *Women and Credit*, 23.

[53] BIHR, Dean and Chapter Wills, vol. 41, fo. 346, Elizabeth Peacock (1630).

[54] SRO, SC 7/1/10–34. The majority of civil pleas heard in Southampton's common court were
suits of debt and trespass upon the case (debt suits that involved breaches of oral rather than written
contracts). In Southampton, nearly three-fourths (99 of 142) of all common court cases in which
singlewomen appeared were to recover debts.

Never-married women initiated debt suits for sums of money ranging from 20s. to £200. Most suits concerned substantial amounts, with only a handful of debt cases (five out of forty-five) involving sums below £10. The most common amounts that singlewomen tried to recover were £10, £20, £40, and £200. It is significant that these were substantial, rounded sums. This shows that never-married women who went to court were attempting to recover unpaid loans or legacies due to them, rather than sales credit or trade debts, which would have involved smaller and more random amounts.[55] In rare instances, the reason for a debt suit is explicit. For example, in 1676, when Joanne Meacham sued John Clements for money due to her, the court clerk helpfully recorded that the debt was a written obligation or bond between the two parties for £200.[56] Meacham and other singlewomen like her who advanced such substantial amounts were by no means small lenders.

Never-married women not only loaned out significant sums, they also often advanced large portions of their total estates. Although early modern England was a commercial economy, keeping cash on hand, or 'ready money' as it was called, was still a rarity. Most wealth was held in inaccessible forms, which meant that any person who did hold ready money could easily find a market for it. Amy Erickson has found that single persons held at least half of their worth in credit or cash, and my evidence indicates that urban singlewomen held an even higher proportion of their estates in this form.[57] For example, Mildred Arnold of Southampton died in 1667 with an estate worth approximately £93. Her property was comprised of apparel and linen, kitchenware, furniture, gold and silver money, some small, old books, and £74 in debts due to her; that is, a striking 79.6 per cent of her estate was in the form of money she had loaned out.[58] In 1601 Southampton appraisers valued Elizabeth Parkinson's property at a little over £274, of which £210 was in the form of outstanding loans.[59] The Bristol singlewoman Deborah James was worth £421 in 1672, £326 of which was money she had loaned out.[60] Over three-quarters of Parkinson's and James' estates were in the form of inaccessible investments. And it was not just middling-class women who tied up so much of their money. In 1682 the Southampton servant Elizabeth Morgan held a more modest estate worth £15, but a full £12 of it was due on bond from her brother.[61] Similarly, Elizabeth

---

[55] Peter Earle has suggested that historians count rounded sums secured by formal instruments (e.g. bonds) as loans rather than sales debt. Earle, *Making of the English Middle Class*, 362 and n. 19.
[56] SRO, SC 7/1/34.
[57] Erickson, *Women and Property*, 81 and n. 12.
[58] HRO, 1641 A100/1–2 and 1667 B1.
[59] HRO, 1601 AD29/1–2.
[60] BRO, W1672/29.
[61] HRO, 1682 B33.

Harrison of York died in 1728 with an estate valued at a little over £11, of which £1 was made up of apparel and ready money in her purse, and the remaining £10 was held in a promissory note.[62]

It is significant that singlewomen were able to loan out nearly all of their estates. Because they had few claims on their money (Elizabeth Parkinson lived with her mother and sisters, and Elizabeth Morgan resided with her brother) they were able to let others enjoy the use of it. This was very different from a widow, who usually had children, a household, and perhaps a business to support, and who needed more ready access to her money rather than tying it up in loans. For instance, a sample of thirty wills made by Southampton widows in the early modern period reveals that while widowed testators loaned out money as often as never-married ones, they did not loan out as much.[63] If a widow and a never-married woman held estates of roughly the same size, the widow did not loan out as large a proportion of her money as did the singlewoman. In Southampton widows loaned out an average of 42 per cent, or less than half, of their recorded wealth. This compares to the never-married women in the port town, who loaned out a full two-thirds of their estates.[64] Single female testators in other towns also loaned out more than the Southampton widows. In Bristol, the majority of singlewomen loaned out 58 per cent of their wealth and in York, two-thirds of such women tied up 70 per cent of their estates in loans.

Secondly, not only did singlewomen loan out more money than widows, they also borrowed money much less than widows did. Only 5 per cent of Southampton's single female testators borrowed money, compared to 20 per cent of widows who did so.[65] The pattern of singlewomen lending money only, and not borrowing, is apparent not only in probate documents but also in the records from Southampton's common court. The never-married women who appeared before this court were almost always (in forty-one out of forty-five cases) the plaintiffs in these debt suits. Singlewomen went to court because they loaned money; they were not taken to court for borrowing it. Widows, who were more likely to be supporting a family and practising a trade than were never-married women, had greater demands on

[62] BIHR, Dean and Chapter Wills, reel 1251, Elizabeth Harrison (1728/29).

[63] These 30 wills are a random sample derived from the 273 extant probate records made by Southampton widows between 1550 and 1750 that were proved in the courts of Winchester diocese. In all, 47% (or 14 out of 30) of Southampton widows had loaned money at the time of their deaths

[64] These figures are based on the wills of singlewomen and widows that mentioned the specific amount of debts due to them and for which there are surviving inventories that recorded the values of the women's estates.

[65] In the Southampton probate sample 3 widows both loaned and owed sums, and 3 widows solely borrowed money, as compared to only 2 singlewomen who both loaned and borrowed money and none who borrowed alone.

their capital, which meant they had less money to loan out and sometimes needed to borrow money themselves. Singlewomen, however, had more disposable income to invest in loans. If they loaned out more of their overall wealth and seldom had to borrow money, this suggests that never-married women were just as, if not more, significant to urban credit networks than were widows.

Not only did singlewomen distinguish themselves by the large amount of their estates that they had on loan, they also loaned out their money using new and formal means. Robert Tittler and Marjorie McIntosh have argued that moneylending in the early modern era was becoming more formalized and professional.[66] It appears that urban singlewoman were in the vanguard of this transformation. Probate documents reveal that never-married women most often loaned money through formal means, which allowed them both to document their loans and to detail the specifics of their investments. For example, the majority of single female lenders used written instruments to record their loans. They engaged in formal transactions that charged a fixed rate of interest, and specified a date for repayment as well as a penalty for non-payment.

In all four provincial towns discussed here, never-married women were prone to recording and thus formalizing their loans. Singlewomen in Oxford employed almost every written instrument available in the early modern era. For example, Sarah Peisley loaned money through bonds, bills, and notes of hand.[67] Bonds were written deeds in which debtors obliged themselves to pay their creditors a certain sum of money by a specific date, along with a fixed rate of interest.[68] Bills and notes of hand also were written (and thus legal) evidence of indebtedness. Other Oxford singlewomen, like Mary Barnes, mentioned debts and securities (documents held by a creditor as a guarantee of money due to them).[69] Compared to Oxford, never-married women in Southampton usually limited their loans to bonds or mortgages, the latter offering real property as collateral. Some were like Gracill Roberts, who had £100 due to her upon specialties (written contracts of debt that were under seal).[70] Single female lenders in York primarily utilized bonds and bills to record their loans. In 1728 Elizabeth Harrison also mentioned holding a promissory note for £10, this was akin to a note

---

[66] Both Marjorie McIntosh and Robert Tittler have argued that moneylending was becoming increasingly formalized by the end of the sixteenth century. Marjorie McIntosh, 'Money Lending on the Periphery of London, 1300–1600', *Albion*, 20: 4 (Winter 1988), 557–71; Tittler, 'Money-lending in the West Midlands', 250

[67] COS, W 100.59 Sarah Piesley (1786).

[68] *Oxford English Dictionary* (1993 online edition); Thomas Fitch, *Dictionary of Banking Terms* (New York: Barron's, 1990).

[69] COS, W 97.147 Mary Barnes (1768).

[70] HRO, 1643 AD43/1–3.

of hand and indicated a promise to pay a certain sum to the creditor. Singlewomen in Bristol were more specific in noting how they loaned money; they utilized bonds, bills obligatory, or securities.

These women's actions illustrate that single female lenders did not have flexible expectations about repayment. Rather, they established payment schedules and penalties for non-payment when they made a loan. For example, in seventeenth-century Southampton Amy Kempe loaned £100 by a written bond that stipulated that she would be paid £103 in six months (a rate of 6 per cent annual interest) or a penalty of £200 for non-payment.[71] Similarly, Elizabeth Cole, who died in Bristol in 1749, had put most of her money into two large loans for which she had arranged to receive interest at prescribed times. Her will carefully stated that her bequest to her mother should consist of 'the interest of £30 now at use, likewise the interest of £80 due from Mr. Haskins to be paid at quarterly payments of five per cent per annum'.[72] Through such written and specific means singlewomen ensured that they would be able to recoup their considerable investments in court if need be. And as we have seen, single female lenders in Southampton were not shy about going to court to recover money that was owed to them. The methods single female lenders employed indicate a level of financial savvy with which we often do not credit women in the early modern era. While singlewomen in provincial towns may not have been what we would term 'professional' moneylenders, this does not mean that they did not act professionally. We should not confuse the two.

Single female lenders in provincial towns provided loans to their urban communities and sometimes even farther afield. Studies of widowed and local moneylenders have shown that these women primarily extended credit to acquaintances, friends (especially females ones), and kin. While relatives also figured among singlewomen's loan recipients, the majority were friends, neighbours, and acquaintances (the majority of whom were male). For instance, the single female lenders in Bristol overwhelmingly made loans to men (ten out of twelve loans). In Oxford most single female testators did not name those persons who owed them money. Nevertheless, of the four who did mention their debtors, all loaned money to local men and one woman loaned money to a male cousin. In Southampton only about half of the single female testators specified to whom they had loaned funds. Of these, the majority mentioned men, an equal number of whom were local men and male relatives. Only one singlewoman listed a sister, and another mentioned a local woman. In York most single female testators were very particular about listing their debtors. The clear majority loaned

---

[71] SRO, SC 2/1/8, fo. 7ᵛ.
[72] BRO, transcript of Bristol wills proved between 1749 and 1751, vol. 1, p. 9.

money to men (eighteen of twenty-two loans). Eight of these male debtors lived locally in York, three resided in other communities, and seven others were male relatives.

The significance of urban singlewomen as moneylenders and investors is borne out not only by the loans these women advanced to private individuals, but also by the credit they supplied to the towns themselves. For example, throughout most of the seventeenth century Southampton's corporation borrowed money from its inhabitants to stay solvent. Town creditors first appeared in Southampton's assembly (or town council) books in the 1610s, and they continued through to the 1690s.[73] Their appearance coincided with the port town's most severe period of financial crisis. The seventeenth century saw a drastic drop in customs revenue, due to Southampton's declining position as a luxury and long-distance trading port and a severe depression in the new draperies cloth industry. Only when Southampton's fortunes began to improve at the end of the seventeenth century did the corporation cease to borrow from its inhabitants. Scholars of the European continent have noted the common nature of municipal borrowing in times of financial distress, but little work has been done on this phenomenon in English towns. This means we do not yet know if the practice was common in provincial towns other than Southampton.[74]

To be sure, Southampton turned to its substantial merchants and tradesmen in this moment of financial crisis. More surprisingly, the largest percentage of municipal creditors were singlewomen. Women described as 'spinsters' and 'daughters' (in this instance indicating women of marriageable age rather than minor children) made up anywhere between one-fourth to more than three-quarters of all lenders to the corporation over the seventeenth century. More importantly, they comprised an average of 48.6 per cent of the creditors throughout this period. This is in comparison to men, who averaged 28.1 per cent of the municipal lenders, and widows, who came in a distant third, averaging only 14.5 per cent of the corporation's creditors. The remaining 8.8 per cent of lenders was comprised of children of both sexes.[75] Never-married women were also consistent lenders to Southampton over the entire seventeenth century. This was in contrast to widows, who figured as municipal lenders in only five of the nine decades

[73] SRO, SC 2/1/6–9.

[74] Historians of continental Europe, such as W. K. Jordan and James Collins, have studied municipal borrowing, and especially women's role within it.

[75] SRO, SC 2/1/6, 8–9. These percentages are based on a sample of all of the town creditors listed in the assembly books from the time the lenders began to appear in the 1610s to when they disappeared in the 1690s. I sampled one year out of each decade between 1610 and 1700. Singlewomen made up 50% of all creditors listed in the 1610s; 25% of those in the 1620s; 25% of those in the 1630s; 44% of those in the 1640s; 30% of those in the 1650s; 80% of those in the 1660s; 69% of those in the 1670s; 60% of those in the 1680s; and 25% of those in the 1690s.

between 1610 and 1690. What could account for the predominance of never-married women among Southampton's municipal creditors?

One explanation for the significant number of single female creditors is that Southampton's corporation was functioning as a bank for orphan's portions. This was a common practice in other towns, such as London and Bristol, where courts of orphans claimed custody of both the orphaned children of freemen as well as their portions, which they then loaned out to private individuals. The investment of children's portions also occurred in smaller towns, such as Lincoln, Hull, and Burton. Amy Erickson has characterized such municipal lending 'as a civic service, and not as a profit-making venture'.[76] But Southampton's situation does not fit these models. First, the town only safeguarded children's portions when it was experiencing monetary pressures in the seventeenth century; in the centuries before and after there was no tradition of a dowry or portion bank. Secondly, adult men and women loaned money to Southampton's corporation as much as children had their portions loaned out for them. Southampton differed markedly from London, where the corporation's records show that only the legacies of minors were used as investment income.[77] While Southampton was not operating a dowry bank per se, girls were more likely than boys to receive their inheritance as a cash portion, so it stands to reason that the money singlewomen and their families invested was comprised of their cash portions. This may also explain why singlewomen rather than single men functioned as the primary creditors to Southampton's corporation.

Through the practice of municipal investment, Southampton's corporation obtained the use of considerable sums of money belonging to both minor and adult singlewomen. For example, in 1618 John Mullens, the stepfather of Sarah and Elizabeth Cornish, delivered their legacies of £15 each to the assembly.[78] Executors or kin might have felt the two daughters' portions were safer with the town than with their new stepfather, who could not be trusted to keep himself from taking money his predecessor had left to his two young, defenceless girls. The inheritances of the Cornish girls were at the more humble end of the spectrum of sums loaned to Southampton, although some portions advanced to the corporation were as low as £6 or £7. More typical were the £100 dowries belonging to Katherine, Anne, and Dorothy, the daughters of John Mayor, who, while he was still alive, invested these sums with the corporation.[79] Out of the sixty singlewomen who extended credit to Southampton's corporation,

---

[76] Erickson, *Women and Property*, 81–2.
[77] Corporation of London Record Office, Orphan's Fund Records.
[78] SRO, SC 2/1/6, fo. 182ᵛ.
[79] SRO, SC 2/1/6, fos. 186ᵛ, 210ᵛ, 229ᵛ.

fifteen loaned sums of less than £50, nineteen invested amounts between £50 and £100, and twenty-six gave sums of between £100 and £200. Most amounts loaned to the corporation were equal to £50, £100, or £200. Sums of this size indicate that it was the daughters of skilled craftsmen, shopkeepers, and merchants who most often bankrolled Southampton's corporation.[80]

Significantly, many of the singlewomen who loaned money to Southampton did so as adults, and of their own volition rather than their parents'. For example, in 1642 Amy Kempe loaned the town £100 at 6 per cent interest, and in 1645 Mary Heath invested £50 of her money in the corporation. The money Kempe and Heath loaned came out of their inheritances, but it was they, and not their families, who made the decision to lend this money out at interest. In addition, middle-aged and older singlewomen invested sums in the corporation and received annuities in return. For example, in 1659 the assembly sealed a bond of £160 to a 40-year-old singlewoman named Elizabeth Searle, promising to pay her a £10 annuity during her natural life. In the same year Elizabeth's slightly younger sister Ann loaned the town £50. Three years later the town assembly also promised Ann an annuity of £6. 10s. in return for the money she had loaned them. The corporation received a tidy sum up front from the two single sisters, but it may have come to rue these arrangements. Elizabeth Searle received her annuity for at least thirteen years (so the corporation may have made a few pounds off of her), but by 1679 they had to buy off her sister Ann's annuity for £40. 15s.[81] Over a period of seventeen years Ann Searle received the sum of £151. 5s. for an original loan of £50, thereby tripling her investment.[82] Southampton singlewomen of all ages were prominent in municipal investment because it provided an annuity or steady income on which a never-married woman could support herself.[83]

At the same time that singlewomen earned investment income they were also assisting their town and illustrating their importance among the local citizenry. Never-married women were often long-term investors in Southampton's corporation, loyally loaning their money for periods of up to thirty-one years. These lengthy investments were partly attributable to parents investing their minor daughters' portions until they turned 21 or married. When a singlewoman reached the age of majority, or married, she

---

[80] For the average inheritances of urban daughters, see Erickson, *Women and Property*, 87–9.

[81] SRO, SC 2/1/8, fos. 7ᵛ, 19, 148ᵛ, 183ᵛ, 283ᵛ, and SC 2/1/9, 17.

[82] Local and central governments desperate for money often abandoned schedules based on the age of an investor when offering annuities to female creditors. Jordan, *Women and Credit*, 74.

[83] This was also true on the continent; however, Collins found that widows were the women who most commonly participated in municipal and government lending in France. Collins, 'Economic Role of Women', 456–7, Jordan, *Women and Credit*, 71–6.

could claim her money. In fact the circumstance most likely to lead a never-married woman to call in her debts from the corporation was marriage. Out of the sixty singlewomen who loaned money to Southampton's corporation in the seventeenth century, thirty-three remained single the entire time their money was on loan, while another sixteen married during this time.[84] Almost all of the women who married (thirteen out of sixteen) cancelled their bonds within two years of marriage.[85] Those adult women who did not marry kept their investment in the corporation of their own volition. For example, Elizabeth Odber had her bond reissued in her own name when she reached the age of majority; in Odber's case she made the decision to leave her money with the town for another ten years after her bond was put into her own name in 1681.[86] Odber illustrates how, even if a parent or guardian had made the original loan, many singlewomen chose to keep their money invested in the town, and they were the ones who ultimately decided how long the corporation enjoyed their credit.

Singlewomen like Elizabeth Odber loaned their money to Southampton's corporation for decades at a time because it seemed a good investment. In the early seventeenth century single female creditors earned as much as 8 per cent on these municipal bonds. From the 1630s onward they received 6 per cent interest, a rate that was at or near the maximum established by parliamentary statute.[87] The interest from a municipal investment was greater than that from a private one, which hovered at around 5 per cent.

This shows a level of financial savvy among Southampton's singlewomen, but perhaps no story better illustrates this than that of Mary Stevens. As a single, pregnant woman, the assembly warned Stevens to depart from Southampton in 1637. Instead, Stevens offered to put the generous sum of £30 in the corporation's hands to discharge them of any expenses that she and her future child might incur. Mary Stevens continued to negotiate her circumstances. Three months later not only had the town's officials given back a third of her money, but they had also agreed to pay her 6 per cent interest on the remaining £20.[88] Here was an unwed mother, perhaps in the

---

[84] A further 11 women appeared only once in the assembly books, so there is no indication of whether they remained single or married during the duration of their investment.

[85] Two other women had their loans paid back within three or four years of marriage, while one woman who married waited seven years to cancel her bond.

[86] SRO, SC 2/1/6, fo. 308ᵛ and SC 2/1/9, 33.

[87] The interest paid by Southampton's corporation was close to the statutory maximum. In 1571 parliament had begun to condone usury by establishing the precedent of fixing a maximum interest rate. The first maximum interest rate was 10%, falling to 8% in 1624, to 6% in 1652, and to 5% in 1713. Norman Jones, *God and the Moneylenders: Usury and Law in Early Modern England* (Oxford: Basil Blackwell, 1989), 19, 63, 79, 174; Erickson, *Women and Property*, 81 and n. 13; C. G. A. Clay, *Economic Expansion and Social Change: England 1500–1700*, 2 vols. (New York: Cambridge University Press, 1984), ii. 274, 278–9, 281.

[88] SRO, SC 2/1/6, fo. 294ᵛ.

most vulnerable position a woman in the early modern period could find herself, who managed to turn dire straits into an investment opportunity!

Not all singlewomen (or anyone else for that matter) had the bravado of Mary Stevens. Some never-married women, knowing that they had only themselves to depend on for support, were looking for safe and certain investments. Such women may have left their money with the corporation because they viewed municipal lending as a secure investment.[89] Unfortunately, as time would tell, entrusting one's inheritance to the town of Southampton was not always the safest move. In 1688 Southampton's charter of incorporation was renewed under King James II. It seems that the town officials took advantage of this situation to back out of any contracts they had made under the former charter. In June of 1688 six persons from Southampton sent a petition to the attorney-general in London. The petitioners consisted of three singlewomen, two widows (one of whom had originally loaned money to the town when she was single), and one man, whose loans had not been paid back. Not only was the town reneging on women without husbands, but one of the single-women was Dorothy Schreckenfox, who was both deaf and dumb and whose physician father was deceased. In their petition the six stated that their friends had originally 'lent their portions to the Mayor, Bailiffs, and Burgesses of Southampton at interest, taking bonds under the town seal, and [they had been] informed that on renewing the charter the new Mayor, etc., will refuse to pay them their interest or principal'.[90] They asked that a clause be inserted into the new charter requiring the payment of bonds that were signed under the former charter.

The women's petition was partially successful. The corporation did end up honouring the debts of the six petitioners to some extent; however, they did not pay back the obligations in full. In 1691 Elizabeth Odber, one of the protesting singlewomen, received £100 from the corporation in full discharge of a debt of £383. 6s. 8d. In other words, Odber received about only one-fourth of the money owed to her. Two years later Dulcibella Matthews, a woman who had loaned several sums of money to the corporation over a period of thirty-one years, spanning her single, married, and widowed life, received only £60 toward the £125 debt owed her.[91] South-ampton did little to repay the civic consciousness of women like Matthews, who had kept their money invested in the corporation for decades. Perhaps,

[89] Historians such as William Jordan assume (but have not proven) that women in the early modern era were probably not risk-takers and that they desired safe investments. While investing in municipalities was more risky than investing in real estate, it was less so than investing in trade. Jordan, *Women and Credit*, 69, 71, 73.

[90] *Calendar of State Papers, Domestic Series, of the Reign of James II, 1687–1689*, 3 (London: HM Stationery Office, 1972), 219.

[91] SRO, SC 2/1/9, 182, 202.

in retrospect, this was not a wise investment. But all investments involve risk, and singlewomen like Elizabeth Odber and Dulcibella Matthews took the prudent steps available to them to minimize that risk. They invested where their parents had, they were wise enough to use written bonds to record their loans, and they were not afraid to petition the central government when they felt that Southampton's officials were treating them unfairly.

It is perhaps not an accident that it was singlewomen, the very persons who had bankrolled Southampton for the better part of the seventeenth century, who found themselves on the wrong end of a bad investment in 1688. The town assembly singled out unmarried women for less than creditable treatment, for none of the men who invested in the town received less than their due when they cancelled their bonds in the late seventeenth century. Southampton's corporation was more than happy to take the money of singlewomen, but it seemed uneasy about being indebted to such women. By loaning money and assisting Southampton, these women provided an implicit challenge to patriarchy—the town fathers needed the help of singlewomen to run the town. Although the men who ran Southampton might want to deny it, some of the town's most useful citizens were women, and single ones at that.

Female Citizens

The singlewomen who held real property, loaned money, and invested in England's provincial towns performed important civic roles. As independent householders, never-married women, like married men and widows, also paid the taxes and rates that were the life's blood of any municipality. In addition, middling singlewomen were significant philanthropists in their urban communities. Never-married women were also aware of how they contributed to civic life. The poet Jane Barker wrote of how singlewomen like herself aided their churches, neighbours, and communities:

> The neighboring poor are her adopted heirs,
> And less she cares, for her own good than theirs.
>   And by obedience testifies she can
>   Be's good a subject as the stoutest man.
>   She to her church, such filial duty pays,
> That one wou'd think she'd lived ith' pristine days.
> Her whole lives business, she drives to these ends,
> To serve her god, her neighbour, and her friends.[92]

---

[92] Jane Barker, 'A Virgin Life', in *Poetical Recreations* (London, 1688).

In this section I look at never-married women's participation as urban citizens. I argue that, as middling singlewomen took on more civic duties, they also demanded the privileges of citizenship. In particular, I explore the political roles that these women began to exercise based on their status as householders, property holders, and tax- and ratepayers. Over the early modern era Englishwomen, single ones especially, attempted to exercise their political voice through office-holding, voting, and oath-taking.

Never-married women of the middling sort took up an increasing proportion of the urban tax and rate burden over the seventeenth and eighteenth centuries. For instance, singlewomen who owned and leased property in Southampton began to pay more taxes in the 1700s. In All Saints Infra parish, ninety-two people paid land tax in 1729; eight were female, and three of them were single. By 1754 the number of overall taxpayers in the parish had dropped to sixty-seven, but the number of women had risen to twenty, three of whom were single. This means that never-married women rose from 3 to 5 per cent of the taxpayers in All Saints Infra parish between 1729 and 1754. In St Michael's parish the story was the same. In 1729, 188 people paid land tax; thirty-six were women, and four of them were single. By 1754 there were 179 taxpayers in St Michael's parish, thirty-one of who were women, but now ten (or one-third) of them were single. Over the first half of the eighteenth century singlewomen rose from 2 to 6 per cent of the taxpayers in this parish: a threefold increase. Although these numbers are small, they do illustrate the growing proportion of singlewomen who contributed to the tax base in Southampton.[93]

Never-married women who held property in Southampton not only paid taxes, they also contributed to parish poor rates. From at least the 1730s onward, singlewomen figured prominently among those who paid for the upkeep of the poor and contributed to the repair of parish churches. For instance, the All Saints Parish Rate Book lists four singlewomen paying rates between 1743 and 1746; while the Holy Rood Rate Book for 1732–50 includes up to eleven never-married women paying assessments. And when St Michael's church was repaired in 1741–2, six singlewomen contributed between 2s. and 12s. on an assessment of 2s. to the pound.[94] Southampton's local authorities were holding singlewomen of the middling sort accountable for duties commonly reserved for urban householders or property holders.

The philanthropy of never-married women did not stop at compulsory rate giving. Mary Sibron, a female property holder in Southampton, involved herself in the distribution of poor relief to the local Huguenot

[93] SRO, SC 14/2/1–370, *passim*.
[94] SRO, SC/AG 8/3/1; SC/AG 8/6/1; PR 7/5/1.

congregation's female members. She transferred an annuity of £80 to the church for the use of these women.[95] While it was common for individuals to leave bequests of a few pounds to the poor of the parish or to their parish church, Louise Bretin left much more to Southampton's Huguenot church. She bequeathed £36 in her will, £20 of which went to the congregation.[96] Charity to Nonconformist churches was not just limited to never-married women in Southampton. In 1709 the diarist Celia Fiennes endowed the Nonconformist chapel at Barnet in Hertfordshire, and in her 1738 will she left her residual estate to the fund for Dissenting country ministers.[97] Singlewomen were also likely to leave money to schools and to set up homes for needy persons. For instance, Sarah Gledhill bequeathed £200 (or one-fourth of her estate) to establish a school for poor children in Barkisland (Yorks.).[98] Men and widows also bequeathed money to religious and educational causes in their wills, but singlewomen were unique in directing charity to women who shared their marital status. For instance, in 1736 Elizabeth Daniel of Oxford left the profits of £5 a year to clothe six poor widows or 'old maids'.[99] In the town of Lancaster, Mrs Anne Gillison, a 'maiden lady' aged 71, bequeathed £100 to the Lancaster Dispensary, the same amount to the town's charity school for girls, and another £50 each to the infirmaries in Manchester and Liverpool. More importantly, she left the enormous sum of £1,600 to build and endow houses for eight distressed 'old maids'.[100] But it is York that yields the most examples of single female philanthropy from the early modern period. Here women such as Mary Fothergill left money to a charity girls school, Anne Wright bequeathed one of her houses for a freeman's widow or single daughter to live in rent free, and Edith Park endowed a house for two poor spinsters or widows.[101]

These examples illustrate the kind of economic impact that never-married women of means could make on provincial towns. Singlewomen with property propped up the tax base, and those with disposable income provided much-needed capital, in the form of loans and charity. But

[95] Edwin Welch (ed.), *The Minute Book of the French Church at Southampton 1702–1939*, Southampton Record Series, 23 (Southampton, 1980), 74.

[96] HRO, W 1692.

[97] Christopher Morris (ed.), *The Journeys of Celia Fiennes* (London: Cresset Press, 1949), appendix.

[98] John William Clay, *Abstracts of Yorkshire Wills in the Time of the Commonwealth*, Yorkshire Archaeological and Topographical Society, 4 (Worksop: The Society, 1890).

[99] Oxfordshire Record Office, W 206.57, Elizabeth Daniel (1710); Alan Crossley (ed.), *A History of the County of Oxford*, Vol. 4: *The City of Oxford* (Oxford: Oxford University Press, 1979), 471.

[100] *Gentleman's Magazine*, 60: 1 (Jan. 1790), 87.

[101] BIHR, Dean and Chapter Wills, reel 1250, Mary Fothergill (1718), reel 1245, Anne Wright, (1670), reel 1244, Edith Park (1664).

urban authorities were faced with a double-edged sword. Requiring single-women to perform the duties of urban citizens was implicitly acknowledging their economic and civic power. Citizens not only had duties, they also earned privileges.

In the early modern period contemporaries increasingly recognized female property holders and householders as part of the urban citizenry. In London those who paid the local rates, such as scot and lot or watch and ward, were free of the city and enjoyed certain duties and privileges. We normally associate the freedom with those who were members of gilds, but these examples remind us that individuals also earned it through ownership of freehold property, whether by inheritance or purchase, and through paying local rates and taxes.[102] While some towns recognized as urban citizens the singlewomen who headed households, held property, and paid taxes, others tried to deny never-married women this status. For example, in the sixteenth-century borough of Maidstone, Kent, a singlewoman named Rose Cloke was admitted to be 'one of the corporation and body politique of the same town and parish, from henceforth to enjoy the liberties and franchise of the same in every respect, as others the freemen of the said town'. But in 1621 the town of Leicester decided that 'neither is it thought fit that any woman be hereafter made free of the corporation'.[103]

One of the privileges (and duties) of holding freehold property was to serve in various capacities as well as hold local office. Once we start looking, it is possible to find many examples of female freeholders who were expected to attend county courts where free suitors chose the knights of the shire and sat on grand juries. While the common-law theorist Sir Edward Coke later said this was not expected of female freeholders, he provided no authority or precedent for his opinion.[104] Women also served as constables, churchwardens, overseers of the poor, and reeves by right of residence or tenancy. Such women attended and voted in local meetings of the parish vestry.[105] It seems likely (but has not been fully interrogated) that a woman had to be a *feme sole* to hold office. It is also possible that most female officeholders were the widows and daughters

---

[102] Charlotte C. Stopes, *British Freewomen: Their Historical Privilege* (London: S. Sonnenschein & Co., 1894), 77, 84, 86–7.

[103] Ibid. 89–90.

[104] Ibid. 61, 64–7; Hilda Smith, 'Women as Sextons and Electors: King's Bench and Precedents for Women's Citizenship', in her *Women Writers and the Early Modern British Political Tradition* (New York: Cambridge University Press, 1998), 336.

[105] Karl von Den Steinen, 'The Discovery of Women in Eighteenth-Century Political Life', in (ed.), Barbara Kanner *The Women of England From Anglo-Saxon Times to the Present* (Hamden, Conn.: Archon Books, 1979), 241; Smith, 'Women as Sextons', 324–42.

of elite men, who inherited real property and its associated duties before quickly passing them on to another male. What is less clear is if office-holding was something a woman, especially a singlewomen, did in her own right.

Female office-holding was something that opened the door to female voting. Contemporaries seem to have viewed office-holding by women as more acceptable than voting, most likely because there was already a precedent of women holding many private offices. Office-holding by women (of all marital states) was upheld in a 1739 legal case heard before the King's Bench. In addition to allowing women to hold office, *Olive* v. *Ingram* also established that a woman who was *feme sole* might both hold a local office such as church sexton and vote for that office. The judges based their decision on various factors and precedents, such as women paying scot and lot, or local rates and parish assessments. While the justices doubted the sense of women voting because of their 'supposedly limited judgment in public matters', they did at least acknowledge the possibility.[106]

The ability of women to vote was also based on their holding personal or real property, and in boroughs it was based on paying local rates or trading. As early as 1617 the case of *Holt* v. *Lyle* had affirmed that a *feme sole* with a freehold could vote for a parliament man.[107] In 1720 the local governors of Dorchester stipulated that 'the right of electing burgesses to serve in Parliament for the borough of Dorchester is in the inhabitants of the borough paying to church and poor in respect of their personal estates and in such persons as pay to church and poor in respect of their real estates within the said borough'.[108] In other words, those persons who resided in Dorchester, and who paid parish and poor rates, according to how much personal or real estate they held, had the right to vote for their representative to parliament. Nevertheless, legal theory was often at odds with urban customs and reality; and it was the latter that impacted women more. As Karl von Den Steinen has asserted for the eighteenth century: 'The exclusion of women from the franchise rested on shaky legal grounds at best, and women theoretically held more rights in eighteenth-century England than they usually exercised. The absence of women from the eighteenth-century electorate rested primarily upon social constraints rather than legal prohibitions.'[109]

---

[106] Smith, 'Women as Sextons', 324–42.
[107] Stopes, *British Freewomen*, 95–6.
[108] Charles Herbert Mayo and Arthur William Gould, *The Municipal Records of the Borough of Dorchester* (Exeter: William Pollard, 1908), 439.
[109] Den Steinen, 'The Discovery of Women', 240.

There were moments when singlewomen chose to test legal theory and exercise their right to vote based on their status as property holders. For example, in the 1640 election of two knights of the shire from Suffolk to the Long Parliament, a number of never-married women in Ipswich took it upon themselves to vote. This was a contested election in which the high sheriff, Sir Simon D'Ewes, was accused by the Royalist Sir Roger North of favouring the Puritan candidates. A clerk explained the incident:

Tis true that by the ignorance of some of the clarkes at the other two tables the oaths of some *singlewomen that were freeholders* were taken without the knowledge of the said High Sheriff who as soon as he had notice thereof instantly sent to forbid the same, conceiving it a matter very unworthy of any gentleman and most dishonorable in such an election to make use of their voices *although they might in law have been allowed* nor did the said High Sheriff allow of the said votes . . . [but] cast them out.[110]

What is significant about this episode is not that single female property holders failed to have their voices heard, but that they tried to vote at all, and that the sheriff admitted that by law women who controlled freehold property were allowed to do so. Nevertheless, legal right and social practice were not one and the same. The sheriff both forbade these singlewomen to cast their votes and deemed their doing so dishonourable. He did not, as one might assume, call into question the honour of the women who voted; rather, he singled out the men who had presumably made 'use of their voices'. In the sheriff's mind no woman was capable of performing such a civic act on her own volition, or had enough knowledge to do so. Unfortunately, we do not know if his was a correct assumption.

The participation of women in the Suffolk election was not entirely unique. In the same 1640 election Sir Thomas Littleton filled the polling place in Worcestershire with 'boyes, women, and poore people'. Almost forty years later, at an election in Richmond in 1678, women were not allowed to vote directly but were allowed to assign their votes to male deputies.[111] These three examples provide us with a tantalizing glimpse into a little-known arena of female political activity. The only reason we know women tried to vote in the two elections of 1640 is because in disputed elections voters' names were recorded. Unfortunately, we do not know if

---

[110] British Library, Harleian MS. 158, fo. 286a. I am grateful to Cynthia Herrup for bringing this source to my attention. Also see Stopes, *British Freewomen*, 102. Italics are my own.

[111] Sara Mendelson and Patricia Crawford, *Women in Early Modern England, 1550–1720* (Oxford, 1998), 347, 396.

female property holders also exercised their legal right to vote in undisputed elections, but it is a distinct possibility.

While the singlewomen who attempted to vote in seventeenth-century elections were not successful, never-married women were able to exercise their citizenship by signing political oaths. Emphasizing the political nature of such acts, Sara Mendelson and Patricia Crawford have referred to oath-taking as 'covenantal suffrage'.[112] Such suffrage became more common for women over the early modern era. For instance, women sometimes appeared among those who took the Protestation of Faith of 1641/2 and vowed to maintain and defend with their 'life, power, and estate, the true Reformed Protestant Religion...against all Popery and Popish Innovations'. There was some ambiguity over who was to make the Protestation. In some areas, such as West Sussex, the term 'inhabitants' was construed as male. Here all office-holders, as well as all males aged 18 and over, made the Protestation at their local church (few actually signed the returns; instead, a clerk subscribed the names). But women were not required to exhibit their loyalty to Protestantism.[113] In the Palatine of Durham, however, office-holders as well as all the inhabitants, both householders and others above the age of 18, were expected to take the Protestation oath. Durham's officers were following parliament's instructions, which did not specify that only 'males' should make the oath. While women do appear in the Durham and Northumberland returns, they are not numerous. In Auckland St Andrew parish, for instance, four women signed their names along with fifty-two men. Three of these women appear to have been either single or widowed, and one woman was recorded as a widow.[114] David Cressy has found that 'female subscription [to the Protestation Oath] occurred occasionally in more than half a dozen parishes' throughout the country. For example, in West Shefford (Berks.) and St Mabyn and St Tudy (Cornwall) equal numbers of men and women took the Protestation. And in Lettcomb Bassett (Berks.) two singlewomen refused to make the Protestation (proof that some localities expected women to do so), 'professing themselves to be but simple unlearned maidens'.[115]

My findings for Oxfordshire indicate that it was more common for women to make the Protestation than Cressy asserts, although female

---

[112] Ibid. 399.

[113] R. Garraway Rice (ed.), *West Sussex Protestation Returns 1641–2*, Sussex Record Society, 5 (Lewes: Farncombe & Co., 1906); A. J. Howard (ed.), *The Devon Protestation Returns 1641* (Pinner: A. J. Howard, 1973).

[114] *Durham Protestations*, Surtees Society, 135 (Durham & London: Andrews & Co., 1922).

[115] David Cressy, 'The Protestation Protested, 1641 and 1642', *Historical Journal*, 45: 2 (2002), 272.

inclusion still varied widely by parish. For instance, out of the 151 oath-takers in Asthall parish, an astonishing 45 per cent (or sixty-eight persons) were women. The marital state of these women was not recorded, but the officials listed only eight women following men with the same surnames (suggesting that they were the men's wives or daughters), and recorded women largely as a second group. The churchwardens of Cockthorpe, Hardwicke, and Yelford were more detailed, recording twenty-four wives, eight widows, and what appear to be twelve singlewomen out of the eighty-six inhabitants above the age of 18 who took the oath. Here women made up about half of those persons making the Protestation, and wives comprised over half of the female oath-takers. In parishes such as Longe Combe, Steeple Barton, and Minster Lovell the proportions of men and women taking the oath were also fairly equal. The officials in South Leigh parish listed inhabitants by family group, which makes it somewhat easier to ascertain marital status. Out of 148 inhabitants who made the Protestation, half (or seventy-three) were women, of whom fourteen were single, six were widowed, sixteen were either single or widowed, and thirty-seven were married. Nevertheless, there were Oxfordshire hundreds, such as Banbury, Binfield, and Bloxham, where no women at all appeared among the oath-takers.[116]

The Protestation Returns of the 1640s reveal that female oath-taking was a legal grey area and varied by locality. When women did take the oath, it was not just as *femes soles*, for married women were just as likely to do so as unmarried ones. This suggests that the Protestation was not something a man could make for his wife. If it was a political oath he would have been able to do so, but the Protestation was fundamentally a religious oath. Men were legally and politically responsible for their wives, but female and male Christians were equal in the eyes of God, and had to act according to their own consciences. This interpretation is backed up by the inclusion of women in oaths with both religious and political connotations, such as the Vow and Covenant, the Solemn League and Covenant, the Engagement, and the 1696 Association Oath.[117]

The question of whether women also took oaths of a more political nature, such as pledges of loyalty to specific monarchs, is less studied. There are few extant oaths of allegiance. One that exists from the North Riding of Yorkshire reveals that in this locality only men pledged their

[116] Christopher S. A. Dobson (ed.), *Oxfordshire Protestation Returns 1641–2*, Oxfordshire Record Society (Banbury: Cheney, 1955).
[117] I would like to thank Ted Vallance for bringing the inclusion of women in these oaths to my attention. I have only found a few widows listed in the Association Oath Rolls taken in the British Colonies. Wallace Gandy (ed.), *The Association Oath Rolls of the British Plantations, 1696* (London: privately printed, 1922).

loyalty to the monarchs William and Mary, Anne, and George I (except for one widow who seems to have been standing in for her husband, a local office-holder).[118] By contrast, Sarah, duchess of Marlborough, and other ladies in the princess's household did sign a loyalty oath to William III in 1696. These women pledged their loyalty, however, not because of their gender or social status but due to their status as office-holders at Court.[119] The question is, did ordinary women in towns also pledge their loyalty to the monarch? It appears that some urban women in the eighteenth century did.

Southampton boasts one of the few extant and complete loyalty oaths from the period. In the months of October through December 1723 the citizenry of the port town signed their names to an oath professing loyalty to King George I and denouncing the Pretender to the throne, James III. Among the 492 signers of the oath were 186 women, meaning that nearly 38 per cent of those who professed their political loyalty were female.[120] Such a finding flies in the face of accepted wisdom that only those who held or might potentially hold secular and ecclesiastical office (in other words, men) needed to profess loyalty to the monarch and sign such a political document. In Southampton women numbered among the citizens with a political voice.

The women who signed Southampton's loyalty oath were primarily *femes soles*. The oath did not indicate marital status, but I have been able to identify it for 124 of the 141 female signees. These women were either singlewomen or widows, women who as *femes soles* were allowed to represent themselves. Out of these 124 women, sixty-one were single, forty were widowed, and a further twenty-three were either singlewomen or widows. Never-married female signees outnumbered those who were widowed three to two. These two groups of women pledged their loyalty in proportion to their numbers in the larger adult female population.[121] This was exceedingly rare. Despite their smaller numbers, widows almost always outnumbered singlewomen in other early modern sources that recorded heads of household, workers, or property holders.

Who were the Southampton singlewomen who pledged their loyalty to George I? First, most had advanced to their middling or older years. Never-married women of all ages did sign the oath. For instance, the

[118] Revd J. C. Atkinson (ed.), *Quarter Sessions Records*, North Riding Record Society, 8 and 9 (London: The Society, 1884).

[119] Mendelson and Crawford, *Women in Early Modern England*, 371.

[120] SRO, SC 9/1/24.

[121] In the 1696 Marriage Duty assessments for Southampton, adult singlewomen comprised between 25.7 and 34.6% of the adult female population, while widows made up between 16.3 and 25.2% (the remaining 8.9% were either singlewomen or widows and 49.1% were wives). This means singlewomen outnumbered widows about 3 to 2.

youngest signee I have identified was Ann Fleet, the daughter of the prosperous clothworker Christopher Fleet, and later a property owner in her own right. As Fleet was baptized on 7 January 1705/6, she was just shy of 18 years old in the autumn of 1723, suggesting a minimum age of 18 for the signers of the oath. But most female signees were not as young as Ann Fleet. Older singlewomen outnumbered their younger counterparts, with nearly 75 per cent of them in their middle or old age (mid-thirties onward). There was a reason why most of these signers were older. Age granted all women, single ones included, authority, and in this case political clout. But there were also practical reasons that explain the age of the women who pledged their loyalty. Older women who had never married were more likely to head households, hold property, lend money, dispense charity, and pay taxes and rates than were younger singlewomen. This was because never-married women either inherited property and businesses in their middle or old age when their parents and older kin died, or because they had purchased property and built up businesses by their later years. It was precisely these older singlewomen who would have numbered among the significant urban citizens for whom it was necessary to profess loyalty.

The singlewomen who signed Southampton's loyalty oath were advantaged by wealth and status as much as by age. For instance, over one-half of the single female signees were property holders, businesswomen, or members of prominent families in the town. Of the sixty-one never-married women who pledged their loyalty, twenty-two held property in Southampton, and six of these women also paid Stall and Art to trade in the town. Seventeen of the sixty-one singlewomen who signed their name to the oath shared a surname with a Southampton burgess or office-holder in Southampton—the elite men of the town. An additional thirteen never-married women had male kin admitted as free commoners in the town. Such men were all prosperous artisans, including a number of clothworkers, a few cordwainers, a cutler, an ironmonger, and a carpenter. The singlewomen related to freemen were more likely to hold property than the never-married women related to burgesses. This seems to indicate that the relatively lower social status of these women was offset by their property holding status.

Literacy was also an indicator of the status of the never-married women who pledged their loyalty in 1723. Only twelve of the sixty-one single-women signed the oath with a mark rather than with a signature. This suggests a literacy rate of 80 per cent for the single female signees, evidence that these women were of middling to elite status. This number can be compared to twenty-one out of forty widows who made their mark on the loyalty oath. Because only 20 per cent of singlewomen signed with a mark while over half of the widows did so, the never-married women who took the oath seem to have been significantly more literate than the widows. This was despite the fact that the widows who signed the oath came from substantial families and held property as well. This might suggest that singlewomen had to be of higher status than widows to earn the privilege of political oath-taking; or it could indicate that never-married women, who did not have husbands to aid them with their businesses and investments, had more of a need to be literate.

The mature and middling-status singlewomen who comprised the majority of the women who signed the 1723 oath of loyalty reveal that such women had a political voice in Southampton by the early eighteenth century. We can compare this to the situation in York, which also boasts an extant and complete oath of allegiance for 1723.[122] While 492 people took the oath in Southampton, approximately 1,538 people did so in York. These numbers are not surprising, since York was a much larger provincial centre. Another difference was that more women signed the oath of loyalty in York than in Southampton. In Southampton 186 of the 492 signers were women (or 37.8 per cent), compared to York, where 684 of the 1,538 signers were women (or 44.5 per cent). And while almost half of the signees in York were female, fewer of the women were single; 186 (or 27.2 per cent) of the oath-takers were singlewomen. This compares to Southampton, where between sixty-one and eighty-four (or between 43.3 and 59.6 per cent) of the 141 female signees were singlewomen. In Southampton *femes soles*, especially those who were never married, were the majority of female signees. In York *femes soles* also dominated, but in this city it was widows who outnumbered singlewomen. Widowed signees made up 253 (or 37 per cent) of the 685 women on the oath rolls. Also in York, where proportionately more women pledged their loyalty, married women were much more a part of the oath rolls than in Southampton. Of the 684 female signees, 232 (or 33.9 per cent) were listed as 'the wife of so and so', whereas in Southampton only a handful of women seem to have been wives. It is worth noting that the marital status of the York women was more clearly delineated in the oath rolls than in Southampton. All but thirteen (or 1.9 percent) of the women had the designation of spinster, widow, or wife following their name. In sum, the majority of women who claimed a political voice in Southampton were singlewomen, followed by widows and wives; while in York it was widows, followed by wives and singlewomen. And in both towns singlewomen comprised somewhere between over one-fourth and one-half of female oath-takers.

What is significant about Southampton and York's oaths of loyalty is the sheer number of women who signed an oath of a political (rather than a religious) nature. This was a political statement open only to legal adults

[122] York City Archives, YCA F12.

and heads of household. The inclusion of certain townswomen in an oath of loyalty indicates that these women enjoyed some civic status. Not every adult inhabitant was included among the oath-takers. In Southampton only about 28 per cent of adult inhabitants pledged their loyalty. The proportion of singlewomen in the population who pledged theirs was a bit lower, between 21 and 23 per cent.[123] Where town officials drew the line between those who needed to profess their loyalty and those who were unimportant in civic terms is difficult to say. And it cannot be ruled out that the oath may have been a voluntary gesture, with anyone who wished to do so being allowed to sign. Nevertheless, the track record of urban authorities suggests that they left little to chance when it came to never-married women in their towns. Rather, it seems that by the eighteenth century the townspeople of Southampton and York included a select group of singlewomen among the prominent citizenry of the town. Such civic recognition was unprecedented in the early modern era.

The inclusion of women among the takers of political oaths in the early eighteenth-century is significant in that it goes against the prevailing theories that there was a decline in women's political involvement after the Civil Wars, and that arguments were hardening against the voting rights of women in the 1690s.[124] These oaths reveal that in some provincial towns the political role of unmarried women was increasing rather than declining in the early eighteenth century. We need more research on the political activity of middling and urban women to assess whether our assumptions have been wrong. Marital status may once again be the critical factor here. The political and civic involvement of singlewomen seems to have been increasing, even if that of married women was under attack.

This chapter has shown that if a woman never married it was far better for her, both personally and publicly, to have some money. As Jane Austen's eponymous heroine put it in *Emma*, 'it is poverty only which makes celibacy contemptible to a generous public! A single woman, with a very narrow income, must be a ridiculous, disagreeable, old maid! . . . but a single woman, of good fortune, is always respectable.' Not only did money make an urban singlewoman respectable, it allowed her to play an important civic role. The popular notion of the female citizen's role was to (re)produce

---

[123] It is uncertain what Southampton's population was in 1723, but the Marriage Duty assessments of 1696 record a figure of 3,001, which included 1,751 adults. This means the 492 oath-takers would have constituted about 28% of Southampton's adult population. Southampton's Marriage Duty assessments also included between 286 and 371 adult singlewomen. Since between 61 and 84 singlewomen signed the oath, this was somewhere between 21 to 23 % of the never-married women in Southampton.

[124] See Lois G. Schwoerer, 'Women and the Glorious Revolution', *Albion*, 8: 2 (1986), 195–218.

children and care for the family. A never-married woman could not fulfill this, but she could be a useful citizen in other ways. She could establish a business or manage property, lend money, pay taxes, assist the poor, and in all these ways prove her worth to herself and her community. Single female householders, rentiers, moneylenders, and philanthropists were important members of their communities, performing the same functions that made a man an upstanding citizen.

And yet such women were not always recognized or appreciated for their usefulness. Towns such as Southampton were happy to let singlewomen pay taxes, care for the poor, and even bankroll the corporation, but their gratitude was not always evident. Just because Southampton's officers did not appreciate the assistance of the never-married women who lived in their town, however, does not mean that they went unappreciated in their families, neighbourhoods, and churches. It is difficult to uncover the standing an average person held in their community in the early modern era, especially when that person was single and female, but we do know that money bought power, if not authority, in this period, and the never-married women examined here did enjoy some of that. Sometimes this power was translated into political terms, as when the mature and middling-status singlewomen of Southampton and York joined with the men and widows in these towns to pledge their loyalty to their king. A person's loyalty was only needed if they had the money and clout to cause problems if they chose to be disloyal. Never-married women of property were among those citizens whose loyalty mattered, both to the king and to their urban communities.

Up until recently studies of singlewomen have largely focused on them as dependants (servants) or as agents of public disorder (prostitutes, fornicators, and bastard-bearers). How much of this focus reflects what early modern town fathers wanted us to see? This chapter reveals that urban singlewomen could also be independent, knowledgeable, and prosperous property holders and creditors, as well upstanding citizens who had much to contribute to their localities. Why have we overlooked the civic and economic contribution of never-married women in the early modern era for so long? Perhaps it is because the stereotypes of dependent, useless 'spinsters' and 'old maids' have had such staying power and have blinded us to the reality of singlewomen's usefulness in the past. The next chapter examines popular representations of never-married women, and attempts to discover both their origins and meanings. We will see that it is no coincidence that the first negative depictions of never-married women began to circulate at the same moment that singlewomen were increasing their economic and civic significance in England.

6
Spinsters, Superannuated Virgins, and Old Maids: Representations of Singlewomen

Even today, when children play the card game 'Old Maid', in which they match as many pairs as possible while avoiding the card with no mate, they are being socialized to believe that married couples are winners and single-women (but not men) are losers. The 'old maid' is something to be avoided at all costs. Where did these ideas come from, and when did the figure of the 'old maid' originate? Recently scholars have produced some provocative work on the representations of young singlewomen in the medieval period, but have not found evidence for stereotypes about lifelong singlewomen. There is some equally excellent research on the stereotype of the spinster in the eighteenth century. But we do not have any studies of how contemporaries represented never-married women in the period between the medieval and modern eras. Without any research on the origins and changing depictions of never-married women, we might assume that the negative caricature of lifelong singlewomen is one of those cultural constants. But this is not, in fact, the case. This chapter shows how popular representations of singlewomen markedly changed in England during the early modern period. We will see how and when 'spinster' became a derogatory term, and how the 'singlewoman' was replaced with the concept of the 'old maid'.

A cultural history of the lifelong singlewoman is a complicated project to attempt. Trying to identify cultural trends is always difficult and never certain, but this chapter uses literature—much of it fictional and satir-ical—to posit some long-term shifts in the ways that English people thought about never-married women. I identify three phases in the repre-sentation of the never-married woman. The first phase was the lack of recognition of older and lifelong singlewomen in the literary representa-tions of the Middle Ages. Only young maidens inhabited the minds of writers until the Reformation, a Virgin Queen, and demographic trends altered the cultural landscape. The second phase began in the seventeenth century, when never-married women of all ages (not just young maidens) began to turn up in various literary genres. Contemporaries not only began to acknowledge the existence of lifelong singlewomen, they also began to debate the place and role of what they deemed poor, pathetic women who had *failed* to marry. The third phase began at the end of the seventeenth century, when the first truly negative stereotypes about lifelong single-women appeared and the word 'spinster' took on a negative cast. During the eighteenth century the fully formed trope of the 'old maid' emerged in various literary genres. This lifelong singlewoman was no longer hapless and pathetic, but was now satirized, scorned, and even derided as a menace to English society. While there was some overlap in these second and third phases (not all representations of never-married women were negative in the eighteenth century, for instance), the overall trajectory was, first of recognition, and then of scorn towards lifelong singlewomen.

This chapter makes use of a range of literary sources. I have sought representations of singlewomen in ballads, pamphlets, proverbs, poems, essays, periodicals, and novels. There are some genres, such as drama and art, that would also be particularly fruitful to explore, although there is not space to do so here. There are, of course, some methodological concerns with fictional sources such as these. How should we read satirical sources, for instance? How do we guard against taking them too literally? What about the multiple aims of literature that may have been written for amusement as well as social commentary, or perhaps simply to sell? How do we discern between transformations in stereotypes versus changes in genre? And where is the line between imagined and real when a fictional source references real events, peoples, and places? Although these issues cannot all be dealt with here, what is significant is that various sources and genres all supported the same chronology. In English culture, lifelong singlewomen moved from absence to presence and then emerged as a common satirical trope over the early modern period.

From Absence to Presence

Singlewomen were represented in various genres in the Middle Ages, but these depictions largely focused on life-cycle singlewomen, that is, young females who would presumably marry. Young maidens figured in romances, the lives of heroic virgin martyrs, dramatic cycles, fabliaux, ballads, and songs.[1] Kim Phillips's work shows that popular representations of single-women in the medieval period were frequently religious ones. The Virgin Mary and virgin martyr saints such as St Katherine and St Margaret were

---

[1] See Katherine J. Lewis, Noel Menuge, and Kim Phillips (eds.), *Young Medieval Women* (New York: St Martin's Press, 1999); Cindy Carlson and Angela J. Weisl (eds.), *Constructions of Widowhood and Virginity in the Middle Ages* (New York: St Martins Press, 1999); Kim M. Phillips, *Medieval Maidens: Young Women and Gender in England, 1270–1540* (Manchester: Manchester University Press, 2003).

some of the most familiar and beloved figures to English people. Phillips also suggests that young maidenhood was represented as the perfect age in medieval art and literature, both secular and religious. In terms of secular literature, Roberta Krueger has explored how the courtly romances of the High Middle Ages are replete with adolescent females engaged in autonomous adventures who are ultimately reined in and channelled into appropriate female roles through marriage.[2] Judith Bennett has explored the voices of young maidens in the songs and ballads of the later Middle Ages. In these songs singlewomen are depicted in various poses—chaste and lusty, autonomous and passive, cheerful and rueful—but in all cases these singlewomen are young.[3] Medieval representations of singlewomen focused on their youth, their virginity and sexuality, their romances and courtships, and ultimately their marriages. Contemporaries paid very little, if any, attention to women who never married, because singleness was viewed as a life stage, not a life choice.

The terms that contemporaries used to describe singlewomen echoed these same presumptions. For instance, a never-married woman summoned before the diocese of Winchester's consistory court in the sixteenth century was likely to appear as a servant, a *puella* (maiden), a *puera* (young woman), or a *virgo* (virgin). These were all terms that emphasized the youthfulness and chastity of never-married women.

But change was on the horizon. In 1558 Elizabeth I ascended the throne as a 25-year-old singlewoman. She never married throughout her long reign, during which she transformed from life-cycle to lifelong singlewoman before she died at the age of 69. The presence of a never-married woman on the throne could have increased the visibility of such women and led to more positive depictions of them. It is true that literary representations of Elizabeth that focused on her singleness were largely positive. Male courtiers such as John Lyly and Edmund Spenser figured her as the classical goddesses Diana and Cynthia or the poet Sappho. Elizabeth represented herself as a Protestant alternative to the Virgin Mary.[4] And yet Elizabeth's reign produced very little public commentary on singlewomen in general. One of the reasons is that Elizabeth expected people to think of her as exceptional rather than representative of all women. As Elizabeth informed

[2] Roberta Krueger, 'Transforming Maidens: Singlewomen's Stories in Marie de France's Lais and Later French Courtly Narratives', in Judith M. Bennett and Amy M. Froide (eds.), *Singlewomen in the European Past, 1250–1800* (Philadelphia: University of Pennsylvania Press, 1999), 146–91.

[3] Judith M. Bennett, 'Ventriloquisms: When Maidens Speak in English Songs, *c.*1300–1550', in Anne Klinck and Anne Marie Rasmussen (eds.), *Cross Cultural Approaches to Medieval Women's Song* (Philadelphia: University of Pennsylvania Press, 2001), 187–204.

[4] Philippa Berry, *Of Chastity and Power: Elizabethan Literature and the Unmarried Queen* (London and New York: Routledge, 1989), 111–61; Roy Strong, *The Cult of Elizabeth: Elizabethan Portraiture and Pageantry* (Berkeley: University of California Press, 1987).

her parliament, she chose to live out of the state of marriage and desired the word 'virgin' to be carved on her tombstone. Nevertheless, Elizabeth did not advocate singleness for the average Englishwoman.

While Elizabeth I's marital status may have had little effect on English attitudes toward lifelong singleness, her Church did. The Reformation led to a distinctly more negative view of singleness.[5] Before the dissolution of the monasteries Englishwomen had a religious alternative to lay marriage: they could dedicate their lives to the Church. Nevertheless, contemporaries viewed nuns not so much as singlewomen but as brides of Christ; their celibacy was of a sexual nature rather than a marital one. After the Reformation the option of being a nun was legally closed off to Englishwomen and marriage became virtually compulsory. Luther and Calvin both encouraged marriage among Protestants, and Merry Wiesner has speculated that 'this may have led to a great suspicion of unmarried persons . . . especially unmarried women'. In England celibacy became associated with Catholicism.[6] The Puritan minister William Gouge's popular treatise *Of Domesticall Duties* (first published in 1622) argued that 'we shall find single life too light to be compared with honest marriage'. Gouge believed that if one had to choose between virginity and marriage, it was better to marry so as to escape the possibility of sin through fornication. Since contemporaries believed women were more likely to be susceptible to sin, it was even more important for them to marry. According to Gouge, the only acceptable reason to remain single was if a person suffered from lameness, impotence, or had a contagious disease such as leprosy; in other words, anything that would prevent procreation, 'for by those signs of impotence God shows that he calls them to live single'.[7]

It was around this same time that contemporaries began to view single persons as likely candidates for damnation. Such views are found in a proverb of murky origins that made its first appearance in the English language in *The Book of Fortune* (*c*.1560). The saying went: 'A mickle truth it is I tell | Hereafter thou'st lead Apes in Hell: | For she that will not [marry] when she may, | When she will she shall have nay.' This proverb stated that the punishment for women who rejected marriage, and thus God's plan for humankind, was to lead apes in hell. By the 1590s the phrase was popping up in a number of Shakespeare's plays, including *The Taming*

---

[5] For the scant literature on early modern Protestant views of celibacy, see: Merry Wiesner-Hanks, *Christianity and Sexuality in the Early Modern World* (New York: Routledge, 2000); Eric Seeman, ' "It is Better to Marry Than to Burn": Anglo-American Attitudes Toward Celibacy, 1600–1800', *Journal of Family History*, 24: 4 (1999), 397–419; and Christine Peters, 'Single Women in Early Modern England: Attitudes and Expectations', *Continuity and Change*, 12: 3 (1997), 325–30.

[6] Wiesner-Hanks, *Christianity and Sexuality*, 64.

[7] William Gouge, *Of Domesticall Duties*. 2nd edn., (London, 1626), 123–4, 105–6.

of the Shrew and *Much Ado about Nothing*. In 1600 John Donne remarked that: 'There is an old proverb, that, they that die maids, must lead Apes in Hell.' By 1670 John Ray's *Collection of English Proverbs* recorded the saying as 'Old Maids lead apes in Hell', and it is this phrase that stuck.[8] While the notion of eternal punishment for singlewomen is obvious in the proverb, scholars continue to debate the meaning of the apes. One theory is that the apes signify the husbands or children that singlewomen never had on earth, or perhaps their counterparts, the old bachelors. Another is that the apes are the only consorts that old maids can obtain, and even then they have to be led. Apes were associated with lechery as well, so they may have signified the inverse of the lifelong singlewoman's celibacy.

Virginity emerged as a common literary subject in the early seventeenth century. The popular Protestant perception was that, while virginity was a necessary virtue in a young woman, it was something to be traded for marriage, not kept by the woman. Shakespeare made some pointedly negative remarks on lifelong virginity in *All's Well That Ends Well*. The play's character Paroles, who is attempting to bed Helen, tells her that holding on to one's virginity is against nature and a slap in the face of one's mother. He remarks that virginity 'is a commodity [that] will lose the gloss with lying; the longer kept, the less worth', and he compares 'old virginity' with 'French withered pears: it looks ill, it eats drily'.[9] Such double entendres reveal the assumption that virginity was sexually desirable only in the young. Like fruit, it existed only to be plucked and devoured, otherwise it was wasted.

The same assumption informed both popular and theoretical medical diagnoses of 'the disease of virgins', or what English people more commonly referred to as the greensickness. John Dunton included an entry on green-sickness in *The Ladies Dictionary*. He explained that women who did not use their reproductive functions suffered from this disease. Sufferers experienced difficulty breathing, headaches, heart palpitations, and other aches due to the 'inordinate efflux of the menstrous blood'. Dunton claimed that greensickness also manifested itself by 'the folly of such virgins, who covet to eat coals, chalk, wax, nutshells, whited wall, starch, tobacco pipes, and such like unaccountable trash'.[10] Medical historian Helen King has found that this disease that specifically targeted virgins emerged in England in the 1550s, and she posits a connection between an illness that only occurred in

---

[8] Burton Stevenson, *The Macmillan Book of Proverbs, Maxims, and Famous Phrases* (New York: Macmillan, 1968), 76–7; F. P. Wilson, *The Oxford Dictionary of English Proverbs* (Oxford: Clarendon Press, 1970), 590; Morris P. Tilley, *A Dictionary of the Proverbs in England in the Sixteenth and Seventeenth Centuries* (Brooklyn, NY: AMS Press, 1983), 405; and Johannes Hoops, 'Old Maids Lead Apes in Hell', *Englische Studien*, 70 (1935/6), 337–51.

[9] William Shakespeare, *All's Well That Ends Well* (c.1603), I.i. 135–65.

[10] John Dunton, *The Ladies Dictionary* (London, 1694); *Oxford English Dictionary*.

virgins and could only be cured by marriage and motherhood to 'Protest-antism favouring marriage'. This disease continued to be diagnosed in England, as well as in Europe and North America, up until 1930, and went under the labels of the greensickness, as well as chlorosis and, by the mid-nineteenth century, anaemia.[11] It is significant that the victims of greensickness were young, life-cycle singlewomen who were close to puberty. Older singlewomen were not imagined as victims, even though presumably they too would not have exercised their reproductive functions and so could become diseased.

In the second half of the sixteenth century, however, there was an important change in the terms contemporaries used to describe single-women. Instead of using words that assumed virginity, youth, or eventual marriage, such as 'virgin' and 'maiden', words such as *soluta* (single) and 'spinster' began to appear in court, probate, and administrative records. The word 'spinster' was an important innovation. It referred to a never-married woman without assuming a premarital status, and it was appropriate to both young and old women, as well as to women before they married or women who never married. It also emphasized these women's economic independence. In the medieval period 'spinster' had been an economic or occupational term denoting a female spinner, but by the seventeenth century this economic term was adopted as the legal term for a woman on her own. Although our present-day definition of the term 'spinster' emphasizes lifelong celibacy, there is no evidence that early modern people restricted the word to older or lifelong singlewomen. For instance, the clerk of Winchester's consistory court recorded the marital status of women as young as 17 and as old as 50 as 'spinster'. As a legal term, 'spinster' was a neutral descriptor. It did not become a derogatory term until the eighteenth century, as we will see below.

Although 'spinster' was a new term in the early modern era, the term 'singlewoman' (usually written as a compound word) had a much longer history. In the Middle Ages a 'singlewoman' could connote a prostitute, and was sometimes used to refer to any woman who was not married—widowed as well as never-married.[12] But by the early modern period the meaning of 'singlewoman' changed and became synonymous with spinster. The words 'spinster' and 'singlewoman' were significant because they recognized a new

---

[11] Helen King, *The Disease of Virgins: Greensickness, Chlorosis and the Problems of Puberty* (London and New York: Routledge, 2004), esp. the introduction.

[12] Ruth Karras, 'Sex and the Singlewoman', in Bennett and Froide (eds.), *Singlewomen in the European Past*; and Cordelia Beattie, 'The Problem of Women's Work Identities in Post Black Death England', in James Bothwell et al. (eds.), *The Problem of Labour in Fourteenth-Century England* (York: York Medieval Press, 2000), 7 and n. 21. Beattie argues that both *soluta* and single woman were umbrella terms for never-married and widowed women in the Middle Ages. I do not see this in the early modern period, however.

group in society. No longer were never-married women assumed to be daughters or maidens awaiting marriage; instead, they were now represented as a distinct adult group. This terminology became even more common as the numbers of never-married women rose in the seventeenth century. The independence associated with the terms may also reflect the increase in the opportunities for householder status, employment, self-maintenance, and civic duty that never-married women enjoyed in the second half of the seventeenth century and that have been traced in Chapters 3 through 5. It is interesting to note that 'spinster' and 'single-woman' became the accepted terms in legal, testamentary, and civic records, while words like 'virgin' and 'maid' lingered on much longer in literary parlance.

The terms used to describe women who never married were not the only change in the representation of such women in the seventeenth century. In the 1640s, at the same time as England experienced civil war, public awareness of lifelong singlewomen came to the fore. For instance, in 1648 Robert Herrick published his well-known poem 'To Virgins, to Make Much of Time'. His poem was a warning to women to 'Gather ye rosebuds while ye may' and 'Then be not coy, but use your time, | And while ye may, go marry; | For having lost but once your prime, | You may for ever tarry'. Herrick's advice to women to marry when they could, and not to delay or they might find themselves 'losing out' to lifelong singleness, signalled the arrival of a new social concern in England: women who never married.

Also beginning in the 1640s, and continuing into the 1690s, a genre of political-themed literature emerged that expressed the concerns of single-women. At this time real women were petitioning parliament, significant numbers of women were speaking and writing publicly for the first time, and English people were debating the extension of the franchise.[13] Into this context emerged a number of fictional petitions and complaints by women and tales of fictional female parliaments. These pamphlets were all anonymous but written in the voice of various female Londoners, including virgins, maids, daughters of citizens, and servants. Literary scholars doubt that these works were really written by young singlewomen.[14] But what has been missed is that these fictional complaints, petitions, and female parliaments all focused on one issue: the lack of male marriage partners in England and the consequent rise in the number of never-married women

---

[13] Patricia Higgins, 'The Reactions of Women, With Special Reference to Women Petitioners', in Brian Manning (ed.), *Politics, Religion and The English Civil War* (London: Edward Arnold, 1973), 179–222.

[14] See e.g. R. J. Fehrenbach, 'A Letter sent by Maydens of London (1567)', *English Literary Renaissance*, 14 (1984), 285–304.

in the second half of the seventeenth century. Fiction and reality collided in the person of the singlewoman.[15]

The first of these singlewomens' petitions appeared in 1642. It was entitled *The Virgin's Complaint for the Losse of their Sweet-hearts, by these Present Wars, and their owne Long Solitude, and Keeping their Virginities against their Wills: Presented in the Names and Behalfes of all the Damsels both of Country and City, January 29, by Sundry Virgins of the City of London*. In this pamphlet singlewomen of every social status—from wealthy citizens' daughters to maiden water-bearers—complain that the wars have taken away all the young men, so that they have none to marry except old usurers 'that are as cold in their constitutions and performance, as they are in their charities'. The sexual innuendo illustrates the satirical nature of this petition, and yet, as in all satires, there are serious matters lurking beneath the surface. The petition is presented by 205,000 maids throughout the kingdom, who plead that if the wars are ended and their sweethearts restored to them they will 'be good girls and please our fathers, and in no way injure...our husbands, when we shall have the happiness to have them'.[16] The author underscores that this is the plight of a large number of women who are finding it difficult to marry. These fictional women were not choosing singleness; rather, they were demanding their right to heterosexual relationships. Nevertheless, this pamphlet differs from medieval ballads about maidens pining for love, for these singlewomen are represented not as individuals looking for sweethearts, but rather as a group of women who lack men to marry. This pamphlet marks a new recognition of singlewomen as a collective social group; a group, moreover, that was having difficulty fulfilling the expected female roles of wifehood and motherhood.

The petitions and complaints of never-married women continued as a literary theme throughout the seventeenth century. While in the 1640s the fictional singlewomen had complained that the wars were to blame for the loss of prospective mates, by the 1650s the women were beginning to grumble that it was the men themselves who were the obstacle to marriage. Female complaints about the inability to marry began to be represented not only in petitions but also through fictional female parliaments or assemblies. *Now or Never: or, A New Parliament of Women Assembled* (1656) was aimed at all 'London-prentices, young men and batchelors', and included

[15] These pamphlets include: *The Virgin's Complaint* (1642); *The Maids' Petition* (1647); *Now or Never, or a New Parliament of Women* (1656); *The Ladies Remonstrance* (1659); *A Declaration of the Maids* (1659); *The Maids' Complaint against the Batchelors* (1675); *An Account of the Proceedings of the New Parliament of Women* (1683); *The Young Women and Maiden's Lamentation* (1690); *The Petition of the Ladies for Husbands* (1693); and *A Humble Remonstrance of the Batchelors* (1693).

[16] *The Virgin's Complaint*, 2, 8.

speeches by the 'City-Virgins and eight several Acts, Orders, and Decrees, touching a free choice in marriage'. One of the laws passed by this fictitious female parliament was that young men should 'be forced to marry within the age of 24 years, and that if they continue single longer than the time limited, that for every year they shall forfeit three pounds'.[17] *The Maid's Complaint against the Batchelors: or an Easter-Offering for Young Men and Apprentices* (1675) appeared twenty years later, but continued the argument that men were 'slighting the good old way of matrimony'. The fictional singlewomen in this piece railed against men who neglected them or who were 'willing enough to break bulk but not pay custom', leaving them to bear and raise up bastards alone.[18] The never-married women represented in these pamphlets did not choose to eschew marriage; they were forced to remain single because men did not wish to marry. This trope permeated the literature on never-married women for the entire early modern era—never-married women were seldom seen as being single by choice.

In the later seventeenth century fictional petitions transformed into complaints in which singlewomen blamed their failure to marry on other women. In *The Maid's Complaint Against the Bachelors* (1675) singlewomen argue that men do not marry because married women and whores lure them away from proper wedlock. The London maids also complain that when men do marry they forgo virgins, and instead 'are glad merely for a wretched livelihood, to wed some ugly deformed most abominable old widow of fourscore'.[19] Likewise, in *The Young Women and Maiden's Lamentation* (*c*.1690) never-married women complain that older women, wives, and widows have more access to men than do they.[20] These maids are perturbed at the loss of male companionship, but also claim that older women, who have had their turn, who cannot produce children, and who should not be interested in sex at their age anyway, still get all the young men. Similarly, *An Account of the Proceedings of the New Parliament of Women* (1683) features the 'distressed maids of the nation' presenting a petition of complaint against 'widows, who, against reason, have been over-occupied by several husbands, while, on the contrary, these poor maidens were ready to starve for a bit of man's flesh'. The (matronly) members of the female parliament respond that it is not possible to 'make an act that we should all have husbands', but they propose to set up 'public places, where lovesick maids may find ease, by the association of merry boys'. The members of the women's parliament also vote to condone sexual 'liberty

[17] *Now or Never, or a New Parliament of Women*, 6.
[18] *The Maid's Complaint against the Batchelors: or an Easter-Offering for Young Men and Apprentices*, 1, 4–5.
[19] Ibid. 7.
[20] *The Young Women and Maiden's Lamentation* [no pagination].

for maidens that could get no husbands, and that they might accept of what kindnesses were offered to them'.[21] The (probably male) authors of these pamphlets had fun representing women as lusty rivals who want to marry men primarily for sexual satisfaction. But these writers also demonstrated a growing awareness that more and more Englishwomen were having trouble finding marriage partners in the later seventeenth century, and thus were remaining single.

Moreover, fictional female petitions and parliaments acknowledged not only that women were having difficulties securing marriage partners, but also that some women were remaining single for life. These pamphlets were innovative in entertaining the possibility of older and perhaps lifelong single-women. For example, *A New Parliament of Women* (1656) features speeches made by an ancient maid as well as a young maid. Old and young single-women are represented as having differing experiences and concerns. The young maid boasts that women like her are 'fresh, young, handsome, and lusty'. But she says that men's desire for money, the control a woman's friends have over her marital choices, and the customs that restrain chaste women from pursuing and encouraging bashful men are what stand in the way of young maids marrying. In contrast to her younger counterpart, the ancient maid reveals a good amount of bitterness and self-pity in her speech. She states that 'This makes many of us (poor souls) not to be looked upon, so that we live in a despairing condition: nay a Case of consumption I may term it, may I not? If we lose our teeming time.' She blames whores and adulterous wives ('I profess such women are our greatest enemies') for her missed chance at marriage and childbearing, and demands that the female parliament severely punish all whores and limit the time men are allowed to remain bachelors.

In addition to the popular recognition of lifelong singlewomen, there is another significant change that appears over time in this ephemeral litera-ture. The social status or class of the fictional singlewomen changed by the end of the seventeenth century. In the 1640s the pamphlets represented never-married women as servants, waiting gentlewomen, and chamber-maids, but by 1693 fictional petitions are being issued by singlewomen who call themselves 'ladies'. Gone are serving-maids pining for apprentices and young men lost to war, and in their place are single ladies angry at urban gentlemen who prefer coffee houses, whores, and taverns to settling down. In *The Petition of the Ladies* singlewomen aim to encourage marriage by appealing to biblical texts (Increase and Multiply), classical history (only married men governed the states of Athens and Sparta), and nationalism: 'We therefore humbly petition you, that, for the Increase of their Majesties liege People, in whom the Power and Strength of a Nation consists, and for

---

[21] *An Account of the Proceedings of the New Parliament of Women* [no pagination].

the utter Discouragement of Celibacy, and all its wicked Works, you would be pleased to enact, First, that all men, of what quality and degree soever, should be obliged to marry as soon as they are One and Twenty.' Those men who did not would be forced to pay a yearly sum, half of which would go to the king to pay for the wars in Flanders and the remainder to poor housekeepers to maintain their families. The single ladies also suggested 'That no excuse be admitted but only that of natural Frigidity or Impotence', and that a jury of matrons or midwives would be called in to assess such cases. Taxing a bachelor's wealth and questioning his masculinity were presented as the ways for genteel singlewomen to gain husbands.

How should we account for the increasing cultural presence of never-married women in the second half of the seventeenth century? These popular representations supplied a few reasons: Englishwomen were remaining single due to men going to war; wives, widows, and prostitutes were keeping men from 'lawful' marriage; or men were simply choosing not to marry. By the end of the century this was represented as a problem not just for the average Englishwoman, but for urban and genteel women especially. Although the reasons offered for people remaining single may not have been accurate, popular culture was commenting on what demographic historians have verified as a reality: the numbers of people who never married were increasing in seventeenth-century England.

Singlewomen as Society's Victims

In the last three decades of the seventeenth century popular representations of never-married women moved from acknowledging their existence to offering advice and assistance to these 'hapless victims'. By the 1670s older and lifelong singlewomen became the subject of non-fictional genres. Advice manuals for singlewomen had long been aimed at young women and daughters, and conduct books for women were conventionally divided into sections on maids, wives, and widows. But a change occurred in the later seventeenth century, when advice literature began to distinguish between life-cycle and lifelong singlewomen. For instance, in *The Ladies Calling* (1673) Richard Allestree separated his section on never-married women into distinct discussions of 'superannuated virgins' and 'the younger sort of virgins'.[22] Likewise, in his entry on 'virgins' in *The Ladies Dictionary* (1694), John Dunton divided the commentary on virgins between those who were on 'in years' and those 'of the younger sort'. Dunton also advocated a scheme for assisting all 'young maids, who are under forty

²² Richard Allestree, *The Ladies Calling* (London, 1673), pt. 2, p. 4.

years of age' to marry. Singlewomen over the age of 40 were no longer marriageable in Dunton's eyes, most likely because of their proximity to menopause and thus their inability to reproduce.[23]

John Dunton's scheme probably owed much to the profusion of pamphlets that appeared at the end of the seventeenth century debating the institution of marriage. The main intent of this literature seems to have been humorous entertainment, making use of jokes that had been around since the fabliaux of the Middle Ages. Between the 1680s and 1730s a flurry of pamphlets addressed themselves to the debate between the pleasures of the single life and the comforts of marriage. Some, like *The Pleasures of a Single Life: or, The Miseries of Matrimony*, were typical misogynistic rants about scolding wives and crying babies leaving a man with no peace. Responses written by authors claiming to be female were in no way feminist. For instance, *The Women's Advocate: Or, the Fifteen Real Comforts of Matrimony* (1683) purports to defend wives by instructing men that even though wives are spendthrifts, busybodies, and shrews, they are only trying to keep up appearances and household affairs for their husbands' sake.[24]

And yet there was something new in these literary debates: a number of contributions now criticized marriage from a sympathetic female point of view. *The Ladies Choice*, a direct answer to *The Pleasures of a Single Life*, critiques vain beaux, drunken wits, greedy businessmen, and ambitious courtiers but does not reject wedlock entirely. The 'female' author admits that 'marriage is bondage', but if a woman marries a sensible, temperate, and well-bred man 'the yoke is easie; glorious are the chains; | His fetters please, nor wish we to be free | But glory in the loss of liberty...' Other pamphlets from a female subject position were more negative about marriage. In *The Maid's Vindication: or, The Fifteen Comforts of Living a Single Life* (1707) the 'gentlewoman' author calls husbands jailers and says women are only released from this prison through death or adultery. She shakes her head at silly, blind maids who long to get rid of their maidenhoods and so run into marriage, which they will find to their disappointment is quicksand. *Matrimony; or, Good Advice to the Ladies to Keep Single* (1739) echoed these sentiments thirty years later. The author warns women that men are adulterous drunks who abuse their wives in private and challenge their authority in front of the household.[25] What these pamphlets reveal is that,

---

[23] Distinguishing between singlewomen by age may not have been Dunton's own idea, since it seems he derived much of his material from Allestree's *The Ladies Calling*. Dunton, *Ladies Dictionary*, 238.

[24] *The Women's Advocate: or, The Fifteen Real Comforts of Matrimony... Written by a person of quality of the female sex*, 2nd edn. (London, 1683).

[25] *The Maid's Vindication: or, The Fifteen Comforts of Living a Single Life... Written by a Gentlewoman* (London, 1707); *Matrimony: or, Good Advice to the Ladies to Keep Single* (London, 1739).

by the late 1600s and into the early 1700s, there was a growing recognition
that women as well as men might choose to reject, or think hard before
choosing, marriage.

While we could dismiss these pamphlets as seventeenth-century versions
of the age-old man versus woman debate, if we read them in tandem with
other literature from the time we will recognize a serious note under
the humour. Commentators and clergy certainly feared that such anti-
marriage literature reflected and maybe contributed to a real decline
in marriage rates. In response came several ideas on how to encourage
and increase marriage in Britain. Some of these proposals were satirical in
nature, but others were quite serious. Several schemes for increasing marriage rates focused on taxing or penalizing bachelors and, to a lesser extent,
widowers. For example, the author of *Marriage Promoted* (1690) warned
'that the neglect of marriage (if not timely prevented) will occasion the
destruction of these kingdoms', because the inevitable result will be de-
population.[26] John Dunton, an admirer of that treatise, also bemoaned the
fact that people were remaining single. Similarly, he advocated a tax on
those men and women who chose to remain single, and stated that the
money raised should be used to ensure that all young maids below the age of
40 could marry.[27] Dunton's proposal to tax not only single men but also
singlewomen with adequate portions was unique.[28] He ascribed an agency
to never-married women that contemporaries seldom acknowledged.
Nevertheless, Dunton only worried about giving women of childbearing
age the opportunity to marry since these women would produce the next
generation. His concern was not for women, but for the nation in general.

Anxieties about declining marriage rates, and thus population rates,
continued into the eighteenth century. At this time they became inextric-
ably linked to pro-natalism, because Britain was continually at war or in
economic competition with its neighbours and thus required a continual
supply of military men and workers. Into this context appeared *The
Levellers: A Dialogue between two young ladies, concerning Matrimony, pro-
posing an Act for Enforcing Marriage, for the Equality of Matches, and Taxing
Single Persons. With the Danger of Celibacy to a Nation* (1703). This fictional
conversation takes place between Politica and Sophia, two young, single
ladies of beauty and wit but small fortune. Sophia worries that they are 'not
answering the end of our Creation in the propagation of our Species', and as
such they sin. But Politica argues that it is not their fault, for they are willing
but, as her friend puts it: 'the matrimonial knot [is] tied only by the
pursestring' and 'my money will not grow to the height of a husband,

---

[26] *Marriage Promoted in a Discourse of its Ancient and Modern Practice* (London, 1690), 24.
[27] *The Ladies Dictionary*, 236–9.
[28] Ibid.

though I water it with Tears'. In other words, they remain single because men will not marry a woman unless she has a large enough dowry. Sophia and Politica resolve to think of some way to get rid of the 'grievance of celibacy, under which the nation groaneth'. They worry that the wars consume men and yet there is no supply of the same, so that 'our ships and armies, in a short time, will want soldiers' if people do not marry and have children. Politica argues that the answer to this national dilemma is a compulsory law enforcing matrimony. This Act will require every bachelor over 24 years of age and every widower under 50 to pay 20*s*. a year. She computes that this would add £2,500,000 to the queen's treasury and help defray the costs of war, 'for the unmarried people are, as it were, useless to the State'. Since single people do not produce soldiers they can at least pay for the war, argues Politica.[29] This pamphlet represents singlewomen arguing that marriage is important to save the nation, not themselves, and that as single persons they are useless to their country. They are victims, but even more so is Britain.

It is significant that contemporaries did not view the ideas set forth in *Marriage Promoted* and *The Levellers* as pure fantasy. In some respects their proposals reflected actual government policy. For instance, during the reign of William and Mary parliament enacted the Marriage Duty tax, to fund foreign wars. Among other provisions this Act included a tax on bachelors over 25 years of age and on childless widowers. The Marriage Duty tax stayed in effect for eleven years, from 1695 to 1706.[30] Although there is no proof that it encouraged men to marry and to change the marital status of the country's singlewomen, it does reveal the popular view that unmarried men should be singled out and penalized for contributing to the nation's problems by not marrying and procreating. Government policy, like literature, blamed men for not marrying, and assumed that women were remaining single because men did not ask rather than by choice. If singlewomen had not been viewed as society's victims, they would presumably have been taxed too.

Other proposals claimed that taxes would not increase marriage, and so they advocated a carrot rather than a stick approach. By the early eighteenth century fiction presented a new answer to low marriage rates: a lottery with marriage as the prize. Such schemes provide another example of the blurred line between fiction and reality. In the late seventeenth and early eighteenth centuries lotteries were one of the most popular forms of entertainment and financial speculation. They were used to fund private philanthropic

---

[29] *The Levellers* (1703), in the *Harleian Miscellany*, vol. 5, pp. 416–33.
[30] For the best overview of the Marriage Duty tax, see Kevin Schurer and Tom Arkell (eds.), *Surveying the People: The Interpretation and Use of Document Sources for the Study of Population in the Later Seventeenth Century* (Oxford: Leopard's Head Press, 1992).

schemes and by the British government to fund foreign wars, so it was not much of a stretch to advocate a lottery for another needy cause: in this case, singlewomen. One of the first of these marital lotteries, *The Love-Lottery: Or, A Woman the Prize* (1709), proposed that maids and widows should venture 10*s.* to win a husband or a £500 portion. While bachelors and widowers could also play if they wished, the author depicted women as the individuals desperate to marry. This project was aimed at beautiful women without fortunes, daughters of tradesmen, servants, exchange-girls, sempstresses, and others in the clothing trades. The author was concerned about the marital prospects of poor and working women, but they also had to be young. For example, the women who were not permitted to play were those who were unchaste; virgins over 25 years of age and widows over 35, unless they had 'money enough to supply the defects of age'; no maids who chew charcoal or widows who smoke tobacco or drink gin; and no women with eyesores or imperfections. In fact, women 'must be straight, agreeable, and free from disease (greensickness excepted), not deformed in body or mind and not hiding deformities under their clothing'. According to this author, some women were not suitable for marriage even if it was a game of chance.

Another *Proposal for a Matrimonial Lottery; From the Record Office* appeared on 14 February or Valentine's Day, 1710.[31] The need for this project was ascribed to the wars, which were causing damsels to labour 'under the torments of an insupportable solitude'. The proposal specifically allowed both young and old women who had never married, or 'maids' and 'singlewomen', to enter this game and win the prize of 'a good husband'. This scheme was supposedly so popular, that a month later an advertisement warned of traffic outside the Record Office due to the 'great numbers of maids, widows, and singlewomen resorting there'. Although a satire, this proposal made use of real lottery practices, such as newspaper advertisements and record offices where tickets could be purchased.

Other lottery schemes proposed to auction off singlewomen instead of letting them play for husbands. An example of this method is *A scheme for disposing of (by way of Lottery) a dozen and a half of Old Maids, resident in or near Covent Garden...* [32] These older singlewomen are represented as less than desirable marriage partners. Those men who entered the lottery did not have to pay; rather, they were rewarded with a marriage portion for taking one of the 'old maids'. In 1734 *A Bill for a Charitable Lottery for the Relief of the Distressed Virgins in Great Britain* appeared. This pamphlet

---

[31] *The Records of Love: or, Weekly Amusements for the Fair Sex*, 1: 7 (18 Feb. 1710); 1: 9 (4 Mar. 1710).

[32] British Library, c. 116 i. 4/11 (no date). I am grateful to Beverly Lemire for bringing this source to my attention.

depicted singlewomen as charity cases in need of relief, and singleness as the cause of suffering for both the women and the nation. The author explains: 'Whereas by the melancholy disuse of holy matrimony in these kingdoms, an infinite number of his Majesty's female subjects are left upon the hands of their parents, in the un-natural state of virginity, to the prejudice of the commonwealth, the unsupportable burdening of private families, and the unspeakable affliction of the said females...' The concern here was for the nation, the family, and the individual, in that order. The supposed 'affliction' never-married women laboured under was listed last. Age and class also influenced which singlewomen were eligible to be auctioned off or considered the best 'prize':

All the Virgins in Great Britain from fifteen to forty shall be disposed of by lottery. The greatest prizes will be ladies of fortune, the second prizes will be Beauties, Pretty Girls, Agreeables, Wits, Ladies of quality, Huswifes, and Relations of the first minister or his mistress. The lowest prizes will be women of fashion and breeding, card players, misses of accomplishments, parsons' daughters, saints and good conditioned girls, alias friskies [non-virginal singlewomen].

The plight of never-married women was not only mocked in the marital lotteries but also in a number of proposals for dating services. These satirical schemes urged never-married women to advertise themselves for marriage. For example, *The Love-Lottery* (1709) recommended the establishment of an 'Office of Intelligence' where unmarried men and women could post their names, fortunes, and characters and be advised of suitable matches.[33] Then, in the 1740s lists of eligible men and women began to appear. Of the two lists of eligible wealthy women, one was entitled:

A master-key to the rich ladies treasury; or, The widower and batchelor's directory. Containing an exact alphabetical list of the duchess, marchioness, countess, viscountess, baroness dowagers, ladies by curtesie, daughters of peers, baronets widows, widows, and spinsters in Great Britain. With an account of their places of abode, reputed fortunes, and fortunes they possess in the stocks. By a younger brother.

This guide represented never-married women as commodities that would aid a man in making his fortune. Men were only interested in marriage for monetary purposes, and so the answer was for singlewomen to advertise their worth. With their emphasis on wealth, these dating services were aimed at aiding elite singlewomen only. This change in focus from ordinary singlewomen to those of genteel or elite status was common to eighteenth-century literary depictions of never-married women.

The literature we have examined so far sought to eliminate the existence of lifelong singlewomen by finding husbands for them. But beginning in

---

[33] *The Love-Lottery: Or, A Woman the Prize* (London, 1709).

the 1670s a radically different policy emerged. A growing chorus began to accept that singlewomen might not be able, or might not even want to change their marital state. If never-married women were now a fixture of British society, what was to be done with them? Writers began to suggest various schemes for educating, employing, and housing lifelong single-women. It is important to note that while most schemes to increase marriage rates were satirical, the projects for accommodating never-married women were of a more serious nature, written in the form of essays and social commentaries.

From the late seventeenth century onward a number of writers began to advocate academies or colleges for singlewomen.[34] In 1671 Edward Chamberlayne presented his scheme for *An Academy or Colledge, wherein Young Ladies and Gentlewomen may at a very Moderate Expense be Duly Instructed in the True Protestant Religion, and in all Vertuous Qualities that may Adorn that Sex.* He said he modelled his idea on Protestant colleges in Germany. Chamberlayne both saw a need for young maidens to be instructed in virtues and believed that there should be an equivalent to male collegiate life for young women. Nevertheless, he did not just envision these seminaries as training grounds for young singlewomen. He also thought that they would serve as havens 'for sober, pious, elder virgins and widows, who desire to separate themselves from the vanities of the world, and yet employ their talents to the benefit of the public'. Edward Chamberlayne asked any 'elder virgins, who intend not to marry' and who desire 'to lead the rest of their days without cares and troubles of the world, to live with honour and reputation, to devote themselves to the service of God and the good of the country, by contributing their advice and assistance in the training up of young ladies and gentlewomen', to apply to him for a position. One of these 'grave' and 'discreet' ladies would serve as the governess of the college, and other matrons, 'having taken up a resolution to live a retired, single, and religious life', would assist her in governing the institution.[35]

Chamberlayne's proposal of 1671 was the first institutional and vocational plan for Englishwomen who never married. Chamberlayne differed from his contemporaries not only in his interest in engaging with single-women's concerns rather than trying to marry them off, but also in his respect for such women and his acknowledgement that a woman might make a 'resolution', or choose, to remain single. Chamberlayne was not alone for long. Four years later Clement Barksdale put forward *A Letter*

---

[34] Bridget Hill, 'A Refuge from Men: The Idea of a Protestant Nunnery', *Past & Present*, 117 (1987), 107–30.

[35] Edward Chamberlayne, *An Academy or Colledge, wherein Young Ladies and Gentlewomen may at a very Moderate Expense be Duly Instructed in the True Protestant Religion, and in all Vertuous Qualities that may Adorn that Sex* (London, 1671), title-page, 2, 4–7.

Touching a Colledge of Maids, or, a Virgin Society. The author said this proposal had come about at a meeting at which 'half a dozen fair young ladies, rich, and virtuous' were present. While Barksdale authored the proposal, he claimed it had originated in the minds of young, wealthy singlewomen. This scheme specifically aimed to emulate the halls of commoners at Oxford for a single female clientele. Unlike Chamberlayne, Barksdale's proposal seems to have been intended for young singlewomen, although he did not specifically exclude older ones from the college. But he was clear about including young women of modest means in the scheme. Such poor singlewomen could wait at the tables, as well as on 'the ladies in their chambers'.[36]

What is perhaps the best-known proposal for an institution catering to never-married women came from the pen of Mary Astell. She wrote her works on singleness while she was still relatively young, publishing *A Serious Proposal* (1694) at the age of 28 and *Some Reflections upon Marriage* six years later. Astell died in 1731 at the age of 65, having never married.[37] In her *Serious Proposal* Astell argued that female education would improve women's usefulness, draw them away from foolish pursuits and behaviours, and increase their virtue. She envisioned an educational institution that would be a place where 'heiresses and persons of fortune may be kept secure from the rude attempts of designing men' until they wished to marry. With such women paying between £500 and £600 to enter the institution, they would help defray the costs for 'daughters of gentlemen who are fallen into decay'. Women would be able either to stay until marriage or to be 'received into the House if they incline to it'. The institution would also provide a place for 'persons of quality who are over-stocked with [female] children', to 'honourably dispose of them' for a dowry much less than a marriage portion. Most significantly, Astell suggested that the house would also provide an alternative for women, so that they would not have to marry hastily and imprudently simply because they were ageing and feared 'the dreadful name of *Old Maid*'.[38]

Astell recognized that marriage was not an option for every woman. According to her, the main reason was dowry inflation and the inability of singlewomen of modest means to secure partners. Although Astell seems to have been happy with her never-married status, she did not assume that most singlewomen actively chose never to marry. Nevertheless, she did

---

[36] [Clement Barksdale], *A Letter Touching A Colledge of Maids, or, a Virgin Society* (London, 1675) [no pagination].

[37] Bridget Hill (ed.), *The First English Feminist: Reflections upon Marriage and Other Writings by Mary Astell* (New York: St Martin's Press, 1986), 4–7.

[38] Mary Astell, *A Serious Proposal to the Ladies*, 4th edn. (London, 1701; repr. New York: Source Book Press, 1970), 4–6, 35–6, 39–40.

believe that it was often better for a woman to stay single than to marry badly. And she recognized that such women, especially 'fallen' (or impoverished) gentlewomen, needed a viable alternative to marriage in order to remain single. This meant that Astell's proposed foundation was the only one to provide for lifelong singlewomen as much as young, life-cycle ones.

It is significant that at the end of the seventeenth century the popular answer to the plight of singlewomen was institutionalization of a religious sort. With the Reformation, Britain had abolished the convent, and with it a place for singlewomen. But a century-and-a-half later some High Churchmen proposed that it was time to institute Anglican nunneries. George Wheler's *A Protestant Monastery* (1698) included a chapter on convents for women, in which he argued that these institutions were suitable 'for all times and countries, and are by far less dangerous' if rules and precautions are followed. He thought that the liberty of the women in the convents must be preserved and that those that entered in their youth to be educated should be free to leave and 'marry when convenient offers are made ... as long as the vigour of their youth remains'. In other words, a Protestant nunnery should not be seen as taking the place of marriage, at least for those women who were pre-menopausal and still able to procreate. But Wheler did deem some women unmarriageable, and thought that these nunneries would benefit the state, the church, and the many families 'burdened with daughters, their parents cannot, either for want of beauty, [or] money, dispose of in marriage, or in any other decent manner provide for ...'

And yet the religious nature of female retirements is what made such plans controversial and ultimately prevented their implementation. On the one hand, conduct writers advocated religious roles for singlewomen. For instance, Richard Allestree had some advice for such 'calamitous creatures' as women who 'failed to' marry in *The Ladies Calling*. He told such women to 'addict themselves to the strictest virtue and piety, [so] they would give the world some cause to believe, 'twas not their necessity, but their choice which kept them unmarried, that they were pre-engaged to a better amour, espoused to the spiritual bridegroom; and this would give them among the soberer sort, at least the reverence and esteem of matrons'.[39] On the other hand, religious retirements for singlewomen were denigrated as too Catholic and dismissed as unnecessary. Allestree noted that there were no societies of nuns in England, and believed this was not a problem since those of his countrywomen interested in 'voluntary virginity' were only a small minority. His contemporary, John Dunton, did not take seriously the type of singlewomen who would enter a convent. His entry on 'vows' in *The Ladies Dictionary* stated that 'most of those young ladies, who in an ill

---

[39] *The Ladies Calling*, pt. 2, 3–4.

humour by being crossed in love, or in some other worldly affairs, or in a sudden fit of zeal, thrust themselves into monasteries, and vow a single life; are not many months there before they repent their rashness'.[40] Such views did not take into account the thousand or so Catholic singlewomen in seventeenth-century England who exiled themselves from family and country to follow a religious vocation, or the pious Protestant singlewomen who did not even have this option.[41]

Due to anti-Catholic sentiment in England none of the institutions proposed by Chamberlayne, Barksdale, or Astell came to fruition. Almshouses or schools were one thing, but nunneries were another. Astell supposedly obtained an offer of £10,000 to make her proposal a reality, but the donor (who may have been her friend Lady Elizabeth Hastings, or even Princess Anne) was persuaded to retract the funds because the institution looked like it would be 'preparing a way for Popish orders' and would be seen as a nunnery.[42]

More acceptable to English opinion were secular academies for singlewomen. One of Daniel Defoe's proposed schemes in *An Essay upon Projects* (1697) was an academy for women. He was quick to distinguish his idea from that 'Method propos'd by an Ingenious Lady [Astell], in a little Book, call'd Advice to the Ladies'. He deemed Astell's idea impractical, since 'youth, will not bear the restraint; and I am satisfi'd, nothing but the height of Bigotry can keep up a Nunnery'.[43] For Defoe, 'religious confinement and vows of celibacy' were not what singlewomen needed; instead, education would provide for them. For a man dismissive of the claustration of women, Defoe ironically spends most of his treatise describing the high walls and moat that would encircle his female academy. His treatise did promote education for women, but as a way to make women better companions to their spouses, not for a woman to support herself. Defoe's plan had few answers for singlewomen looking to change their marital state, except the hope that education would make them more attractive to a prospective spouse, and he offered nothing to those women who faced lifelong singleness.

Nevertheless, Defoe's focus on education as a panacea for singlewomen was echoed by other writers. In 1738 the *Gentleman's Magazine* ran a piece on 'How widows and young gentlewomen may live comfortably on £15 a year'. A group of London merchants said that they intended to establish a

[40] *The Ladies Dictionary*, 45, 458–9, 448–9.

[41] Claire Walker, *Gender and Politics in Early Modern Europe: English Convents in France and the Low Countries* (New York: Palgrave, 2003).

[42] George Ballard, *Memoirs of Several Ladies of Great Britain* (Oxford, 1752), 445.

[43] Michael F. Shugrue (ed.), *Selected Poetry and Prose of Daniel Defoe* (New York: Holt, Rinehart & Winston, 1968), 29–38.

large house where any gentlewomen of good character could lodge for free provided they could weave lace, spin, knit, embroider, or do plain sewing. As a concession to this class of women, they would only be expected to do as much in a day as common, working women did in half that time. They would also be supplied with tea and sugar at breakfast and a doctor to attend them 'in all distempers but the vapours'. In response to a young gentlewoman who said she was too well bred to live off 'so small a pittance', the author stated that if young women were given an education in 'honest employments' this singlewoman would not think herself too good to work for a living.[44] Apparently others agreed, for in the following year 'A Method to Make Women Useful' appeared in the same magazine. The author was purportedly a mother concerned about the numbers of gentlemen and tradesmen who had too many daughters and not enough money to provide them with dowries. Despite this problem, these parents were educating their daughters at boarding schools that taught them to be gentlewomen but provided them with few, if any, useful talents. This author advocated female education in bookkeeping and writing, as well as in needlework, so if need be a singlewomen could establish herself in trade. This article optimistically noted the plethora of businesses suitable for genteel singlewomen, who could set themselves up as linen- or woollen-drapers, haberdashers, mercers, glovers, perfumers, grocers, confectioners, and milliners. 'By this means a single woman may get a handsome and reputable living, and not be forced to a disagreeable match, or even to marry at all', although, 'when men see a woman can live in a decent manner without them, there will be enough glad to have her', for such a woman would be a good companion to a man of business.[45] In these articles education is represented as the answer for women without husbands, as well as the way to get a husband.

At the end of the seventeenth and beginning of the eighteenth centuries, then, popular representations of never-married women focused on how to assist these women and end their (and the nation's) plight. Some literary proposals were serious, like those of Astell or Wheler, while others were more satirical, like the marital lotteries and offices for marriages. But even when mocking, the assumption was that never-married women should be pitied since they were society's victims. By contrast, representations of lifelong singlewomen in the eighteenth century became increasingly mean-spirited; they focused less on pitying or helping never-married women and more on blaming them. While not all depictions were negative, the majority became so.

---

[44] *Gentleman's Magazine*, 8 (Feb. 1738), 85.
[45] Ibid. 9 (Oct. 1739), 525–6.

Singlewomen As Society's Villains

The term 'old maid' began to appear in various types of literature in the late seventeenth century. It soon surpassed in popularity the mocking but clumsy title of 'superannuated virgin'. Richard Allestree used both terms in *The Ladies Calling*. His 1673 publication claimed: 'An old Maid is now thought such a Curse as no Poetic fury can exceed...' Susan Lanser has pointed out that Allestree's use of the word 'now' indicates that in 1673 the negative view of the old maid was relatively new.[46] It did not take long for the term to be taken up by the pens of singlewomen themselves. It appeared in Jane Barker's poem 'A Virgin Life', which was published in 1688. Here she wrote of hoping she could remain 'Fearless of twenty-five and all its train, | Of slights or scorns, or being called Old Maid...' Echoing Barker's thoughts six years later, Mary Astell wrote in her *Serious Proposal* that ageing singlewomen feared 'the dreadful name of *Old Maid*'. The negative perception of the lifelong singlewoman was already in place by the end of the seventeenth century, as singlewomen such as Barker and Astell could attest, but the fully formed caricature of the 'old maid' only emerged in the early eighteenth century.

The figure of the 'old maid' began to appear with increasing frequency and in increasing detail in various genres of literature in eighteenth-century Britain. Lanser cites the poem a *Satyr Upon Old Maids* (1713) as an example of what she sees as a new, pejorative view of singlewomen. This poem called never-married women 'odious' and 'impure' 'dunghills', and accused them of being 'nasty, rank, rammy, filthy sluts' who would throw themselves at diseased and mentally unstable men just to avoid lifelong singleness. Lanser notes the particular focus on singlewomen's bodies as impure, diseased, and 'morally and physically repugnant'.[47]

The sheer ubiquity of the 'old maid' in all types of eighteenth-century genres is notable. Monthly and weekly periodicals such as the *Gentleman's Magazine*, the *Tatler*, and the *Spectator* made the lifelong singlewoman a common target of their satires. For example, in 1737 the 'Convocation of Old Maids' appeared in the *Gentleman's Magazine*, a popular monthly that had begun publishing out of London in 1731.[48] Reminiscent of the fictional female parliaments that had appeared a century earlier, this article featured an assembly of singlewomen gathered together to discuss their

---

[46] Susan S. Lanser, 'Singular Politics: The Rise of the British Nation and the Production of the Old Maid', in Bennett and Froide, *Singlewomen in the European Past*, 298.

[47] Ibid. 297–300.

[48] The 'Convocation' originally appeared in the *Universal Spectator*, a periodical started coincidentally by Defoe's son-in-law.

marital state. The injunction that no women under 35 are to have a vote and none under 30 to hold office gives some insight into contemporary notions of the age at which a woman became an 'old maid'. The single female assembly argues that they are being victimized for actions for which they are not responsible: 'And if we are so unfortunate as never to be asked the question, or to refuse the only deformed wretch who perchance opens his mouth, it is such an evidence of our guilt, that we are branded with infamy for being old maids, and doomed to scorn and contempt here, and Apes and Devils hereafter.' The convocation resolves that the great number of maidens in Great Britain is a 'national grievance' and is 'contradictory to the natural ends of society'.[49]

In this piece, the seventeenth-century problem of low marriage rates has transformed into the eighteenth-century problem of superfluous single-women. Never-married women are now represented as the source of trouble to both the Church and the State in Britain. These fictional singlewomen complain that they are also now scorned and viewed with contempt. In the *Spectator* never-married women are referred to by such derogatory names as Sarah Lately, Charity Frost, and Susannah Lovebane. Addison also re-proached never-married women for 'censoriousness, gossiping, and trouble-making', characteristics that would come to define the 'old maid'.[50]

While Addison and Steele mocked 'old maids', Defoe produced the most severe satires of never-married women in the periodical press. In 1719–20 Defoe took on the subject positions of both an old maid and her critics in a series of satirical pieces for *Mist's Journal*. In his support of 'An Office for Marriages' he says that such a design 'would be particularly useful to a set of despicable creatures, called Old Maids'. While ladies of fortune, wit, and beauty have no need of such a scheme, 'as for those wretches who had languished out their insipid lives, perhaps without ever having an offer of a Husband; 'tis no wonder, if they, (lost to all sense of modesty, and at their last cast), should (rather than sink with the heavy luggage of Virginity into their graves)' want to use this office.[51] Here again is the theme of a dating service for never-married women. But in Defoe's hands these women are no longer charity cases, they are 'despicable, insipid wretches'. Gone is the hapless, pathetic figure replaced by a negative figure whose faults account for her singleness.

[49] *Gentleman's Magazine*, 7 (Feb. 1737), 99–102.
[50] *Spectator*, nos. 7, 272, 296, 483. Cited in Gwendolyn B. Needham, 'The "Old Maid" in the Life and Fiction of Eighteenth-Century England', Ph.D. dissertation, University of California (1938), 156–7.
[51] 'An Office for Marriages' (4 Apr. 1719), in William Lee (ed.), *Daniel Defoe, His Life and Recently Discovered Writings*, vol. 2 (1869; repr. New York: Burt Franklin, 1969), 115–16.

Defoe provided more sympathetic, albeit patronizing, depictions of younger singlewomen. Again in *Mist's Journal* he wrote as 'A female distressed for a fortune and a husband'. This young, sensible, pretty woman lacks money, and so 'for this twelve years, put money into the Lotteries, and for what think you, but to buy this haughty, saucy thing, called a HUSBAND ...' It seems that Defoe was more kind when considering a young singlewoman faced with greedy suitors and high dowry prices. Perhaps this was because he was the father of four marriageable daughters, two of whom never married. Defoe was less sympathetic, however when representing 'A Female Quixote' who, although not so young, is still picky about a spouse, and 'would rather run the Hazard of leading Apes [in hell], according to the old Fable, than join [herself] with a Mechanick'.[52]

In the 1720s Defoe continued to build up the caricature of the older singlewoman in various issues of *Applebee's Journal*. His first foray was a 'Satire on Censorious Old Maids' (1723). Defoe describes a tea-table court not unlike the Spanish Inquisition, where single ladies sit in judgement of their own sex. These women 'alarmed me much, because I was told they were of another Species of Women, and particularly such, as were more cruel and merciless than the other, being a furious and voracious kind of females; nay, even a kind of Amazonian Cannibals, that not only subdued, but devoured those that had the misfortune to fall into their hands'. Here Defoe represents lifelong singlewomen as another species, both animalistic and cannibalistic. Then he admits that the 'reason old maids are without compassion to their fellow-creatures ... [is] that nobody having had compassion upon them, and the Age having been so cruel to them, as to shew them no mercy', they only practice *lex talionis*. But he goes on to exhibit exactly the type of mercilessness he exposes, stating that sour and acrimonious liquids run in the veins of old maids instead of blood, and if 'an old maid should bite any body, it would certainly be as mortal, as the bite of a Mad-Dog'. Singlewomen are no longer subjects of pity, or even figures of fun; now they are evil.

The subject of lifelong singlewomen was so popular in the press that it resulted in a periodical called *The Old Maid* (1755). This serial publication was different, however, in that it was written by a woman and offered an alternative to the largely negative depictions of lifelong singlewomen. Frances Brooke produced this periodical under the pseudonym of Mary Singleton. While Brooke was a singlewoman when she published *The Old Maid*, she married a clergyman the following year, at the age of 32. Because she married slightly later than the popular notion of age at first marriage,

---

[52] 'On Old Maids' (29 Aug. 1719), 'A Female Distressed for a Fortune and a Husband' (30 Jan. 1720), and 'A Female Quixote' (19 Mar. 1720), in ibid. 143–4, 187–9.

Brooke may well have thought she was destined to be a lifelong single-woman; but she certainly was not the elderly virgin that Mary Singleton represented. Despite her own singleness, or perhaps because of it, Brooke's representations of 'old maids' are conflicted, but by no means as derogatory as Defoe's.

While many male authors assumed that most women stayed single because they had to, Brooke presented another side to the story. Mary Singleton explains how she came to be a lifelong singlewoman. At the age of 23 she had promised herself to a suitor of whom her father disapproved. When Singleton's father died two years later her lover deserted her for a wealthier woman. Singleton fled England, living abroad with her sister's family for three years. She was wary of other marriage offers, and when her sister died, leaving an infant daughter to her care, Singleton 'determined... to remain single'.[53] Unrequited love contributed to, but did not force, Mary Singleton's decision to stay single. After other offers, she chose this path. While Singleton's 'life story' is fictional, as we will see in the next chapter, her account of marital choice is strikingly similar to that provided by real women who never married.

The caricature of the 'old maid' appeared in various literary and artistic mediums other than periodicals. Engravers and printmakers, beginning with Hogarth in his *Time of Day* and *The Rake's Progress* series, made the lifelong singlewoman a visual figure of fun. Popular plays, such as Arthur Murphy's *The Old Maid. A Comedy in Two Acts* (1761), placed the lifelong singlewoman at the centre of satire.[54] And the eighteenth-century novel made a stock figure of the 'old maid', who was cast as the foil to the young, single heroine of the ubiquitous marriage plot. Katherine Kittredge has explored some of the best-known caricatures of never-married women in the novel. Samuel Richardson's *Pamela* (1740) featured the ugly, masculine, and evil-natured Mrs Jewkes. Miss Tabitha Bramble of Tobias Smollett's *Humphry Clinker* (1771) and Bridgit Allworthy of Henry Fielding's *Tom Jones* (1749) were notoriously ungrateful singlewomen, dependent on the brothers with whom they resided. In contrast, independent singlewomen such as Mrs Western in *Tom Jones* and Elisinda in *The Prude, A Novel by a Young Lady* (1724) were often represented as overly masculine in nature. Novelists also frequently portrayed lifelong singlewomen as pushy, nosey, greedy, and either sexually promiscuous or prudish.[55]

---

[53] Mary Singleton, *The Old Maid* (London, 1755–6), nos. 1, 5.

[54] Murphy's *The Old Maid* was performed 25 times at Drury Lane theatre and was a popular piece well into the nineteenth century. Lanser, 'Singular Politics', 320, n. 22.

[55] Katharine Kittredge, ' "Tabby Cats Lead Apes in Hell": Spinsters in Eighteenth Century Life and Fiction', Ph.D. dissertation, SUNY, Binghamton (1992), 165, 181–9, 193, 244, 249, 260, 289, 310, 317–18, 321–2.

It was not just male novelists who depicted lifelong singlewomen in a negative light; for example, Fanny Burney's novel *Camilla* (1796) featured the conniving and grasping Mrs Mittin. Nevertheless, it was female authors who provided the few positive representations of never-married women. Sarah Scott's *Millenium Hall* (1762) depicted strong and contented single-women within a supportive female community. In this novel, the aged singlewoman Miss Mancel and her widowed friend, the former Miss Melvyn, retire together and establish a home for young women. With Mancel, Scott created one of the most positive single female characters in eighteenth-century fiction. While Miss Mancel does not challenge the norms of female virtue, she does make a happy and worthy life for herself without having a relationship with a man. Kittredge has argued that the community is 'a setting in which [the singlewoman] regains the identity and usefulness that the man/marriage dominant society denies her'.[56] As we saw with the literature on academies and colleges for singlewomen, writing about such women outside of the marriage paradigm seems to have been one of the few ways to create a more positive portrayal of them.

While Scott's *Millenium Hall* is admired by feminist literary critics, contemporary taste seems to have leaned more toward the poet William Hayley's popular representation of singlewomen. In 1785 Hayley published *A Philosophical Essay on Old Maids*, a three-volume poem, with the first volume devoted to cataloguing the chief faults of 'old maids'. Hayley's contribution was nothing new; rather, it synthesized the eighteenth century's negative caricature of the 'old maid'. He represented singlewomen as credulous creatures who believed that all men were in love with them and that they might yet gain a husband. He depicted them as obsessed with sex, promiscuous if they could be, envious of others if they could not. Hayley's singlewomen were 'maimed' because they lacked husbands, and unnatural because they were deprived of their roles as wife and mother. He claimed the chief faults of 'old maids' were their nosiness, affectations (of youth especially), envy, and ill nature.[57] Hayley's poem was so popular it went through six editions and was translated into French and German.[58] This says something about the popularity of satirizing never-married women during the eighteenth century.

How should we explain the transformation of lifelong singlewomen from English society's victims to its villains? What happened in England for these popular representations to become so negative? And why did the English develop a negative 'old maid' stereotype a century earlier than other Euro-

---

[56] Ibid. 13, 119, 368, 374–7, 382–3.

[57] William Hayley, *A Philosophical Essay on Old Maids* (London, 1785); Kittredge, '"Tabby Cats"', 25–8, 41.

[58] Needham, 'The Old Maid', 163–7.

pean countries? Lanser has suggested that the negative representation of never-married women was tied to the pro-natalist concerns of the British nation, which was at war and in need of soldiers during the eighteenth century. Pro-natalism certainly affected popular perceptions of never-married (read, non-reproductive) women; however, I do not think it entirely explains the emergence of the 'old maid' stereotype, its particularity to Anglo-American culture, and its persistence. If we cast our eye over the entire early modern period, rather than focusing just on the eighteenth century, other possible explanations emerge. First, if we think back to the urban singlewomen of earlier chapters we will remember that their economic power (in terms of business-owning, property holding, and money-lending) grew from the 1690s through the first half of the 1700s. It is probably no coincidence that, as singlewomen became more independent and powerful, popular depictions of them became more pejorative. After all, if women who never married were successful in life, this might encourage other women to remain single.

This leads to the second reason why lifelong singlewomen may have been negatively stereotyped as 'old maids'. The seventeenth century shows that there were alternative representations. In that century singlewomen were victims, particularly of circumstance and of men, and as such were worthy of pity. That century's discourse had suggested that women were forced to remain single because of a lack of male suitors. The change in the eighteenth century was that singlewomen were no longer represented as victims; rather, they were now blamed for their marital status. Why the blame? Because there was a recognition that some women might choose to never marry instead of being forced into singleness. If this was the case, what better way to ensure that more women did not choose to never marry (and upset the patriarchal model of heterosexual marriage and reproduction) than to characterize such women as 'old maids'? The necessity for women to marry and produce the next generation may well account for the staying-power of the 'old maid' stereotype up until the present day.

There is a third reason that helps explain why the 'old maid' stereotype emerged in England in particular. Nineteenth-century feminists such as Frances Cobbe were aware of this reason when they referred to the figure of the 'Protestant Old Maid'.[59] England largely lacked a space (both conceptual and real) for singlewomen in its society. The Protestant Reformation abolished the nunnery, and did not replace it with any other institution for never-married women in the early modern period. Other European

[59] Frances Power Cobbe, 'Social Science Congresses and Women's Part in Them', *Macmillan's Magazine* (Dec. 1861), 90. Quoted in Eileen Janes Yeo, 'Virgin Mothers: Single Women Negotiate the Doctrine of Motherhood in Victorian and Edwardian Britain', paper presented to Rutgers Center for Historical Analysis (Fall 2003).

countries provided spaces for singlewomen, including convents, alms-houses, beguinages, and Magdalen houses. But Protestant England preferred to blame singlewomen for their own inability to 'fit' into English society, rather than to create a place in which for them to fit. England's refusal to accommodate the singlewoman led to something akin to a blame-the-victim mentality in the eighteenth century.

The early modern period was a true watershed in the popular representation of never-married women. Before the seventeenth century single-women figured in ballads as young virgins pursuing love, sex, and courtship. But in the mid-seventeenth century there began to be an acknowledgement that not all Englishwomen were marrying, and that a sizeable group of older singlewomen now existed in English society. The later seventeenth century witnessed a literary focus on solving the 'problem' of singlewomen, either by marrying them off through lotteries and match-making schemes, or providing them with an alternative to the nuclear family household, whether it was a college or nunnery. Never-married women were hapless charity cases in need of relief. Another change came in the early eighteenth century, as the popular conception of never-married women became much more negative and vitriolic. The stereotype of the spinster or old maid emerged, and the never-married woman became a figure of scorn, contempt, and even abuse. In the early modern era popular conceptions of lifelong singlewomen changed from recognition, to pity, to ridicule.

How did never-married women live with the ridicule, contempt, and scorn aimed at them? And how did they create a space for themselves in English society, since the culture did not do it for them? In the next chapter I will look at singlewomen's own words and how they chose to represent themselves, in contrast to how English society represented them. And I will explore the issue of whether never-married women chose singleness, as contemporaries feared, or had it thrust upon them.

7

The Question of Choice: How Never-married Women Represented Singleness

As we saw in the last chapter, seventeenth- and eighteenth-century stereo-types portrayed never-married women as single because of a lack of male partners or outright rejection by men. Richard Allestree, in his popular conduct book *The Ladies Calling* (1673), had some words of advice for never-married women, or as he liked to call them, those 'calamitous creatures' who had 'failed to' marry. Allestree told these women to 'addict themselves to the strictest virtue and piety, [so that] they would give the world some cause to believe, 'twas not their necessity, but their choice which kept them unmarried, that they were pre-engaged to a better amour, espoused to the spiritual bridegroom; and this would give them among the soberer sort, at least the reverence and esteem of matrons'.[1] The underlying assumption here was that singlewomen, of course, had not chosen their marital status but they should pretend to have done so in order to avoid pity and scorn.

The question of choice has been an important one in the study of singlewomen. Our fascination with the issue of choice, however, may have more to do with our modern-day preoccupation with individualism and free will than with the experiences of never-married women in early modern England. In a country where the Anglican Church accepted (to some extent) Calvinistic notions of God's will, and Dissenting sects only more so, never-married women may not have thought of their singleness as an active decision. In a Protestant country where marriage was expected of almost all, most women assumed they would get married, whether they desired to or not. The marriage process and the series of negotiations and constraints that governed courtship in early modern England have recently been the subject of study.[2] Most lifelong singlewomen had proceeded down some portion of this courtship path, but for various reasons these women were either tripped up or they stopped short. They then diverted to an

---

[1] Richard Allestree, *The Ladies Calling* (London, 1673), pt. 2, pp. 3–4.
[2] Diana O'Hara, *Courtship and Constraint: Rethinking the Making of Marriage in Tudor England* (Manchester and New York: Manchester University Press, 2000).

alternative path, that of singlehood. How and why this occurred for some women is the topic of this chapter.

To examine why women remained single and what they thought about their single status it is necessary to analyse their own words and actions. Surprisingly, this has not been done to any degree, researchers having preferred instead to chronicle the stereotypes others had about women who never married. A number of sources can illuminate never-married women's attitudes toward their marital state. These include wills, which shed some light on the ideas of non-elite singlewomen, as well as letters, journals, diaries, and poetry, which are skewed toward the middling sort. Because sources by singlewomen (particularly non-elites) are not overly plentiful, this chapter stretches this book's 1750 endpoint and includes a few women who wrote after the mid-eighteenth century, but I have only included examples that are particularly illuminating.

The wills, journals, letters, and poems written by early modern single-women reveal that these women constructed an identity for themselves based on their marital status. From their writings it appears that never-married women may have necessarily had more of a sense of the individual self than married women or even some men. Without the requisite female identity of wife or mother, singlewomen wrote alternative identities for themselves. Personal writing may have been especially important to never-married women. In a society that tried to deny them a place, they had to create one themselves. They did so through their words as well as their actions. By neglecting the study of marital status and the study of single-women in particular, scholars may have missed a fruitful area in the search for the origins of the 'modern, individual self'. The emergence of the individual self has most often been associated with the bourgeois male of the late eighteenth century, but this notion could be altered by examining the single female of the seventeenth and eighteenth centuries.[3]

Examining the personal writings of singlewomen also sheds some light on why women remained single and their attitudes toward their marital status. The first section of this chapter illustrates how women rarely made a straightforward choice to never marry; rather, they usually made a series of decisions and non-decisions that led to lifelong singleness. It is possible to discern a pattern of factors that seem to have predisposed some women to remain single. The most common of these circumstances included sickness or deformity, the demands of care-giving and family responsibilities, the loss or lack of financial means, the pursuit of religious vocations, and the early death of the singlewoman herself or her prospective spouse.

---

[3] See e.g. the work of Michael Mascuch, *Origins of the Individualist Self: Autobiography and Self-identity in England, 1591–1791* (Stanford, Cal.: Stanford University Press, 1996).

The second section of this chapter examines never-married women's attitudes toward singleness. In particular, I explore how never-married women were affected by the negative depictions of themselves in the popular literature of the period; whether it was possible for them to carve out more neutral or even positive roles for themselves; and if they saw themselves as active choosers of their marital status or as victims of fate. What we will see is that, whether it was a choice or not, remaining single was neither simply a positive or negative experience. Many never-married women recognized and pointed out the benefits of being single—the time for themselves, the absent burdens of a husband and children, the liberty to follow a vocation, and the ability to develop deep friendships. Nevertheless, all the singlewomen included here acknowledged that they lost something by forgoing marriage. That something may have been the social status reserved to married matrons, the normative experience of a married life, the companionship obtained by membership in a nuclear family, or the fulfillment of what early modern people commonly viewed as a woman's destiny. Singlewomen's personal writings reveal that the concept of marital 'choice' hides a complex, long-term, and fraught process.

Factors Leading to Singleness

Families, and singlewomen themselves, commonly viewed illness and infirmity as impediments to marriage. Contemporaries considered household duties, childbearing, and child-rearing hard work that an ill or lame woman would not be able to perform. William Stout noted this in his autobiography when discussing his sister Elin, who was plagued with ulcers and sickness from her teens onward: 'My sister had the offers of marriage with several country yeomen, men of good repute and substance, but being always subject to the advice of her mother, was advised, considering her infirmities and ill state of health, to remain single, knowing the care and exercises that always attended a married life.'[4] Elin Stout did remain a lifelong singlewoman. Nevertheless, we should note that her 'ill health' did not prevent her natal family from calling on her to nurse various kin, keep house for her brothers, raise her nieces and nephews, and manage her brother William's shop and apprentices. Elin Stout's case reveals that a singlewoman's 'ill health' could be used as a convenient excuse to keep her single and keep her labour in the natal family, rather than losing it to a new family created by marriage.

---

[4] J. D. Marshall (ed.), *The Autobiography of William Stout of Lancaster 1665–1752* (New York, 1967), 87–8.

While sickness itself might cause a woman to remain single, illness could also result in deformity, another reason that factored into a woman's marital opportunities. Many diseases, smallpox most prominent among them, might mar a woman's physical appearance. Early modern people had very different standards of beauty from our own age, yet by the eighteenth century singlewomen were being represented as ugly 'old maids'. The central character of William Hogarth's engraving of 'Morning' from his *Times of the Day* series (1738) was an old maid. A number of characteristics identified her as such, most notably her prudish distaste at the revellers coming out of Tom King's coffeehouse, her gaunt but overdressed figure, and her face, which was marred with pockmarks. The assumption behind the depiction of a gaunt, pockmarked singlewoman was that her marital status was due to her unattractiveness. While this was by no means true (numbers of lifelong singlewomen were conventionally attractive, not least among them Hogarth's two never-married sisters), for some women this may have been a self-fulfilling prophecy. While many plain women married, women deformed in face or body might have been more likely to remain single. Religious commentators even named deformity as one of the few condoned reasons for a person to remain single. In his treatise *Of Domesticall Duties*, the Puritan minister William Gouge said the only time it was acceptable not to marry was if a person was lame, impotent, or had a contagious disease such as leprosy, which would prevent that person from procreating: 'for by those signs of impotence God shows that he calls them to live single'.[5] Evidently, the adage 'be fruitful and multiply' did not apply to those who were not 'whole'.

Gertrude Savile provides an example of a singlewomen whose physical appearance played a role in her not marrying, but not necessarily in the way we might think. Savile, a gentlewoman resident in eighteenth-century London, suffered from an 'unhappy malady in [her] face'. In her diary Savile chronicled the doctors she consulted and remedies she attempted throughout her youth and middle age to cure this mystery ailment. Savile blamed her malady for her depression and for her shyness and discomfort when it came to being in company. She wrote: 'I have thought my more than common dispiritedness was from the distemper in my face, [that] has broke my spirit. Such a continual mortification all my youth and gay part of life, not only cut me off from pleasures of it, but has cowed and depressed me'.[6] By keeping her from the social activities where genteel women met husbands, Savile's 'deformity' contributed to her single status. Savile's physical appearance did contribute to her singleness, but it did not lead to outright rejection by a male

[5] William Gouge, *Of Domesticall Duties*, 2nd edn. (London, 1626), 123–4, 105–6.
[6] Alan Saville (ed.), *Secret Comment: The Diaries of Gertrude Savile 1721–1757*, Thoroton Society Record Series, 41 (Nottingham, 1997), 21, 87.

suitor, as we might assume, rather it caused her fear and avoidance of social situations. The reason for Savile's single state was complicated; it was not just due to a man, for she had agency in the decision as well.

Deformity also impacted on the marital prospects of the Bath milliner Mary Chandler. Her brother Samuel bluntly stated that Chandler 'had nothing in her shape to recommend her, being grown, by an accident in her childhood, very irregular in her body'. According to him, Chandler dealt with this 'irregularity' by making it 'the subject of her own pleasantry'. Not only did she joke about her appearance, she also compensated for it by 'cultivat[ing] her mind to make herself agreeable'. Samuel Chandler also felt his sister's 'shape [was] such as gave her no reasonable prospect of being happy in a married state, and therefore [she] chose to continue single'.[7] But rather than relying on her brother's perceptions alone, it is possible to see what Chandler herself said about her physical appearance. Chandler did choose to foreground her deformity in the poetry that she published. She dedicated one poem about her experience of childhood disease to Dr Oliver. In another, 'My Own Epitaph', Chandler represented deformity as part of her posthumous identity: 'Here lies a true maid, deformed and old; | Who, that she never was handsome, never needed be told'.[8] Chandler represented her physical appearance and her irregular spine as impediments to marriage, or at least as excuses for not engaging in matrimony. When she was 54 years old an even older gentleman, who had read and admired her poems, proposed marriage to her. Chandler joked about the proposal in verse: 'Fourscore long miles, to buy a crooked wife | Old too! I thought the oddest thing in life'.[9] Like Savile, Chandler's own feelings about her appearance may have had more, or just as much, to do with her singleness as any assumed (on her or our part) rejection by male suitors.

While her physical condition could affect her marriage prospects, shouldering family responsibilities was one of the most common reasons why a woman might marry late in life. And, the later a woman waited the less likely she was to marry at all. In early modern England daughters, more than sons, often remained with their parents or siblings to help generate income, do housework, and care for young, sick, or elderly kin. Delaying marriage until family responsibilities were over meant that a woman might be past childbearing age and less likely to marry. Mary Capper provides a good example of how a singlewoman could find herself burdened with

[7] Robert Shiels, *Account of the Lives of the Poets of Great Britain and Ireland* (1753), cited in David Shuttleton, '"All Passion Extinguish'd": The Case of Mary Chandler, 1687–1745', in Isobel Armstong and Virginia Blain (eds.), *Women's Poetry in the Enlightenment: The Making of a Canon, 1730–1820* (New York: St Martin's Press, 1999), 33–49.

[8] Mary Chandler, *The Description of Bath. A Poem*, 3rd edn. (London, 1736), 21–3, 40–1.

[9] Janet Todd (ed.), *A Dictionary of British and American Women Writers 1660–1800* (Totowa, NJ: Rowman & Allanheld, 1985), 80–1.

family duties during her prime marriage years. Capper hailed from a middling background, with brothers who were clergymen and London merchants. In her early teens Capper wrote that 'nursing and needlework were my proper employments'. At the age of 27 she was sent to live with her married brother, partly because her Quaker religious views offended her parents, but also to assist the newly married couple. The following year another brother, this one unmarried, requested that Capper come and live as his housekeeper. Capper remained with her brother until her father died, and then, in her early thirties, she went to live with and care for her widowed mother. It was at this point that Capper contemplated marrying a fellow Quaker in London, but having to leave the metropolis to care for her mother may have been one of the reasons why she rejected the match. Capper remained with her mother until the latter's death. In the 1790s, and at the age of 39, Capper found herself free from family duties for the first time ever. Instead of starting her own family she opted to become a Quaker minister, a path she continued for the next fifty years. This career allowed her to travel and to focus on her own talents, two things she had probably not done in her years of care-taking. And when she was not ministering, Capper lodged alone in Birmingham.[10] Mary Capper illustrates how the burden of family and household responsibilities might lead a singlewomen to reject marriage and its familial duties.

Finances were a factor influencing lifelong singleness. The woman doomed to a life of singleness due to the lack of a marriage portion was a common trope in eighteenth-century literature, but it is still not clear how much this reflected reality. Certainly, dowry inflation plagued the elite in the seventeenth and eighteenth centuries, but it is uncertain how far down the social scale this was a factor.[11] Amy Erickson has found that the gentry, along with wealthy tradesmen and yeomen, saw marriage portions increase threefold, from £200 in the late sixteenth century to £500–£600 by the second half of the next century. But she has suggested that dowry inflation was not a concern for women below the gentry.[12] Diana O'Hara has found some compelling evidence to the contrary for rural daughters of husband-men and yeomen in Kent. Looking at bequests that these daughters received 'toward marriage' or at the 'age of marriage', O'Hara found that between the mid-fifteenth and late sixteenth centuries dowries increased fivefold.[13]

---

[10] William and Thomas Evans (eds.), 'A Memoir of Mary Capper, Late of Birmingham. A Minister of the Society of Friends', *Friends Library*, 12 (Philadelphia, 1848), 2, 15, 17, 20–2.

[11] Between the second quarter of the sixteenth and the third quarter of the seventeenth centuries dowries for daughters of the aristocracy increased tenfold. Lawrence Stone, *The Crisis of the Aristocracy*, abridged edn. (Oxford: Oxford University Press, 1967), 290–2.

[12] Amy Erickson, *Women and Property in Early Modern England* (London and New York: Routledge, 1993), 120–2.

[13] O'Hara, *Courtship and Constraint*, esp. 190–226.

Although the question of how general dowry inflation was is not entirely settled, it is relatively easy to find examples of women who associated their lifelong singleness with economic need. The seventeenth-century poet known as 'Ephelia' explicitly represented money, or a lack thereof, as the impediment to her marital chances.[14] Ephelia emphasized her marital status in poems such as 'Maidenhead' and 'The Green-Sickness Cure', which she included in her collection *Female Poems on Several Occasions* (1679). She also wrote several poems on the subject of Mr J. G., whom she styled 'her dearer half'. Ephelia related how J. G. had travelled abroad and failed to visit her on his return. After lamenting how she had loved J. G. for four years, she admitted that she now had a rival. J. G. proceeded to marry this rival, which Ephelia attributed to the fact that, 'as her numerous flocks decayed, His passion did so too'.[15] Likewise, the lack of a portion is one of the reasons why the poet Elizabeth Thomas (1675–1731) put off marriage. Her father died when she was 2, leaving her and her mother in what she termed poverty. Thomas's mother did remarry, but this stepfather only depleted the family funds further. When her mother developed breast cancer, Thomas had to sell things off, including her valuable book collection which she had purchased with gifts from godmothers and other relations. Thomas was engaged to Richard Gwinnet throughout her mother's sickness, but one of the reasons why they could not marry was that Gwinnet's father viewed her as a disadvantageous connection and postponed his son's inheritance. When her mother finally died after fourteen years of sickness she left Thomas £333 in debt, rather than with any money for a portion. Thomas was then in her mid-forties, and remained single until her death at 56.[16]

The governess Agnes Porter believed her lack of suitors was due to a similar lack of funds. At the age of 40 she became interested in one Dr McQueen, but the next year she reported in her journal that he was 'on the point of matrimony with a lady of fortune'. It was at about this same time that Porter decided to invest in a lottery. More than a month later she found a story she had heard from Mr Nichols, the writing master, important enough to note down in her journal. A woman's father had died in debt and

---

[14] Todd, *Dictionary*, 115–16. Ephelia's identity is an enigma. Literary scholars have posited that she was from an 'upper class London family', while others have identified her as Joan or Katherine Phillips (the only daughter of the poet Katherine Phillips (who was the daughter of a successful London merchant and the wife of a landed gentleman and MP). The most recent theory, put forward by Maureen Mulvihill, is that she was Mary Villiers Stuart, duchess of Richmond and Lennox and daughter to the first duke of Buckingham.

[15] Ephelia, *Female Poems on Several Occasions*, 2nd edn. (London, 1684), 6, 77–9.

[16] *Pylades and Corinna: or, Memoirs of the Lives, Amours, and Writings of Richard Gwinnet Esq. of Great Shurdington in Gloucs. and Mrs. Elizabeth Thomas Junior of Great Russell St., Blooms-bury... to which is prefixed The Life of Corinna, Written by Herself* (London, 1731), 4–6, 32, 39–44, 69–73.

the woman had decided to go into service. Passing by a lottery office, she bought a sixteenth share of a ticket (the same amount Porter had recently bought). The next day the woman found out that she had won a £1,200 prize. She went to board with a merchant's family, where she met a man of fortune to whom she was married in a matter of weeks. For Agnes Porter 'fortune' was the means that allowed a woman like herself to marry.[17] Porter worked hard to ensure financial stability for herself in old age. She died worth £2,000, which she had invested in navy stock so that it produced about £150 a year for her to live on.[18] Porter had amassed this sum through twenty-five or so years as a governess and companion. The sad irony is that a woman worth £2,000 felt she had missed out on marriage because of her lack of money.

Religion was another contributing factor in lifelong singleness. Even though the Protestant Reformation officially ended the option of monastic life for women in England, Catholic women still found ways to dedicate themselves to a life of pious celibacy. Some exiled themselves to the continent, where they joined or founded convents; others secluded themselves at home and carved out a life of lay piety; and a handful of followers of Mary Ward founded covert English nunneries at Hammersmith and York.[19] Although they might be the first to come to mind, Catholic women were not the only ones to embrace a life of religious celibacy. Single female members of the Church of England also followed lives of religious retirement. The philanthropist Elizabeth Hastings seldom left her estate at Ledsham. Living in seclusion there, she devoted herself to rigorous piety and charity. And as we saw in the last chapter, Hastings's single friend Mary Astell wrote about the need for Protestant nunneries in England, so that pious gentlewomen who never married would have a place to go.

Dissenting women, however, may have been the most likely to combine lives of religiosity and singleness. For reasons historians have yet to fully explore, many Nonconformist women married late, or sometimes not at all. As mentioned above, the Quaker minister Mary Capper remained single throughout her ninety-one-year life. In her journal Capper mentioned marriage only once. This was when she was 33, and just after her conversion to Quakerism. She was living in London with her brother when she formed a 'strong attachment to a young man Friend, to whom she expected to be married'. But she decided that her prospective mate did not value the Quakers and their principles highly enough, so she broke things off,

---

[17] Jeanna Martin (ed.), *A Governess in the Age of Jane Austen* (London: Hambledon Press, 1998), 103–4, 109, 39.

[18] Public Record Office, PROB 11/1560/530, cited in Martin, *Governess*, 28–9.

[19] For Catholic singlewomen, see Claire Walker, *Gender and Politics in Early Modern Europe: English Convents in France and the Low Countries* (New York: Palgrave, 2003).

'though it nearly cost her her life; and she could never afterwards entertain the prospect of matrimony'.[20] Capper exemplifies how a woman who was not against marriage per se might only find one person in the course of her life for whom she was willing to alter her marital status—and in Capper's case even then her religious principles won out over her affections. In later years Capper criticized female Friends who married non-Quakers; she expected other women to act as she had and put religion before marriage.

The fact that Mary Capper restricted prospective partners to those who shared her religious beliefs may well have contributed to her singleness. Religious endogamy was a significant factor in the lives of women in minority sects. Marjorie Reeves's study of several Nonconformist families living in south-western England reveals a high level of intermarriage among co-religionists. This resulted in both late marriages and a striking number of women who did not marry at all in these families. Jane Attwater and her cousin Mary Steele did not marry co-religionists until they reached the ages of 37 and 44 respectively. Attwater, at least, debated long and hard in her journal before marrying at all. In 1785 she wrote to her cousin Mary for advice. It seems that after her mother's death she began to consider setting herself up in business rather than marrying.[21]

Mary's aunt, Anne Steele (1717–78), a writer of Baptist hymns and religious poetry, provided her with a model of lifelong singlehood. Engaged early in life, Steele's intended husband drowned and she never married thereafter. Even though she was a Dissenter, it is significant that Anne Steele called on Catholic imagery to describe her life as a pious singlewoman. She named her outhouse retreat at her father's home in Broughton her 'cell', and referred to herself as a nun. In 'To Melinda' (the poetical name for her sister), Steele made use of the same imagery, contrasting her conventual life to the one of courtship in which her sister was engaged:

> Melinda Now Returns Victorious
> Three Hearts Subdued too much by half
> D'ye think such News can make me laugh
> *While I poor solitary Nun*
> Moping at home can't rise to one...
> Methinks t'would be but just and due
> To spare your Sister one or two
> But this is only spoke in jest
> On second thoughts and those are best
> Your Vict'ry since I cannot share

[20] Evans, 'Memoir of Mary Capper', 21, 25.
[21] Marjorie Reeves, *Pursuing the Muses: Female Education and Nonconformist Culture, 1700–1900* (Leicester: Leicester University Press, 1997), 98, 118.

I want no slaves that you can spare
Lone quiet in a humble Cell
Will suit my temper full as well.[22]

Steele's poem intimates that she is jealous of her sister's romantic conquests, but then she states that she is just jesting and that she prefers a simple life of solitude and quiet. The poem may reflect ambivalence on her part, but it also stakes a claim for a different sort of life for a young singlewoman.

Fate, and the relatively high mortality rate of the early modern era, also influenced whether a woman died single or married. Some women intended to marry, but ill health and sudden death meant that instead they ended their lives as singlewomen. For example, in 1701 Elizabeth Raleigh 'of Portsmouth, spinster, being sick and weak of body', made her testament. Among her bequests was a piece of clothing 'which was to have been my wedding shift'.[23] In 1651 Joanne Rowte of Portsmouth left nearly half her estate to her 'intended husband' John Compton. Similarly, Eleanor Percy, of the Isle of Wight, divided her estate equally between her 'intended husband' Samuel Churchill and his daughter Elizabeth.[24] These three women made their wills as 'spinsters', and thus are counted as lifelong singlewomen, but they had obviously meant to marry.

A woman might remain single for life because of a partner's death rather than her own. Some women were not averse to marriage per se, but once they lost a particular lover their interest ended. For example, Anne Steele never married, but at one point she had been engaged to a young man who had drowned while swimming in the River Avon.[25] For the poet Elizabeth Thomas a multitude of factors may have led to her singleness. For instance, she was sickly throughout her life, financially insecure due to the death of her father and the shady business schemes of her stepfather, burdened with a sick mother whom she nursed into her own forties, and fond of a solitary life of reading and writing poetry. And yet Thomas did almost marry the gentleman Richard Gwinnet, with whom she carried on a passionate courtship for sixteen years. In her memoir *The Life of Corinna*, Thomas wrote that she and Gwinnet struck up a friendship and 'mutual esteem' which was not extinguished on Gwinnet's part even after Thomas explained that she had no marriage portion and that she had to care for her mother. Thomas and Gwinnet agreed to wait until marriage might be possible, and proceeded to write and visit one another for sixteen years. Then, in 1717, Gwinnet's father

---

[22] Ibid. 69. Italics my own.
[23] Hampshire Record Office (hereafter HRO), 1701 A 80/1–2.
[24] HRO, 1651 A45/1–2; 1732 A96.
[25] Reeves, *Pursuing the Muses*, 27, 62.

finally handed over his inheritance and said he could marry whom he pleased. Gwinnet rode immediately to see Thomas, but she asked him to put off the marriage for another six months while she nursed her mother who was on her deathbed. Unfortunately, her lover died before her mother did.[26] Elizabeth Thomas never married between the time Gwinnet died (while she was in her forties) and her own death at the age of 56. For her, the man she had loved, and perhaps the opportunity for marriage in general, had both disappeared.

Interestingly, some of the women who spoke out most vociferously against marriage ended up marrying. This was the case for Alice Thornton, the daughter of the Yorkshire gentleman Christopher Wandesforde. Alice and her family suffered due to the untimely deaths of her Royalist father and eldest brother, and because of parliament's sequestration of the family estates during the Civil Wars. Alice Thornton began to write her autobiography at the age of 42, when she was a widow. In it, she described her years as a singlewoman as a series of marital near-misses. She recorded that she survived several attempts by Scottish soldiers to kidnap and marry her during the Civil Wars. When she was 24, her uncle proposed that if she married her cousin he would try to gain back her family's sequestered estates from the Puritan government. Alice agreed to the match for her family's own good, although she said it was 'contrary to my own inclination to marriage' and that she had hoped not 'to change *my happy estate* for a miserable encumbered one in the married'.[27] Although Alice was able to disentangle herself from this arrangement, her mother then began to pressure her to marry. This was most likely because she was past her early twenties, the marriageable age for a gentlewoman. Thornton wrote:

As to myself, I was exceedingly satisfied in that happy and free condition, wherein I enjoyed my time with delight abundantly in the service of my God and the obedience I owed to such an excellent parent . . . nor could I, without much reluctance, draw my thoughts to the change of my single life, knowing too much of the cares of this world sufficiently without the addition of such incident to the married estate.

Despite her antipathy toward marriage, Thornton said she eventually was persuaded to it only because her mother found her a 'godly, sober, and discreet' mate, and because she viewed it as her duty. 'And if it pleased God so to dispose of me in marriage, making me a more public instrument of good to those several relations, I thought it rather [my] duty in me to accept my friends' desires for a joint benefit, than my own single retired content.'[28] Here Thornton represented her marriage not as an active choice but as an

---

[26] Thomas, *Pylades and Corinna*, 71–3.
[27] *The Autobiography of Mrs. Alice Thornton Of East Newton, co. York*, Surtees Society, 62 (1875), 62. Italics my own.
[28] Ibid. 75, 77.

acceptance of God's plan. In fact, if she had been able to decide she would have opted for singleness, but Thornton believed she did not have the agency, God did. This is a telling example of how our present-day focus on the issue of choice can be misleading, if not anachronistic.

Alice Thornton's preference for singlehood seems to have manifested itself psychosomatically. She married William Thornton just before her twenty-fifth birthday. She wrote that, on her wedding day, 'Having been in health and strength for many years before, I fell suddenly so ill and sick' with a headache, stomach-ache, vomiting, and 'sickness at my heart' for eight hours.[29] It is significant that Thornton emphasized that years of good health deserted her on the symbolic day when she changed her marital state. Her satisfaction with being single and devoting her life to God and to her mother, and her reluctance to enter into the cares of married life, may have made the transition to wife rougher for Alice Thornton than for many women.

Like Alice Thornton, when the Bluestocking Elizabeth Robinson Montagu was a young woman she envisioned never marrying. Montagu was very close to her sister, Sarah (Robinson Scott), whom she wrote to at the age of 20 while on a visit in 1740: 'A slice of the apartment I live in would make you and I a comfortable house in the state of our virginity when we are poor old maidens.'[30] Perhaps Montagu's mind was changed when Anne Donnellan, herself a lifelong singlewoman, assured her that marriage 'is the settlement in the world we should aim at, and the only way we females have of making ourselves of use to society and raising ourselves in the world'. Although Montagu married at the young age of 22, she described her transition as 'changing from old maid's pink to bridal pink and silver'. At the time she was fearful of her decision and worried about losing her close female friendships. Montagu's marriage did not prove to be particularly happy. Twenty years later she told Lord Lyttleton that she thought she had married too quickly, and she suggested that his own daughter should wait until the more mature age of 28 (a late age for a gentlewoman to marry at this time) before changing her marital status.[31] For Montagu, singleness was not something a woman should abandon too early or too easily.

Some women expressed no desire to marry for a much longer period of their lives than Alice Thornton or Elizabeth Montagu, and then suddenly changed their marital state. Such a woman was Catherine Payton Philips (*c.*1726–94), who was called into the Quaker ministry at the young age of 18. For the next fifty years she kept busy travelling and preaching throughout

[29] Ibid. 83.
[30] Letter written in 1740, quoted in Sylvia H. Myers, *The Bluestocking Circle: Women, Friendship, and the Life of the Mind in Eighteenth-Century England* (Oxford: Clarendon Press, 1990), 34.
[31] Ibid. 85, 96.

Britain and America. Philips's memoirs reveal that she obviously enjoyed her vocation and that she felt resentment when she returned home and was expected to take up family responsibilities. In 1760 she said she was 'endeavouring to discharge my duty in domestic cares a greater weight whereof than heretofore rested upon me since my sister's marriage; through which, and my brother's continued indisposition, my way in leaving home was straightened; yet I know not that any clear manifestation of duty was omitted; although sometimes it was discharged with difficulty'. Two years later Philips moaned, 'a load of domestic concerns devolved on me'. Her words reveal that she did not shirk her duty, but also that it did not weigh lightly on her shoulders.

And then suddenly, after forty-five years of singleness and with little explanation in her memoirs, Catherine Philips got married. She said that she had not married earlier because:

> my mind had been, and was under strong restrictions in regard to entering into the marriage state, should I be solicited thereto; for as it appeared that for a series of years I should be much engaged in travelling for the service of truth, I feared to indulge thoughts of forming a connection, which from its encumbrances, might tend to frustrate the intention of Divine wisdom respecting me. This caution tended to keep me reserved in my conduct, towards such as might be likely to entertain views beyond friendship.

What had occurred so that Philips no longer felt that marriage might constrain her vocation as a Quaker preacher? My reading is that, by taking a spouse, Philips escaped the duty of caring for her natal household, because she would now have one of her own. In addition, because she married at around the age of menopause, Philips never had children during her thirteen-year marriage, meaning that she only had to care for her husband and herself. How much she had to do even that was uncertain, since she continued to preach and travel with female companions after her marriage. The only exception to this pattern was a ten-month stretch which, she noted, 'was the longest period I remember to have been *confined*'.[32] Philips seems to have been an independent woman who, by finding a supportive spouse, was able to use both singlehood and marriage to ensure her continued enjoyment of freedom and career.

Attitudes Toward Singleness

As the last section has shown, there were various reasons why a woman might find herself single in middle or old age. She may not have made a

---

[32] William and Thomas Evans (eds.), 'Memoirs of the Life of Catharine Philips', *Friends Library*, 11 (Philadelphia, 1847), 188, 231, 247, 253, 261. Italics my own.

definitive decision or choice never to marry and yet still find herself single, or she may have decided early in life or at a more mature stage that she did not favour changing her marital state. This section examines the words of never-married women to see how they constructed their single selves. It begins by examining the wills of singlewomen for the evidence they provide on the construction of a never-married identity. Wills are useful because they provide a window onto non-elite women's attitudes toward singleness. Then we move on to the journals, poetry, and letters written by single-women from the middling sort and gentry, to examine the light they shed on the construction of the single female self in the early modern period.

The personal writings of early modern women have been well studied, but scholars have looked almost exclusively at the writings of ever-married women, both wives and widows. Women often produced these works for their own children, and placed marriage and the creation of a family at their narrative centre. By focusing on the personal writings of women who never married, this chapter forces us to ask some very different questions. If, as Mary Beth Rose has asserted, 'attempts by women to define themselves as integrated individuals in a male-dominant society' were problematic, how much more difficult were they for singlewomen, who experienced a double burden?[33] A woman who never married had to construct her identity without recourse to such roles as wife and mother. A singlewoman who wrote a journal or a memoir did so with no direct descendents to whom she could pass it on. This would have affected the meaning of such an enterprise. Never-married women may have been more apt to write because they had more time than wives and mothers, or because of what Barbara Lewalski has called the relationship 'between authoring a text and authoring a self'.[34] Singlewomen needed to find a place for themselves in early modern England, and writing was one of the ways they could do so. And if we accept the link between individuality and modernity posited by some literary scholars, a singlewoman's identity, which was by definition more individual, may also have been more modern.

One of the most common moments for singlewomen to reflect on their identity and their single status was when they faced their demise. Historians have recently begun to read wills as autobiographical texts. Read in this light, we see that single female testators frequently chose to emphasize their marital status and represent themselves as never-married women in their wills. One of the most telling portions of the early modern will was the

[33] Mary Beth Rose, 'Gender, Genre, and History: Seventeenth-Century English Women and the Art of Autobiography', in Rose (ed.), *Women in the Middle Ages and the Renaissance* (Syracuse, NY: Syracuse University Press, 1986), 249.

[34] Barbara Lewalski, *Writing Women in Jacobean England* (Cambridge, Mass.: Harvard University Press, 1993), 6.

section in which the testator made arrangements for their funeral and burial. Some willmakers were quite terse, while others had definite ideas about memorializing their life. It was in this part of their wills, more than any other, that singlewomen chose to draw attention to their marital status.

Singlewomen most frequently represented their marital status at burial through the choice of never-married women as pallbearers or chief mourners, and by their stress on the colour white. For example, Margaret Yalden of Winchester gave gloves and a ribbon to each of the eight poor maidens that she specified should carry her to her burial. She also provided alms to unmarried women in particular, including three widows and two old mistresses.[35] Jane Bracebridge of Southampton asked that Mary, Ann, and Jane Clutterbuck, as well as Sarah Poole, all Nonconformist singlewomen like herself, 'bear up the four corners of the sheet [shroud]' at her funeral. She also wanted each of them to have a ring, gloves, and a silk hood to remember her by.[36] Elizabeth Wainwright of Oxford asked to be buried as her executors determined, 'only my desire is that six unmarried women shall bear the Pall over me to ye church'. Toward the end of her will Wainwright added a bequest of 10s. to the minister for preaching her funeral sermon, and ordered her executor and trustees to 'new furnish ... the gravestones belonging to my family putting my name and age upon them and to keep [them] decently covered'.[37] Other singlewomen called attention to their marital status by privileging the virginal colour white at their funerals. Elizabeth Holmes of Bristol wrote that she wanted her body to be interred in the family vault in Bristol, and she asked the Reverend and five Masters to 'be the supporters of my pall and that they have each a white lutestring hatband and pair of white kid gloves and that on the Sunday after my funeral the Reverend Master Evans do preach a funeral sermon for me at the Meeting House at Turveys Corner'.[38] Through the colour white the deceased woman's maidenly status would be memorialized. It is significant that Bracebridge and Wainwright were older singlewomen, not young maids, and yet they still desired a burial emphasizing their virginal state.[39]

These single female testators seem to have been proud of, or at least comfortable with, their singleness. Moreover, they chose to foreground

[35] HRO, 1642 A75.

[36] HRO, 1723 A119.

[37] Centre for Oxfordshire Studies (hereafter COS), W 94.64, Elizabeth Wainwright, (2 Dec. 1725).

[38] Bristol Record Office, unpublished transcript of Bristol wills, Elizabeth Holmes, (15 Nov. 1749).

[39] It was a common custom in the seventeenth century for bachelors, maids, children, and women who died in childbed to have a white pall at their funerals. Claire Gittings, *Death, Burial and the Individual in Early Modern England* (London: Croom Helm, 1984), 118. Gittings assumes that any deceased virgins were 'girls' or 'young', but my evidence shows that these customs resonated with lifelong singlewomen as well.

their marital status as part of their identity. The mere act of planning a public funeral also reveals that some singlewomen, despite their marginal marital status and lack of direct descendants, had enough of a sense of self to want their funeral to be a moment of public note. For example, Elizabeth Coles of Oxford desired 'a hearse to carry me and two coaches to carry the holders up and the bearers if required'. She asked for her corpse to be carried to Upper Hayford and laid by her mother, and she bequeathed gloves and hatbands to the men 'who carry me to the grave', and 'for the women who bear up the pall I bequeath gloves and scarves, and two glasses of wine a piece for both men and women'.[40]

Wills provide a tantalizing, if brief, glimpse at how ordinary towns-women represented singleness, and more work is needed in this area. For the remainder of this chapter I will focus on some longer forms of life writing, and on how three particular singlewomen created a single self through such writing. All three of these never-married women lived in the late seventeenth and first half of the eighteenth centuries and hailed from the middling sort and gentry. The first, Gertrude Savile, produced a series of journals that provide a rich source for exploring how one woman's views of singleness altered over her life-cycle. The second, Mary Chandler, wrote poetry and used self-deprecating humour to represent her never-married self. And the last, Mary Masters, penned both poems and letters in which she constructed a self who was single by choice.

Gertrude Savile (1697–1758) is a prime example of a never-married woman who worked out her single identity through her writing. She began life as the daughter of an Anglican rector, but due to various deaths in the family, her older brother George became the seventh Baronet Savile. Ger-trude Savile had no title herself, but her brother settled a £3,000 marriage portion on her when she was 20. When she neared 25 and had not yet married he began to pay her, first an annual loan, and then an annuity. The deaths of Savile's mother, married sister, and a male cousin increased her annual income to over £335 in the 1730s. The economic independence Savile gained in her forties allowed her to lease, first a house near her brother's family in Yorkshire, and then a fine residence on Great Russell Street in London.[41] Despite her relatively advanced social and financial position, Savile did not represent her life positively in her journal.

Savile's journal was a secular one, in which she wrote about her own personal life as well as recording the events of the day. It is also one of the more detailed journals written by a singlewoman in early modern England. Savile began her journal in her mid-twenties and kept it, on and off, until

---

[40] COS, W 210.285 Elizabeth Coles, (24 Mar. 1736).
[41] 'Account Books of Gertrude Savile, 1736–58', *Thoroton Society Record Series*, 24 (1965), 100–1, 107; and Savile, *Secret Comment*, 19.

three months before her death at the age of 60. Savile's entries, especially those in which she represented her thoughts and feelings, varied in detail, but one of the most valuable things about the long-running journal is that it allows us to trace how her attitude toward her marital status changed over time.

Savile's journal indicates a certain level of self-awareness. While she never gave any indication that her journal was for anything more than personal use, passages in which she criticized others or talked about men she admired were written in code. Savile seems to have been close to her nieces and nephew, when they were young at least, but it is unlikely that she produced her journal for them. And yet she seems to have felt the need to leave a legacy. When her brother had his family portrait painted he included their mother but not Gertrude, so she paid to have her individual portrait done. She wrote: 'I was so silly to have my own picture [painted] because nobody else thought it worthwhile', but her actions contradict her words.[42] While Savile had no children who would place her portrait on their walls, she had enough of an identity to wish to be remembered, and tried to ensure this both through her portrait and her journal.

As a gentlewoman, Gertrude Savile may have especially felt the sting of society's disdain. Women of this social status had no obvious alternative to marriage, and were the particular targets of the 'old maid' stereotype. Savile wrote of her own family reproaching her for what she thought of as her failure to marry. During one of their frequent mother–daughter quarrels, Savile wrote that: 'Mother threw out many vexing galling things, but after dinner upon her saying something I took to be a ridicule and reproach for my not being married (prodigiously unkind) I gave the reins to my brutist terrible passions'.[43] Savile interpreted her mother's words as proof that even her kin were disappointed in her, and that they dwelled on her 'failure' to marry or 'lack' of a husband.

Close to her twenty-fifth birthday, Savile wrote in code:

I was never so convinced of the reasons for a young woman's making marriage a shelter from the insults, scorns and the thousand ills she is exposed to while single...an old maid is the very butt for ridicule and insults. Miserable are women at the best, but without a protector she's a boat upon a very stormy sea without a pilot; a very cat, who, if seen abroad is hunted and worried by all the curs in the town.[44]

The age of 25 was significant for early modern women. In 1688, thirty-four years before Savile's comment, Jane Barker mentioned some of the same

[42] Savile, *Secret Comment*, 196.
[43] Ibid. 191.
[44] Ibid. 21.

concerns in her poem 'A Virgin Life': 'But in this happy life let me remain, | Fearless of twenty five and all its train, | Of slights or scorns, or being called Old Maid.'[45] Barker constructed singlehood as a 'happy life', and yet she worried that social pressure might make marriage impossible to resist. She was torn; from her autobiographical novels, it appears that Barker had entertained and then rejected a suitor sometime before her mid-thirties.[46] But her poetic works also indicate that she feared societal scorn for reaching the age of 25 without marrying. Singlewomen did not live in a vacuum, they could not help but come into contact with popular ideas about singleness. How much they assimilated these sentiments and became victims of self-contempt varied by individual. While Jane Barker did not project the self-hatred that Savile did, she did share Savile's concern about how others viewed her marital status. In this respect, singleness was not just an individual choice, it was a decision made in a social context.

Gertrude Savile presented a very negative view of the single life, one that she began to apply to herself over the years. At the age of 30 she recorded thoughts of her death in her journal. She emphasized her marital status, saying that her gravestone would bear the words 'Gertrude Savile, spinster'. And she composed an epitaph for herself:

> Here Lyes a Maid; who only try'd that State,
> The easiest Lott perhaps assign'd by Fate;
> And should be least obnoxtious to the hate
> Of a malicious World. But I have mett
> Hard usage in my Life; you now are in my debt.
> You owe me some forebearance in my Grave . . .
> I bore an Honest Heart and Vertuous Mind;
> Not to wrong nor any Ill inclined,
> And had I had a Friend (but there I ne'er was try'd)
> I had a Grateful Friendly heart that could have dyed
> Or Sacrificed my all for such a one . . .
> Therefore I'm better here, and let me rest in peace;
> Rake not my Ashes; let your censure sease;
> Let this thought stop your Judging; she is gon
> To answer for her faults to Him alone
> Who knew them.[47]

Savile was not unique in writing her own epitaph. It was one of the three 'dominant modes of autobiographical writing' by early modern women,

---

[45] Jane Barker, 'A Virgin Life', *Poetical Recreations* (London, 1688), pt. 1 [no pagination].
[46] Carol Shiner Wilson (ed.), *The Galesia Trilogy and Selected Manuscript Poems of Jane Barker* (Oxford: Oxford University Press, 1997), p. xxxviii.
[47] Savile, *Secret Comment*, 58–9.

along with the dream vision and the mother's legacy.[48] But the content of
her epitaph may be more unique. The narrative thread of Savile's autobiography is the wrongs done to a woman who was 'hated' by a 'malicious
world', 'censured', and 'judged' for her 'faults'. She emphasized two points:
that she was friendless, by which she seems to mean spouseless; and that the
world was in her debt and owed her 'some forbearance' in her death. Savile
represented that death as an escape from her marital state which had caused
her such 'hard usage'.

Gertrude Savile had not wished to remain single, and this coloured her
depiction of singleness, which she presented as a negative and depressing
experience. While Savile pursued marital options into her mid-twenties,
over time she stopped mentioning the possibility in her journal. In her late
twenties and early thirties she began to record her mood each day, with
phrases such as 'not happy', 'miserable', or 'very miserable'. She exhibited
what we today would term classic signs of psychological distress: fatigue,
lack of interest in life, as well as anxiety and fear about going out of the
house and interacting with people. She resented her dependence on her
brother and mother, and became combative with both kin and her servants.
The latter, perhaps not surprisingly, exhibited a high turnover rate, which
then further contributed to Savile's distress.

While Savile became resigned to her marital state over time, she rarely
projected happiness or contentment in her writing. The belief she expressed
in her early thirties never seems to have changed: 'What must I do when I
am a very old woman? As I have done while young—keep out of the world.
O that I could obtain that which alone is happiness in all ages and
circumstances!'[49] What was it that Savile equated with happiness? It may
have been marriage, but it could have also been social acceptance or
economic security. Contemporaries, of course, associated these rewards
with marriage, but the distinction was an important one. Singlewomen
may not have necessarily wished for a male partner, but they did hope for
the social and economic privileges enjoyed by a wife.

Although Savile's depression never led her to commit suicide, this was
not unheard of among singlewomen. In 1716 Dudley Ryder commented in
his diary that:

a young relation of Mrs. Walles the school[mistress] hanged herself on Sunday night
last. The reason of it seems to have been a too sensible resentment of her unhappy
circumstances which reduced her to the necessity of receiving her subsistence from
her uncle. She had been a great while melancholy... but last Sunday she several times

[48] Robert C. Evans, 'Deference and Defiance: The "Memorandum" of Martha Moulsworth', in
Claude J. Summer and Ted-Larry Pebworth (eds.), *Representing Women in Renaissance England*
(Columbia: University of Missouri Press, 1997), 178.
[49] Savile, *Secret Comment*, 68–9, 114.

expressed her thoughts about self murder, that she thought it was reasonable where a person was neither serviceable to the world nor herself.

Her family watched her after these words, but 'she slipped away and hanged herself with her garters'.[50] The Oxford-educated clergyman Robert Burton particularly associated what contemporaries termed 'melancholy' with women who were single. He believed that 'noble virgins, nice gentlewomen, such as are solitary and idle, live at ease, lead a life out of action and employment... are generally melancholy, such for the most part are misaffected, and prone to this disease'. Burton suggested that only financially secure singlewomen suffered from depression: 'For seldom shall you see a hired servant, a poor hand-maid, though ancient, that is kept hard to her work and bodily labour, a coarse country wench, troubled in this kind...'[51] Because Burton believed idleness negatively affected a person's mental health, he associated melancholy with the genteel and not the labouring singlewoman. Burton implicitly argued that never-married women of elite status should involve themselves in work or appropriate activities, as both a panacea for their ills and to provide a place for themselves in society.

Robert Burton would have viewed Gertrude Savile as a textbook case. She never found much to do with her time and energy. A lack of activity made her feel superfluous and useless, just as society told her she was. In 1728 she wrote: 'I must thank my mother that I am grown so much into the love of cards, having nothing to please me or amuse me. I fear I shall grow more into it, and that it will become my whole pleasure. 'Tis the only one for a friendless, forsaken old maid.'[52] Savile was an avid reader, journal writer, and a lover of animals, and yet she differed from other singlewomen of the same social and marital status, who busied themselves with religion, charity, family, or business. It is probably not a coincidence that such active women expressed resignation and even contentment with their lives, while Savile rarely did so. But the act of writing may also have helped Savile to persevere. As Barbara Lewalski has stated, 'authorship may be the process as well as the product of asserting subjectivity and agency'.[53] Her journal allowed the shy Savile a place to assert, explain, and defend her single self, and ultimately to soldier on.

There are not many extant diaries or journals, at least lengthy ones, kept by singlewomen in the early modern era, so we have little with which to compare Savile. The available source material increases tremendously,

[50] William Matthews (ed.), *The Diary of Dudley Ryder 1715–1716* (London, 1939), 194.
[51] Robert Burton, *The Anatomy of Melancholy*, ed. Floyd Dell and Paul Jordan-Smith (London, 1621; repr. New York: Farrar & Rinehart, 1927), 355–6.
[52] Savile, *Secret Comment*, 141.
[53] Lewalski, *Writing Women*, 11.

however, by the end of the eighteenth century. For example, the governess
Agnes Porter kept a journal that allows us a perspective on singleness from a
woman of a lower social status than Gertrude Savile. Agnes Porter was born
the daughter of a clergyman around 1750. After her father's death, and near
the age of 30, she took a position as a governess to help maintain herself, her
mother, and a troubled sister. Porter's position was a good one, serving first
the earl of Ilchester's family and then looking after the children of Ilchester's
daughter, Mary Talbot. She remained with the family until her mid-fifties,
when her health began to interfere with her duties. Until her death eight
years later, Porter moved around, staying first with her married sister, then
with her friends Mrs and Miss Lucy Lloyd, and finally with a clergyman's
family. She found her final resting place in her friends the Lloyds' family
burial plot in Somersetshire.

Porter kept a journal on and off from 1794 to 1814, that is, from
her forties to her sixties. This was a significant time-period in a singlewoman's life-cycle, since this was when she would confront the likelihood
of lifelong singleness. Porter's writing reveals a level of self-awareness;
she seems to have viewed her journal as a conversation with herself.[54]
Porter also appears to have intended her journal for public consumption,
if not publication. She deleted some words, cut out several sections, and
lapsed into French when she was discussing personal concerns. Two years
before Porter died she sent two journals 'about educating mother and
daughter' to her former pupil and friend, Mary Talbot, and after she died
her friend Miss Lucy Lloyd sent a further volume along to Mary's sister,
Harriot Frampton.[55] Both this self-awareness and her methods of self-
presentation in her writing had implications for how she represented her
singleness.

Porter's journal and letters reveal that she did not choose to remain single.
At the end of 1790, when she was near 40 years old, she was eagerly
anticipating letters from her friend Dr McQueen. When they did not
come she recorded being 'pensive all day, bordering a little on ill
humour... and it all originated in disappointment at not receiving from a
particular correspondent'. Porter's discontent deepened when she did finally
hear from Dr McQueen, and found he was 'on the point of matrimony with
a lady of fortune...' In July, 1791 Porter recorded that Dr MacQueen had
wed on 8 June, and that her friend Miss Baillie had also recently married:
'N.B. my acquaintances are marrying very fast off my hands. They will leave
me in the lurch, *n'importe, je serai toujours heureuse en depit du célibat* [No
matter, I will always be happy despite being a celibate]'.[56] In her journal

[54] Martin, *Governess*, 172, 242.   [55] Ibid. 322, 332.
[56] Ibid. 97, 100, 118, 121.

Porter constructed an image of singlewomen as the ones who are left behind. It is also significant that she switched to French when describing this; Porter was always a little embarrassed when she discussed her singleness. When her younger sister Fanny married a clergyman, Agnes noted that 'just such another man, with ten years more over his age, would make me a very happy woman'. A few years later she wrote to one of her former pupils that she hoped her sister would enjoy 'the blessing of an affectionate husband, which our sex, both married and single, are apt to name, or esteem tacitly as the *sumum bonum* [supreme good] of worldly happiness'.[57] Here Porter may have extended her own positive beliefs about marriage to all singlewomen, but it is significant that she constructed a husband as the provider of a woman's earthly happiness.

Like Gertrude Savile, Porter began to contemplate lifelong singlehood when she reached her forties. She rejoiced at the marriage of her friend Miss Mitchell, although she noted 'it breaks into my future prospect of ending my evening of life with her'. And in her late forties Porter wrote to one of her pupils asking her to address her letters to *Mrs* rather than *Miss* Porter. She added: 'I know, my love, I am not yet an old woman, though I begin to be rather advanced in life for a Miss. Do not suppose that being styled Mrs. will spoil my marriage—on the contrary, I may be mistaken for a little jolly widow and pop off when you least expect it.' Porter's joke belies the reality that advancing age did lessen her marriage prospects. It also illustrates how popular ideas about widows were more positive than those about 'spinsters'. As Porter aged, she constructed herself as part of a group of women whose identity was based on their singleness. Writing to her former pupil, she said: '*Ainsi va le monde* [thus the world goes] for the singleton tribe, of which an unworthy member is your affectionate Po'.[58]

Agnes Porter was painfully aware of the possibilities that faced an elderly singlewoman. Commenting in her journal in 1791, she said, 'I could not forbear partially and deeply reflecting on the ills that singlewomen are exposed to, even at the hour of death, from being the property of no one. My will is long since made, of what little I possess, and I hope it will please Infinite Goodness that my last breath shall be received by a tender and humane person, if not a friend.'[59] It is significant that while Porter's primary heir was her married sister, two cousins who were both singlewomen and governesses inherited the remainder of her estate. Although Porter's journal was not full of complaints and recriminations like Gertrude Savile's, it was replete with instances of the difficult and insecure position of the working singlewoman. For early modern

[57] Ibid. 30, 186   [58] Ibid. 36, 320.   [59] Ibid. 37–8.

women it was often a challenge to construct lifelong singleness in a positive light.

While journals provided one genre in which never-married women could represent themselves and their marital status, Mary Chandler chose poetry as her medium. Poetry was one of the most common forms in which women wrote in the early modern period. It was a genre particularly suited to introspection and the exploration of the self. Two things that made Chandler unusual among female poets were that she was also a trades-woman, and that she published poetry about her single marital status. Representing and defining singleness in a private journal was one thing, but publishing poetry on the subject of singleness indicates that Chandler may have had even more of a desire for self-presentation.

Mary Chandler (1687–1745) was born in Malmesbury but lived most of her life in Bath. Her father Henry and brother Samuel were Dissenting ministers, while her brother John was a doctor. Denied the vocations of religion and medicine that were open to her male siblings, Mary Chandler supported herself by setting up a millinery shop near Bath's Pump Room. She engaged in trade for some thirty years and held several properties in the town. While Chandler mentioned no formal schooling, she did allude to reading the classics. It also helped that the shopkeeper next door was James Leake, bookseller and brother-in-law to the author Samuel Richardson. Leake published Chandler's topographical poem *The Description of Bath* (1733), making her a first-time author at the age of 47. Another edition published three years later included a collection of personal poems. Chandler's poetry proved quite popular, and went through six editions in the first half of the eighteenth century alone. She was quite self-deprecating about her writing (like most female authors), and continued to work in the millinery trade until close to her death.[60] In April 1745 Chandler advertised two houses to let, one with a 'well and long accustomed milliner shop', and the sale of her stock of millinery goods. Six months later she died at the age of 58. Chandler's single female kin benefited from her estate and continued her legacy. Her sisters Abigail Chandler and Susanna Axford inherited her property, and her nieces Mary and Elizabeth Chandler continued her millinery trade. The Bath community also remembered Mary Chandler. An elegy written in her honour was published in the *Bath Journal*, attesting to Chandler's local celebrity.[61]

While Gertrude Savile and Mary Chandler shared the use of words to define the single state, Chandler did not share Savile's bitterness. Instead,

---

[60] Reeves, *Pursuing the Muses*, 38–9, 45, n. 79.
[61] *Bath Journal*, 8 Apr. 1745 and 7 Oct. 1745; Bath Record Office, Corporation Leases, F 1656, 1922, 244.

she expressed resignation and sometimes even contentment with her marital status. Like Savile, Chandler composed 'My Own Epitaph':

> Here lies a true maid, deformed and old;
> who, that she never was handsome, ne'er needed be told.
> Tho' she ne'er had a lover, much friendship had met;
> and thought all mankind quite out of her debt.
> She ne'er could forgive, for she ne'er had resented,
> as she ne'er had deny'd, so she never repented.
> She lov'd the whole species, but some had distinguish'd;
> but time and much thought had all passion extinguish'd.
> Tho' not fond of her station, content with her lot;
> a favour receiv'd she had never forgot.
> She rejoic'd in the Good that her Neighbour possess'd,
> and Piety, Purity, Truth she profess'd.
> She liv'd in much Peace, but ne'er courted pleasure;
> her book and her pen had her moments of leisure.
> Pleas'd with Life, fond of health, yet fearless of death;
> believing she lost not her soul with her breath.[62]

Chandler differed from most early modern female writers whom scholars have studied, because she did not define herself as a daughter, wife, or mother.[63] Instead, she constructed herself as a friend, a neighbour, a learned woman, and a Christian. This was how Mary Chandler represented her identity as a never-married woman. But she also framed her life in the negative. In her epitaph she used the words 'never' eight times and 'not' three times: 'never was handsome', 'not fond of her station', and so on. Here the word 'station' could refer both to Chandler's socio-economic status as well as to her marital status. In either case, she had not attained the standing for which she had once hoped. But Chandler also hastened to add that she was not bitter. In contrast to Savile, Chandler said she had enjoyed 'much friendship' in her time and 'thought all mankind quite out of her debt'. The tone of Chandler's epitaph was more positive and grateful than Savile's, although it was wistful about her physical and financial difficulties.

At other times Chandler used humour to represent the singlewoman's condition. In a poem entitled 'A letter to the right honorable the Lady Russell', Chandler adopted an amusing tone to recount how Sir Harry and

---

[62] Chandler, *Description of Bath*, 40–1.

[63] Helen Wilcox has suggested that 'the Renaissance Englishwoman was rarely her own self, but always someone's daughter, someone's mother, or, of course, someone's wife'. Helen Wilcox, '"My Soule in Silence"?: Devotional Representations of Renaissance Englishwomen', in Summers and Pebworth (eds.), *Representing Women*, 18. Mary Chandler is an exception to this notion.

his Lady decided one day that Chandler needed to marry, and proposed two men for her to choose between. Chandler responded with:

> Soon I accepted, either was my choice;
> most votes shall carry't. Mine's a neutral voice.
> So I may wed, I'm not exceeding nice;
> my humble wishes, sir, no higher rise,
> than that the man be honest, free from vice;
> improv'd by learning both of books and men;
> his genious witness'd by his well-known pen;
> true to his country, and fair virtue's cause;
> unaw'd, unbrib'd, by pow'r or by applause;
> from superstition, and prophaneness free;
> his fortune equal, to himself and me . . .

Then she changed to a more serious tone:

> Thus far in mirth. But now for steady truth,
> I'm climbed above the scale of fickle youth.
> From pain of love I'm perfectly at ease,
> my person nature never formed to please.
> Friendship's the sweetest joy in human life,
> 'tis that I wish—and not to be a wife.[64]

In the poem Chandler described her ideal partner, a virtuous, loyal, and pious genius; no doubt a man who would be little short of impossible to find. If this did not distance her from marriage enough, she then became explicit and said she was no longer interested in love, but only in friendship.

Mary Chandler's representation of singleness differed from Gertrude Savile's in other ways. Chandler focused on how never-married women could fulfill their own needs. Her poem 'My Wish' provides a detailed vision of what one early modern singlewoman desired for her future. It is significant that she chose a pastoral theme for this poem; Josephine Roberts has argued that women in particular were attracted to the pastoral because its coded nature allowed them to use it 'to experiment with the social system'. If this is the case, Chandler's poem seems to allow for a questioning of the need for marriage, and constructs the possibility of a cheerful existence as a singlewoman:[65]

---

[64] Chandler, *Description of Bath*, 24–7.
[65] Josephine Roberts, 'Deciphering Women's Pastoral: Coded Language in Wroth's *Love's Victory*', in Summers and Pebworth (eds.), *Representing Women*, 163.

Would heaven indulgent grant my wish
for future life, it should be this;
health, peace, and friendship I would share
a Mind from business free, and care...
a fortune from encumbrance clear,
about a hundred pounds a year;
a house not small, built warm and neat,
above a hut, below a seat...
and near some neighbours wise and good...
There should I spend my remnant days,
review my life, and mend my ways...
A friendly cleric should be near...
My thoughts my own, my time I'd spend
in writing to some faithful friend...
delight me with some useful book...
Some money still I'd keep in store,
that I might have to give the poor...
Thus calmly see my sun decline;
my life and manners thus refine.
And acting in my narrow sphere,
in cheerful hope, without one care,
I'd quit the world, nor wish a tear.[66]

Chandler's poem illustrates the practical needs of a singlewoman: an income and a home of her own (requirements that had not changed when Virginia Woolf wrote 200 years later). Chandler's allusion to a £100 annual income and a home smaller than a gentry estate illustrate that she was hoping to maintain a middling-class lifestyle in old age. She had worked as a shopkeeper for thirty years to support herself; yet she still envisioned the possibility of retirement, or spending her time from 'business free', and instead devoting herself to piety, learning, and charity. Chandler constructed the singlewoman's life as a solitary one; there is no mention of family here, and she lives alone, but she does hope for the companionship of friends, neighbours, and the clergy. This was her 'Wish', the contented life that she envisioned for herself; a life with no mention of marriage, that could still be a cheerful and even fulfilling one. The only discordant phrase here is 'acting in my narrow sphere'. This might have been a reference to what Chandler represented as her narrow role in life, with its lack of spousal and maternal responsibilities. Alternatively, it could have been a reference to her modest financial and social circumstances, and not at all a negative comment on her marital status.

[66] Chandler, *Description of Bath*, 65–7.

The vision of singleness that Mary Chandler created in her poetry is echoed in the poems of Jane Barker. Barker was born in 1652, the daughter of a former official at the court of Charles I. Her education included a stint at a girl's school in Putney. After her father's death in 1681, Barker helped her mother manage the family estates, and added money to the family coffers by selling a cure for the gout. In 1688 her career as a writer took off with the publication of *Poetical Recreations*, a collection to which she contributed over fifty poems. Out of economic necessity Barker tried another genre, publishing the novel *Love Intrigues* in 1713. She wrote a number of other books before she died of a tumor in 1732. Literary scholars consider Jane Barker one of the first women to write for a living, and one of the foremothers of the novel.[67]

Jane Barker's representations of the single life changed as she aged. As a 25-year-old she had written about her misgivings about choosing to never marry, but by the time she was in her seventies Barker penned a more positive poetic vision of the single life:

> Ah! Happy State! how strange to see,
> What mad conceptions some have had of thee!
> As if being was all wretchedness,
> Or foul deformity, in vilest dress ...
> A Virgin bears the impress of all good ...
> The Business of her life to this extends,
> To serve her God, her neighbour and her friends.[68]

In the 1720s, when Barker wrote this poem, the stereotype of the 'old maid' was common in England. For Barker writing was a way to resist this characterization of her marital state. Her representation of female singlehood assertively opposed the negative stereotypes of wretchedness, deformity, and vileness that were circulated by her contemporaries. Instead she emphasized the good works—piety, charity, friendship—performed by never-married women. In doing so, she created a positive role for singlewomen like herself. Chandler and Barker both were aware of the popular construction of the singlewoman but, unlike Savile, they used writing to resist it.[69]

Mary Masters (*fl.* 1733–55) also wrote about singleness in her poems as well as in her prose. Masters's writing makes it possible to see whether constructions of singleness varied by genre; if poetry produced less auto-

---

[67] This biographical summary is based on Carol Shiner Wilson's introduction to Barker's *The Galesia Trilogy*. Also see Kathryn R. King, *Jane Barker, Exile: A Literary Career 1675–1725* (Oxford: Oxford University Press, 2000).
[68] Wilson, *The Galesia Trilogy*, 140.
[69] Lewalski, *Writing Women*, 2–3.

biographical and more fanciful representations than correspondence, for instance. Mary Masters hailed from the provincial town of Norwich, but spent much of her later years in Otley (Yorks.). We do not know much about her background, except that she had friends who were Dissenting ministers. In her publications Masters mentioned that her parents died early in her life. She also noted: '[my father] would not permit me to receive [learning], but endeavored to prevent me from acquiring the use of the pen, or a proper pronunciation in reading; and those glorious lessons of wisdom . . . were by him neglected, through a notion that women ought to be instructed in nothing but common household affairs, and the management of the needle.'[70] Masters had continual financial difficulties, which she said led a suitor to reject her. Explaining the reason for her publication of *Poems on Several Occasions* (1733), she said: 'As I entered the world ill-provided with the gifts of fortune, I was, in the early part of my life, persuaded to increase my little stock by subscription, in which I succeeded beyond my merit, and for a while lived contentedly and quiet . . .' At the age of 50, Masters needed to publish again to supplement her income, because 'the death of some friends, and treachery of others, rendered my situation very inconvenient and uncomfortable: In hopes of redressing it, I was prevailed upon to make a second attempt, several gentlemen and ladies assuring me they would not only honour me with their own names, but use their utmost influence in my favour.' This need resulted in her multi-genre work, *Familiar Letters and Poems on Several Occasions* (1755).[71]

Mary Masters never married, and her stated preference for female friendship over marriage was a common theme in her poetry.[72] She wrote a number of amatory poems to her female friends. In 'To Marinda, at Parting' she addressed her best friend:

> Think it not strange, that I profess a love . . .
> In my fond heart a tender friendship grew,
> Ere yet I could your pleasing image view . . .
> Your conversation gives a solid joy,
> Which absence will too cruelly destroy . . .
> —why must I lose her sight?
> O transient pleasure! O too short delight![73]

Masters was by no means unique among early modern woman in describing a female friend using words such as 'love', 'pleasure', 'beauty', and 'delight';

---

[70] Mary Masters, *Familiar Letters and Poems on Several Occasions* (London, 1755), 52–3.
[71] Ibid., Preface.
[72] Mary Masters, *Poems on Several Occasions* (London, 1733), 63.
[73] Ibid. 12–15.

words that to modern ears sound like language one would use to address a lover. Masters's use of the language of amatory friendship indicates that she was woman-identified in her relationships. Connections with women were of clear emotional import to her, but as discussed in Chapter 3, it is unclear if such relationships could or should be labelled as lesbian. Nevertheless, woman-identified singlewomen such as Mary Masters may have not missed or needed a marital relationship in order to enjoy companionship or emotional support. It is significant that in her writing Masters does not focus on missing out on marriage, like Savile, Barker, and even Chandler did.

While Mary Masters did not represent marriage as something she desired for herself, she was not anti-marriage. She wrote many poems celebrating the weddings of friends, and in her letters she spoke in favour of marriage for others. For example, when her correspondent 'Evadne' wrote that love and marriage could not coexist, and that the title of husband made a lover into a tyrant, Masters (or 'Maria') responded: 'I am so far from thinking the hymeneal tye and love incompatible', and she warned that if Evadne's 'platonic system' prevailed it would cause 'general destruction' and the 'whole world would be a desart'. In later letters to 'Evadne' Masters went so far as to call singleness an 'error' and an 'inferior state', and platonic love 'no more than a shadow'. In her letters Masters did not advocate a general rejection of marriage, because of what she saw as a need to populate the earth, but she seems to have viewed her own singleness as an exception. Masters reconciled this seeming contradiction through the imprimatur of religion. She urged 'Evadne' to 'bear calmly the fate which heaven has allotted'. Evidently, however, 'fate' meant for Masters to remain single. When staying with friends in Yorkshire, in a house built on the remains of an ancient monastery, she wrote, 'the house I lived in last at [Norwich] was part of the deanery and formerly a monastery; so I am translated from one cloister to another, and in a fair way of dying a nun'.[74]

Should we read Masters's poetry differently from her letters, assuming that the latter were autobiographical but not the former? The two genres may not have been so distinct in her eyes. Like many female correspondents she included verses within her letters to express and describe herself. For example, she wrote to a friend that she had been 'gloomy and low' due to a false friend, but that now she had a more 'happy tenour of mind.' Then she turned to verse:

> An active mind, and spirits gay,
> Turn my September into May.

---

[74] Masters, *Familiar Letters*. 15–17, 37–9, 54, 56, 64.

Higher health and livelier bloom,
Promise still an age to come,
Charming prospects rise in sight,
And thrill my heart with new delight,
I feel fresh life in every vein,
And sprightly youth returns again.[75]

It is also significant that Masters's correspondents chose to search her poetry for autobiographical information. One of her poems was entitled: 'An answer to a poetical letter from Miss——, in which she informs me of a warm debate, in a senate of ladies, upon the question, whether I had ever been in love? And not being able to decide it by a volume of poems I formerly published, she appeals to me for a determination.' Masters's response to this woman's letter was in verse:

And really, my dear,
I'll be very sincere,
And make you an honest reply;
For since life began,
I never knew the man,
For whom I could languish and die ... [76]

With these lines Masters constructed herself as single by choice. A male friend of hers also inferred that her marital status was due to choice; a poem he addressed to her included the words 'when you condescend to wed'.[77]

Even though Mary Masters wrote of choosing her marital status, she did not always represent her life as a happy one. This is an important point. We cannot reflexively associate choice with happiness and the lack thereof with discontent for early modern women. Masters's poem 'Maria in Affliction' reveals that agency did not preclude discontentment:

But I, unhappy, see no prospect near,
To give me hope and dissipate my fear...
Removed from every joy, deprived of all
That I could fair, or good, or pleasant call ...
The Years, on which my largest hopes were placed
Drew near, then came, and like the former passed ...
Increasing hours but aggravate my pain ...
Add to the pressure, which I felt before...
And circling bring another round of woe.[78]

[75] Ibid. 83–5.   [76] Ibid. 216–19.
[77] Masters, *Poems*, 206–9.   [78] Ibid. 101–3.

Masters represented herself as a woman who believed her life and prospects had passed her by, and who now felt nothing but fear and pressure. Her words reveal that even choosing one's marital status did not prevent remorse over hopes and time that had passed by. What exactly Masters had missed out on is not clear, however. Nowhere in her verse did she represent her unhappiness as due to the lack of a man or a lover. It is likely that Masters did not mention love because this is not what she had missed out on. Rather, her regret might have stemmed from the social status and economic security that a woman was deprived of when she chose not to marry. This is exactly what Masters mentioned in a letter she wrote to a 'reverend friend'.

> my circumstances do really acquire an addition to make my situation easy, and place me in the happy! happy! state of independency... Were I a villager near some post-town in a peaceful retirement, I could live to God and myself, and enjoy the correspondence of two or three sincere friends. I think I should be then as happy as this world could make me: I should be as fond of my apartment as a hermit of his cell, and care seldom to quit it: There would I wait the last important hour with content and cheerfulness, while I was daily making a due preparation for it. This is the most ardent desire of... M. Masters.[79]

Here, Masters represented the path to happiness and cheerfulness as independence, but not freedom from marriage; rather, freedom from financial concerns. Also important were friendship and piety, but not male companionship. Masters's depictions of singleness were largely consistent between genres; her letters and her poems projected the same image. Mary Masters seems to have chosen singleness and friendship over marriage, or at least been comfortable with lifelong singleness, but this did not mean that she presented her decision as free from complications.

Like Mary Masters, Anna Seward was a poet who wrote about her singleness in her correspondence. While Seward lived most of her formative years in the second half of the eighteenth century, she provides a telling example of how a singlewoman might respond to the 'old maid' stereotype. Seward was the daughter of the canon of Lichfield, who provided her with a liberal education. When her mother died in 1780 Seward remained with her father as housekeeper and nurse until his death ten years later. Although she had a number of marital near-misses and interest from various suitors, Seward chose singlehood. On her father's death (when she was nearly 50), she came into an income of £400 and remained living in the Bishop's Palace. This provided Seward with a comfortable lifestyle until her death at the age of 67.[80]

---

[79] Masters, *Familiar Letters*, 112–17.

[80] Margaret Ashmun, *The Singing Swan: An Account of Anna Seward and Her Acquaintance with Dr. Johnson, Boswell & Others of Their Time* (New Haven, Conn.: Yale University Press, 1931), *passim*.

Anna Seward's correspondence opens a revealing window onto how a singlewoman both defined herself as a member of a social group, in this case 'old maids', and how she responded to stereotypes directed at the group. Seward's friend and patron was the poet William Hayley, who, as we saw in Chapter 6 penned *An Essay on Old Maids*. This satire put Seward in a difficult position. She was a firm admirer of Hayley, and yet he had published a work making fun of women such as herself. Seward's first response was to use humour to handle the uncomfortable situation. She joked to her friend Mrs Knowles that a mutual friend was a 'prudent wife, a kind mother, and a cheerful desirable neighbour. Ah! How much a more useful creature than such a celibaic cypher as myself! You coin a word now and then, so pray welcome my stranger-epithet...' In the same letter she mentioned: 'My curiosity is on fire to become acquainted with my sisters, the old maids, of whom I hear so much, and which are said to be the bard's.'[81]

But Seward's humour soon gave way to ambivalence and discomfort in the face of Hayley's verbal assault. In a letter to a male friend she wrote: 'As to the Old Maids, I still rely upon internal evidence respecting the author of that work. Perhaps I wish no man had written it, while I feel that no woman would; but I persevere in believing there is but one man in Europe, since it lost Voltaire, whose species of wit is responsible for that very uncommon composition.' The next month she wrote to another male friend: 'The Essay on Old Maids; certainly the production of that pen, whose genius, wit, and learning, throws most of its literary rivals at immeasurable distance. This whimsical work, richly illuminated by all those emanations, so lightly, so wantonly betrays the cause it affects to defend, that I could wish it had never passed the press.'[82]

Seward was in a bind; should she stand up for her 'sisters, the old maids', and possibly risk her friendship with Hayley, or should she stay silent? She seems to have decided that self-respect outweighed any further assistance Hayley might have given to her poetic career. By March of 1786 she had written to him about his *Essay*:

Its author has not yet answered my letter on the subject of that witty, but ungenerous sport of fancy, the Old Maids. He is, I fear, displeased with my ingenuousness on that subject; yet I cannot repent of it, but sincerity is the first duty of friendship... Should dear Mr. Hayley be offended, I shall be deeply grieved, since words are weak to say how much I love, admire, and honour his genius and his virtues. Well! His continued silence, or the style of his next letter will shew...

---

[81] A. Constable, *Letters of Anna Seward: Written between the years 1784 and 1807*, 6 vols. (Edinburgh, 1811), i. 109, 104.
[82] Ibid. i. 115, 129.

Anna Seward was worried about losing Hayley's friendship, and six months later it appears that her fears were realized. She wrote to a female friend: 'You inquire after my correspondence with the illustrious [Hayley]. It is not what it was; but the deficiency, or cause of deficiency, proceeds not from me. I honour and love him as well as ever; yet I feel that the silver cord of our amity is loosening at more links than one.' Seward continued to promote Hayley's 'genius' and was proud of her four-year correspondence with him, but she did not stop ribbing him for his satire on singlewomen. Responding to his idea for a lamp that would shed light on the statue of the poet Howard, Seward said she 'should like to have the office of guarding it from extinction.—Priestess to the lamp of benevolence! Such an appointment might exalt, to some degree of dignity, the derided state of stale maidenhood.'[83]

Where did Anna Seward gain a sense of self strong enough to stand up to the old maid stereotype of her age? Hayley was not the only man she went up against, for her criticism of her one-time neighbour Samuel Johnson was also very public. We can attribute some of her comfort with being an outspoken singlewoman to her relatively secure social and financial situation. Her identity as a poet also seems to have aided her representation of herself. Anna Seward quite literally substituted her identity as a poet for that of wife and mother. Early on she wrote to William Hayley: 'And now, my dear bard . . . Suffer me, then, to express my gratitude for the kind attention and ardent welcome with which *my poetical offspring* has been received in its lovely precincts . . . and for the generous, the discriminating approbation which has so highly gratified *their parent*'.[84] For Seward, singleness did not preclude procreation, but hers was of the literary rather than biological variety.

So far we have been examining how never-married women represented singleness, but married women also wrote about singlehood. Women who had experienced both the single and the marital states had the ability to compare them, something a singlewoman could not do. But was the grass always greener? The poet Katherine Phillips wrote an ode to singlehood after she had become a wife. Her poem 'A Married State' (1667) is one of the best comparisons of singlehood and wifehood we have from the early modern period. Philips emphasized the many familial duties and cares of wives, implicitly representing singleness as a state of individuality, freedom, and happiness:

> A married state affords but little ease;
> The best of husbands are so hard to please.

---

[83] Ibid. i. 147–8, 168, 179–80; ii. 158.
[84] Ibid. i. 16–17. Emphasis my own.

This in wives' careful faces you may spell,
Though they dissemble their misfortunes well.
A virgin state is crowned with much content,
It's always happy as it's innocent.
No blustering husbands to create your fears,
No pangs of childbirth to extort your tears,
No children's cries for to offend your ears,
Few worldly crosses to distract your prayers.
Thus are you freed from all the cares that do
Attend on matrimony and a husband too.
Therefore, madam, be advised by me:
Turn, turn apostate to love's levity.
Suppress wild nature if she dare rebel,
There's no such thing as leading apes in hell.[85]

Philips concluded her poem by proclaiming that the eternal punishment that supposedly awaited women who did not marry did not exist. She represented singleness as better than marriage for women here on earth and in the hereafter.

The writings of the poet Anne Steele, a lifelong singlewoman, and her married sister Mary Wakeford reveal how each believed her marital state to be the best. In a poem to her sister, Wakeford referred to the nine muses as 'silly old Maidens'. Steele responded with 'On Amira calling the Muses Old Maids': 'Old Maids indeed Amira you are wrong | Those lovely Sisters are forever young... | Then be the beauties of the fair consign'd | And let the charming Muses deck the Mind.' In an undated set of verses the sisters produced a discussion of the pros and cons of marriage. The never-married Steele wrote against marriage, rather than for singleness:

If all the soft pleasures you (married folks) talk of in love
Can balance the pains which in absence you prove
If you would confess 'em how gloomy your fears
How great your anxieties troubles and cares
What endless perplexities torture your breast
Can happiness dwell in a heart without rest...
Fate has joined love and care and they never can part.

The married Mary Wakeford responded that single people had cares as well as married ones, who at least had partners to help them:

No doubt but in wedlock there's plenty of fears
But if they would own it ha[ve]n't single folk cares...
If our minds with strange whimseys wild fancy supplies

---

[85] Katherine Phillips, 'A Married State', in N. H. Keeble (ed.), *The Cultural Identity of Seventeenth-Century Woman: A Reader* (New York: Routledge, 1994), 255–6.

What terrours from wrinkles in yours must arise...
And since Married and Single you'll surely find pain
As well you may peaceably yield up your heart
And in every care let a husband take part.

Steele retorted that if singlewomen lost their power as they aged, married women lost it even earlier, upon their marriage. And she suggested that a partner would not share or ease her troubles, but only double them:

If Spinsters with beauty must soon lose their sway
Wives give up their freedom in one fatal day...
Unless I am fated to yield up my heart
Can I wish to be wretched and double my part.[86]

Anne Steele and Mary Wakeford provide us with some telling insight on the position of eighteenth-century women. Both constructed life as full of care and trouble, and admitted that women lost power to men, but both also represented their own marital status as the preferable condition. Perhaps this is the lesson we should take from the writings of early modern women. Life was challenging for both wives and singlewomen; the challenges just differed. And a woman could construct her life as positive or negative no matter what her marital state. How much did any woman in early modern England really choose to remain single or to marry? Her individual desires were only one part of a whole spectrum of opportunities and constraints that included family, religion, economics, demographics, and yes, even fate. How a woman responded to her situation was where the individual choice occurred.

The voices of singlewomen make it apparent that, whether they chose to never marry or had singleness thrust upon them, their marital status came with a price, both social and economic. The struggles singlewomen faced seem to have induced some of them to reflect on their condition in poetry and prose. Through these women's words we get a glimpse of how singlewomen negotiated a patriarchal system that, while antagonistic toward them, also allowed some room for manoeuvre. And we gain a sense of how these women constructed a single female identity. Never-married women represented themselves as individuals rather than as wives, mothers, or even daughters. In this sense, the self-writing of singlewomen may have more in common with that of the men rather than the ever-married women of the period. If we are to look for the origins of the modern self, the writings of early modern singlewomen are as valid a place to start as the writings of their male contemporaries.

---

[86] Reeves, *Pursuing the Muses*, 87–90.

8
Epilogue

This book has revealed how successfully singlewomen have been expunged from our historical consciousness. Contemporary records often rendered these women invisible, but historical scholarship has only perpetuated and exacerbated the neglect. Such a successful erasure of women who did not marry, always making them appear to be aberrations or small in number, has allowed the supposed norm—the marital couple and nuclear family—to appear unchallenged. And when we have acknowledged singlewomen, it has been almost always in a negative light: as spinsters or old maids. For all its cultural particularity, the English figure of the spinster was exported abroad to Europe and the United States and has lasted until the present day. Three hundred years later, being called an old maid still has cultural resonance, and this means that the singlewomen of early modern England still have relevance.

Looking back, I am struck by three historical constants that emerge from this study. The issue of change over time, the relationship between representation and reality, and the chimera of English exceptionalism are all pertinent to this topic. This book has revealed a distinct change in the lives of never-married women at the end of the seventeenth century. Demographers long ago found that numbers of lifelong singlewomen were at their highest level of the early modern period in the later part of that century. And this study has shown that urban singlewomen were increasingly active in trade, property holding, and moneylending by the end of the 1600s. In addition, the literature of the later seventeenth century began to address the topic of lifelong singlewomen for the first time in a variety of genres and ways. And from the 1680s onward women like Jane Barker, Mary Chandler, and Mary Masters began to write positively about what it meant to choose lifelong singleness. The later seventeenth century seems to have been a watershed moment for never-married women in England. And yet, tracing such change over time in the experiences of singlewomen does not mean that this group disproves the notion that women's lives in the past were characterized more by continuity than by change. For even as singlewomen's socio-economic opportunities increased and popular notions about never-married women emerged, the overriding experience for these women was one of continued marginalization. While the ways in which this was achieved did change over the early modern era, never-married women were always relegated to the margins. In the sixteenth century lifelong single-women did not even exist as a meaningful social category. Such erasure made never-married women into de facto liminal figures. By the eighteenth century lifelong singlewomen had become acknowledged as a social group, but they continued to be marginalized. Now they were made into figures of fun or blamed for their own problematic position in society, if not society's ills in general. While changes in singlewomen's lives did occur in early modern England, they did so within a continual context of singleness being viewed as different from the norm.

The history of singlewomen in early modern England also reveals a considerable rift between perception and reality. The negative stereotypes about spinsters and old maids claimed that such women were useless, lonely, barren, and bereft individuals; and that they were either to be pitied or scorned. But such characterizations are not borne out by the never-married women in these pages. Rather than being functionless and friend-less, singlewomen in early modern England were critical care-takers for their extended families and important workers, taxpayers, and citizens in their communities. They had so much power in places such as Southamp-ton that they bankrolled the corporation when it was in debt and swore loyalty to the monarch when his throne was in peril. The power wielded by singlewomen explains the disjuncture between representation and reality. Powerful women without men were a threat to English society. Acknow-ledging the influence and significance of singlewomen might encourage more women not to marry. Better instead to characterize never-married women as either pathetic or evil, to ensure that singleness remained a marginalized social and marital status. The increasing negativity of the stereotypes about never-married women correlated directly to the growing power and significance of real singlewomen in English society. And the negative representations targeted that class of singlewomen—middling and genteel women—who had the means to exercise the most influence.

This study of singlewomen also returns us to the historical trope of 'English exceptionalism'. In recent decades historians have fought against the once-accepted notion that the English were in all ways different from continental Europeans. Rather than focusing on English distinctiveness, we have inserted England back into British, European, and Atlantic world contexts. This is especially true of historians of women in early modern Europe, who have not allowed national borders and bodies of water to stand in the way of comparative dialogue. In the case of never-married women, however, a comparative awareness reveals that early modern England may have been an exceptionally difficult place to be a singlewoman. As this book has shown, the social and familial structure, economy, religious environment, and legal system combined to make singleness particularly incompatible with early modern English values and society.

The emphasis on the nuclear family in early modern England cannot be underestimated in its impact on singlewomen. Both culturally and politically, the household headed by the marital couple was considered the basis of English society and English order. This household was established at marriage, meaning that social adulthood and householder status in England were tied to marriage. Early modern England's focus on the nuclear family and its de-emphasis of both the multi-family household and ties of extended kinship, rendered never-married women out of place. Singlewomen struggled throughout the early modern era to position themselves as adult women without being wives and mothers, as well as to head their own households and enjoy the civic rights and privileges attached to householder status. They also strove to define themselves as members of families, albeit non-nuclear ones. In societies with more of an emphasis on extended kinship, singlewomen may not have had as much difficulty fitting in as they did in early modern England.

The household was not only the cultural and familial foundation of early modern England, it was also the economic basis. A pre-modern economy based on the household rather than the individual had severe repercussions for women who did not marry. Families, headed by married men or their widows, received all of the economic assistance and support from their communities. Singlewomen were expected to work to support themselves, and yet as individuals they had the least amount of economic opportunities and assistance available to them. It was assumed that all never-married women should be servants, working as dependants in someone else's household, and yet service in England was viewed as a life-cycle occupation for young people only. This left lifelong singlewomen in England without obvious economic options, whereas in other regions of Europe it was possible to remain in service as an older woman.

England's transformation into a Protestant country had a significant effect on women who never married. The loss of the Catholic convent had both a real and an ideological impact. Historians have noted that the number of nuns in England just before the Reformation was not particularly high, but it was not just the opportunity to enter into a convent that was lost with England's Protestant turn, it was the loss of a sanctioned alternative to marriage. Also lost was the acceptability of institutionalized or communal living for unmarried women. In other parts of Europe, where the convent was still an option and there was a history of beguinages, Magdalen houses, and other living arrangements for women who were single, such women were less out of place. England's particular Protestant history also gave rise to emigration, civil wars, and various Dissenting sects, all factors that contributed to numbers of women remaining single, either due to the loss of men or to religious endogamy.

The flurry of publication that also occurred during and just after the Civil Wars gave rise to the literary figure of the older or superannuated singlewoman. Beginning in the second half of the seventeenth century, English authors spilled a good amount of ink on the issue of what to do with women who never married, and by the turn of the eighteenth century English writers produced some of the first and most virulent stereotypes about the never-married woman. In both textual and visual form the spinster and the old maid became stock characters of the English experience. In fact, the ubiquity of the old maid in novels, plays, prints, and ballads belies her supposed marginality. The English were unique in registering the earliest concern about and the harshest scorn for what they termed the spinster or old maid. It was not until the later eighteenth and the nineteen centuries that other European countries also produced any sustained critique of singlewomen.

The one area in which English singlewomen seem to have benefited compared to their continental counterparts was the law. English common law divided women into *femes soles* and *femes coverts*, women alone and women covered by their husbands' legal identity. As *femes soles*, English singlewomen enjoyed certain legal rights and the ability to represent themselves once they were of age, something that was less true for never-married women in countries under Roman or civil law. The ability to make one's own legal and economic decisions may have contributed to the number of English singlewomen, making marriage less appealing to a never-married woman who controlled her own business or property. Singlewomen also were able to bequeath their wealth to whomever they chose because of the individual nature of English property rights. And because of never-married women's involvement in legal affairs, the term 'spinster' emerged in the early seventeenth century as the legal term for such women. This was originally a neutral descriptor and one that applied to singlewomen of all ages, without assuming a premarital state as did terms such as 'virgin' or 'maid'. The common law differentiated the experiences of English singlewomen from those on the continent, who required male proxies to represent them in court, lived under systems of communal inheritance, and were less legally distinct from married women.

More comparative work is needed to situate the singlewoman in early modern England into a British, European, and Atlantic context. And yet the research on early modern England itself has only begun. I view this book as an introduction to this subject rather than a definitive statement. I hope others will continue to explore singleness, and that they will take my findings and both refine and question them. We need much more original, archival work, especially on never-married women in rural areas and in the metropolis. And we need studies of singlewomen in the period previous to the seventeenth and eighteenth centuries. There are also still numerous issues related to singlewomen and singleness in pre-modern Europe that merit further study. We need more work on the sexuality of never-married women, both in terms of what we today define as heterosexuality and homosexuality. Although a woman in the past might have been single in terms of her marital status, she may not have perceived herself as single in terms of partnership status. We need to further explore the role of religion in never-married women's lives, and whether we have perhaps erected a too distinct barrier between the study of lay and religious single-women. Questions of marital status also require further elaboration. While I have argued for differences between widowed and never-married women, we have yet to explore separation and divorce in terms of singleness. By my typology a divorced woman was 'ever married', but she also became a singlewoman once again; so where did she fit in the continuum of female marital status? And perhaps most importantly, we need a comparison of singlewomen and men and of male and female singlehood. While marital status did not influence the lives of men in the same ways that it did women, in a patriarchal society never-married men also were not idealized. This book has shown the significance of marital status for women in the past, but the gendered nature of marital status merits study in and of itself.

Lastly, the study of singlewomen and singleness is not a historical end-point, rather it is an opening. Focusing on single people allows for a greater appreciation of how age, partnership status, and household position affected people's lives in the past. The study of singlewomen further illustrates how societal differences complicated and enriched the past and how we cannot fully comprehend what a society presents as a norm without recognizing what it represents as marginal.

Bibliography

Primary Sources

MANUSCRIPTS

BATH

Bath City Record Office

Corporation Leases, 1581–1776

BRISTOL

Bristol Record Office

Transcript of Bristol Wills, 1749–51
Bristol Wills and Inventories, 1610–1750
Indices to Bristol Probate Records

LONDON

British Library

Harleian MS 158, f286a

OXFORD

Centre for Oxfordshire Studies

Oxford Diocese and Archdeaconry Courts, Probate Records, 1550–1775
Indices to Oxfordshire Probate Records

Oxford City Record Office

Consistory and Archdeaconry Courts of Oxford, Probate Records, 1550–1775
D.5/6–10, Books of Leases

SOUTHAMPTON

Southampton Record Office

Charity Records
D/MC 5/1, Thomas White Charity Account Book
D/MC 6/1, William Wallop Gift Account Book
D/MC 7/1, Lynch's Gift Account Book
D/MC 8/1, Steptoe's Account Book
D/MC 9/3, Nathaniel Mill's Account Book
D/TH 1/1, Thorner's Charity Account Book
Court Records
SC 6/1/16–108, Court Leet Records

SC 6/2/1–37, Stall and Art Leet Estreats
SC 7/1/10–37, Town and Piepowder Court Records
SC 7/2/1–52, Town Court Papers
SC 9/1/1–208b, Sessions Rolls
SC 9/2/1–13, Sessions Order, Petty Sessions, and Recognizance Books
SC 9/3/4–14, Examination Books
SC 9/4/1–401, Sessions Papers
Municipal Administrative Records
SC 2/1/6, 7–10, Assembly Books and Corporation Journal Books
SC 2/6/6, Book of Instruments
SC 3/1/1–2, Burgess admissions
SC 3/5/1, Book of Free Commoners
SC 5/1/41–54, Steward's Books
SC 5/2/1-2, Book of Debts
SC 5/3/1–52, Book of Fines, Mayor's Account Books
SC 5/17/1–35, Scavage Books
Unpublished index of town officers
Parish Records
D/ABC 1/1–2, Above Bar Church Book
PR 4/2/1, St Lawrence's and St John's Churchwardens Accounts
PR 5 11/1/1–26, 11/2, 11/4, St Mary's Parish Records
PR 7/5/1, St Michael's Churchwardens Accounts
PR 9/12, 14/1, South Stoneham Churchwardens Accounts and Vestry Book
PR 9/15/1–6, St Mary/South Stoneham Account Books and Poor Rate Books
SC/AG 8/3/1–2, All Saints Parish Rate Book
SC/AG 8/6/1, Holy Rood Parish Rate Book
Transcript of the Above Bar Independent Chapel registers, 1688–
Transcript of the Parish Registers of All Saints, 1653–63, 1723–70
Transcript of the Parish Registers of Holy Rood, 1653–1812
Transcript of the St Mary's Parish Church Registers, 1675–
Transcript of the St Mary Extra Parish Registers, 1681–
Transcript of the St Michael's Parish Registers, 1552–1812
Transcript of the Parish Registers of South Stoneham, 1663–
Poor Relief Records
SC/AG 6/1–2, Settlement Examinations
SC 10/1/1–19, Poor Relief Records
Property Records
D/LY, D/MC, D/MH, D/PM, D/SDF, D/Z, Miscellaneous Property Records
SC 4/1/2, Survey of the Town of Southampton, 1617
SC 4/1/5, Book of Entry of Leases
SC 4/1/7, Rental of Corporation, 1738
SC 4/2/353–88, Various Deeds, Bonds, and Agreements
SC 4/3/31–541, Corporation Leases
Unpublished Calendar of Corporation Leases
Unpublished Calendar of Various Deeds, Bonds, and Agreements

Unpublished Catalogue of Deeds to Various Properties in Southampton
Unpublished Topographical Lists to Various Areas and Parishes in Southampton
Tax Records
SC 14/2/1–35, 39, 43, 55–61, 83–8, 97, Assessment Books
SC 14/2/37a & b, 38, 42b, 48–53, 68a, Poll Tax Assessments
SC 14/2/47, 62–82b, Marriage Duty Tax Assessments
SC 14/2/97, 118–370, Land Tax Assessments

WINCHESTER
Hampshire Record Office

Q 1, 3, 4, 9, Quarter Sessions Records, 1550–1750
Consistory and Archdeaconry Courts of Winchester, Probate Records, 1550–1750
21M65 C3/2–14, Consistory Court of Winchester, Depositions

YORK
Borthwick Institute of Historical Research

Dean's and Chapter Courts of York, Probate Records, 1620–1750
Prerogative and Exchequer Courts of the Archbishop of York, Probate Records, 1620–1750

York City Record Office
YCA F12 York Oath of Allegiance, 1723

PRINTED PRIMARY SOURCES

'Account Books of Gertrude Savile, 1736–58', *Thoroton Society Record Series*, 24 (1965).
Advice to the Women and Maidens of London (London, 1678).
ALLESTREE, RICHARD, *The Ladies Calling. In Two Parts* (Oxford, 1673).
An Account of the Proceedings of the New Parliament of Women (London, 1683).
An answer to the pleasures of a single life, or, the comforts of marriage confirm'd and vindicated (London, 1701).
ANDERSON, R. C. (ed.), *Assize of Bread Book 1477–1517*, Southampton Record Society, 23 (Southampton: Cox & Sharland, 1923).
—— (ed.), *Books of Examinations and Depositions 1601–1602*, Southampton Record Society, 26 (Southampton: Cox & Sharland, 1926).
—— (ed.), *Books of Examinations and Depositions 1622–1627*, Southampton Record Society, 29 (Southampton: Cox & Sharland, 1929).
—— (ed.), *Books of Examinations and Depositions 1627–1634*, Southampton Record Society, 31 (Southampton: Cox & Sharland, 1931).
—— (ed.), *Books of Examinations and Depositions 1634–39*, Southampton Record Society, 34 (Southampton: Cox & Sharland, 1934).

—— (ed.), *Books of Examinations and Depositions 1639–1644*, Southampton Record Society, 36 (Southampton: Cox & Sharland, 1936).

ASHMUN, MARGARET (ed.), *The Singing Swan: An Account of Anna Seward and Her Acquaintance with Dr. Johnson, Boswell & Others of Their Time* (New Haven, Conn.: Yale University Press, 1931).

ASTELL, MARY, *A Serious Proposal to the Ladies*, 4th edn. (London, 1701; repr. New York: Source Book Press, 1970).

ATKINSON, Revd. J. C. (ed.), 'Quarter Sessions Records', *North Riding Record Society*, 8 and 9 (London, 1890–2).

The Autobiography of Mrs. Alice Thornton Of East Newton, co. York, Surtees Society, 62 (Durham, 1875).

BALLARD, GEORGE, *Memoirs of Several Ladies of Great Britain* (Oxford, 1752).

BARKER, JANE, 'To Mr. G. P. My Adopted Brother; on the Nigh Approach of his Nuptials', in *Poetical Recreations* (London, 1688).

—— 'A Virgin Life', in *Poetical Recreations* (London, 1688).

[BARKSDALE, CLEMENT], *A Letter Touching A Colledge of Maids, or, a Virgin Society* (London, 1675).

BATESON, MARY (ed.), *Borough Customs*, Selden Society Series, 18 and 21 (London: B. Quaritch, 1904, 1906).

The Bath Journal (1744–5).

BERESFORD, JOHN (ed.), *The Diary of a Country Parson: The Rev. James Woodeforde 1758–1781* (Oxford: Oxford University Press, 1926).

BLUNDELL, MARGARET (ed.), *Cavalier: Letters of William Blundell to his friends, 1620–98* (London: Longmans, Green & Co., 1933).

BURTON, ROBERT, *The Anatomy of Melancholy*, ed. Floyd Dell and Paul Jordan-Smith (London, 1621; repr. New York: Farrar & Rinehart, 1927).

Calendar of State Papers, Domestic Series (London: HM Stationery Office, 1895–1960).

CHAMBERLAYNE, EDWARD, *An Academy or Colledge, wherein Young Ladies and Gentlewomen may at a very Moderate Expense be Duly Instructed in the True Protestant Religion, and in all Vertuous Qualities that may Adorn that Sex* (London, 1671).

CHANDLER, MARY, *The Description of Bath, a Poem*, 3rd edn. (London, 1736).

CLAY, JOHN WILLIAM, *Abstracts of Yorkshire Wills in the time of the Commonwealth*, Yorkshire Archaeological and Topographical Society, 4 (1890).

CONNOR, W. J. (ed.), *The Southampton Mayor's Book of 1606–1608*, Southampton Records Series, 21 (Southampton: University of Southampton, 1978).

CONSTABLE, A. (ed.), *Letters of Anna Seward: Written between the years 1784 and 1807*, 6 vols. (Edinburgh, 1811).

A Declaration of the Maids of the City of London (London, 1659).

A Discourse of the Married and Single Life (London, 1621).

DOBSON, CHRISTOPHER S. A. (ed.), *Oxfordshire Protestation Returns 1641–2*, Oxfordshire Record Society (Oxford, 1955).

DODDS, MADELEINE HOPE (ed.), *The Register of Freemen of Newcastle Upon Tyne*, Publications of the Newcastle Upon Tyne Records Commission, 3 (Newcastle: Northumberland Press, 1923).

DUNTON, JOHN, *The Ladies Dictionary* (London, 1694).

Durham Protestations, Surtees Society, 135 (Durham and London, 1922).

EARWAKER, J. P. (ed.), *The Court Leet Records of the Manor of Manchester 1552–1686*, 1 (Manchester, 1884).

EAST, ROBERT (ed.), *Extracts from Records in the Possession of the Municipal Corporation of the Borough of Portsmouth* (Portsmouth, 1891).

EPHELIA, *Female Poems on Several Occasions*, 2nd edn. (London, 1684).

EVANS, WILLIAM and EVANS, THOMAS (eds.), 'Memoirs of the Life of Catharine Philips', *The Friends Library*, 11 (Philadelphia, 1847).

—— (eds.), 'A Memoir of Mary Capper, Late of Birmingham. A Minister of the Society of Friends', *The Friends Library*, 12 (Philadelphia, 1848).

Extracts from the Leeds Intelligencer, Thoresby Society, 33 (Leeds, 1935).

EYRE, ADAM, 'A Diurnal', in *Yorkshire Diaries and Autobiographies in the Seventeenth and Eighteenth Centuries*, Surtees Society, 65 (Durham, 1877).

'A Family History begun by James Fretwell', in *Yorkshire Diaries and Autobiographies*, Surtees Society, 65 (Durham, 1877).

FERGUSON, R. S. and NANSON, W., *Some Municipal Records of the City of Carlisle*, Cumberland and Westmoreland Antiquarian and Archaeological Society, Extra Ser., 4 (Carlisle, 1887).

GANDY, WALLACE (ed.), *The British Plantations Association Oath Rolls 1696* (London, 1922).

Gentleman's Magazine (London, 1737–9, 1790).

GIDDEN, H. W. (ed.), *Book of Remembrance of Southampton 1440–1620*, Southampton Record Society, 27 (Southampton: Cox & Sharland, 1927).

—— (ed.), *Book of Remembrance of Southampton 1303–1518*, Southampton Record Society, 28 (Southampton: Cox & Sharland, 1928).

—— (ed.), *Book of Remembrance of Southampton 1483–1563*, Southampton Record Society, 30 (Southampton: Cox & Sharland, 1930).

GODFRAY, HUMPHREY MARETT, (ed.), *Registre De L'Eglise Wallonne De Southampton*, Huguenot Society of London, 4 (Lymington, 1890).

GOUGE, WILLIAM, *Of Domesticall Duties*, 2nd edn. (London, 1626).

GROOMBRIDGE, MARGARET (ed.), *Calendar of Chester City Council Minutes 1603–1642*, Record Society of Lancashire and Cheshire, 106 (Blackpool, 1956).

HALSBAND, ROBERT and GRUNDY, ISOBEL (eds.), *Lady Mary Wortley Montagu, Essays and Poems and Simplicity a Comedy* (Oxford: Clarendon Press, 1977).

HAMILTON, G. H. (ed.), *Books of Examinations and Depositions A.D. 1570–1594*, Southampton Record Society, 16 (Southampton: Cox & Sharland, 1914).

HAYLEY, WILLIAM, *A Philosophical Essay on Old Maids* (London, 1785).

HEARNSHAW, F. J. C. and D. M. (eds.), *Southampton Court Leet Records, A.D. 1550–1577*, Southampton Record Society, 1 (Southampton: Cox & Sharland, 1905–6).

—— (eds.), *Southampton Court Leet Records, A.D. 1578–1602*, Southampton Record Society, 2 (Southampton: Cox & Sharland, 1905–6).

—— (eds.), *Southampton Court Leet Records, A.D. 1603–1624*, Southampton Record Society, 4 (Southampton: Cox & Sharland, 1906–7).

HEYWOOD, THOMAS (ed.), *The Diary of the Rev. Henry Newcombe*, Chetham Society, 18 (Manchester, 1847).

HILL, BRIDGET (ed.), *The First English Feminist: Reflections Upon Marriage and Other Writings by Mary Astell* (New York: St Martin's Press, 1986).

HORROCKS, J. W. (ed.), *Assembly Books of Southampton 1602–8*, Southampton Record Society, 19 (Southampton: Cox & Sharland, 1917).

—— (ed.), *Assembly Books of Southampton 1609–10*, Southampton Record Society, 21 (Southampton: Cox & Sharland, 1920).

—— (ed.), *Assembly Books of Southampton 1611–1614*, Southampton Record Society, 24 (Southampton: Cox & Sharland, 1924).

—— (ed.), *Assembly Books of Southampton 1615–1616*, Southampton Record Society, 25 (Southampton: Cox & Sharland, 1925).

HOWARD, A. J. (ed.), *The Devon Protestation Returns 1641* (Pinner, Middlesex, 1973).

A Humble Remonstrance of the Batchelors (London, 1693).

INGAMELLS, JOHN and EDGECUMBE, JOHN (eds.), *The Letters of Sir Joshua Reynolds* (New Haven, Conn.: Yale University Press, 2000).

JAMES, T. B. (ed.), *The Third Book of Remembrance of Southampton, 1514–1602*, 4 vols., Southampton Records Series, 22 (Southampton: University of Southampton, 1979).

'The Journal of Mr. John Hobson', in *Yorkshire Diaries and Autobiographies*, Surtees Society, 65 (Durham, 1877).

KAYE, J. M. (ed.), *The Cartulary of God's House, Southampton*, Southampton Records Series, 19–20 (Southampton: University of Southampton, 1976).

The Ladies Remonstance (London, 1659).

LATTER, MARY, *The Miscellaneous Works, in Prose and Verse, of Mrs. Mary Latter* (1759).

LEE, WILLIAM, *Daniel Defoe, His Life and Recently Discovered Writings*, 2 vols. (1869; repr. New York: Burt Franklin, 1969).

The Levellers (London, 1703), in *Harleian Miscellany*, vol. 5, pp. 416–33.

LEWIS, Lady THERESA, *Extracts of the Journal and Correspondence of Miss Berry from 1783–1852*, 3 vols. (London, 1865).

The Love-Lottery, Or, A Woman the Prize (London, 1709).

The Maiden's Plea (London, 1684).

The Maid's Complaint against the Batchelors, or an Easter-Offering for Young Men and Apprentices (London, 1675).

The Maid's Petition (London, 1647).

The Maid's Vindication, or, The Fifteen Comforts of Living a Single Life . . . Written by a Gentlewoman (London, 1707).

Marriage Promoted in a Discourse of its Ancient and Modern Practice (London, 1690).

MARSHALL, J. D. (ed.), *The Autobiography of William Stout of Lancaster 1665–1752* (New York, 1967).

MARTIN, JEANNA (ed.), *A Governess in the Age of Jane Austen* (London: Hambledon Press, 1998).

MASTERS, MARY, *Poems on Several Occasions* (London, 1733).

—— *Familiar Letters and Poems on Several Occasions* (London, 1755).

MATTHEWS, WILLIAM (ed.), *The Diary of Dudley Ryder 1715–1716* (London, 1939).

Matrimony, or, Good Advice to the Ladies to Keep Single (London, 1739).

MERSON, A. L. (ed.), *The Third Book of Remembrance of Southampton, 1514–1602*, Southampton Records Series, 2 and 3 (Southampton: University of Southampton, 1952, 1955).

—— (ed.), *The Third Book of Remembrance of Southampton, 1514–1602*, Southampton Records Series, 8 (Southampton: University of Southampton, 1965).

'Memorandum Book of Sir Walter Claverley, Esq', in *Yorkshire Diaries and Autobiographies*, Surtees Society, 77 (Durham, 1886).

MILLIGAN, PERCY, *The Register of the Freemen of Norwich 1548–1713* (Norwich, 1934).

MORRIS, CHRISTOPHER (ed.), *The Journeys of Celia Fiennes* (London: Cresset Press, 1947).

Now or Never, or, A New Parliament of Women (London, 1656).

PENNINGTON, MONTAGU (ed.), *A Series of Letters between Mrs. Elizabeth Carter and Miss Catherine Talbot from the year 1741 to 1770*, 3rd edn. (London, 1819).

The Petition of the Ladies for Husbands (London, 1693).

PHILLIPS, KATHERINE, 'A Married State', in N. H. Keble (comp.), *The Cultural Identity of Seventeenth-Century Woman: A Reader* (New York: Routledge, 1994).

PICTON, JAMES A., *City of Liverpool: Selections from the Municipal Archives and Records* (Liverpool, 1830).

POUND, J. F. (ed.), *The Norwich Census of the Poor*, Norfolk Record Society, 40 (Norwich, 1971).

RALEIGH, WALTER (ed.), 'The Lady's New-Year's Gift, Or, Advice to a Daughter', in *The Complete Works of George Saville, First Marquess of Halifax* (Oxford: Clarendon Press, 1912).

The Records of Love, or, Weekly Amusements for the Fair Sex, 1: 7 (18 Feb. 1710) and 1: 9 (4 Mar. 1710).

Records of the Borough of Nottingham, 4 (London, 1889).

RICE, R. GARRAWAY (ed.), *West Sussex Protestation Returns 1641–2*, Sussex Record Society, 5 (Lewes: Farncombe & Co., 1906).

—— *Sussex Apprentices and Masters 1710 to 1752*, Sussex Record Society, 28 (London: Mitchell, Hughes & Clarke, 1924).

ROBERTS, EDWARD and PARKER, KAREN (ed.), *Southampton Probate Inventories 1447–1575*, Southampton Records Series, 34 and 35 (Southampton: University of Southampton, 1992).

ROGERS, TIMOTHY, *The Character of a Good Woman both in a Single and Married State* (London, 1697).

ROWE, MARGERY M. and JACKSON, ANDREW M. (eds.), *Exeter Freemen 1266–1967*, Devon and Cornwall Record Society, Extra Ser., 1 (Exeter, 1973).

SALTER, H. E., *Oxford City Properties*, Oxford Historical Society, 83 (Oxford, 1926).

SAVILLE, ALAN (ed.), *Secret Comment: The Diaries of Gertrude Savile 1721–1757*, Thoroton Society Record Series, 41 (Nottingham, 1997).

SCOTT, SARAH, *A Description of Millenium Hall* (New York: Garland, 1974).

SHILTON, DOROTHY and HOLWORTHY, RICHARD, *Wells City Charters*, Somerset Record Society, 46 (London, 1932).

SHUGRUE, MICHAEL F. (ed.), *Selected Poetry and Prose of Daniel Defoe* (New York: Holt, Rinehart & Winston, 1968).

SINGLETON, MARY, *The Old Maid* (London, 1755–6).

THOMAS, ELIZABETH, *Poems on Several Occasions*, 2nd edn. (London, 1727).

—— *Pylades and Corinna, or, memoirs of the lives, amours, and writings of Richard Gwinnet Esq.... and Mrs. Elizabeth Thomas Junr... to which is prefixed the life of Corinna written by herself* (London, 1731).

VERNEY, Lady FRANCES P. (ed.), *Memoirs of the Verney Family during the Seventeenth Century* (London, 1892–9).

VERNEY, Lady MARGARET MARIA, (ed.), *The Verney Letters of the Eighteenth Century from the MSS at Claydon House* (Edinburgh, 1930).

The Virgin's Complaint (London, 1642).

WALLES, JOHN, *A Maiden's Lamentation for Being Unmarried*, in Thomas Wright (ed.), *Songs and Ballads, With Other Short Poems, Chiefly of the Reign of Philip and Mary* (London: J. B. Nichols & Sons, 1860).

WALLIS CHAPMAN, A. B. (ed.), *The Black Book of Southampton c. 1388–1620*, 3 vols., Southampton Record Society, 13, 14, and 17 (Southampton: Cox & Sharland, 1912, 1915).

WELCH, EDWIN (ed.), *The Admiralty Court Book of Southampton 1566–1585*, Southampton Records Series, 13 (Southampton: University of Southampton, 1968).

—— (ed.), *The Minute Book of the French Church at Southampton 1702–1939*, Southampton Records Series, 23 (Southampton: University of Southampton, 1980).

WILLIS, A. J. (comp.) and MERSON, A. L. (ed.), *A Calendar of Southampton Apprenticeship Registers, 1609–1740*, Southampton Records Series, 12 (Southampton: University of Southampton, 1968).

—— (comp.) and HOAD, MARGARET J. (ed.), *Borough Sessions Papers 1653–1688*, Portsmouth Record Series, 1 (Chichester: Phillimore, 1971).

[CASSANDRA (WILLOUGHBY), Duchess of Chandos], *An Account of the Willoughby's of Wollaton*, 2 vols., in W. H. Stevenson (comp.), *H.M.C. Report, Middleton* (1911).

WILSON, CAROL SHINER (ed.), *The Galesia Trilogy and Selected Manuscript Poems of Jane Barker* (New York: Oxford University Press, 1997).

The Women's Advocate, or, The Fifteen Real Comforts of Matrimony... Written by a person of quality of the female sex, 2nd edn. (London, 1683).

WOOD, A. C. (ed.), *The Continuation of the History of the Willoughby Family. by Cassandra, Duchess of Chandos* (Eton, Windsor: Shakespeare Head Press, 1958).

The Young Women and Maiden's Lamentation (London, 1690).

Secondary Works

AMUSSEN, SUSAN, *An Ordered Society: Gender and Class In Early Modern England* (New York: Columbia University Press, 1988).

ANDERSON, MICHAEL, 'The Social Position of Spinsters In Mid-Victorian Britain', *Journal of Family History*, 9: 4 (1984), 377–93.

ANDREADIS, HARRIETTE, *Sappho in Early Modern England: Female Same-Sex Literary Erotics, 1550–1714* (Chicago: University of Chicago Press, 2001).

ASHTON, ROBERT, *The Crown and the Money Market, 1603–1640* (Oxford: Clarendon Press, 1960).

BACKSCHEIDER, PAULA, *Daniel Defoe: His Life* (Baltimore, Md.: Johns Hopkins Press, 1989).

BAKER, J. H., *An Introduction to English Legal History* (London: Butterworths, 1990).

BARRON, CAROLINE and SUTTON, ANNE (eds.), *Medieval London Widows, 1300–1500* (New York: Hambledon Press, 1994).

BEATTIE, CORDELIA, 'A Room of One's Own? The Legal Evidence for the Residential Arrangements of Women Without Husbands in Late Fourteenth- and Early Fifteenth-Century York', in Noel James Menuge (ed.), *Medieval Women and the Law* (Woodbridge: Boydell Press, 2000), 41–56.

—— 'The Problem of Women's Work Identities in Post Black Death England', in James Bothwell et al. (eds.), *The Problem of Labour in Fourteenth-Century England* (York: York Medieval Press, 2000), 1–19.

BEIER, A. L., 'Vagrants and the Social Order in Elizabethan England', *Past & Present*, 64 (1974), 3–29.

BEN-AMOS, ILANA KRAUSMAN, 'Women Apprentices in the Trades and Crafts of Early Modern Bristol', *Continuity and Change*, 6: 2 (1991), 227–52.

—— *Adolescence and Youth in Early Modern England* (New Haven: Yale University Press, 1994).

BENNETT, JUDITH M., 'Medieval Women, Modern Women: Across The Great Divide', in David Aers (ed.), *Culture and History, 1350–1600: Essays on English Communities, Identities and Writing* (New York: Harvester Wheatsheaf, 1992), 147–75.

—— *Ale, Beer and Brewsters in England: Women's Work in a Changing World 1300–1600* (New York: Oxford University Press, 1996).

—— ' "Lesbian-Like" and the Social History of Lesbianisms', *Journal of the History of Sexuality*, 9: 1–2 (2000), 1–24.

—— 'Ventriloquisms: When Maidens Speak in English Songs, c.1300–1550', in Anne L. Klinck and Ann Marie Rasmussen (eds.), *Medieval Women's Song: Cross-Cultural Approaches* (Philadelphia: University of Pennsylvania, 2002), 187–204.

—— and FROIDE, AMY M. (eds.), *Singlewomen in the European Past, 1250–1800* (Philadelphia: University of Pennsylvania Press, 1999).

BERG, MAXINE, 'Women's Property and the Industrial Revolution', *Journal of Interdisciplinary History*, 24: 2 (1993), 233–50.

BERRY, PHILIPPA, *Of Chastity and Power: Elizabethan Literature and the Unmarried Queen* (London and New York: Routledge, 1989).

BOULTON, JEREMY, 'London Widowhood Revisited: The Decline of Female Remarriage in the Seventeenth and Early Eighteenth Centuries', *Continuity and Change*, 5: 3 (1990), 323–56.

BRADDICK, M. J., *Parliamentary Taxation in the Seventeenth Century* (Rochester, NY: Boydell Press, 1994).

BREE, LINDA, *Sarah Fielding* (New York: Twayne Publishers, 1996).

BRODSKY ELLIOTT, VIVIEN, 'Single Women in the London Marriage Market: Age, Status, and Mobility, 1598–1619', in R. B. Outhwaite (ed.), *Studies in the Social History of Marriage and Society* (New York: St Martin's Press, 1981), 81–100.

—— 'Widows in Late Elizabethan London: Remarriage, Economic Opportunity and Family Orientations', in Lloyd Bonfield, Richard M. Smith, and Keith Wrightson (eds.), *The World We Have Gained* (New York: Basil Blackwell, 1986), 122–54.

BROWN, W. NEWMAN, 'The Receipt of Poor Relief and Family Situation, Aldenham, Hertfordshire, 1630–90', in R. M. Smith (ed.), *Land, Kinship and Life-Cycle* (New York: Cambridge University Press, 1984), 405–22.

BROWNE, JOHN, *History of Congregationalism and Memorials of the Churches of Norfolk and Suffolk* (London, 1877).

BURGESS, L. A., 'Southampton in the Seventeenth Century', in J. B. Morgan and P. Peberdy (eds.), *Collected Essays on Southampton* (Southampton: County Borough of Southampton, 1968), 66–81.

CARLTON, CHARLES, 'The Widow's Tale: Male Myths and Female Reality in 16th and 17th Century England', *Albion*, 10: 2 (1978), 118–29.

CASTLE, TERRY, 'Sister, Sister', *London Review of Books*, 17: 5 (3 Aug. 1995).

CAVALLO, SANDRA and WARNER, LYNDAN (eds.), *Widowhood in Medieval and Early Modern Europe* (New York: Longman, 1999).

CHAMBERS-SCHILLER, LEE, *Liberty, A Better Husband: Single Women in America. The Generations of 1780–1840* (New Haven, Conn.: Yale University Press, 1984).

CHAYTOR, MIRANDA, 'Household and Kinship: Ryton in the Late 16th and Early 17th Centuries', *History Workshop Journal*, 10 (1980), 25–60.

CHESTER WATERS, R. E., 'A Statutory List of the Inhabitants of Melbourne, Derbyshire in 1695', *Journal of the Derbyshire Archaeological and Natural History Society*, 7 (1885), 1–30.

CHILD, ELIZABETH, ' "To Sing the Town": Women, Place, and Print Culture in Eighteenth-Century Bath', *Society for Eighteenth Century Studies*, 28 (1999).

CHOJNACKI, STANLEY, 'Measuring Adulthood: Adolescence and Gender in Renaissance Venice', *Journal of Family History*, 17: 4 (1992), 371–96.

CIONI, MARIA, *Women and Law in Elizabethan England, With Particular Reference to the Court of Chancery* (New York: Garland, 1985).

CLAPHAM, SIR JOHN, *The Bank of England: A History* (New York: The Macmillan Co., 1945).

CLARK, ALICE, *Working Life of Women in the Seventeenth Century*, 3rd edn. (New York: Routledge, 1992).

CLARK, PETER, 'The Migrant in Kentish Towns 1580–1640', in Peter Clark and Paul Slack (eds.), *Crisis and Order in English Towns 1500–1700* (London: Routledge & Kegan Paul, 1972), 117–63.

—— and SLACK, PAUL, 'Introduction', in Peter Clark and Paul Slack (eds.), *Crisis and Order in English Towns 1500–1700* (London: Routledge & Kegan Paul, 1972), 1–56.

CLAY, C. G. A., *Economic Expansion and Social Change: England 1500–1700*, 2 vols. (New York: Cambridge University Press, (1984).

COLEMAN, D. C., *The Economy of England 1450–1750* (New York: Oxford University Press, 1977).

COLLINS, JAMES B., 'The Economic Role of Women in Seventeenth-Century France', *French Historical Studies*, 16: 2 (Autumn 1989), 437–70.

COOPER, DI and DONALD, MOIRA, 'Households and "Hidden" Kin in Early-Nineteenth-Century England: Four Case Studies in Suburban Exeter, 1821–1861', *Continuity and Change*, 10: 2 (1995), 257–78.

CORFIELD, PENELOPE, 'A Provincial Capital in the Late Seventeenth Century: The Case of Norwich', in Peter Clark and Paul Slack (eds.), *Crisis and Order in English Towns 1500–1700* (London: Routledge & Kegan Paul, 1972), 263–310.

CRAWFORD, PATRICIA, 'Menstruation in Seventeenth-Century England', *Past & Present*, 91 (1981), 47–73.

—— *Women and Religion in England 1500–1720* (New York: Routledge, 1993).

—— and MENDELSON, SARA, 'Sexual Identities in Early Modern England: The Marriage of Two Women in 1680', *Gender & History*, 7 (1995), 362–78.

CRESSY, DAVID, 'Kinship and Kin Interaction In Early Modern England', *Past & Present*, 113 (Nov. 1986), 38–69.

DAVIDOFF, LEONORE, DOOLITTLE, MEGAN, FINK, JANET, and HOLDEN, KATHERINE, *The Family Story: Blood, Contract and Intimacy, 1830–1960* (Harlow, Essex: Longman, 1999).

D'CRUZE, SHANI, '"To Acquaint the Ladies": Women Traders in Colchester *c*.1750–*c*.1800', *Local Historian*, 17: 3 (1986), 158–61.

DEN STEINEN, KARL VON, 'The Discovery of Women in Eighteenth-Century Political Life', in Barbara Kanner (ed.), *The Women of England From Anglo-Saxon Times to the Present*, (Hamden, Conn.: Archon Books 1979).

DIEFENDORF, BARBARA, 'Women and Property in Old Regime France', in John Brewer and Susan Staves (eds.), *Early Modern Conceptions of Property* (New York: Routledge, 1995), 170–93.

DONOGHUE, EMMA, *Passions Between Women: British Lesbian Culture 1668–1801* (New York: HarperCollins, 1993).

EARLE, PETER, 'The Female Labour Market in London in the Late Seventeenth and Early Eighteenth Centuries', *Economic History Review*, 2nd ser., 42: 3 (1989), 328–53.

—— *The Making of the English Middle Class* (Berkeley: University of California Press, 1989).

ERICKSON, AMY LOUISE, *Women and Property in Early Modern England* (New York: Routledge, 1993).

EVANS, ROBERT C., 'Deference and Defiance: The "Memorandum" of Martha Moulsworth', in Claude J. Summer and Ted-Larry Pebworth (eds.), *Representing Women in
Renaissance England* (Columbia, Mo.: University of Missouri Press, 1997).

FARMER, SHARON, ' "It is not Good that [Wo]man Should Be Alone": Elite Re-
sponses to Singlewomen in High Medieval Paris', in Judith M. Bennett and Amy
M. Froide (eds.), *Singlewomen in the European Past, 1250–1800* (Philadelphia:
University of Pennsylvania Press, 1999).

FEHRENBACH, R. J., 'A Letter sent by Maydens of London (1567)', *English Literary
Renaissance*, 14 (1984), 285–304.

FROIDE, AMY M., 'Singlewomen, Work and Community in Southampton, 1550–
1750', Ph.D. Dissertation, Duke University (1996).

—— 'Marital Status as a Category of Difference: Singlewomen and Widows in Early
Modern England', in Judith M. Bennett and Amy M. Froide (eds.), *Singlewomen
in the European Past, 1250–1800* (Philadelphia: University of Pennsylvania Press,
1999).

—— 'Old Maids: The Lifecycle of Singlewomen in Early Modern England', in L. A.
Botelho and Pat Thane (eds.), *Women and Ageing in British Society Since 1500*
(New York: Longman, 2001).

—— 'Hidden Women: Rediscovering the Singlewomen of Early Modern England',
Local Population Studies, 68 (Spring 2002), 26–41.

GEREMEK, BRONISLAW, *The Margins of Society in Late Medieval Paris* (New York:
Cambridge University Press, 1987).

GILLIS, JOHN, *For Better, For Worse: British Marriages, 1600 to the Present* (New York:
Oxford University Press, 1985).

GINTER, DONALD, 'The Incidence of Revaluation', in Michael Turner and Dennis
Mills (eds.), *Land and Property: The English Land Tax 1692–1832* (New York:
St Martin's Press, 1986), 180–8.

—— *A Measure of Wealth, The English Land Tax in Historical Analysis* (Montreal:
McGill-Queen's University Press, 1992).

GITTINGS, CLAIRE, *Death, Burial and the Individual in Early Modern England*
(London: Croom Helm, 1984).

GLASS, D. V., 'Two Papers on Gregory King', in D. V. Glass and D. E. C. Eversley
(eds.), *Population in History: Essays in Historical Demography* (Chicago: Aldine,
1965), 159–220.

—— 'Notes on the Demography of London at the End of the Seventeenth Century',
Daedalus, 97: 2 (1968), 581–93.

—— 'Socio-Economic Status and Occupations in the City of London at the End of
the Seventeenth Century', in A. E. J. Hollaender and William Kellaway, *Studies in
London History* (London: Hodder & Stoughton, 1969), 373–89.

GOLDBERG, P. J. P., *Women, Work, and Life Cycle in a Medieval Economy: Women in
York and Yorkshire c.1300–1520* (Oxford: Clarendon Press, 1992).

—— (ed.), *Women in England c.1275–1525* (New York: Manchester University
Press, 1995).

GOWING, LAURA, 'Gender and the Language of Insult in Early Modern London',
History Workshop Journal, 35 (Spring 1993), 1–21.

GOWING, LAURA, *Domestic Dangers: Women, Words, and Sex in Early Modern London* (Oxford: Oxford University Press, 1996).

GRASSBY, RICHARD, *Kinship and Capitalism: Marriage, Family and Business in the English-Speaking World, 1580–1740* (New York: Cambridge University Press, 2001).

GRIFFITHS, PAUL, *Youth and Authority: Formative Experiences in England 1560–1640* (Oxford: Clarendon Press, 1996).

HAJNAL, J., 'European Marriage Patterns in Perspective', in D. V. Glass and D. E. C. Eversley (eds.), *Population in History: Essays in Historical Demography* (Chicago: Aldine, 1965), 101–43.

HARMAN, CLAIRE, *Fanny Burney: A Biography* (New York: A. Knopf, 2001).

HARRIS, BARBARA J., *English Aristocratic Women 1450–1550: Marriage and Family, Property and Careers* (New York: Oxford University Press, 2002).

HIGGINS, PATRICIA, 'The Reactions of Women, with Special Reference to Women Petitioners', in Brian Manning (ed.), *Politics, Religion and the English Civil War* (London: Edward Arnold, 1973), 179–222.

HILL, BRIDGET, 'A Refuge From Men: The Idea of a Protestant Nunnery', *Past & Present*, 117 (1987), 107–30.

—— 'The Marriage Age of Women and the Demographers', *History Workshop Journal*, 28 (Autumn 1989), 129–47.

—— *Women, Work, and Sexual Politics in Eighteenth-Century England* (New York: Basil Blackwell, 1989).

—— *Servants: English Domestics in the Eighteenth Century* (Oxford: Clarendon Press, 1996).

—— *Women Alone: Spinsters in England, 1660–1850* (New Haven, Conn.: Yale University Press, 2001).

HITCHCOCK, TIM, ' "Unlawfully begotten on her body": Illegitimacy and the Parish Poor in St. Luke's Chelsea', in Tim Hitchcock, Peter King, and Pamela Sharpe (eds.), *Chronicling Poverty: The Voices and Strategies of the English Poor, 1640–1840* (New York: St Martin's Press, 1997), 70–86.

HOLDERNESS, B. A., 'Elizabeth Parkin and Her Investments, 1733–66: Aspects of the Sheffield Money Market in the Eighteenth Century', *Transactions of the Hunter Archaeological Society*, 10: 2 (1973), 81–7.

—— 'Credit in a Rural Community, 1660–1800: Some Aspects of Probate Inventories', *Midland History*, 3: 2 (1975), 94–115.

—— 'Credit in English Rural Society Before the Nineteenth Century, with Special Reference to the Period 1650–1720', *Agricultural History Review*, 24: 2 (1976), 97–109.

—— 'Widows in Pre-Industrial Society: An Essay Upon their Economic Functions', in Richard M. Smith (ed.), *Land, Kinship and Life-Cycle* (New York: Cambridge University Press, 1984), 423–42.

HOOPS, JOHANNES, 'Old Maids Lead Apes in Hell', *Englische Studien*, 70 (1935/6), 337–51.

HOULBROOKE, RALPH, 'Women's Social Life and Common Action in England from the Fifteenth Century to the End of the Civil War', *Continuity and Change*, 1: 2 (1986), 171–89.

HOWELL, CICELY, 'Peasant Inheritance Customs in the Midlands, 1280–1700', in Jack Goody, Joan Thirsk, and E. P. Thompson (eds.), *Family and Inheritance: Rural Society in Western Europe, 1200–1800* (New York: Cambridge University Press, 1976), 112–55.

HUFTON, OLWEN, 'Women Without Men: Widows and Spinsters in Britain and France in the Eighteenth Century', *Journal of Family History,* 9: 4 (1984), 355–76.

—— *The Prospect Before Her: A History of Women in Western Europe*, Vol. 1: *1500–1800* (London: HarperCollins, 1995).

HUNT, MARGARET R., *The Middling Sort: Commerce, Gender and the Family in England, 1680–1780* (Berkeley: University of California Press, 1996).

—— 'The Sapphic Strain: English Lesbians in the Long Eighteenth Century', in Judith M. Bennett and Amy M. Froide (eds.), *Singlewomen in the European Past, 1250–1800* (Philadelphia: University of Pennsylvania Press, 1999), 270–96.

HUTTON, DIANE, 'Women in Fourteenth Century Shrewsbury', in Lindsey Charles and Lorna Duffin (eds.), *Women and Work in Pre-Industrial England* (London: Croom Helm, 1985), 83–99.

INNES, JOANNA, 'Prisons For the Poor: English Bridewells, 1555–1800', in Francis Snyder and Douglas Hay (eds.), *Labour, Law, and Crime: An Historical Perspective* (New York: Tavistock Publications, 1987).

JACKSON, MARK, *New-Born Child Murder: Women, Illegitimacy and the Courts in Eighteenth-Century England* (New York: Manchester University Press, 1996).

JOHANSEN, HANS CHRISTIAN, 'Never-married Women in Town and Country in Eighteenth-century Denmark', in John Henderson and Richard Wall (eds.), *Poor Women and Children in the European Past* (New York: Routledge, 1994).

JONES, NORMAN, *God and the Moneylenders: Usury and Law in Early Modern England* (Oxford: Basil Blackwell, 1989).

JORDAN, WILLIAM, *Women and Credit in Pre-Industrial and Developing Societies* (Philadelphia: University of Pennsylvania Press, 1993).

KARRAS, RUTH, *Common Women, Prostitution and Sexuality in Medieval England* (New York: Oxford University Press, 1996).

—— 'Sex and the Singlewoman', in Judith M. Bennett and Amy M. Froide (eds.), *Singlewomen in the European Past, 1250–1800* (Philadelphia: University of Pennsylvania Press, 1999).

KENT, D. A., 'Ubiquitous But Invisible: Female Domestic Servants in Mid-Eighteenth Century London', *History Workshop Journal*, 28 (1989), 111–28.

KING, W. J., 'Punishment For Bastardy in Early Seventeenth Century England', *Albion*, 10 (1978), 130–51.

KITTREDGE, KATHARINE OTTAWAY, '"Tabby Cats Lead Apes in Hell": Spinsters in Eighteenth Century Life and Fiction', Ph.D. Dissertation, SUNY, Binghamton (1991).

KRUEGER, ROBERTA, 'Transforming Maidens: Singlewomen's Stories in Marie de France's *Lais* and Later French Courtly Narratives', in Judith M. Bennett and Amy M. Froide (eds.), *Singlewomen in the European Past, 1250–1800* (Philadelphia: University of Pennsylvania Press, 1999).

KUSSMAUL, ANN, *Servants in Husbandry in Early Modern England* (New York: Cambridge University Press, 1981).

LACEY, KAY E., 'Women and Work in Fourteenth and Fifteenth Century London', in Lindsey Charles and Lorna Duffin (eds.), *Women and Work in Pre-Industrial England* (London: Croom Helm, 1985), 24–82.

LANE, PENELOPE, 'Women, Property and Inheritance: Wealth Creation and Income Generation in Small English Towns, 1750–1835', in Jon Stobart and Alastair Owens (eds.) *Urban Fortunes: Property and Inheritance in the Town 1700–1900* (Burlington, Vt.: Ashgate, 2000), 186 and Table 8.2.

LANSER, SUSAN S., 'Singular Politics: The Rise of the British Nation and the Production of the Old Maid', in Judith M. Bennett and Amy M. Froide (eds.), *Singlewomen in the European Past, 1250–1800* (Philadelphia: University of Pennsylvania, 1999).

LASLETT, PETER, 'Size and Structure of the Household in England Over Three Centuries', *Population Studies*, 23: 2 (1969), 199–223.

—— *The World We Have Lost: England Before the Industrial Age*, 2nd edn. (New York: Scribner, 1971).

—— 'Introduction', in Peter Laslett and Richard Wall (eds.), *Household and Family in Past Time* (Cambridge: Cambridge University Press, 1972), 1–89.

—— 'Mean Household Size in England Since the Sixteenth Century', in Peter Laslett and Richard Wall (eds.), *Household and Family in Past Time* (Cambridge: Cambridge University Press, 1972), 125–58.

—— OOSTERVEEN, KARLA, and SMITH, R. M. (eds.), *Bastardy and Its Comparative History (Cambridge, Mass: Harvard University Press, 1980).*

LE CLUSE, JANE P., 'The Stranger Congregation in Southampton 1567–1712', dissertation for diploma in English local history, Portsmouth Polytechnic, (1988).

LEMIRE, BEVERLY, *Dress, Culture and Commerce: The English Clothing Trade Before the Factory, 1660–1800* (New York: St Martin's Press, 1997).

LEVER, Sir TRESHAM (ed.), *The House of Pitt: A Family Chronicle* (London: Wyman & Sons, 1947).

LEWALSKI, BARBARA, *Writing Women in Jacobean England* (Cambridge, Mass.: Harvard University Press, 1993).

LEWIS, KATHERINE J., MENUGE, NOEL JAMES, and PHILLIPS, KIM M. (eds.), *Young Medieval Women* (New York: St Martin's Press, 1999).

LYNCH, KATHERINE A., 'The European Marriage Pattern in the Cities: Variations on a Theme by Hajnal', *Journal of Family History*, 16: 1 (1991), 79–96.

MCINTOSH, MARJORIE K., 'Servants and the Household Unit in an Elizabethan English Community', *Journal of Family History*, 9: 1 (1984), 3–23.

—— 'Money Lending on the Periphery of London, 1300–1600', *Albion*, 20: 4 (Winter 1988), 557–71.

MASCUCH, MICHAEL, *Origins of the Individualist Self: Autobiography and Self-identity in England, 1591–1791* (Stanford, Cal: Stanford University Press, 1996).

MASTEN, VIKTORIA L., 'Taking the Waters: Elite Women in English Spa Towns 1700–1800', MA thesis, California State University at Long Beach (1993).

MAYHEW, GRAHAM, *Tudor Rye* (Falmer: University of Sussex, 1987).

—— 'Life Cycle Service and the Family Unit in Early Modern Rye', *Continuity and Change*, 6: 2 (1991), 201–25.

MELDRUM, TIM, 'A Women's Court in London: Defamation at the Bishop of London's Consistory Court, 1700–1745', *London Journal*, 19: 1 (1994), 1–20.

—— *Domestic Service and Gender 1660–1750: Life and Work in the London Household* (New York: Longman, 2000).

MENDELSON, SARA and CRAWFORD, PATRICIA, *Women in Early Modern England, 1550–1720* (New York: Oxford University Press, 1998).

MERSON, A. L., 'Southampton in the Sixteenth and Seventeenth Centuries', in F. J. Monkhouse (ed.), *A Survey of Southampton and its Region* (Southampton: Southampton University Press, 1964), 218–27.

MITCHELL, IAN, 'The Development of Urban Retailing 1700–1815', in Peter Clark (ed.), *The Transformation of English Provincial Towns 1600–1800* (London: Hutchinson, 1984), 259–83.

MORRIS, RUPERT H., *Chester in the Plantagenet and Tudor Reigns* (Chester: n.p., 1894).

MULDREW, CRAIG, 'Credit and the Courts: Debt Litigation in a Seventeenth-Century Urban Community', *Economic History Review*, 46: 1 (1993), 23–38.

—— *The Economy of Obligation* (New York: MacMillan, 1998).

MURRAY, JACQUELINE, 'Kinship and Friendship: The Perception of Family by Clergy and Laity in Late Medieval London', *Albion*, 20: 3 (1988), 369–85.

MYERS, SYLVIA H., *The Bluestocking Circle: Women, Friendship, and the Life of the Mind in Eighteenth-Century England* (Oxford: Clarendon Press, 1990).

NEEDHAM, GWENDOLYN B., 'The "Old Maid" in the Life and Fiction of Eighteenth-Century England', Ph.D. dissertation, University of California (1938).

NOBLE, MARGARET, 'Land Tax Returns and Urban Development', *Local Historian*, 15: 2 (1982), 86–91.

NUTTALL, GEOFFREY, *Visible Saints: The Congregational Way, 1640–1660* (Oxford: Basil Blackwell, 1957).

O'HARA, DIANA, *Courtship and Constraint: Rethinking the Making of Marriage in Tudor England* (Manchester: Manchester University Press, 2000).

PALAZZI, MAURA, 'Female Solitude and Patrilineage: Unmarried Women and Widows During the Eighteenth and Nineteenth Centuries', *Journal of Family History*, 15: 4 (1990), 443–59.

PATTERSON, A. TEMPLE, 'Southampton in the Eighteenth and Nineteenth Centuries', in F. J. Monkhouse (ed.), *A Survey of Southampton and its Region* (Southampton: University of Southampton University, 1964), 227–35.

—— (ed.), *A History of Southampton, 1700–1914. I: An Oligarchy in Decline, 1700–1835*, Southampton Records Series, 11 (Southampton: University of Southampton, 1966).

PETERS, CHRISTINE, 'Singlewomen in Early Modern England: Attitudes and Expectations', *Continuity and Change*, 12: 3 (1997), 325–45.

PHILLIPS, KIM M., *Medieval Maidens: Young Women and Gender in England 1270–1540* (New York: Palgrave/Manchester University Press, 2003).

PINCHBECK, IVY, *Women Workers and the Industrial Revolution, 1750–1850* (London: Virago Press, 1981).

PLATT, COLIN, *Medieval Southampton: The Port and Trading Community, A.D. 1000–1600* (London: Routledge & Kegan Paul, 1973).

PLOMER, H. R. et al., *A Dictionary of Printers and Booksellers 1726–1775* (Oxford: Oxford University Press, 1932).

POWER, M. J., 'East London Housing in the Seventeenth Century', in Peter Clark and Paul Slack (eds.), *Crisis and Order in English Towns 1500–1700* (London: Routledge & Kegan Paul, 1972), 237–62.

PRIOR, MARY, 'Women and the Urban Economy: Oxford 1500–1800', in Mary Prior (ed.), *Women in English Society 1500–1800* (London: Methuen, 1985), 93–117.

RANCE, ADRIAN, *Southampton: An Illustrated History* (Portsmouth: Milestone Publications, 1986).

REEVES, MARJORIE, *Pursuing the Muses: Female Education and Nonconformist Culture, 1700–1900* (Leicester: Leicester University Press, 1997).

RICHARDS, ERIC, 'Women in the British Economy Since About 1700: An Interpretation', *History*, 59 (1974), 337–57.

RIZZO, BETTY, *Companions Without Vows: Relationships Among Eighteenth-century British Women* (Athens: University of Georgia Press, 1994).

ROBERTS, JOSEPHINE, 'Deciphering Women's Pastoral: Coded Language in Wroth's *Love's Victory*', in Claude J. Summer and Ted-Larry Pebworth (eds.), *Representing Women in Renaissance England* (Columbia: University of Missouri Press, 1997).

ROBERTS, MICHAEL, ' "Words they are Women, and Deeds they are Men": Images of Work and Gender in Early Modern England', in Lindsey Charles and Lorna Duffin (eds.), *Women and Work in Pre-Industrial England* (London: Croom Helm, 1985), 122–80.

—— 'Women and Work in Sixteenth-Century English Towns', in Penelope Corfield and Derek Keene (eds.), *Work in Towns 850–1850* (New York: Leicester University Press, 1990), 86–102.

ROSE, MARY BETH, 'Gender, Genre, and History: Seventeenth-Century English Women and the Art of Autobiography', in Rose (ed.) *Women in the Middle Ages and the Renaissance* (Syracuse, NY: Syracuse University Press, 1986).

ROSEN, ADRIENNE B., 'Economic and Social Aspects of the History of Winchester 1520–1670', D.Phil. thesis, University of Oxford (1975).

ROTHERY, ELIZABETH ANNE, 'Poverty in Southampton 1540–1640', dissertation for diploma in English local history, Portsmouth Polytechnic (1989).

SANDELL, ELSIE M., 'Georgian Southampton: A Watering Place and Spa', in J. B. Morgan and P. Peberdy (eds.), *Collected Essays on Southampton* (Southampton: County Borough of Southampton, 1968), 74–81.

SANDERSON, ELIZABETH C., *Women and Work in Eighteenth-Century Edinburgh* (New York: St Martin's Press, 1996).

SCHOFIELD, ROGER, 'English Marriage Patterns Revisited', *Journal of Family History.* 10: 1 (1985), 2–20.

SCHURER, KEVIN and ARKELL, TOM (eds.) *Surveying the People: The Interpretation and Use of Document Sources for the Study of Population in the Later Seventeenth Century* (Oxford: Leopard's Head Press, 1992).

SCHWOERER, LOIS, 'Women and the Glorious Revolution', *Albion*. 18: 2 (1986), 195–218.

SEEMAN, ERIC, '"It is Better to Marry Than to Burn": Anglo-American Attitudes Toward Celibacy, 1600–1800', *Journal of Family History*. 24: 4 (1999), 397–419.

SHARPE, J. A., *Defamation and Sexual Slander in Early Modern England: The Church Courts at York*, Borthwick Papers, 58 (York: University of York, 1980).

SHARPE, PAMELA, 'Gender-Specific Demographic Adjustment to Changing Economic Circumstances, Colyton, 1538–1837', Ph.D. thesis, University of Cambridge (1988).

—— 'Literally Spinsters: A New Interpretation of Local Economy and Demography in Colyton in the Seventeenth and Eighteenth Centuries', *Economic History Review*, 44: 1 (1991), 46–65.

—— 'Poor Children as Apprentices in Colyton, 1598–1830', *Continuity and Change*, 6: 2 (1991), 253–70.

—— *Adapting to Capitalism: Working Women in the English Economy, 1700–1850* (Basingstoke: Macmillan, 1996).

—— '"The Bowels of Compation": A Labouring Family and the Law, *c*.1790–1834', in Tim Hitchcock, Peter King, and Pamela Sharpe (eds.), *Chronicling Poverty: The Voices and Strategies of the English Poor, 1640–1840* (New York: St Martin's Press, 1997).

—— 'Dealing with Love: The Ambiguous Independence of the Singlewoman in Early Modern England', *Gender & History*, 11: 2 (July 1999), 202–32.

SHUTTLETON, DAVID, '"All Passion Extinguish'd": The Case of Mary Chandler, 1687–1745', in Isabel Armstrong and Virginia Blain (eds.), *Women's Poetry in the Enlightenment: The Making of a Canon, 1730–1820*, (New York: St Martin's Press, 1999), 33–49.

SHOEMAKER, ROBERT, *Prosecution and Punishment: Petty Crime and the Law in London and Rural Middlesex, c.1660–1725* (New York: Cambridge University Press, 1991).

SKEDD, SUSAN, 'Women Teachers and the Expansion of Girls' Schooling in England, *c*.1760–1820', in Hannah Barker and Elaine Chalus (eds.), *Gender in Eighteenth-Century England: Roles, Representations and Responsibilities* (New York: Longman, 1997).

SLACK, PAUL, 'Poverty and Politics in Salisbury 1597–1666', in Peter Clark and Paul Slack (eds.), *Crisis and Order in English Towns 1500–1700: Essays in Urban History* (London: Routledge & Kegan Paul, 1972), 164–203.

—— *Poverty and Policy in Tudor and Stuart England* (London: Longman, 1988).

SLATER, MIRIAM, *Family Life in the Seventeenth Century: The Verneys of Claydon House* (New York: Routledge, 1984).

SMITH, HILDA, 'Women as Sextons and Electors: King's Bench and Precedents for Women's Citizenship', in Hilda Smith, *Women Writers and the Early Modern British Political Tradition* (New York: Cambridge University Press, 1998).

SNELL, K. D. M., *Annals of the Labouring Poor: Social Change and Agrarian England, 1660–1900* (New York: Cambridge University Press, 1985).

SOUDEN, DAVID, 'Migrants and the Population Structure of Later Seventeenth-Century Provincial Cities and Market Towns', in Peter Clark (ed.), *The Transformation of English Towns 1600–1800* (London: Hutchinson, 1984), 133–68.

SPICER, ANDREW PAUL, 'The Walloon Community of Southampton *c.*1567–1600', BA thesis, University of Southampton (1985).

SPICKSLEY, JUDITH, 'The Early Modern Demographic Dynamic: Celibates and Celibacy in Seventeenth-Century England', D.Phil. thesis, University of Hull (2001).

SPUFFORD, MARGARET, 'The Limitations of the Probate Inventory', in John Chartres and David Hey (eds.), *English Rural Society, 1500–1800: Essays in Honour of Joan Thirsk* (New York: Cambridge University Press, 1990), 139–74.

STAVES, SUSAN, 'Resentment or Resignation? Dividing the Spoils Among Daughters and Younger Sons', in John Brewer and Susan Staves (eds.), *Early Modern Conceptions of Property* (New York: Routledge, 1995), 194–218.

STONE, LAWRENCE, *The Family, Sex, and Marriage in England 1500–1800*, abridged edn. (New York: Harper & Row, 1979).

STOPES, CHARLOTTE C., *British Freewomen: Their Historical Privilege* (London, 1894).

STYLES, PHILIP, 'A Census of a Warwickshire Village in 1698', *University of Birmingham Historical Journal*, 3 (1951–2), 33–51.

TADMOR, NAOMI, *Family and Friends in Eighteenth-Century England: Household, Kinship, and Patronage* (Cambridge: Cambridge University Press, 2001).

THOMAS, KEITH, 'Age and Authority in Early Modern England', *Proceedings of the British Academy*, 62 (1976), 205–48.

—— *History and Literature* (Swansea: University College of Swansea, 1988).

TITTLER, ROBERT, 'Money-lending in the West Midlands: The Activities of Joyce Jeffries, 1638–49', *Historical Research*, 67: 164 (1994), 249–63.

TODD, BARBARA J., 'Widowhood in a Market Town, Abingdon 1540–1720', D.Phil. thesis, University of Oxford (1983).

—— 'Demographic Determinism and Female Agency: The Remarrying Widow Reconsidered... Again', *Continuity and Change*. 9: 3 (1994), 421–3.

TODD, JANET (ed.), *A Dictionary of British and American Women Writers 1660–1800* (Totowa, NJ: Rowman & Allanheld, 1985).

TRAUB, VALERIE, *The Renaissance of Lesbianism in Early Modern England* (Cambridge: Cambridge University Press, 2002).

TUDOR-JONES, R., *Congregationalism in England 1662–1962* (Letchworth: Independent Press, 1962).

TURNER, CHERYL, *Living by the Pen: Women Writers in the Eighteenth Century* (London and New York: Routledge, 1992).

TURNER, MICHAEL and MILLS, DENNIS, (eds.), *Land and Property: The English Land Tax 1692–1832* (Stroud: Alan Sutton, 1986).

UNDERDOWN, DAVID, 'The Taming of the Scold: The Enforcement of Patriarchal Authority in Early Modern England', in Anthony Fletcher and John Stevenson (eds.), *Order and Disorder in Early Modern England* (New York: Cambridge University Press, 1985).

VANN, RICHARD T., 'Wills and the Family in an English Town: Banbury 1550–1800', *Journal of Family History*, 4: 4 (1979), 346–67.

VICINUS, MARTHA, *Independent Women: Work and Community for Single Women 1850–1920* (Chicago: University of Chicago Press, 1985).

WAHL, ELIZABETH, *Invisible Relations: Representations of Female Intimacy in the Age of Enlightenment* (Stanford, Cal.: Stanford University Press, 1999).

WALES, TIM, 'Poverty, Poor Relief and the Life-cycle: Some Evidence from Seventeenth-Century Norfolk', in R. M. Smith (ed.), *Land, Kinship and Life-Cycle* (New York: Cambridge University Press, 1984), 351–404.

WALKER, CLAIRE, *Gender and Politics in Early Modern Europe: English Convents in France and the Low Countries* (New York: Palgrave, 2003).

WALL, RICHARD, 'The Age at Leaving Home', *Journal of Family History*, 3: 2 (1978), 181–202.

—— 'Woman Alone in English Society', *Annales de Demographie Historique*, 17 (1981), 303–17.

WATKINS, SUSAN COTT, 'Spinsters', *Journal of Family History*, 9: 4 (1984), 310–25.

WEATHERILL, LORNA, 'A Possession of One's Own: Women and Consumer Behavior in England, 1660–1740', *Journal of British Studies*, 25: 2 (1986), 131–56.

WEIR, DAVID R., 'Rather Never Than Late: Celibacy and Age at Marriage in English Cohort Fertility', *Journal of Family History*, 9: 4 (1984), 340–54.

WELLS, ALISON, 'Southampton in the Spa Period', BA thesis, University of Southampton (1989).

WIENER, CAROLE Z., 'Is a Spinster an Unmarried Woman?', *American Journal of Legal History*, 20 (1976), 27–31.

WIESNER, MERRY, *Women and Gender in Early Modern Europe* (New York: Cambridge University Press, 1993).

—— 'Having Her Own Smoke: Employment and Independence for Singlewomen in Germany, 1400–1750', in Judith M. Bennett and Amy M. Froide (eds.), *Singlewomen in the European Past 1250–1800* (Philadelphia: University of Pennsylvania Press, 1999).

WIESNER-HANKS, MERRY, *Christianity and Sexuality in the Early Modern World* (New York: Routledge, 2000).

WILCOX, HELEN, ' "My Soule in Silence"?: Devotional Representations of Renaissance Englishwomen', in Claude J. Summer and Ted-Larry Pebworth (eds.), *Representing Women in Renaissance England* (Columbia: University of Missouri Press, 1997).

WILLEN, DIANE, 'Guildswomen in the City of York, 1560–1700', *Historian*, 46 (1984), 204–18.

—— 'Women in the Public Sphere in Early Modern England: The Case of the Urban Working Poor', *Sixteenth Century Journal*, 19: 4 (1988), 559–75.

WRIGHT, SUSAN J., 'Family Life and Society in Sixteenth and Early Seventeenth Century Salisbury', Ph.D. thesis, University of Leicester (1982).

WRIGHT, SUSAN J., '"Churmaids, Huswyfes and Hucksters": The Employment of Women in Tudor and Stuart Salisbury', in Lindsey Charles and Lorna Duffin (eds.), *Women and Work in Pre-Industrial England* (London: Croom Helm, 1985), 100–21.

—— 'Confirmation, Catechism and Communion: The Role of the Young in the Post-Reformation Church', in S. J. Wright (ed.), *Parish Church and People: Local Studies in Lay Religion 1350–1750* (London: Hutchinson, 1988), 203–27.

—— '"Holding Up Half the Sky": Women and Their Occupations in Eighteenth-Century Ludlow', *Midland History,* 14 (1989).

—— 'Sojourners and Lodgers in a Provincial Town: The Evidence From Eighteenth-Century Ludlow', *Urban History Yearbook* (1990), 14–35.

WRIGHTSON, KEITH, 'Kinship in an English Village: Terling, Essex, 1550–1700', in Richard M. Smith (ed.), *Land, Kinship, and Life-Cycle* (New York: Cambridge University Press, 1985), 313–32.

WRIGLEY, E. A. and SCHOFIELD, ROGER, *The Population History of England, 1541–1871: A Reconstruction* (London: Edward Arnold, 1981).

Index